Risk Assessment and Management in Cancer Genetics

Risk Assessment and Management in Cancer Genetics

Edited by

Fiona Lalloo
Consultant Clinical Geneticist
St Mary's Hospital, Manchester, UK

Bronwyn Kerr
Consultant Clinical Geneticist
St Mary's Hospital, Manchester, UK

J. M. Friedman
Professor, Department of Medical Genetics,
University of British Columbia, Canada

and

D. Gareth R. Evans
Professor of Clinical Genetics
St Mary's Hospital, Manchester, UK

OXFORD
UNIVERSITY PRESS

OXFORD

UNIVERSITY PRESS

Great Clarendon Street, Oxford OX2 6DP

Oxford University Press is a department of the University of Oxford.
It furthers the University's objective of excellence in research, scholarship,
and education by publishing worldwide in

Oxford New York

Auckland Cape Town Dar es Salaam Hong Kong Karachi
Kuala Lumpur Madrid Melbourne Mexico City Nairobi
New Delhi Shanghai Taipei Toronto

With offices in

Argentina Austria Brazil Chile Czech Republic France Greece
Guatemala Hungary Italy Japan Poland Portugal Singapore
South Korea Switzerland Thailand Turkey Ukraine Vietnam

Oxford is a registered trade mark of Oxford University Press
in the UK and in certain other countries

Published in the United States
by Oxford University Press Inc., New York

British Library Cataloguing in Publication Data

Data available

Library of Congress Cataloging in Publication Data

Data available

Typeset by Newgen Imaging Systems (P) Ltd., Chennai, India
Printed in Great Britain
on acid-free paper by
Biddles Ltd., King's Lynn

ISBN 0–19–852960–0   978–0–19–852960–6

10 9 8 7 6 5 4 3 2 1

Contents

Part 3 **Inherited cancer syndromes**

List of Contributors

Jillian M. Birch, BSc, MSc, PhD
Professor, Cancer Research
UK Paediatric and Familial
Research Group
Royal Manchester Children's Hospital
Manchester, UK

John Burn, BmedSci, MBBS,
MD, FRCP
Professor of Clinical Genetics
Institute of Human Genetics
International Centre for Life
Newcastle upon Tyne, UK

Susan Domchek, MD
Assistant Professor of Medicine
University of Pennsylvania
Philadelphia, PA, USA

Fiona Douglas, MBBS, FRCP
Consultant in Clinical Genetics
Institute of Human Genetics
International Centre for Life
Newcastle upon Tyne, UK

Rosalind Eeles, PhD, FRCR, FRCP
Senior Lecturer in Cancer Genetics
and Clinical Oncology
Institute of Cancer Research and
Honorary Consultant
Royal Marsden Hospital NHS Trust
London, UK

D. Gareth R. Evans, MD FRCP
Professor of Clinical Genetics
Academic Unit of Medical Genetics
and Regional Genetics Service
St Mary's Hospital
Manchester, UK

Jan M. Friedman, MD, PhD, FAAP,
FABMG, FCCMG, FRCPC
Professor, Department of
Medical Genetics
University of British Columbia
Vancouver, Canada

Richard S. Houlston,
MD PhD FRCP FRCPath
Reader in Molecular and Population
Genetics
Institute of Cancer Research
Sutton, UK

Sameer Jhavar,
DNB (RT), MD (RT), DMRT
Clinical Research Fellow in Cancer
Genetics
Institute of Cancer Research and
Royal Marsden Hospital NHS Trust
London, UK

Bronwyn Kerr,
MBBS, FRCAP, FRCPCH
Consultant Clinical Geneticist
Academic Unit of Medical Genetics
and Regional Genetics Service
St Mary's Hospital
Manchester, UK

Fiona Lalloo,
BmedSci, MBBS, MRCP, MD
Consultant Clinical Geneticist,
Academic Unit of Medical Genetics
and Regional Genetics Service
St Mary's Hospital
Manchester, UK

Eamonn R. Maher, BSc MD FRCP
Professor of Medical Genetics, Section of
Medical and Molecular Genetics
Department of Paediatrics and
Child Health
University of Birmingham, UK

Barbara C. McGillivray, MD,
FRCPC, FCCMG
Professor of Medical Genetics
Department of Medical Genetics
Children's and Women's Health Centre
of British Columbia
Vancouver, Canada

Fred H. Menko, MD, PhD
Consultant Clinical Geneticist
Department of Clinical Genetics and
Human Genetics
VU University Medical Centre
Amsterdam, The Netherlands

Pål Møller, MD PhD
Consultant in Clinical Genetics
Unit of Medical Genetics
Norwegian Radium Hospital
Oslo, Norway

Patrick Morrison, MD,
FRCPCH, FFPHMI
Professor of Human Genetics
Department of Medical Genetics
Belfast City Hospital
Belfast, Northern Ireland

Eamonn Sheridan, MB ChB
Consultant in Clinical Genetics
Department of Clinical Genetics
St James Hospital
Leeds, UK

Hans F. A. Vasen, MD
Internest and Medical Director
The Netherlands Foundation Detection
Hereditary Tumours
Leiden, The Netherlands

Barbara L. Weber, MD
University of Pennsylvania
Philadelphia, PA, USA

Part 1

Introduction

Chapter 1

How to evaluate a family history

Bronwyn Kerr

Family history and cancer risk

Cancer is common in the general population, with a lifetime risk of developing cancer in Western Europe, the United States and Australasia of one chance in three. For some of the common cancers, environmental factors are clearly the most important trigger, for example the relationships between papilloma virus infection and cervical carcinoma or cigarette smoking and carcinoma of the lung.

For other of the common cancers (breast, ovary and bowel), although environmental factors may contribute, family history can be the most important determinant of risk. A family history may reflect the presence in the family of a high-risk cancer gene mutation or a predisposition to a particular cancer on the basis of the presumed action of a number of different genes, either acting alone or with environmental factors (Box 1.1). From this perspective, it is worth remembering that family members do tend to share the same environmental exposures, particularly in early life. The pattern of breast cancer observed after Hiroshima, with the highest incidence in women who were adolescents at the time of the explosion, suggests that, at least for breast cancer, early environmental exposures are important (1). Indeed radiotherapy treatment for Hodgkin disease increases breast cancer risk in survivors, with a greater impact in those treated at younger ages, confirming this impression.

It is important to realize that familial factors may be present even in the absence of a family history of the relevant cancer. While only 10 to 15 per cent of women with

---

Box 1.1 Possible contributors to the risks associated with a family history

1 High-risk autosomal dominant mutation

2 A gene or genes of lesser penetrance

3 Multiple genes of low penetrance acting together

4 Environmental factors, contributing to 1–3 above or alone

5 Rarely, autosomal recessive inheritance.

breast cancer have a first or second-degree relative with the disease, up to 27 per cent of breast cancer is attributable to heritable factors from twin studies (2).

How to assess a family history

The initial step in cancer risk assessment is to determine a risk based on family history. In some circumstances, this risk will then be modified by the patient's own circumstances, for example, their age or the presence or absence of known additional risk factors.

Since individuals with a history consistent with autosomal dominant inheritance have the greatest risk, recognition of autosomal dominant inheritance is critical. The number of people with cancer within a kindred affects the likelihood of autosomal dominant inheritance, as do the ages of onset, the types of cancer, the relationships of affected people to one another, ethnic background and whether there is any one in the family who has more than one primary malignancy.

The key to correctly interpreting a family history in all circumstances is the skill of being able to correctly draw a three-generation family tree. In the cancer genetic clinic, when non-penetrance is common due to different malignancy risks in men and women, including both maternal and paternal sides of the family is crucial. It is not uncommon for a consultand to be concerned only with a maternal history of breast cancer, for example, when the paternal family history, once taken, is more worrying (Fig. 1.1).

The symbols and conventions underlying the construction of a family tree are widely available (3). In the cancer clinic, documentation on the pedigree should include types

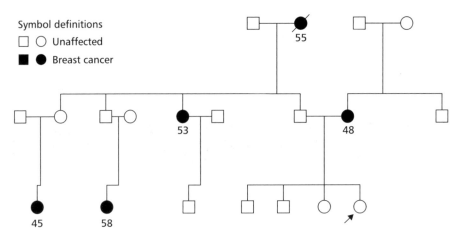

Fig. 1.1 The importance of paternal history. The consultand was referred because of the history of breast cancer in her mother at age 48. However, the family history on the paternal side was highly likely to have an autosomal dominant mutation, on the basis of Consortium Criteria, with the consultand at 25 per cent risk of having inherited it.

Box 1.2 Characteristics of autosomal dominant inheritance

- Condition results from a single copy of a mutant gene, i.e. one member of a gene pair.
- Males and females affected in a 1:1 ratio, unless penetrance is affected by sex.
- Males and females are equally capable of transmitting the disease.
- The condition is vertically transmitted from parent to child.
- The probability that a gene carrier will transmit the trait is 0.5 or 50 per cent.
- The probability that the child of an affected person will manifest the condition may be less than 50 per cent if the mutant gene is not always manifest (incomplete penetrance).
- The effect of the mutant gene may vary widely, even within the same family (variable expressivity).
- An affected person may be the first affected in a family as a result of a new mutation.

of cancer (including bilaterality and multiple primaries of the same organ), age of onset of cancer, and age and cause of death for as many family members as possible. Interpretation of a family tree requires an understanding of the principles of inheritance of single gene disorders, particularly autosomal dominant (Box 1.2) and autosomal recessive inheritance.

For those not used to genetic terminology, the concepts of penetrance and expressivity can be difficult:

- **Penetrance** refers to the probability that a person who inherits an autosomal mutation will ever manifest signs of doing so. Some autosomal dominant conditions, for example achondroplasia, have 100 per cent penetrance. This means that everyone who has the mutation in the gene *FGFR3* that causes achondroplasia will have the condition. Similarly, all people who inherit a disease-causing mutation in the gene that causes Huntington's disease will develop the condition if they live long enough. For most autosomal dominant conditions, however, penetrance is not 100 per cent. Of the cancer-causing autosomal dominant mutations, only Li–Fraumeni syndrome (Chapter 16) and FAP (Chapter 9) are associated with close to 100 per cent penetrance. Mutations in *BRCA1* have an 80 per cent penetrance in women, and virtually no effect in men (Chapter 5).

- **Expressivity** refers to the variable effects that can result from a disease-causing mutation. In *BRCA1* mutations, for example, the same mutation in different family members can be asymptomatic (not fully penetrant), or associated with breast cancer alone, either unilateral or bilateral, associated with ovarian cancer, associated with breast and ovarian cancer, or associated with prostate cancer.

Table 1.1 Malignancies associated with mutations in the common autosomal dominant cancer predisposing conditions

Gene	Malignancy
BRCA1	Breast, ovary, prostate
BRCA2	Breast, male breast, ovary, pancreas, melanoma, stomach
MLH1, MSH2 (HNPCC)	Bowel, uterus, ovary, stomach, upper urinary tract, biliary tree, brain
TP53 (Li–Fraumeni)	Breast, brain, rhabdomyosarcoma, osteosarcoma, soft tissue sarcoma, leukaemia, adrenocortical carcinomas, lung adenocarcinomas
APC (FAP)	Bowel (including duodenum), hepatoblastoma

Abbreviations: HNPCC – hereditary non-polyposis colorectal cancer; FAP – familial adenomatous polyposis.

In interpreting a family tree therefore, it is important to remember the variable expressivity of autosomal dominant cancer-predisposing mutations and to look specifically for a pattern of cancers in the family that are know to be consistent with mutations in the common cancer-predisposing genes (Table 1.1). Similarly, it is important to be alert for the possibility of non-cancer manifestations, also part of variable expressivity, of the cancer predisposing syndromes (Chapters 12–16).

Generally, a reported family history of breast cancer is correct (4–6). It is variable expressivity that contributes to the importance of confirming gynaecological or intra-abdominal malignancies in particular. A confirmed history of ovarian cancer or uterine cancer, rather than cervical, may change the status of a given family tree to almost certainly autosomal dominant.

There are a number of ethical issues that arise when using information from many people in a kindred to clarify risk to an individual. Some of these issues are discussed further in Chapter 18. Often family members will not know initially that their medical history is being discussed and documented. Counselling in this situation requires sensitivity and constant vigilance around confidentiality.

Despite respect for the privacy of other family members, it is sometimes apparent that the details provided are inconsistent or improbable. Factitious family histories have been reported in the cancer genetic clinic (7). Other common, identified factors in these families were a history of benign breast disease, poor communication within the families, long survival with early onset or bilateral disease and lack of detailed knowledge of illness and treatment in close relatives. It is our practice to confirm breast cancer histories where mutation testing or prophylactic surgery is planned.

Autosomal recessive inheritance (Box 1.3) is a rare cause of familial cancer. The concepts of variable penetrance and expressivity do not apply to autosomal recessive conditions. One expects to see similarly affected people in one generation of a family. The importance of this has recently been demonstrated by the identification of biallellic mutations in *MYH1* in about 25 per cent of polyposis patients where *APC* mutation testing is negative (8).

Box 1.3 Characteristics of autosomal recessive inheritance

- Results from a mutation in both members of a gene pair.
- Males and females are equally likely to be affected.
- The birth of an affected child establishes both parents as carriers of a single copy of the gene mutation.
- The chance of a second affected child in the sibship is one in four or 25 per cent in each pregnancy.
- Rarely seen in previous or subsequent generation of the family unless there is consanguinity or a high gene frequency.

Determining risk from the family history

Risk assessment based on family history is a multistep process (Box 1.4). The family history as documented in the pedigree is used to determine, firstly: is this a family where a high-risk, cancer-predisposing, autosomal dominant mutation is likely to be present? If so, what gene (sometimes genes) is likely to be involved? Risks can then be determined from what is known about that particular gene or genes. When such a gene is unlikely, risks can be derived from empiric data (Chapters 5, 6 and 7). For less common cancers, the principles of risk determination are the same, although the genetic basis may be less clear, and little empiric data are available (Chapter 11).

For the common cancers, criteria indicating that an autosomal dominant mutation is likely to be present are available (Boxes 1.5 and 1.6). For the purposes of these criteria, bilateral breast cancer is regarded as two cases.

Ethnicity has an important influence on risk. In some ethnic groups (for example Chinese and Indian ethnic groups for breast cancer) the incidence of common cancers is less, and so a given family history may be more significant. This may also be the case for populations with a known higher frequency of mutations. For example, Ashkenazi, Finnish and Icelandic populations have a higher frequency of mutations in *BRCA1/2*. In these populations, a lesser family history may also be significant and exclusion of the common known mutations can be used to modify risk (Chapter 5).

For the common cancers, it is also important to remember that some cancers in the family may have occurred by chance. This is more likely for cancers occurring in the 70s and 80s, and less likely when cancers have occurred at an age that is considered young (less than age 50 for breast, stomach, pancreas, bowel and prostate). For ovarian cancer, occurrence at an older age is still likely to be significant if in the context of other family members with either ovarian or early breast cancer (Chapter 7). Given that breast cancer is so common, when determining risks in dominant families on the basis of the likelihood of having inherited a given gene, and the risks of breast

Box 1.4 Key steps in interpreting a family history

◆ Construct a three-generation family tree, including both sides of the family.

◆ Remember variable penetrance and expressivity.

◆ Confirm all abdominal malignancies using medical records or death certificates.

◆ Confirm malignancies where the history is inconsistent or unclear, or where mutation testing or prophylactic surgery is planned.

◆ Remember ethnicity.

◆ Determine whether the family meets criteria for autosomal dominant inheritance.

◆ If not, use empiric risk estimation.

Box 1.5 Families that are highly likely to have an autosomal dominant mutation: Consortium data (9–12)

◆ Four or more cases breast, or breast and ovarian cancer diagnosed <60 years

◆ Three cases breast cancer diagnosed <50 years

◆ Two cases breast and one ovarian cancer

◆ Breast cancer in a male with a family history (male breast cancer overall, 10 per cent genetic)

◆ Isolated breast cancer diagnosed <30 years has a 30 per cent chance of being genetic.

Box 1.6 Amsterdam criteria (10) for diagnosis of hereditary non-polyposis colon cancer (see Chapter 10 for modified criteria)

◆ At least three relatives should have histologically verified colorectal cancer; one of them should be a first-degree relative of the other two.

◆ Familial adenomatous polyposis should be excluded.

◆ At least two successive generations should be affected.

◆ One of the relatives should be below 50 years of age when the colorectal cancer is diagnosed.

◆ Tumours should be verified by pathological examination.

cancer based on the penetrance of that gene, population risks need to be included (Chapter 5).

Sometimes, risk can be modified using Bayes theorem (13) to determine the probability that an at-risk but unaffected person in a dominant pedigree is not a mutation carrier (Fig. 1.2). The value of this is in modifying the risk of their descendants. A simplified guide to the use of the theorem can be found in Harper (3).

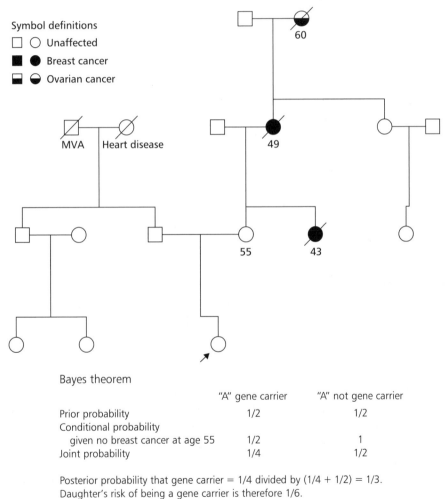

Symbol definitions
□ ○ Unaffected
■ ● Breast cancer
▬ ⊖ Ovarian cancer

MVA | Heart disease

60

49

55   43

Bayes theorem

	"A" gene carrier	"A" not gene carrier
Prior probability	1/2	1/2
Conditional probability		
given no breast cancer at age 55	1/2	1
Joint probability	1/4	1/2

Posterior probability that gene carrier = 1/4 divided by (1/4 + 1/2) = 1/3.
Daughter's risk of being a gene carrier is therefore 1/6.
Daughter's risk of breast cancer = 1/6 × 80% + 1/12 = 1 in 5.

Fig. 1.2 Clearly autosomal dominant pedigree for breast cancer. Consultand's mother, A, at 50 per cent risk of inheriting abnormal gene, but age 55 and well. Bayes theorem was used to calculate the consultand's risk of being a carrier.

Tumour histology and tumour studies

Obtaining a report of the type of ovarian cancer is very important, since some tumour types are very unlikely to be genetic (Chapter 7). Similarly, microsatellite instability studies (MSI) will be abnormal in almost all cases of HNPCC. Breast tumour characteristics may be helpful in families where a *BRCA1* mutation is suspected. Inherited mutations in E-cadherin are nearly always associated with the diffuse type of gastric cancer, and inherited mutations of the *MET* oncogene with papillary renal cancer. It is likely that tumour markers will become more important in risk stratification over the coming decade and new technologies such as tissue microarray may be able to "fingerprint" tumours to determine the underlying gene defects.

Special counselling situations

One of the fortunately rare counselling situations is determining the risk to an identical twin of a cancer that has occurred in the other. In a clearly dominant family, the risk to the unaffected twin is likely to be the penetrance of the gene, as the cancer in the affected twin is equivalent to a presymptomatic gene test. In the presence of a lesser family history, risk determination is difficult. Our approach would be to increase the empiric risk for a first-degree relative, the latter being the risk one would use in non-identical twins.

Another difficult counselling situation is the risk to the well mother of a very young woman with breast cancer. Partly because the tragedy of the situation is unexplained, there is understandable anxiety about breast cancer risks in the whole family. We offer screening for mothers as we would for sisters.

Risk communication

Different agendas frequently exist for counsellors and counselees in the genetic counselling clinic (14). For the counsellor, risk determination and communication may be the most important task, while for the consultand, the object of the appointment may be to find out what to do about a risk already perceived as high (15,16).

In a large study of women's reasons for attending a family history clinic, a variety of motivations for attendance were found, confirming that eliciting a consultand's specific needs is important. It was suggested that an interest in gene testing may be a means for gaining control over a perceived risk. In families where testing is not possible, other means of achieving an increased sense of personal control need to be addressed (16).

A number of studies have highlighted that accurate recall of an actual risk figure following an appointment is poor. Presentation of a risk as an odds ratio is most likely to be accurately recalled, although the perception of the meaning of this risk figure may not be accurate (15). Accurate recall of the risk is more likely in patients sent a summary clinic letter (17). Summary letters written after genetic counselling for breast/ovarian cancer have been found to be useful not only for aiding recall and understanding but also as a means of disseminating information within the family (18).

Concern has been expressed around the psychological sequelae of genetic counselling for cancer risk. In a study comparing a standard psychiatric interview with general health questionnaire (GHQ) to detect affective disorders in a group of women referred to a cancer family history clinic, a psychiatric diagnosis was made in 13.3 per cent. However, in this group, none reported a major concern with breast cancer risk. Relationship difficulties, unresolved grief and issues around loss were common. Women with accurate risk estimation after counselling had lower scores on the GHQ and there was no correlation with level of risk and psychiatric morbidity (19). In the general population, completion of a cancer family history questionnaire to determine risk of breast and colorectal cancer and receipt of risk was not associated with increased anxiety or cancer worry (20).

The risk communication strategies used in cancer genetics have recently been reviewed (21). The risks that might be discussed were summarized as: family and personal history; the probability of a cancer-predisposing gene in the family; the risk of transmitting or inheriting it; and the risk of cancer and the methods of prevention or early detection. Uncertainty, which is an inherent part of all these areas, should be recognized. Two principal methods of risk communication are identified: a probability based approach and a contextual or informational approach. Information tailored specifically to the patient and information aids may also be used.

From this review, it appears that studies of the effectiveness of risk communication strategies have proved difficult, particularly given that conclusions may not be applicable across cultures. There does appear to be consensus that assessing the consultand's *a priori* beliefs, expectations, anxiety and coping styles is important before deciding how information is to be communicated. Information to be imparted should be selected and prioritized, and presented in a number of different ways (absolute and relative risks). Provision of feedback from the consultation to the consultand, either by the use of standard formats (such as leaflets or videos) or by personal letter, appears to be welcome (21). Most important is tailoring the scientific–professional message to the receiver's ability and willingness to cope.

References

1 Land CE, Tokunaga M, Koyama K, Soda M, Preston DL, Nishimori I, *et al.* Incidence of female breast cancer among atomic bomb survivors, Hiroshima and Nagasaki, 1950–1990. *Radiat Res* 2003; **160**:707–717.

2 Peto J, Mack TM. High constant incidence in twins and other relatives of women with breast cancer. *Nat Genet* 2000; **26**:411–414.

3 Harper P. *Practical genetic counselling*, 1998. Oxford: Butterworth Heinemann, Oxford.

4 Eerola H, Blomqvist C, Pukkala E, Pyrhonen S, Nevanlinna H. Familial breast cancer in southern Finland: how prevalent are breast cancer families and can we trust the family history reported by patients? *Eur J Cancer* 2000; **36**:1143–1148.

5 Parent ME, Ghadirian P, Lacroix A, Perret C. The reliability of recollections of family history: implications for the medical provider. *J Cancer Educ* 1997; **12**:114–120.

6 Douglas FS, O'Dair LC, Robinson M, Evans DG, Lynch SA. The accuracy of diagnoses as reported in families with cancer: a retrospective study. *J Med Genet* 1999; **36**:309–312.

7 Kerr B, Foulkes WD, Cade D, Hadfield L, Hopwood P, Serruya C, *et al.* False family history of breast cancer in the family cancer clinic. *Eur J Surg Oncol* 1998; **24**:275–279.

8 Sampson JR, Dolwani S, Jones S, Eccles D, Ellis A, Evans DG, *et al.* Autosomal recessive colorectal adenomatous polyposis due to inherited mutations of MYH. *Lancet* 2003; **362**:39–41.

9 Easton DF, Bishop DT, Ford D, Crockford GP, Breast Cancer Linkage Consortium. Genetic linkage analysis in familial breast and ovarian cancer: results from 214 families. *Am J Hum Genet* 1993; **52**:678–701.

10 Ford D, Easton DF, Peto J. Estimates of the gene frequency of *BRCA1* and its contribution to breast and ovarian cancer incidence. *Am J Hum Genet* 1995; **57**:1457–1462.

11 Ponder BAJ, Easton DF, Peto J. Risk of ovarian cancer associated with a family history: preliminary report of the OPCS study. In: Sharp F, Mason WP, Leake RE, eds. *Ovarian Cancer: Biological and therapeutic challenges*, 1990, pp. 3–6. Cambridge: Chapman Hall.

12 Lalloo F, Varley J, Ellis D, Moran A, O'Dair L, Pharoah P, *et al.* Prediction of pathogenic mutations in patients with early-onset breast cancer by family history. *Lancet* 2003; **361**:1101–1102.

13 Murphy EA, Mutalik GS. The application of Bayesian methods in genetic counselling. *Human Heredity* 1969; **19**:126–151.

14 Shankar A, Chapman P, Goodship J. Genetic counselling: do we recognise and meet the consultands' agenda? *J Med Genet* 1999; **36**:580–582.

15 Watson M, Duvivier V, Wade Walsh M, Ashley S, Davidson J, Papaikonomou M, *et al.* Family history of breast cancer: what do women understand and recall about their risks? *J Med Genet* 1998; **35**:731–738.

16 Brain K, Gray J, Norman P, Parsons E, Clarke A, Rogers C, *et al.* Why do women attend familial breast cancer clinics? *J Med Genet* 2000; **37**:197–202.

17 Evans DGR, Blair V, Greenhalgh R, Hopwood P, Howell A. The impact of genetic counselling on risk perception in women with a family history of breast cancer. *Br J Cancer* 1994; **70**:934–938.

18 Hallowell N, Murton F. The value of written summaries of genetic consultations. *Patient Educ Couns* 1998; **35**:27–34.

19 Hopwood P, Keeling F, Long A, Pool C, Evans G, Howell A. Psychological support needs for women at high genetic risk of breast cancer: Some preliminary indicators. *Psycho-oncology* 1998; **7**:402–412.

20 Leggatt V, Mackay J, Marteau TM, Yates JR. The psychological impact of a cancer family history questionnaire completed in general practice. *J Med Genet* 2000; **37**:470–472.

21 Julian-Reynier C, Welkenhuysen M, Hagoel L, Decruyenaere M, Hopwood P. Risk communication strategies: state of the art and effectiveness in the context of cancer genetic services. *Eur J Hum Genet* 2003; **11**:725–736.

Chapter 2

Guidelines for referral in Europe

Fred H. Menko

Introduction

About 5 per cent of all cancer cases are due to high-penetrance, dominant mutations. A much larger proportion is caused by a combination of weaker susceptibility genes and/or environmental and lifestyle factors. A number of high-penetrance susceptibility genes have been identified and, recently, the clinical significance of genetic alterations in tumours has started to be appreciated.

The recognition of a genetic cause of cancer is important for both patients and relatives. For patients, treatment for hereditary cancer may differ from treatment of sporadic disease. Usually, for individuals with an increased cancer risk because of family history, periodic screening or prophylactic surgery is recommended.

The organization of clinical cancer genetics has developed in different ways in the various European countries. The form of organization is determined by the general organization of health care, the status of clinical genetics as a separate medical specialty, the presence or absence of clinics and registries for families with hereditary cancer, cultural differences, insurance issues and other factors.

In this chapter referral of patients and families for genetic evaluation will be considered from two perspectives: the medical criteria for referral and the organization of cancer genetics services.

Medical criteria for referral

Patient features

Many genetically determined conditions have characteristics that facilitate clinical diagnosis. The presentation of hereditary cancer, however, does not differ from that seen in non-genetic disease in most respects. Some patient characteristics are suggestive of hereditary disease (Table 2.1) and generally will be considered an indication for genetic referral.

Family history and accuracy of data

Occurrence of the same type of tumour or specific combinations of tumours in multiple, close family members is a strong indicator of a hereditary tumour syndrome.

Table 2.1 Patient characteristics which indicate a genetic cause of tumour development (based on Mulvihill (1))

Characteristic	Example
Early age at onset	Breast cancer below age 35 years
Bilateral disease	Bilateral breast cancer/ kidney cancer/ retinoblastoma
Multiple tumours and characteristic combinations of tumours	Multiple colonic cancers Colonic and uterine cancer Colonic cancer and multiple adenomatous polyps Breast and ovarian cancer Childhood cancer and breast cancer Hyperparathyroidism and pancreatic islet tumour
Tumour in the sex not usually affected	Male breast cancer
Association with birth defects	Metastatic cancer and lip pigmentations Wilms' tumour and hemihypertrophy
Rare or unusual tumours types	Medullary thyroid cancer Phaeochromocytoma
Specific ethnic backgrounds	Ovarian cancer and Ashkenazi Jewish ancestry

Table 2.2 The accuracy of family history data (2)

Determinants of accuracy	Higher accuracy	Lower accuracy
Degree of relationship	First-degree relative	Second-degree or third-degree relative
Site of tumour	Breast cancer	Abdominal cancer (bowel, ovary, endometrium, pancreas, prostate) Other cancer

However, a positive family history is not always reliable (Table 2.2). Thus, for medical decision-making it will often be necessary to have a formal pedigree study performed at a clinical genetics centre.

Diagnostic and predictive DNA testing

DNA tests can be either diagnostic (confirming, for example, hereditary disease due to a *RET* germline mutation in a patient with apparently sporadic phaeochromocytoma) or predictive (presymptomatic) when at-risk relatives are tested for a specific mutation diagnosed in affected family members (see Chapter 4). There are several difficulties inherent in diagnostic and predictive DNA testing, and these are summarized in Table 2.3.

Various problems involved in DNA testing can often be solved by evaluating the results of testing along with the clinical data of patients and family members. This may require the skills of a specialist genetic centre or close co-operation between oncologists and geneticists.

Table 2.3 Difficulties involved in diagnostic and predictive DNA testing

Type of testing	Problems	Examples
Diagnostic testing	Mutations of unknown clinical significance	Missense mutations in DNA mismatch repair genes or in *BRCA1/2* may or may not be pathogenic
	Phenocopies	A negative DNA test can be due to testing of a sporadic cancer case which occurs by chance in a family with hereditary cancer
	Genetic heterogeneity	Various genes can be involved in a given case, for example *VHL*, *RET*, *SDHD* and *SDHB* in apparently sporadic phaeochromocytoma
	Psychosocial issues	Demonstration of a *BRCA1* mutation in a breast cancer patient implies risk of recurrent breast cancer, risk of ovarian cancer and cancer risk for offspring
Predictive testing	Diagnostic testing not possible	If all affected family members have died, DNA testing may be started in a healthy relative; when the test is negative (no mutation) usually cancer risk is still high
	Psychosocial issues	Fear of cancer in carriers, cancer risk for offspring; guilt feelings in non-carriers

Predictive testing could also be performed prenatally. A committee of the Dutch Society for Clinical Genetics stated that testing for a *BRCA* mutation in the fetus cannot immediately be judged unacceptable from an ethical point of view (3). In practice, however, requests for prenatal diagnosis of late-onset tumour syndromes are extremely rare.

Genetic profiling of tumours

Until recently, tumour characteristics were of little help in genetic evaluation as histological characteristics in breast and colon cancer were essentially the same in sporadic and familial disease. Pathologists have now identified subtle histological differences between hereditary tumours and their sporadic counterparts. In addition, genetic profiling of tumours is of increasing clinical importance – for example the somatic genetic alterations in hereditary colorectal cancer are well known. Testing for microsatellite instability (MSI) has become a standard procedure in evaluation for possible hereditary non-polyposis colorectal cancer (HNPCC), as MSI is found in almost all HNPCC-associated colorectal cancers but only around 15 per cent of sporadic bowel cancers.

Genetic profiling of tumours may have various clinical applications (Table 2.4):

1 as an indicator of a genetic cause of the disease;

2 as a prognostic marker;

3 as a predictive marker of reaction to therapy.

Table 2.4 Genetic features of malignant tumours and their clinical significance

Clinical significance	Colorectal cancer (4–6)	Breast cancer (7–9)
Indicator of a genetic cause of the disease	MSI-H: indicator of HNPCC	*BRCA1* profile of tumours
Prognostic marker	MSH-H: better prognosis	"Poor prognosis" signature
Predictive marker of response to chemotherapy	MSI status predicts response to adjuvant 5FU chemotherapy	Gene expression profile predicts therapeutic response to docetaxel

In the future, the physician treating a cancer patient may need a genetic profile of the tumour for management decisions, for example on adjuvant chemotherapy in breast cancer. A tumour profile might be indicative of biological behaviour and also suggestive of hereditary disease. Thus, demonstration of a specific genetic profile of a tumour may become a reason for referral for further genetic evaluation.

Organization of cancer genetic services

Awareness of hereditary cancer

Public awareness of hereditary cancer is a relevant factor. In the study of Brain *et al.* (10), 60 per cent of women referred to a familial breast cancer clinic by a medical specialist stated that the referral had been made in response to their own initiative in raising the question of family history. In a cross-sectional study in 1998, Wonderling *et al.* (11) described the pattern of cancer genetics services in the UK. These authors found that most referrals were women with a family history of breast cancer, many of whom did not belong to a high-risk group. Among the clinic attendees, about 25 per cent were categorized as "population level cancer risk or marginally above", about 50 per cent as "risk level sufficient for screening" and 25 per cent as high risk. Eisinger *et al.* (12) argue that the degree of personal concern is also relevant: "A women who has a low risk of being cancer-prone, but who is worried by her family history, should have access to consultation".

The role of primary care

Cancer genetics has now become a field of mainstream clinical medicine. Potentially, general practitioners (GPs) play an important role in the field of cancer genetics. As family doctors they may be aware of a family history of disease and they are the first to be consulted by patients and family members. However, although the majority of GPs feels that their responsibilities include taking a detailed family history, there is no consensus on this matter (Table 2.5).

Several studies have explored the role of GPs in cancer genetics. Emery *et al.* evaluated a computer support system for recording and interpreting family histories of breast and ovarian cancer in primary care (14). A recent Dutch guideline on breast

Table 2.5 General practitioners' views on their role in cancer genetics services (based on Fry *et al.* (13))

The role of the GP	Response (%)		
	Agree	**Neither agree or disagree**	**Disagree**
Taking a detailed family history	61	18	21
Risk calculation if family history is positive	6	10	84
Counselling on cancer risk	24	22	54
Deciding on referral to a cancer genetics clinic	78	13	9
Providing emotional follow-up support	90	7	3
Providing regular clinical examination	39	28	33
Teaching breast self examination	71	18	11
Discussing the need for mammographic or colonoscopic screening	64	17	19

cancer recommends that the GP takes a family history and subdivides patients into various risk categories (15).

The optimal role for both GPs and specialized centres in cancer genetics remains unclear. Stermer *et al.* explored this issue with respect to colorectal cancer and found a wide range of attitudes of GPs and expectations of patients (16). In the UK, a model is being introduced which involves initial referral of all women with a suspected increased risk for breast cancer because of their family history to a dedicated family history clinic (17).

Clinical genetics centres and cancer family clinics

Up to date information on genetic services in Europe can be found at www.eshg.org, the site of the European Society of Human Genetics, and in the ESHG report by Godard *et al.* (18)

When an increased risk of cancer is suspected, an individual may be referred for preventive measures or to a clinical genetics centre for a family study and risk coun-selling. In the latter case, advice on preventive measures will be based on a formal genetic evaluation.

The perspective of clinical genetics includes the individual in the context of his or her family. This aspect of clinical genetics is important in clinical practice for several reasons. Firstly, the facilities of a cancer family clinic to collect and review family data are often needed for proper counselling of the individual. Secondly, if a healthy individual is referred due to familial occurrence of cancer and if, subsequently, the pedigree data indicate hereditary cancer, the next diagnostic step would be to propose DNA studies of affected family members. Affected individuals would be invited to the clinic to discuss

Table 2.6 Subdivision of the first 650 referrals to the clinical genetics department of the VU University Medical Centre, Amsterdam, the Netherlands, 2003: diagnosis at referral

Category	Number	Percentage
All diagnoses	650	100
Cancer/ tumour	271	41.7
Breast/ ovarian cancer	154	23.7
Colorectal/ intestinal tumour	84	12.9
Other or unspecified (4)	33	5.1

the clinical diagnosis and the option of DNA testing. Thus, testing of an affected family member is often crucial for proper counselling of the healthy relative. Thirdly, a pedigree study will also identify additional at-risk family members who may benefit from genetic counselling. According to a recent European recommendation "genetic services should support the identification of and care for relatives who are at risk of serious genetic disorders, but who may not have been directly referred"(18). The exact procedures for DNA testing differ in different countries and regions. The treating physician or the geneticist may request DNA testing. Often, a distinction is made between procedures for diagnostic versus predictive testing. The treating physician may request diagnostic testing whereas predictive testing is restricted to specialists in clinical genetics. In the Netherlands, both diagnostic and predictive DNA testing for hereditary breast and colonic cancer are performed almost exclusively in cancer family clinics.

Breast cancer and colorectal cancer are the main reasons for referral to a clinical genetics centre (Table 2.6). Referral patterns partly reflect the policies recommended in professional national guidelines and the literature on international recommendations (for recent examples see Eisinger *et al.* (19) and Hampel *et al.* (20)). Especially with regard to breast cancer, due to the large number of (predicted) referrals, various ways of regulating referrals have been considered. In the Netherlands strict adherence to the Dutch guidelines for breast cancer would lead to a sharp increase in referrals to clinical genetics centres (21). In the UK, a model has been developed with specific roles for specialized cancer units, clinical genetics centres and general practitioners (Table 2.7).

The use of professional guidelines

The existence of guidelines does not automatically imply that they will be implemented in clinical practice. Illustrative is a recent survey among German gynaecologists on their policies for *BRCA* testing for a 35-year-old healthy woman whose mother died of breast cancer at age 43 years and whose sister was treated for bilateral breast cancer at age 38 years (Table 2.8). Eighty-two per cent of the repondents would perform (basic) genetic counselling and, in the case of indication of patients' interest, would refer the patient for further genetic evaluation.

Table 2.7 Model for management of familial breast cancer (17)

1. Identification of women at suspected increased risk of breast cancer due to their family history

2. Referral to a dedicated family history clinic at a breast cancer clinic

3. Risk assessment by trained specialist nurses; management depending on risk category

Risk category	Management in:
<1 in 6	Primary care
between <1 in 6 and >1 in 4	Breast cancer clinic
>1 in 4	Cancer genetics clinic

Table 2.8 Gynaecologists' policies for *BRCA* testing for a 35-year-old healthy woman with familial early-onset/bilateral breast cancer (22)

Possible options	Percentage of positive answers
Present the pros and cons of testing (offer no opinion)	66
Advise to have the test, irrespective of affected sister's test result	19
Advise to have the test only after a positive test result for the affected sister	11
Advise not to have the test	4

Table 2.9 Colonoscopic screening practice in nine colorectal surgery or gastroenterology units referring patients to the regional genetics centre (26)

Procedures	Application in practice
Confirmation of family history	Usually not
Presence of protocols	Different protocols present in 6/9 units
Adherence to protocols	Often higher or lower frequency of screening than according to protocol

With regard to early-onset or familial colorectal cancer, not only do important differences exist between guidelines of various national societies (23, 24) but also – within a community for which specific guidelines have been developed – application of these recommendations in clinical practice varies considerably (Table 2.9) (25, 26).

Clinical practice is not only determined by evidence-based guidelines. According to a French group of researchers, divergence in medical guidelines "partly reflects the cultural context in which physicians and patients make decisions and health policies are formulated"(27). Acceptability of certain medical interventions differs between different countries (Table 2.10).

Table 2.10 Acceptability (cumulative percentage) of medical interventions for women (n = 355) depending on age and country of origin (modified from Julian-Reynier *et al.* (28))

City/Country	Acceptability of intervention (%)			
	Prophylactic oophorectomy		Prophylactic mastectomy	
	Age 35	Age 50	Age 35	Age 50
Manchester (United Kingdom)	32	65	23	34
Marseilles (France)	8	55	7	24
Montreal (Canada)	20	55	22	28

The role of registries

Initial genetic evaluation of a family takes place within a circumscribed period. However, the follow-up of individuals at high cancer risk is lifelong and requires a specialized form of organization. This can be fulfilled by hospital, regional or national registries.

The Netherlands Foundation for the Detection of Hereditary Tumours was founded in 1985. In the past, families with a suspected hereditary tumour syndrome (especially FAP and HNPCC) were referred to the Foundation for pedigree studies. Subsequently, the referring specialist was advised about the diagnosis and preventive measures. Now, families are primarily referred to one of ten cancer family clinics. If a hereditary tumour syndrome is diagnosed, the family is referred for registration at the Foundation. Representatives of the registry and the clinical genetics centres established guidelines for genetic evaluation and registration. The registration of patients at the national registry ensures that the occurrence of screening is monitored. If a report is not received, a reminder letter is sent to the specialist involved. In addition, if screening recommendations are changed, all treating physicians will be informed.

Future perspectives

The relationship between medical recommendations and daily clinical practice is not straightforward. Often no guidelines for specific subjects are available whereas different guidelines on the same subject may also exist. It should be noted that the quality of guidelines developed by various professional societies has been questioned (29). Finally, the availability of recommendations does not automatically imply that they will be employed in clinical practice.

In a recent study on services for people at increased risk for colorectal cancer, five factors emerged as significant: the poorly defined role of primary care; the need for information and education of professionals and patients; the organization of the follow-up and support of patients at increased risk; the consistency of advice provided to patients; and issues around the communication of risk (16).

The development of new genetic techniques will lead to the emergence of many new prognostic markers, indicators of response to therapy and markers of hereditary cancer, which may directly affect clinical management. Clearly, cancer genetics is a truly multidisciplinary field. Setting up of protocols for cancer genetics services – diagnostic procedures and preventive measures – and implementation of these protocols in clinical practice will be of direct benefit to patients and family members. Moreover, this effort is a prerequisite for a critical evaluation of current approaches.

Acknowledgements

I am grateful to Dr Waltraut Friedl, Bonn, Germany and Professor Annika Lindblom, Stockholm, Sweden for their helpful comments.

References

1 Mulvihill JJ. Prospects for cancer control and prevention through genetics. *Clin Genet* 1989; **36**:313–319.

2 Douglas FS, O'Dair LC, Robinson M, Evans DG, Lynch SA. The accuracy of diagnoses as reported in families with cancer: a retrospective study. *J Med Genet* 1999; **36**:309–312.

3 Cobben JM, Bröcker-Vriends AH, Leschot NJ. [Prenatal diagnosis for hereditary predisposition to mammary and ovarian carcinoma–defining a position]. *Ned Tijdschr Geneeskd* 2002; **146**:1461–1465.

4 De la Chapelle A. Microsatellite instability phenotype of tumors: genotyping or immunohisto-chemistry? The jury is still out. *J Clin Oncol* 2002; **20**:897–899.

5 Hemminki A, Mecklin JP, Järvinen H, Aaltonen LA, Joensuu H. Microsatellite instability is a favourable prognostic indicator in patients with colorectal cancer receiving chemotherapy. *Gastroenterology* 2000; **119**:921–928.

6 Ribic CM, Sargent DJ, Moore MJ, Thibodeau SN, French AJ, Goldberg RM, *et al.* Tumor microsatellite-instability status as a predictor of benefit from fluorouracil-based adjuvant chemotherapy for colon cancer. *N Engl J Med* 2003; **349**:247–257.

7 Van't Veer LJ, Dai H, van de Vijver MJ, He YD, Hart AA, Mao M, *et al.* Gene expression profiling predicts clinical outcome of breast cancer. *Nature* 2002; **415**:530–536.

8 Wessels LF, van Welsem T, Hart AA, van't Veer LJ, Reinders MJ, Nederlof PM. Molecular classification of breast carcinomas by comparative genomic hybridization: a specific somatic genetic profile for BRCA1 tumors. *Cancer Res* 2002; **62**:7110–7117.

9 Chang JC, Wooten EC, Tsimelzon A, Hilsenbeck SG, Gutierrez MC, Elledge R, *et al.* Gene expression profiling for the prediction of therapeutic response to docetaxel in patients with breast cancer. *Lancet* 2003; **362**:362–369.

10 Brain K, Gray J, Norman P, Parsons E, Clarke A, Rogers C, *et al.* Why do women attend familial breast cancer clinics? *J Med Genet* 2000; **37**:197–202.

11 Wonderling D, Hopwood P, Cull A, Douglas F, Watson M, Burn J, *et al.* A descriptive study of UK cancer genetics services: an emerging clinical response to the new genetics. *Br J Cancer* 2001; **85**:166–170.

12 Eisinger F, Alby N, Bremond A, Dauplat J, Espié M, Janiaud P, *et al.* Recommendations for medical management of hereditary breast and ovarian cancer: the French National Ad Hoc Committee. *Ann Oncol* 1998; **9**:939–950.

13 Fry A, Campbell H, Gudmunsdottir H, Rush R, Porteous M, Gorman D, *et al*. GPs' views on their role in cancer genetics services and current practice. *Fam Pract* 1999; **16**:468–474.

14 Emery J, Walton R, Coulson A, Glasspool D, Ziebland S, Fox J. Computer support for recording and interpreting family histories of breast and ovarian cancer in primary care (RAGs): qualitative evaluation with simulated patients. *BMJ* 1999; **319**:32–36.

15 Wiersma T, De Bock GH, Assendelft WJ. [Summary of the Dutch College of General Practitioners' practice guideline 'Diagnosis of breast cancer']. *Ned Tijdschr Geneeskd* 2003; **147**:547–550.

16 Stermer T, Hodgson S, Kavalier F. Patients' and professionals' opinions of services for people at an increased risk of colorectal cancer: an exploratory qualitative study. *Fam. Cancer* 2004; **3**:49–53.

17 McAllister M, O'Malley K, Hopwood P, Kerr B, Howell A, Evans DGR. Management of women with a family history of breast cancer in the North West Region of England: training for implementing a vision of the future. *J Med Genet* 2002; **39**:531–535.

18 Godard B, Kaariainen H, Kristoffersson U, Tranebjaerg L, Coviello D, Ayme S. Provision of genetic services in Europe: current practices and issues. *Eur J Hum Genet* 2003; **11** Suppl 2:S13–S48.

19 Eisinger F, Bressac B, Castaigne D, Cottu P-H, Lansac J, Lefranc J-P, *et al*. Identification and management of hereditary breast/ ovarian cancers (2004 update). *Bull Cancer* 2004; **91**:219–237.

20 Hampel H, Sweet K, Westman JA, Offit K, Eng C. Referral for cancer genetics consultation: a review and compilation of risk assessment criteria. *J Med Genet* 2004; **41**:81–91.

21 Van Asperen CJ, Tollenaar RA, Krol-Warmerdam EM, Blom J, Hoogendoorn WE, Seynaeve CM, *et al*. Possible consequences of applying guidelines to healthy women with a family history of breast cancer. *Eur J Hum Genet* 2003; **11**:633–636.

22 Mehnert A, Bergelt C, Koch U. Knowledge and attitudes of gynecologists regarding genetic counseling for hereditary breast and ovarian cancer. *Patient Educ Couns* 2003; **49**:183–188.

23 Schmiegel W, Adler G, Frühmorgen P, Fölsch U, Graeven U, Layer P, *et al*. [Colorectal carcinoma: prevention and early detection in an asymptomatic population–prevention in patients at risk-endoscopic diagnosis, therapy and after-care of polyps and carcinomas. German Society of Digestive and Metabolic Diseases/Study Group for Gastrointestinal Oncology]. *Z Gastroenterol* 2000; **38**:49–75.

24 Dunlop MG. Guidance on large bowel surveillance for people with two first degree relatives with colorectal cancer or one first degree relative diagnosed with colorectal cancer under 45 years. *Gut* 2002; **51** Suppl 5:V17–V20.

25 Heriot AG, Murday V, Kumar D. Screening relatives of patients with colorectal cancer: the need for continuing education. *J R Coll Surg Edinb* 1999; **44**:13–15.

26 Hill J, Walsh S, Evans DG. Screening of patients at high risk of colorectal cancer. *Colorectal Dis* 2001; **3**:308–311.

27 Eisinger F, Geller G, Burke W, Holtzman NA. Cultural basis for differences between US and French clinical recommendations for women at increased risk of breast and ovarian cancer. *Lancet* 1999; **353**:919–920.

28 Julian-Reynier CM, Bouchard LJ, Evans DG, Eisinger FA, Foulkes WD, Kerr B, *et al*. Women's attitudes toward preventive strategies for hereditary breast or ovarian carcinoma differ from one country to another: differences among English, French, and Canadian women. *Cancer* 2001; **92**:959–968.

29 Grilli R, Magrini N, Penna A, Mura G, Liberati A. Practice guidelines developed by specialty societies: the need for a critical appraisal. *Lancet* 2000; **355**:103–106.

Chapter 3

Guidelines for genetic counselling, testing and referral in North America

Susan Domchek and Barbara L. Weber

Introduction

Cancer is the second leading cause of death in the United States and public interest in risk factors, prevention and screening for cancer is high. Genetic counselling programs are available in most major cancer centres in North America and Europe (www.cancer.gov for sites in the US) and provide an opportunity for individuals to learn more about their risk of cancer, options available for prevention and screening, and the likelihood that their family history is due to an inherited genetic factor, such as mutations in *BRCA1*, *BRCA2*, *APC*, *MSH2* or *MLH1*.

In most centres, individuals can be referred to genetic counselling programs by physicians or be self-referred. However, as recently as 2000, misperceptions by physicians of discrimination risk and confidentiality issues, as well as confusion regarding guidelines for referral for genetic counselling, have occurred (1). Guidelines for genetic counselling were published by the American Society of Clinical Oncology in 1996 and updated in 2003 (2, 3) and include recommendations relating to informed consent, laboratory regulations and circumstances appropriate for genetic testing (e.g. a test which gives answers that will change clinical management). Likewise, definitions of hereditary breast and ovarian cancer (HBOC) (Box 3.1) and hereditary non-polyposis colorectal cancer (HNPCC) (Box 3.2) have also been published. Whilst these definitions are important and can be interpreted as guides to referral for genetic counselling, they rely on detailed pedigrees, including first-, second-, and third-degree relatives, which are rarely obtained in a physician's office. In addition, although most physicians have some knowledge of HBOC and HNPCC, far fewer are aware of other, more rare, hereditary cancer syndromes such as Li–Fraumeni or Cowden syndrome.

In theory, physicians can obtain a family history and calculate a lifetime breast cancer risk using the Gail model to help guide referrals for genetic counselling for breast cancer risk. However, in practice, even in a comprehensive cancer centre, as few as 7 per cent of individuals thought to be at high risk were referred to a counselling

Box 3.1 Definitions of hereditary breast and ovarian cancer

National Comprehensive Cancer Network (NCCN) (v.1. 2003)

- Known *BRCA1* or *BRCA2* mutation in the family.
- Personal history of breast cancer and one or more of the following:
  - diagnosed before 40 with or without family history;
  - diagnosed before age 50 or bilateral, with at least one close blood relative with breast cancer before age 50 or more than one close blood relative with ovarian cancer;
  - diagnosed at any age, with more than two close relatives with ovarian cancer or breast cancer, especially if more than one was diagnosed before age 50 or had bilateral disease;
  - male breast cancer;
  - Ashkenazi Jewish diagnosed at or before age 50.
- Personal history of ovarian cancer and one or more of the following:
  - one or more close relative with ovarian cancer;
  - one or more close relative with breast cancer before age 50 or with bilateral disease;
  - two or more close relatives with breast cancer;
  - one or more male relative with breast cancer;
  - Ashkenazi Jewish descent with no additional family history.
- Personal history of male breast cancer and one or more of the following:
  - at least one close male relative with breast cancer;
  - at least one close female relative with breast or ovarian cancer;
  - Ashkenazi Jewish descent with no additional family history.

program, primarily due to either a failure to collect a complete family history or a failure to recognize a family history as significant (4).

Genetic counselling and testing can lead to targeted interventions that decrease risk of breast (5), ovarian (6, 7) and colon cancers (8). In addition, the identification of family members who are *not* at genetic risk spares these individuals aggressive interventions, such as prophylactic mastectomy, oophorectomy or colectomy and enhanced screening. Who then should be referred for risk assessment and genetic counselling services?

Box 3.2 Definitions of hereditary non-polyposis colorectal cancer (22)

Amsterdam I criteria

After exclusion of FAP and verification of tumour pathology:
- three or more relatives with colorectal cancer, one of whom is the first-degree relative of the other two; AND
- two or more generations affected.
- One or more family member diagnosed before age 50.

Bethesda criteria

- Amsterdam I criteria.
- Two or more HNPCC-associated cancers (colon, uterine, ovarian, gastric, hepatobiliary, small bowel or transitional cell carcinoma of renal pelvis or ureter).
- Individual with colorectal cancer and a first-degree relative diagnosed with colorectal cancer before age 50 or colonic adenoma before age 40 or an HNPCC-associated cancer.
- Colorectal or endometrial cancer diagnosed before age 50.
- Colorectal adenoma diagnosed before age 40.

Referral for calculated breast cancer risk

The Gail model for the estimation of breast cancer risk was developed using data from the Breast Cancer Detection Demonstration Project (BCDDP) of North American women undergoing routine screening mammography (9). This model incorporates the race, age, family history of first-degree relatives, age of menarche, age at birth of first child, number of breast biopsies, and presence of atypia on a breast biopsy. A web-based version of this model is available at http://bcra.nci.nih.gov/brc. The Gail model estimates 5-year and lifetime risk for breast cancer and is useful in selecting women for tamoxifen chemoprevention (10), as the NSABP Breast Cancer Prevention Trial included women older than age 35 with a 5-year Gail risk of greater than 1.7 per cent. Of note, the Gail model is not useful for determining lifetime risk of breast cancer in women with affected second-degree relatives or a paternal history of breast cancer, as these individuals are not included in the calculation. In these cases, the Claus model provides more useful information (11).Women with a lifetime risk of breast cancer of >25 per cent should be considered for referral to a risk assessment/cancer genetics program both to determine whether there is an underlying genetic susceptibility and to encourage enrolment in clinical trials for chemoprevention and screening.

Referral for *BRCA1/ BRCA2* mutation testing

In the United States, genetic testing is considered when an individual has a probability of greater than 5 to 10 per cent of having a detectable mutation. The prior probability of detecting a *BRCA1* or *BRCA2* mutation in women diagnosed with breast cancer under the age of 40 is 6 to 10 per cent (12–14); in unselected men with breast cancer it is 6 to 14 per cent (15,16); in unselected Ashkenazi Jewish women with breast cancer it is 10 per cent (17–19); in Ashkenazi Jewish women with ovarian cancer it is 30 to 60 per cent (17); and in individuals with both breast and ovarian cancer it is more than 50 per cent (20). Therefore, all of these individuals should be referred for genetic counselling. In addition, our patients are strongly counselled to inform other adult family members of their genetic testing results when they become available and are provided with supporting materials to do so. Effective interventions exist, and given the implications for the entire extended family, all first-degree relatives of a documented *BRCA1/2* mutation carrier who are of adult age should be offered counselling and genetic testing.

Prior probability models are used to estimate the likelihood of detecting a *BRCA1* or *BRCA2* mutation and are particularly useful in estimating risk in families with multiple breast cancer cases, with or without ovarian cancer (21). Although these models are routinely used in risk assessment clinics, they generally require information from a three-generation pedigree and familiarity with the limitations of the models. Therefore, they are not commonly used outside this setting. In the absence of this information, families with both breast and ovarian cancer, two or more cases of premenopausal breast cancer, or three or more cases of breast cancer should be referred for accurate assessment of genetic risk; in all of these situations the prior probability of detecting a *BRCA1* or *BRCA2* mutation is often greater than 10 per cent.

Referral for colon cancer risk

Familial adenomatous polyposis (FAP) has a distinct clinical presentation with greater than 100 colonic polyps on colonoscopy, while in attenuated FAP the number of polyps is between 20 and 99 (22, 23). Both are associated with a very high risk for the development of colon and other gastrointestinal cancers, thus all individuals with more than ten polyps should be offered genetic counselling. Although management for an individual with a clinical diagnosis of FAP will not change with the detection of an *APC* mutation (colectomy will be recommended regardless), the results will have profound implications for other family members.

HNPCC is the most common form of hereditary colon cancer susceptibility and accounts for 2 to 5 per cent of all colon cancer (24, 25). Clinical features include multiple affected generations with an early age of onset (mean 45 years), and extracolonic cancers such as uterine, ovarian, stomach, small bowel, pancreatic, hepatobiliary cancers and cancers of the renal pelvis (22). Several definitions of HNPCC exist, including the most stringent Amsterdam I criteria and the more inclusive modified criteria (Chapter 10).

Box 3.3 Referral guidelines for risk assessment and genetic counselling in North America

Breast cancer

- Lifetime risk of breast cancer of at least 25 per cent:
  - Gail model
  - Claus model
  - lobular carcinoma *in situ*.
- Risk of breast cancer susceptibility gene mutation greater than 5 per cent
- Ashkenazi Jewish with ovarian cancer at any age or breast cancer before age 50
- Breast and ovarian cancer in the same family
- Male breast cancer
- Breast cancer diagnosed before age 40
- Two or more breast cancers with at least one before age 50
- Bilateral breast cancer
- Multiple primary tumours in an individual
- Clustering of breast, adrenocortical, leukaemia/lymphoma, brain tumours or sarcomas (Li–Fraumeni Syndrome or Li–Fraumeni syndrome-like) or breast cancer, thyroid cancer, dermatological manifestations (Cowden syndrome) (Chapter 5)
- First-degree relative of affected individual meeting above criteria

Colon cancer

- Any individual with 10 or more colonic polyps
- Colorectal cancer diagnosed before age 50
- Colorectal adenoma diagnosed before age 40
- Endometrial cancer diagnosed before age 50
- Two or more HNPCC-associated cancers.
- Clustering of colon cancer and HNPCC-associated cancer among close relatives

Single cases

- Medullary thyroid cancer
- Adrenocortical carcinoma
- Phaeochromocytoma
- Paraganglioma
- Wilms' tumour
- Retinoblastoma

Virtually all HNPCC tumours have microsatellite instability, which is often used as a screening tool in deciding whether to proceed with testing for germ-line mutations in *MSH2*, *MLH1* and *MSH6* (24, 25).

Referral for specific cancers

The prevalence of germline mutations in specific genes in patients with certain cancers, regardless of family history, routinely exceeds 10 per cent. These cancers include medullary thyroid cancer, phaeochromocytoma and adrenocortical carcinoma. Referral to a cancer genetic counselling service is recommended in all cases (Box 3.3) (26).

Referral for patient concern

Patient concern is a common and valid reason for referral to genetic counselling. Often risk assessment alleviates fear. Even in the setting of a hereditary cancer syndrome, genetic counselling and testing generally results in lower psychosocial distress, both for those individuals who test negative and those who test positive (27).

References

1 Freedman AN, Wideroff L, Olson L, Davis W, Klabunde C, Srinath KP, *et al.* US physicians' attitudes toward genetic testing for cancer susceptibility. *Am J Med Genet* 2003; **120A**:63–71.

2 American Society of Clinical Oncology. Statement of the American Society of Clinical Oncology: genetic testing for cancer susceptibility, Adopted on February 20, 1996. *J Clin Oncol* 1996; **14**:1730–1736.

3 American Society of Clinical Oncology. American Society of Clinical Oncology policy statement update: genetic testing for cancer susceptibility. *J Clin Oncol* 2003; **21**:2397–2406.

4 Sweet KM, Bradley TL, Westman JA. Identification and referral of families at high risk for cancer susceptibility. *J Clin Oncol* 2002; **20**:528–537.

5 Rebbeck TR, Levin AM, Eisen A, Snyder C, Watson P, Cannon-Albright L, *et al.* Breast cancer risk after bilateral prophylactic oophorectomy in BRCA1 mutation carriers. *J Natl Cancer Inst* 1999; **91**:1475–1479.

6 Rebbeck T, Lynch HT, Neuhausen S, Narod S, van't Veer L, Garber JE, *et al.* Prophylactic oophorectomy in carriers of *BRCA1* and *BRCA2* mutations. *N Engl J Med* 2002; **346**:1616–1622.

7 Kauff ND, Satagopan JM, Robson ME, Scheuer L, Hensley M, Hudis CA, *et al.* Risk-reducing salpingo-oophorectomy in women with a BRCA1 or BRCA2 mutation. *N Engl J Med* 2002; **346**:1609–1615.

8 Jarvinen HJ, Aarnio M, Mustonen H, Aktan-Collan K, Aaltonen LA, Peltomaki P, *et al.* Controlled 15-year trial on screening for colorectal cancer in families with hereditary nonpolyposis colorectal cancer. *Gastroenterology* 2000; **118**:829–834.

9 Gail MH, Brinton LA, Byar DP, Corle DK, Green SB, Schairer C, *et al.* Projecting individualised probabilities of developing breast cancer for white females who are being examined annually. *J Natl Cancer Inst* 1989; **81**:1879–1886.

10 Fisher B, Costantino JP, Wickerham DL, Redmond CK, Kavanah M, Cronin WM, *et al.* Tamoxifen for prevention of breast cancer: report of the National Surgical Adjuvant Breast and Bowel Project P-1 Study. *J Natl Cancer Inst* 1998; **90**:1371–1388.

11 Claus EB, Risch N, Thompson WD. Autosomal dominant inheritance of early-onset breast cancer; implications for risk prediction. Ca 1994; **73**:643–651.

12 Fitzgerald MG, Macdonald DJ, Krainer M, Hoover I, O'Neil E, Unsal H, *et al.* Germ-line BRCA1 mutations in Jewish and Non-Jewish women with early-onset breast cancer. *N Engl J Med* 1996; **334**:143–149.

13 Ithier G, Girard M, Stoppa-Lyonnet D. Breast cancer and BRCA1 mutations. *N Engl J Med* 1996; **334**:1198–1199.

14 Krainer M, Silva-Arrieta S, Fitzgerald MG, Shiminda A, Ishoka C, Kanamuru R, *et al.* Differential contributions of BRCA1 and BRCA2 to early onset breast cancer. *N Engl J Med* 1997; **336**:1416–1421.

15 Couch F, Farid LM, Deshano ML, Tavtigian SV, Calzone K, Campeau L, *et al.* BRCA2 mutations in male breast cancer cases and breast cancer families. *Nature Genet* 1996; **13**:123–125.

16 Friedman LS, Gayther SA, Kurosaki T, Gordon D, Noble B, Casey G, *et al.* Mutation analysis of BRCA1 and BRCA2 in a male breast cancer population. *Am J Hum Genet* 1997; **60**:313–319.

17 Abeliovich D, Kaduri L, Lerer I, Weinberg N, Amir G, Sagi M, *et al.* The Founder mutations 185delAG and 5382insC in BRCA1 and 6174delT in BRCA2 appear in 60% of ovarian cancer and 30% of early-onset breast cancer patients among Ashkenazi women. *Am J Hum Genet* 1997; **60**:505–514.

18 Fodor FH, Weston A, Bleiweiss IJ, McCurdy LD, Walsh MM, Tartter PI, *et al.* Frequency and carrier risk associated with common BRCA1 and BRCA2 mutations in Ashkenazi Jewish breast cancer patients. *Am J Hum Genet* 1998; **63**:45–51.

19 King MC, Marks JH, Mandell JB. Breast and ovarian cancer risks due to inherited mutations in BRCA1 and BRCA2. *Science* 2003; **302**:643–646.

20 Martin AM, Blackwood MA, Antin-Ozerkis D, Shih HA, Calzone K, Colligon TA, *et al.* Germline mutations in BRCA1 and BRCA2 in breast-ovarian families from a breast cancer risk evaluation clinic. *J Clin Oncol* 2001; **19**:2247–2253.

21 Domchek SM, Eisen A, Calzone K, Stopfer J, Blackwood A, Weber BL. Application of breast cancer risk prediction models in clinical practice. *J Clin Oncol* 2003; **21**:593–601.

22 Lynch HT, de la Chapelle A. Hereditary colorectal cancer. *N Engl J Med* 2003; **348**:919–932.

23 Lynch HT, Smyrk T, McGinn T, Lanspa S, Cavalieri J, Lynch J, *et al.* Attenuated familial adenomatous polyposis (AFAP). A phenotypically and genotypically distinctive variant of FAP. Ca 1995; **76**:2427–2433.

24 Aaltonen LA, Salovaara R, Kristo P, Canzian F, Hemminki A, Peltomaki P, *et al.* Incidence of hereditary nonpolyposis colorectal cancer and the feasibility of molecular screening for the disease. *N Engl J Med* 1998; **21**:1481–1487.

25 Salovaara BR, Loukola A, Kristo P, *et al.* Population-based molecular detection of herediary nonpolyposis colorectal cancer. *J Clin Oncol* 2000; **18**:2193–2200.

26 Shapiro SE, Cote GC, Lee JE, Gagel RF, Evans DB. The role of genetics in the surgical management of familial endocrinopathy syndromes. *J Am Coll Surg* 2003; **197**:818–831.

27 Aktan-Collan K, Haukkala A, Mecklin JP, Uutela A, Kaariainen H. Psychological consequences of predictive genetic testing for hereditary non-polyposis colorectal cancer (HNPCC): a prospective follow-up study. *Int J Cancer* 2001; **93**:608–611.

Chapter 4

Principles and applications of gene testing for common cancers

D. Gareth R. Evans, Pål Møller and Bronwyn Kerr

This chapter outlines the principles of gene testing for hereditary breast and ovarian cancer and HNPCC. Testing for cancer syndromes is covered in the individual chapters, and ethical and legal issues in Chapter 18.

Utility of gene testing

Breast and ovarian cancer

Particularly for families with a history of breast cancer, there is widespread expectation that gene testing is both available and useful. In fact, the utility of gene testing is relatively small. In a series of 263 women with breast cancer and a family history of the disease, ascertained through a family history clinic, a *BRCA1* mutation was identified in only 16 per cent, and only 7 per cent in the absence of a history of ovarian cancer as well (1).

A *BRCA1* mutation has been found in only 3.6 per cent of female breast cancer patients with onset less than 35 years and without a family history of breast or ovarian cancer (2). Although about 4 to 5 per cent of breast cancer is thought to be due to inheritance of a highly penetrant dominant cancer predisposing gene (3, 4), these genes may only account for about 20 per cent of the familial risk. However, from twin studies, up to 27 per cent of breast cancer has been found to be attributable to heritable factors (5). Even in families with four breast cancers diagnosed at <60 years of age, less than half are due to mutations in *BRCA1/2* (6). Therefore the likelihood of detecting a mutation in *BRCA1/2* will clearly depend on the threshold set for undertaking mutation testing, as well as the sensitivity of the techniques used.

Direct sequencing for mutations in *BRCA1* will only detect approximately 80 to 85 per cent of gene mutations. Guidelines in the US set by the American Society of Clinical Oncology (ASCO) (7) suggest a 10 per cent likelihood of mutation detection is an appropriate threshold for undertaking mutation screening. Thus, isolated cases of breast cancer at any age would not qualify. Such criteria may be relaxed as suggested in Chapter 3. A more realistic threshold in Europe might be 20 per cent for *BRCA1/2* combined or 10 per cent for each gene. Using a scoring system that has been developed in Manchester (see below) a 20 per cent cut off for identifying a mutation in either

BRCA1 or *BRCA2* is possible. Using this threshold, as defined in the NICE (National Institute of Clinical Excellence) guideline for familial breast cancer in the UK (8), a high detection rate for mutations is achieved.

If these guidelines were applied to the 891 samples previously screened for mutations in *BRCA1* and *BRCA2* in Manchester, 434 would be ineligible. However, in this group only 22 mutations (5 per cent) would have been missed. In the remaining 457 samples that would qualify for mutation screening, 157 mutations would have been detected resulting in an overall detection rate of 34 per cent. The potentially eligible families using this threshold would only be about 20 per cent of those that have been assessed as at least moderate risk (1 in 5–6 lifetime risk), in whom a living family member is available.

Hereditary non-polyposis colorectal cancer (HNPCC)

Most centres would screen families fulfilling Amsterdam (including modified) criteria for mutations in *MSH2* and *MLH1* and possibly also *MSH6* (Chapter 10). Detection rates again depend on the techniques used. In particular, the frequency of single or multiple exon deletions necessitates use of a technique such as Multiple Ligation Protection Assay (MLPA), as up to 25 per cent of mutations are of this sort (9).

Using Amsterdam criteria alone, about 50 per cent (30–70 per cent) of families will have a detectable mutation in an affected individual (10, 11). Most centres then use a prescreening tool for lesser family histories fulfilling Bethesda criteria (Chapter 10). By using microsatellite instability and protein staining on tumour specimens from affected individuals, detection frequencies for mutations in excess of 60 per cent can be obtained. Using this combined approach, a high detection frequency is obtained while missing very few mutation-positive families (12). Nonetheless, only about 20 per cent of families that have attended our centre in Manchester with a family history of colorectal cancer would have qualified for such full mutation testing.

Who to test

Once a *BRCA1* or *BRCA2* or HNPCC mismatch repair gene mutation has been identified in an affected family member, a definitive genetic test is available to all blood relatives. An individual testing negative for such a mutation in the family will not be at any substantially increased risk of cancer and will have no risk of transmitting the gene fault to their offspring. Interventions such as early screening and consideration of risk-reducing surgery will no longer be necessary. In practice, even if the initial risk of carrying a mutation is 50 per cent, many women who undertake testing for *BRCA1/2* are in their fifties and so their chance of carrying the mutation will be less as they have not already developed breast or ovarian cancer. As a result, about two in three women test negative for the gene fault in clinical practice.

Clearly some high-risk families will not have a living, affected relative who can be tested. Unfortunately, a negative test for *BRCA1* and *BRCA2* in an unaffected family member will not substantially reduce the risk of breast cancer in that individual in most instances. This is because the majority of families even qualifying for testing (2 in 3) will not have a detectable *BRCA1* or *BRCA2* mutation (see above). Therefore a negative test is likely to be uninformative.

For bowel cancer, while gene testing requires the presence of a living affected person, microsatellite instability and immunohistochemistry on tumour specimens can be useful in determining how likely HNPCC is, and therefore the appropriate type of screening and screening intervals.

Mutation screening scores

Breast and ovarian cancer

The likelihood of finding a mutation in *BRCA1* is increased by a family history of both breast and ovarian cancer, an average age of diagnosis of less than 55 years for breast cancer, the presence of breast and ovarian cancer in the same woman and Ashkenazi ancestry (1). Recently, other tumour-related factors, such as lack of oestrogen receptors, grade 3 and p53 staining, have also been shown to correlate highly with germline *BRCA1* mutation status (13). Although ovarian cancer is still a predictor for identifying a *BRCA2* mutation, a young age at breast cancer diagnosis is less compelling. Tumour-related characteristics are less clear cut for *BRCA2*, although tissue microarray shows promising signs. The presence of early onset prostate cancer or pancreatic cancer is a further indicator of a possible *BRCA2* mutation.

A scoring system has been developed to aid the prioritization of samples for mutation screening of *BRCA1/2* (Table 4.1). This has been shown to outperform other manual scoring systems, including Couch (1) and two models developed by Myriad (Frank 1 and Frank 2) (14, 15). In particular, it appears to be superior to the computer based scoring system, BRCAPRO (16), especially for *BRCA2*, and has much higher sensitivity and specificity than the older models at both the 10 and 20 per cent predicted mutation detection thresholds (17).

To use the scoring system, a score for each cancer (bilateral cancers are considered as 2) is summated for each lineage within the family, extending from the affected person to be tested. The highest score is then used to assess the overall chances of a *BRCA1* or *BRCA2* mutation being detected (Table 4.2):

- A score of 10 points or greater for each gene is equivalent to at least a 10 per cent chance of identifying a mutation.
- A combined score (by summating scores for *BRCA1* and *BRCA2*) of 20 points is equivalent to at least 20 per cent chance of identifying a mutation.
- A combined score (by summating scores for *BRCA1* and *BRCA2*) of 17 points is equivalent to at least a 10 per cent chance of identifying a mutation.

The gene with the highest score should be tested first unless scores are equal, in which case *BRCA2* should be tested first as the overall percentage likelihood for each score is higher for *BRCA2*.

Table 4.1 Scoring system for identification of a pathogenic *BRCA1/2* mutation

Cancer (age)	BRCA1	BRCA2
FBC <30	6	5
FBC 30–39	4	4
FBC 40–49	3	3
FBC 50–59	2	2
FBC >59	1	1
MBC <60	5 (if *BRCA2* already tested)	8
MBC >59	5 (if *BRCA2* already tested)	5
Ovarian cancer <60	8	5 (if *BRCA1* already tested)
Ovarian cancer >59	5	5 (if *BRCA1* already tested)
Pancreatic cancer	0	1
Prostate cancer <60	0	2
Prostate cancer >59	0	1

FBC = female breast cancer (each breast cancer in bilateral disease is counted separately and DCIS is included); MBC = male breast cancer.

Scores should be summed counting each cancer in a direct lineage, for example:

Proband breast cancer aged 29 years (*BRCA1*–6, *BRCA2*–5); mother breast cancer aged 61 years (*BRCA1*–1, *BRCA2*–1 discounted as not the highest score in direct lineage); father MBC 54 (*BRCA1*–5 only if *BRCA2* negative; *BRCA2*–8); Paternal aunt breast cancer bilateral aged 43 and 52 years (*BRCA1* –5; *BRCA2* –5).

Total score: *BRCA2* = 18; *BRCA1* = 16 only after *BRCA2* testing.

Table 4.2 Proportion of pathogenic mutations found in both genes by scoring in 644 samples

Score	BRCA1 (%)	BRCA2 (%)
25+	40/51 (78)	9/12 (75)
20–24	21/42 (50)	7/14 (50)
15–19	36/99 (36)	20/61 (33)
12–14	20/101 (20)	15/71 (21)
10–11	9/76 (11.8)	10/64 (15.6)
8–9	4/104 (3.8)	3/70 (4.3)
1–7	2/141 (1.4)	3/136 (2.2)
Total	132/614 (21.4)	67/428 (15.7)

Screening for founder mutations

Many countries or ethnic groups have particular founder mutations that are not seen in other populations. In countries with a small founder population, a few mutations may account for the vast majority of breast cancer families. For example 2 per cent of the Ashkenazi Jewish population carry either the 185delAG or 5382insC mutation (*BRCA1*) or the 6174delT mutation (*BRCA2*). One study showed that one of these three mutations is present in 59 per cent of high-risk Ashkenazi families (18). In particular, these three mutations represent over 95 per cent of *BRCA1/2* involvement in the Ashkenazi Jewish community (19).

In Iceland, the *BRCA2* 995de15 mutation accounts for most familial breast cancer (20). In Norway, a small number of founder mutations in *BRCA1* account for more than half of *BRCA1/2* involvement (21). A duplication in exon 13 of *BRCA1* appears to be a founder mutation that originated from the UK (22). However, this mutation is unlikely to account for a high proportion of familial breast cancer in the UK. A possible founder mutation in *BRCA2* (2157delG) has been reported (23), which accounts for around 20 per cent of *BRCA2* mutations in the north-west England population. However, there are no founder mutations occurring at high enough frequencies in the UK or USA, outside the Jewish population, to substantially increase the proportion of breast cancers attributable to *BRCA1/2*.

Screening for common founder mutations in certain populations may have clinical utility, even in the absence of an available sample from an affected individual. For instance in an Ashkenazim family with breast and ovarian cancer, the risks of both cancers would be substantially reduced by a negative genetic test for the three Jewish mutations.

Founder mutations have been reported in the mismatch repair genes that cause HNPCC in populations such as Finland and Newfoundland (24, 25). However, in practice, these have little impact on mutation screening of these genes.

Mutation testing

A number of principles have been widely adopted in molecular genetic laboratories to improve the quality of mutation testing in cancer families (Box 4.1).

The appropriate mutation screening method depends on the types of mutations seen. Several hundred different mutations in *BRCA1* and *BRCA2* have been identified, and these occur almost throughout their sequence. Although some mutations are found in multiple families, there is no one predominant mutation in the UK (as, for example, in the case of cystic fibrosis). Consequently, screening for *BRCA1* and *BRCA2* mutations requires screening of the entire coding sequence, except in the case of founder mutations.

In order for genetic testing to be informative, mutation screening is usually undertaken first on an individual affected with breast or ovarian cancer, who is likely to carry a mutation if one is present in the family. When a mutation is found all other affected family members with an appropriate cancer should be tested, if possible, to ensure that no other significant genetic factors are likely to be present in the family. After demonstration that the mutation identified is the cause of the cancer risk in the family, other related unaffected individuals may be offered a "predictive" genetic test to determine

Box 4.1 Principles of gene testing in familial cancer

- Mutation screening is subject to informed consent (Box 4.2).
- Liberal access to testing for locally frequent mutations.
- Search for mutations in specific genes according to priority derived from probability calculations as described in Table 4.1 and Table 4.2, after exclusion of locally frequent mutations.
- Acceptable turnaround time (from when the laboratory receives a sample until the analysis is completed). This may be a few weeks when testing for a known mutation. For an extended mutation search, acceptable turnaround time may be a few months.
- Predictive testing for mutations demonstrated in the families should be verified in a second test in a new sample.
- When predictive testing for mutations demonstrated in the families fails to demonstrate such mutations, locally frequent mutations should be excluded as well to increase negative predictive power of the test results.

Box 4.2 Informed consent

- Informed consent for genetic testing should be in writing.
- Consent to genetic testing may not be considered 'informed' unless based on a counselling session where the results of an adequate family history are discussed, as well as the nature of the disease, its natural course, available health care modalities to modify with the natural course, and their effects.
- A copy of the informed consent should be given to everyone who has signed one. A written description of the assumed inherited disorder in the family, including its genetic transmission, penetrance and expression of the underlying mutations, as well as available health care, should be given all patients and is part of the informed consent.
- Informed consent for research should always be separate from informed consent for health care. It should be stated in writing that access to health care is not dependent on collaboration for research.
- Communication, including obtaining informed consent, when the patient is mentally disabled, may be done through their relatives, or primary care physician (in Europe), or others as appropriate.
- Informed consent from elderly persons without capacity to collaborate may be obtained from their close relatives in Europe, but only if the individual is incompetent in North America.

whether or not they carry the mutation. Since this test is based on a single mutation, it is much more straightforward than the initial screen. In the absence of a prior mutation demonstrated within a family member, predictive genetic testing is usually inconclusive and of no value, as discussed above, unless in a population with a high frequency of founder mutations.

There are several different types of sequence alteration in *BRCA1* and *BRCA2*. The most common alterations seen in high-risk families are those that are predicted to cause a truncated protein. These mutations are known to be associated with increased cancer risk and are the basis of most genetic testing. Many other alterations are also found particularly those substituting a single amino acid (so-called missense mutations). A few of these (particularly in *BRCA1*) are known to be associated with cancer risk and are used in predictive testing, but the risks associated with most missense changes are either low or not known, and these are not utilized clinically. It is hoped that the pathogenicity of such mutations will be resolved in the next few years by functional and other assays.

Sequencing of the entire coding regions of *BRCA1* and *BRCA2* can reliably detect most, but not all, the relevant mutations. In particular, sequencing is not able to detect various large rearrangements of part or all of the gene sequence. These alterations explain approximately 10 per cent of *BRCA1* mutations (they are rare in *BRCA2*). Relatively easy, quick techniques for detecting large rearrangements have recently been developed (MLPA) and adding such techniques is likely to boost sensitivity to close to 95 per cent. As sequencing is relatively expensive for these genes, many laboratories in the UK have previously relied on other techniques for screening. The sensitivities of these techniques (compared to full sequencing) for detecting deleterious mutations vary but are probably in the range 60 to 90 per cent, but this would drop to below 50 per cent with some techniques if a deletion strategy was not incorporated (26).

As already mentioned above, a dual strategy for screening in HNPCC is required with an exon screening strategy – ideally direct sequencing plus a large deletion strategy such as MLPA (9).

Problems of capacity

The process of genetic testing is expensive and time consuming. Where testing is dependent on a government-funded health service there are bound to be constraints on the finances and therefore capacity of the health system to undertake testing. In the UK, a testing threshold of 20 per cent for *BRCA1/2* has been introduced. In North America, where health insurance largely pays for testing, a 10 per cent threshold is typical. However, both insufficient insurance and patients without insurance will limit demand for testing. Issues such as the ability to obtain critical illness policies that include cancer will also limit demand.

Predictive testing

There are many different reasons for requesting predictive mutation testing: concern about children or family; concern with health surveillance; curiosity; consideration of prophylactic surgery; relief of anxiety; and altruistic reasons such as to help research (27).

A large study of women referred because of a family history of breast cancer demonstrated that those who were primarily interested in genetic testing perceived themselves at greater risk than women who were not as interested in genetic testing. Women interested in genetic testing were more likely to have been self referred, to have a relative currently being treated for cancer, to perceive fewer limitations of testing and to be interested in prophylactic mastectomy. It was suggested that an interest in testing might be a means of gaining control over a perceived threat (28).

The uptake of predictive testing for *BRCA1/2* is greater in women than in men – 48 per cent versus 22 per cent of those eligible in a large European series (29). In women, DNA testing was significantly more common at young age, in the presence of children of their own and a high pretest risk. Uptake of mutation testing for HNPCC is, in general, very high although there are few reports in the literature (30).

The predictive testing process

Genetic counselling is generally accepted as a prerequisite for predictive mutation testing. The process is generally separated in time and content from an initial genetic consultation and typically involves two counselling sessions, at least a month apart. The protocol is based on that first developed for Huntington's disease (31), where emotional preparation and time for reflection are considered central to informed decision making about testing for a condition where no treatment is available.

The medical implications of gene testing in families with an increased risk of cancer are different, however, because of the availability of screening. Shortening of the testing protocol has been suggested. A recent review of protocols for predictive testing in HNPCC in the UK (32) demonstrated that 25 per cent of centres were already, or were considering, shortening their protocol and others would in some circumstances, depending on the amount of prior contact with genetic services and individuals awareness of personal risk. There was general agreement across centres, however, that there were three crucial components of pretest counselling: education, reflection and impact of test results. There is, however, little empiric data that establishes which components of pretest counselling are essential for good psychological outcomes and whether a shortened protocol could achieve favourable outcomes (32).

A randomized trial of an educational approach or counselling approach (education plus counselling) to *BRCA1* testing in women at low or moderate risk demonstrated with both methods that there was a significant increase in knowledge, in comparison to a control group. There was no impact on intention to have the test, although women in the counselling group had significant increases in the perceived limitations and risks of *BRCA1* testing, and decreases in perceived benefits (33).

The following principles should be considered during the predictive testing process:

- Initial contact is usually during the process of working out the family history. The time needed to obtain a conclusive family history varies widely, depending on such factors as the complexity of the family history, the availability of medical files for verification of diagnoses and the family's ability to co-operate.

- Re-counselling of all family members may be necessary whenever conclusions, available health services or information about the outcome of preventive modalities change.

- In kindreds with known mutations, the minimum counselling required is one pre- and one post-test counselling session. Although the patient may have been well informed by relatives, in most centres an initial genetic counselling session is also required.

- Initial and pretest counselling may be given in self-established family groups. Mutation test disclosure should ideally always be done separately, and the patient should be invited in writing to bring one person of her/his choosing to the result session if she/he so wishes. This person should not be a close relative simultaneously receiving a test result.

- A written description of the assumed inherited disorder in the family, including its genetic transmission, penetrance and expression of the underlying mutations, as well as available health care, should be given to each patient.

- Disclosure of the interpretation of all information obtained, with or without genetic testing, should be done as a genetic counselling session, concluding in referral(s) to appropriate health care facilities when indicated.

- The results of a mutation test should only be disclosed during a counselling session, and it should always be followed up in writing. During the pretest counselling session the patient should explicitly agree to this procedure.

- Minors are not at risk and should not be subjected to either counselling or mutation testing.

- The counsellor is responsible for identification of the patient's personal perception of the situation, for adjusting it when necessary, and for helping the patient sort out the arguments relevant to the choices. This implies exploring the patient's personal system of values to facilitate their choice (non-directive counselling).

- The counsellor is responsible for the identification of arguments from relatives and others which may be in conflict with the patient's autonomy, and—whenever necessary—to initiate a process to ensure that the patient's choice is in accordance with the patient's own wish. Whenever necessary, the counsellor should split a group to talk to each family member separately (individuation versus group support).

- The patients should be asked to inform their relatives at risk to approach the genetic department for counselling. In most European countries it is forbidden to address relatives without the patient's permission, and it is advisable to not address relatives directly but wait for them to come forward on their own. Written information sheets about the family mutation may help facilitate this communication.

Outcomes of predictive testing

In a study of 105 women who had received pre- and post-test genetic counselling and who were demonstrated to have a *BRCA1/2* mutation, most were satisfied with the information they had received, although 19 per cent felt they needed more support, and women who had had cancer wanted more information related to cancer treatment (34). Screening practices changed in 58 per cent after the result, and two-thirds considered prophylactic surgery of the breasts or ovaries. Prophylactic oophorectomy has been performed in 54 per cent and prophylactic mastectomy in 28 per cent (34). One-third of women reported that there had been a change in family relationships as a result of testing, with beneficial and adverse effects equally reported. A wide range of emotional responses to testing was found, but 92 per cent would recommend testing to women in a similar situation.

In a European series (29), 51 per cent of unaffected women with an identified mutation underwent bilateral mastectomy, and 64 per cent prophylactic oophorectomy. Parenthood was a predictor prophylactic mastectomy, and age of oophorectomy. However, interest in risk-reducing mastectomy varies across Europe and North America, with low uptake in many centres in the US and Southern Europe (35).

For male mutation carriers, the principal motivation for seeking gene testing was concern for their daughters (36). Most believed they were at increased risk of various cancers, but prostate cancer screening practices after testing changed in less than half. More than half had intrusive thoughts about cancer risk. Most participated in family conversations about breast and ovarian cancer risk, and nearly half in conversations about prophylactic surgery. This latter finding contrasts with a small qualitative study of Irish men whose actual or potential daughters had a significant increase in breast cancer risk. Whilst these men, ascertained through an oncology clinic, had concerns about their own and their daughters' risks of cancer, most felt excluded from family conversations about cancer (37).

In contrast to *BRCA1* and *BRCA2*, predictive testing for HNPCC has a high level of uptake. This may reflect the more straightforward decisions regarding the proven benefit of screening colonoscopy.

A number of factors have been identified as associated with a greater risk of post-test distress, as conceptualized by intrusion and avoidance. These factors include pretest intrusion, female gender and having children and depression prior to testing (38). It should be noted, however, that not only predictive DNA testing but also diagnostic testing in individuals affected with cancer may have important psychosocial consequences (39).

Potential pitfalls in genetic testing

There are a number of different reasons why errors can occur in the process of mutation testing:

- Phenocopies are individuals with breast cancer (more rarely ovarian cancer) in a family with a known *BRCA1* or *BRCA2* mutation, or occasionally colorectal cancer in a family with an HNPCC mutation, who do not carry the familial pathogenic change. Assuming that the mutation is present may lead to false reassurance of their descendants who are tested for this familial mutation. Occasionally two high-risk genes can segregate in the same family, but a negative test even without a family history on the non-mutation side does not exclude the presence of other, lower risk genes. Where affected relatives are available for testing, therefore, it is helpful to confirm that all affected relatives carry the mutation. Care should be taken in testing relatives in families where the nearest proven affected mutation carrier is a second or more distant relative, as a negative test may not be as reassuring with regard to cancer risks.

- In populations with founder mutations it is possible to inherit such a mutation from the non-affected side. The typical situation is a mutation-affected mother, where a common founder mutation may also be present in the father. Testing for these mutations should be included as part of a predictive test for a specific different mutation, especially in the Ashkenazim.

- As a precaution, testing of two separate samples from the same individual will lessen the small risk of a sample mix up.

References

1 Couch FJ, DeShano ML, Blackwood MA, *et al. BRCA1* mutations in women attending clinics that evaluate the risk of breast cancer. *New Eng J Med* 1997; **336**:1409–1415.

2 Ellis D, Greenman J, Hodgson S, *et al.* Low prevalence of germline *BRCA1* mutations in early onset breast cancer without a family history. *J Med Genet* 2000; **37**:792–794.

3 Newman B, Austin MA, Lee, M, King M. Inheritance of human breast cancer: evidence for autosomal dominant transmission in high-risk families. *Proc Natl Acad Sci* 1988; **85**:3044–3048.

4 Claus EB, Risch N, Thompson WD. Autosomal dominant inheritance of early onset breast cancer: implications for risk prediction. *Cancer* 1994; **73**:643–651.

5 Peto J, Mack TM. High constant incidence in twins and other relatives of women with breast cancer. *Nat Genet* 2000; **26**:411–414.

6 Ford D, Easton M, Stratton S, *et al.* Genetic heterogeneity and penetrance analysis of the *BRCA1* and *BRCA2* genes in breast cancer families. *Am J Hum Genet* 1998; **62**:676–689.

7 American Society of Clinical Oncology. Statement of the American Society of Clinical Oncology: genetic testing for cancer susceptibility. *J Clin Oncol* 1996; **14**:1730–1736.

8 McIntosh A, Shaw C, Evans G, *et al. Clinical guidelines and evidence review for the classification and care of women at risk of familial breast cancer*, 2004. London: National Collaborating Centre for Primary Care/University of Sheffield.

9 Taylor CF, Charlton RS, Burn J, Sheridan E, Taylor GR. Genomic deletions in MSH2 or MLH1 are a frequent cause of hereditary non-polyposis colorectal cancer: identification of novel and recurrent deletions by MLPA. *Hum Mutat* 2003; **22**:428–433.

10 Wijnen J, Khan PM, Vasen H, *et al.* Hereditary nonpolyposis colorectal cancer families not complying with the Amsterdam criteria show extremely low frequency of mismatch-repair-gene mutations. *Am J Hum Genet* 1997; **61**:329–335.

11 Park JG, Vasen HF, Park YJ, *et al.* Suspected HNPCC and Amsterdam criteria II: evaluation of mutation detection rate, an international collaborative study. *Int J Colorectal Dis* 2002; **17**:109–114.

12 Wahlberg SS, Schmeits J, Thomas G, *et al.* Evaluation of microsatellite instability and immunohistochemistry for the prediction of germ-line MSH2 and MLH1 mutations in hereditary nonpolyposis colon cancer families. *Cancer Res* 2002; **62**:3485–3492.

13 Lakhani SR, Van De Vijver MJ, Jacquemier J, *et al.* The pathology of familial breast cancer: predictive value of immunohistochemical markers estrogen receptor, progesterone receptor, HER-2, and p53 in patients with mutations in *BRCA1* and *BRCA2*. *J Clin Oncol* 2002; **20**:2310–2318.

14 Frank TS, Manley SA, Olopade OI, *et al.* sequence analysis of *BRCA1* and *BRCA2*: correlation of mutations with family history and ovarian cancer risk. *J Clin Oncol* 1998; **16**:2417–2425.

15 Frank TS, Deffenbaugh AM, Reid JE, *et al.* Clinical characteristics of individuals with germline mutations in *BRCA1* and *BRCA2*: analysis of 10,000 individuals. *J Clin Oncol* 2002; **20**:1480–1490.

16 Parmigiani G, Berry DA, Aquilar O. Determining carrier probabilities for breast cancer susceptibility genes *BRCA1* and *BRCA2*. *Am J Hum Genet* 1998; **62**:145–148.

17 Evans DGR, Eccles DM, Rahman N, *et al.* A new scoring system for the chances of identifying a *BRCA1/2* mutation outperforms existing models including BRCAPRO. *J Med Genet* 2004; **41**:474–480.

18 Levy-Lahad E, Catane R, Eisenberg S, *et al.* Founder *BRCA1* and *BRCA2* mutations in Ashkenazi Jews in Israel: frequency and differential penetrance in ovarian cancer and in breast-ovarian cancer families. *Am J Hum Genet* 1997; **60**:1059–1067.

19 Phelan CM, Kwan E, Jack E, *et al.* A low frequency of non-founder *BRCA1* mutations in Ashkenazi Jewish breast-ovarian cancer families. *Hum Mutat* 2002; **20**:352–357.

20 Arason Johannesdottir G, Gudmundsson J, Bergthorsson JT, *et al.* High prevalence of the 999de15 mutation in Icelandic breast and ovarian cancer patients. *Cancer Res* 1996; **56**:3663–3665.

21 Møller P, Heimdal K, Apold J, *et al.* Genetic epidemiology of BRCA1 mutations in Norway. *Europ J Cancer* 2001; **37**:2428–2434.

22 The *BRCA1* exon 13 duplication screening group. The exon 13 duplication in the *BRCA1* gene is a founder mutation present in geographically diverse populations. *Am J Hum Genet* 2000; **77**:207–212.

23 Davies JF, Redmond EK, Cox MC, Lalloo FI, Elles R, Evans DGR. 2157delG: a frequent mutation in *BRCA2* missed by PTT. *J Med Genet* 2000; **37**:e42.

24 Froggatt NJ, Green J, Brassett C, *et al.* A common MSH2 mutation in English and North American HNPCC families: origin, phenotypic expression, and sex specific differences in colorectal cancer. *J Med Genet* 1999; **36**:97–102.

25 Salovaara R, Loukola A, Kristo P, *et al.* Population-based molecular detection of hereditary nonpolyposis colorectal cancer. *J Clin Oncol* 2000; **18**:2193–2200.

26 Evans DGR, Bulman M, Young K, *et al.* Sensitivity of *BRCA1/2* mutation testing in breast/ovarian cancer families from the North West of England. *J Med Genet* 2003; **40**:e107.

27 Lynch HT, Lemon SJ, Durham C, *et al.* A descriptive study of *BRCA1* testing and reactions to disclosure of test results. *Cancer* 1997; **79**:2219–2228.

28 Brain K, Gray J, Norman P, *et al.* Why do women attend familial breast cancer clinics? *J Med Genet* 2000; **37**:197–202.

29 Meijers-Heijboer EJ, Verhoog LC, Brekelmans CTM, *et al.* Presymptomatic DNA testing and prophylactic surgery in families with a *BRCA1* or *BRCA2* mutation. *Lancet* 2000; **355**:2015–2020.

30 Atkan-Collan K, Mecklin J-P, Jarvinen H, *et al.* Predictive genetic testing for hereditary non-polyposis colorectal cancer: uptake and long-term satisfaction. *Int J Cancer (Pred Oncol)* 2000; **89**: 44–50.

31 Crauford D, Tyler A. Predictive testing for Huntington's disease: protocol of the UK Huntington's Prediction Consortium. *J Med Genet* 1992; **29**:915–918.

32 Brain K, Soldan J, Sampson J, *et al.* Genetic counselling protocols for hereditary non-polyposis colorectal cancer: a survey of UK regional genetics centres. *Clin Genet* 2003; **63**:198–204.

33 Lerman C, Biesecker B, Benkendorf JL, *et al.* Controlled trial of pretest education approaches to enhance informed decision making for *BRCA1* gene testing. *J Natl Cancer Institute* 1997; **89**:148–157.

34 Metcalfe KA, Liede A, Hoodfar E, *et al.* An evaluation of the need of female *BRCA1* and *BRCA2* mutation carriers undergoing genetic counselling. *J Med Genet* 2000; **37**:876–873.

35 Evans DGR, Howell A, Baildam A, Brain A, Lalloo F, Hopwood P. Risk-reduction mastectomy: clinical issues and research needs. *J Natl Cancer Inst* 2002; **94**:307.

36 McAllister MF, Evans GDR, Ormiston W, *et al.* Men in breast cancer families: a preliminary qualitative study of awareness and experience. *J Med Genet* 1998; **35**:739–744.

37 Liede A, Metcalfe K, Hanna D, *et al.* Evaluation of the needs of male carriers of mutations in *BRCA1* or *BRCA2* who have undergone genetic counselling. *Am J Hum Genet* 2000; **67**:1494–1504.

38 DudokdeWit AC, Tibben A, Duivenvoorden HJ, *et al.* Predicting adaptation to presymptomatic DNA testing for late onset disorders: who will experience distress? *J Med Genet* 1998; **35**:745–754.

39 Bish A, Sutton S, Jacobs C, *et al.* Changes in psychological distress after cancer genetic counselling: a comparison of affected and unaffected women. *Br J Cancer* 2002; **86**:43–50.

Part 2

Risk assessment of common malignancies

Chapter 5

Risk estimation in breast cancer

D. Gareth R. Evans, Bronwyn Kerr and
Fiona Lalloo

Introduction

Breast cancer is the most common form of cancer affecting women. One in nine to twelve women will develop the disease in their lifetime in the developed world. Every year 39 000 women develop the disease in England and Wales (population 55 million) and as a result, 13 000 will die (Cancer Research Campaign Statistics). While the general population risk of breast cancer that is widely quoted of 1 in 10, is a lifetime risk, the risk in any given decade is never greater than 1 in 34. This needs to be considered in the context of death rates from other causes (1) (Table 5.1).

Risk factors

Family history

Family history is the most important risk factor for the development of breast cancer. About 4 to 5 per cent of breast cancer is thought to be due to inheritance of a dominant cancer predisposing gene (2, 3). Whilst hereditary factors are virtually certain to play a part in a proportion of the rest, these are harder to evaluate.

In evaluating family history, the important features are:

- age at onset;
- bilateral disease;
- multiple cases on one side of the family;
- other related early-onset tumours;
- number of unaffected individuals (large families are more informative);
- ethnic origin.

It is possible to estimate the likelihood of a given history being genetic using the total number of relevant and related cancers. The following lists family histories of breast cancer that are likely to be genetic:

1 four cases diagnosed <60 years is likely to be autosomal dominant (80 per cent chance of a detectable mutation);

2 three cases if diagnosed before the age of 50;

3 two cases diagnosed less than 60 years, plus one ovary;

4 Ashkenazi with a family history – risk of being genetic increases;

5 isolated case diagnosed under 30 years has a 30 per cent chance of being genetic;

6 male breast diagnosed less than 60 years with a family history.

Remember – bilateral diagnosis is regarded as two cases. It should also be remembered that in populations with a lower background incidence of breast cancer, a family history is more significant.

Table 5.1 General population risks of dying

Age	Risk of breast cancer	Risk of dying of breast cancer	Risk of dying of cardiovascular disease
30	1/10	1/24	1/3.4
40	1/11	1/25	1/3.4
50	1/12	1/26	1/3.4
60	1/18	1/30	1/3.3
70	1/29	1/37	1/3.2
80	1/57	1/48	1/3.2

Hormonal and reproductive risk factors

The incidence of breast cancer within the general population is increasing, and this may in part be related to the increasing use of exogenous hormones. Hormonal and reproductive factors have long been recognized as important in the development of breast cancer. It has been demonstrated that prolonged exposure to endogenous oestrogens is an adverse risk factor for breast cancer (4). Breast cancer is, therefore, very uncommon in Turner's syndrome, as these women rarely ovulate. Early menarche, as it prolongs exposure to oestrogens, increases the risk of breast cancer, as does late menopause.

Exogenous oestrogens, either the combined oral contraceptive (COC) or hormone replacement therapy (HRT), also confer increased risks of breast cancer. The oestrogen element of the COC, although suppressing ovulation, will still stimulate the breast cells; however, the extent of this increased risk is still controversial. The risks associated with HRT are now well recognized (4) (Table 5.2).

The age at first pregnancy influences the relative risk of breast cancer as pregnancy transforms breast parenchymal cells into a more stable state, resulting in less proliferation in the second half of the menstrual cycle. As a result, early first pregnancy offers some protection, whilst women having their first child over the age of 30 have double the risk of women delivering their first child under the age of 20 years (5).

Table 5.2 Risks associated with hormone replacement therapy for women age 50–65 (adapted from:*Current Problems in Pharmacovigilance* 2003: 29)

	Cases per 1000 non-HRT users	Extra cases in 1000 users over the same period	
		5-year use	10-year use
Cumulative breast cancer risk over 15 or 20 years	32	1.5 (oestrogen only) 6 (combined HRT)	5 (oestrogen only) 19 (combined HRT)

It is important to emphasize that these hormonal factors will, in most cases, alter risks only marginally, and even at the extremes only by a factor of two (6). Many women who have most of the unfavourable factors will not develop breast cancer and some, particularly if they have a germline mutation, will develop the disease despite favourable reproductive and hormonal factors. Hormonal factors may indeed have different effects on different genetic backgrounds. It has been suggested that in *BRCA2* mutation carriers, for example, an early pregnancy does not confer protection against breast cancer (7).

Proliferative breast disease

◆ Proliferative benign breast disease (ADH, atypical ductal hyperplasia; ALH, atypical lobular hyperplasia) doubles the risk of breast cancer (8).

◆ Fibroadenoma on a biopsy has no impact on risk.

◆ Atypical hyperplasia increases the risk by a factor of 4.4 (8.9 in the presence of a family history) for the next 10 years only and should be confirmed.

◆ Multiple (but not single) intraductal papillomas also increase the risk. Radial scars appear to be an independent risk factor for breast cancer.

Ductal carcinoma *in situ* (DCIS) is a true precursor of invasive ductal carcinoma, in the same breast, with a 30 to 50 per cent risk of breast cancer within 10 years. It has been reported in *BRCA1* and *BRCA2* carriers, but may be under-represented as a proportion of all tumours in comparison with the general population.

Lobular carcinoma *in situ* (LCIS) is associated with an increased risk of breast cancer in *both* breasts, with an incidence of breast cancer of 30 per cent over a mean follow-up of 24 years. It is not known if this risk is increased in the presence of a family history but LCIS is under-represented in familial cases, including *BRCA1* and *BRCA2* cases. However, this may be a marker for families with mutations in the putative *BRCA3* gene. (*BRCAx* are the genes that must account for the non-*BRCA1/2* families).

When interpreting a pedigree, LCIS and DCIS cannot be considered equivalent to a breast cancer case, as cancer may never occur. However, it seems reasonable to increase the risk a little.

Medullary or atypical medullary carcinoma appears to be highly associated with *BRCA1* mutations. Histology of *BRCA1* cancers is most likely to be high grade with more pleomorphism, solid sheets and necrosis.

Risk estimation

Clearly, autosomal dominant pedigrees allow risk assessment based on the penetrance of likely genetic mutations. Epidemiological studies have demonstrated that approximately 80 per cent of mutation carriers in known predisposing genes (*BRCA1* and *BRCA2*) develop breast cancer in their lifetime (9, 10). Therefore, unless there is significant family history on both sides of the family, the maximum risk counselled to an unaffected woman is 40 to 45 per cent (including population risk) on the basis of pedigree information alone.

In the absence of a dominant family history, risk estimation is based on large epidemiological studies. These demonstrate a 1.5 to 3-fold increased risk with a family history of a single affected relative (2, 3). The risk then increases with the increasing number of affected relatives. These risks also increase with the decreasing age at diagnosis of the affected relatives. Within Europe, risk estimation in the family history

Table 5.3 Variables used in the Gail, Claus, Ford and Tyrer models

Variable	Gail (11)	Claus (3)	Ford (9)	Tyrer	Manual
Personal information					
Age	Yes	Yes	Yes	Yes	Yes
Body mass index	No	No	No	Yes	No
Hormonal factors					
Menarche	Yes	No	No	Yes	Yes
First live birth	Yes	No	No	Yes	Yes
Menopause	No	No	No	Yes	Yes
Personal breast disease					
Breast biopsies	Yes	No	No	Yes	Yes
Atypical hyperplasia	Yes	No	No	Yes	Yes
Lobular carcinoma *in situ*	No	No	No	Yes	Yes
Family history					
1st degree relatives	Yes	Yes	Yes	Yes	Yes
2nd degree relatives	No	Yes	Yes	Yes	Yes
Age of onset of cancer	No	Yes	Yes	Yes	Yes
Bilateral breast cancer	No	No	Yes	Yes	Yes
Ovarian cancer	No	No	Yes	Yes	Yes
Male breast cancer	No	No	Yes	No	Yes

setting is based mainly on the Claus data set (3). However, within the US the Gail model of risk estimation is widely used (11).

Specific computer programmes, including Cyrillic™ and BRCAPRO, can be used to estimate risks (12). These programmes take into consideration varying permutations of age of onset of diagnosis, number of affected and unaffected women and hormonal factors, and, as a consequence, different programmes will result in different risk estimations (13, 14). The Gail model does not take into account age of relatives or second-degree relatives. A new model, Tyrer–Cuzick, incorporates all the currently known risk factors.

A major deficiency of the current genetic models is the assumption that all inherited breast cancer is due to just one or two high-risk, dominant genes (*BRCA1* and *BRCA2*). A review of all these methods has demonstrated that one of the most reliable, and certainly the quickest method, is the manual model of risk estimation (15). Indeed the Gail model and BRCAPRO substantially underestimate risk in the family history setting.

Manual risk estimation

Geneticists should be able to assess risk from a pedigree without the use of a computer programme in order to ensure that results from the programme are within the correct "ball park". Risk should be determined on the basis of family history. Particular care should be taken with a history of abdominal malignancy in any family members and confirmation of the diagnosis should be obtained through medical records or cancer registries. Families with strong histories of both breast and ovarian cancer are likely to have mutations in *BRCA1* or *BRCA2*. If the family history is suggestive of a dominant inheritance, risks are based on the penetrance of *BRCA1* and *BRCA2*. If not, risks should be based on the empirical data described below, using the Claus tables.

Examples

Example 1 – risk to a proband with a mother diagnosed with breast cancer at 30 years.

Step 1: Claus Table 1 (one first-degree relative) (see page 56).

Step 2: Read off lifetime risk = 1 in 6 (16.5 per cent).

Example 2 – risk to proband with mother and aunt affected at ages of 57 and 43 years.

Step 1: Claus Table 3 (one first- and one second-degree relative) (see page 57).

Step 2: Read across to age of first relative of 40–49, and then down column of second relative age 50–59. Lifetime risk = 1 in 3–4 (30 per cent).

This risk can also be calculated using the curves in the manner explained in figure 5.2.

In families not fitting the Claus tables and where a dominant inheritance cannot be assumed, risk estimation can be carried out using the Claus curves. These are particularly useful where concern is about a paternal history or when the history is of a single breast and single ovarian cancer.

Example 3 – two paternal aunts with breast cancer at ages 45 and 55 years (Fig. 5.1).

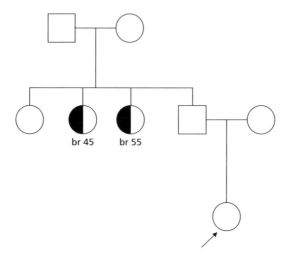

Fig. 5.1 Example 3 pedigree; br = breast cancer.

Step 1: Average age at diagnosis.

Step 2: From graph determine probability of being genetic (50 per cent) (Fig. 5.2).

Step 3: Risk that father is mutation carrier is 1/2 × 50 per cent = 1/4.

Step 4: Determine risk to proband of being gene carrier (1/2 of fathers 1/4 = 1 in 8).

Step 5: Determine risk of breast cancer including general population risk (1/8 × 8/10 [penetrance 80 per cent] + 1/10 [population risk] = 1 in 5 to 1 in 6 (18 per cent).

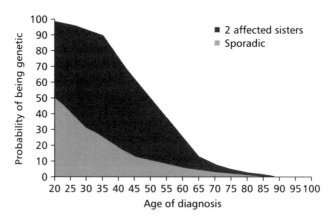

Fig. 5.2 Genetic predisposition – importance of age.

Example 4 – two maternal aunts; one with ovarian cancer age 60, one with breast cancer age 70 (Fig. 5.3).

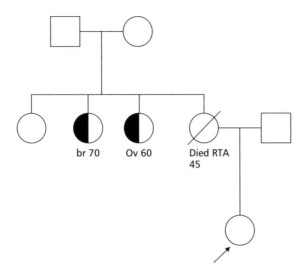

Fig. 5.3 Example 4 pedigree; br = breast cancer, ov = ovarian cancer.

Step 1: Take 10 years off age of ovary diagnosis and average age of diagnosis (60 years).

Step 2: Read from graph probability of being genetic (20 per cent) (Fig. 5.2).

Step 3: If cancer is genetic, mother's risk of being a carrier is 1/2 × 20 per cent = 10 per cent.

Step 4: Determine risk to proband of being gene carrier (1/2 of mothers 10 per cent risk = 1 in 20).

Step 5: Determine risk of breast cancer including general population risk (1/20 × 8/10 + 1/10 = 1 in 7(14 per cent).

The second curve (Fig. 5.4) demonstrates the penetrance of gene mutations. It is possible therefore to modify the likelihood of an individual inheriting a mutation based on their age. Therefore, if there is an intervening unaffected female relative (with intact breasts) the risk to the proband can be decreased.

Example 5 – Two maternal aunts with breast cancer at ages 45 and 55 years (Fig. 5.4).

Step 1: Average age at diagnosis.

Step 2: From graph determine probability of being genetic (50 per cent) (Fig. 5.2).

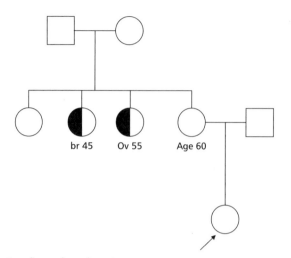

Fig. 5.4 Example 5 pedigree; br = breast cancer.

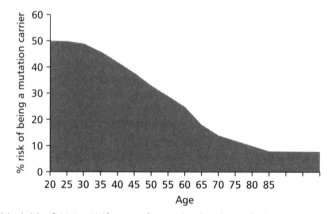

Fig. 5.5 Residual risk of *BRCA1/2* if cancer free and a daughter of a known mutation carrier.

Step 3: Determine mother's risk of being a gene carrier if well at age 60 years (Starts at 1 in 4 and decrease by 50 per cent using graph [Fig. 5.5], as residual risk is 1/2 original risk from graph. Therefore risk of being gene carrier is 1 in 8).

Step 4: Determine risk to proband of being gene carrier (1/2 of mother's 1 in 8 risk = 1 in 16).

Step 5: Determine risk of breast cancer including general population risk (1/16 × 8/10 [penetrance 80 per cent] +1/10 [population risk] = 1 in 7 (15 per cent).

At the extremes, hormonal factors may then be used to modify risk to an individual woman. For dominant families, an individual's risk to health is determined from the known associations of *BRCA1* and *BRCA2* mutations (Table 5.4).

Table 5.4 Risks associated with *BRCA1* and *BRCA2*

| Gene | Lifetime cancer risk (%) | | |
	Breast risk	Ovary risk	Other
BRCA1	80	50	Minimal
BRCA2	80	10–20	Prostate – 14, Male breast – 10

With both genes, mutation carriers have a lifetime risk of a second breast primary of 60%.

With *BRCA2* mutations the risk of a number of other malignancies are increased, including lymphomas and gastric, pancreatic, thyroid and gallbladder malignancies (16).

Ethnic populations and risk assessment of breast cancer

There is little information available on risk estimation in women of different ethnic backgrounds. The Claus data were derived from a population that included women of Anglo-Saxon and Afro-Caribbean origin. Outside Western Europe, Australia and North America, the background incidence of breast cancer is lower. A family history of breast cancer in these populations may therefore be more significant, and risk figures should be increased to take account of this.

The Ashkenazi Jewish population has an increased incidence of breast cancer and there are a number of issues specific to this population. This is due to the high frequency of founder mutations – 185delAG and 5382insC in *BRCA1* and 6174delT in *BRCA2* (combined frequency of 2.5 per cent). Therefore a gene mutation is more likely with a less significant family history (17). Among Ashkenazi women, there is a 10 per cent chance of a *BRCA1* mutation with:

- a single breast cancer <50 years;
- two breast cancers <60 years;
- breast cancer less than 70 years with an ovarian cancer in a first or second-degree relative.

Overall, these three mutations appear to account for at least 50 per cent of the hereditary component of breast cancer and 66 per cent of ovarian cancer in the Jewish population. Therefore excluding these mutations can halve the risk.

The implications of these data are:

- In predictive testing in Ashkenazi families, all three founder mutations should be looked for on both sides of the family.
- In the presence of a family history excluding 185delAG, 6174delT and 5382insC in an unaffected patient would reduce the risk in those families where there are no living affected patients.
- In Jewish women, the risk figures given should take account of the fact that the hereditary component is about doubled, that is 20 per cent of breast cancer in the

40s is hereditary rather than 10 per cent. This increases lifetime risk to first-degree relatives from 1 in 8 to 1 in 6 and therefore changes the family history at which screening would be considered.

Appendix

Risk assessment for women with a family history of breast cancer (from Claus *et al. Cancer*, 1994; 73: 643–651. Reproduced by permission of Wiley-Liss Inc., a subsidiary of John Wiley and Sons Inc.).

Claus Table 1 Predicted cumulative probability of breast cancer for a woman who has one first-degree relative (FDR) affected with breast cancer, by age of onset of the affected relative

Age of woman	Affected FDR with age of onset (years)					
	20–29	30–39	40–49	50–59	60–69	70–79
29	.007	.005	.003	.002	.002	.001
39	.025	.017	.012	.008	.006	.005
49	.062	.044	.032	.023	.018	.015
59	.116	.086	.064	.049	.040	.035
69	.171	.130	.101	.082	.070	.062
79	.211	.165	.132	.110	.096	.088
lifetime risk	1 in 5	1 in 6	1 in 8	1 in 9	1 in 10	1 in 12

Claus Table 2 Predicted cumulative probability of breast cancer for a woman who has one second-degree relative (SDR) affected with breast cancer, by age of onset of the affected relative

Age of woman	Affected SDR with age of onset (years)					
	20–29	30–39	40–49	50–59	60–69	70–79
29	.004	.003	.002	.001	.001	.001
39	.014	.010	.007	.006	.005	.004
49	.035	.027	.021	.017	.017	.013
59	.070	.056	.045	.038	.038	.032
69	.110	.090	.076	.067	.067	.058
79	.142	.120	.104	.094	.094	.083
lifetime risk	1 in 7	1 in 8	1 in 10	1 in 11	1 in 11	1 in 12

Claus Table 3 Predicted cumulative probability of breast cancer for a woman who has two first-degree relative (FDR) affected with breast cancer, by age of onset of the affected relatives

Age of woman	Age of onset of first relative										
	20–29						30–39				
	Age of onset of second relative										
	20–29	30–39	40–49	50–59	60–69	70–79	30–39	40–49	50–59	60–69	70–79
29	.021	.020	.018	.016	.014	.012	.018	.016	.014	.012	.009
39	.069	.066	.061	.055	.048	.041	.062	.056	.048	.040	.032
49	.166	.157	.146	.133	.117	.099	.148	.134	.116	.096	.077
59	.295	.279	.261	.238	.210	.179	.265	.239	.209	.175	.143
69	.412	.391	.366	.335	.297	.256	.371	.337	.296	.251	.207
79	.484	.460	.434	.397	.354	.308	.437	.399	.353	.302	.252
lifetime risk	1 in 2	1 in 2	1 in 2–3	1 in 2–3	1 in 3	1 in 3	1 in 2–3	1 in 2–3	1 in 3	1 in 3	1 in 4

	Age of onset of first relative									
	40–49				50–59			60–69		70–79
	Age of onset of second relative									
	40–49	50–59	60–69	70–79	50–59	60–69	70–79	60–69	70–79	70–79
29	.014	.012	.009	.007	.009	.006	.005	.004	.003	.002
39	.048	.039	.030	.023	.030	.022	.016	.016	.012	.008
49	.117	.096	.075	.058	.075	.056	.042	.041	.030	.023
59	.210	.174	.139	.108	.138	.105	.081	.080	.061	.049
69	.298	.249	.202	.161	.200	.157	.124	.122	.098	.081
79	.354	.300	.246	.200	.245	.195	.158	.156	.128	.109
lifetime risk	1 in 3	1 in 3	1 in 4	1 in 5	1 in 4	1 in 5	1 in 6	1 in 6	1 in 8	1 in 9

Claus Table 4 Predicted cumulative probability of breast cancer for a woman who has a mother and maternal aunt* affected with breast cancer, by age of onset of the affected relatives

Age of woman — **Age of onset of mother**

20–29

Age of woman	Age of onset of maternal aunt*					
	20–29	30–39	40–49	50–59	60–69	70–79
29	.019	.018	.017	.016	.014	.012
39	.064	.062	.058	.054	.047	.040
49	.153	.148	.141	.129	.115	.098
59	.273	.265	.251	.232	.206	.178
69	.382	.371	.353	.327	.293	.254
79	.450	.437	.417	.388	.349	.305
lifetime risk	1 in 2	1 in 2–3	1 in 2–3	1 in 2–3	1 in 3	1 in 3

30–39

Age of woman	Age of onset of maternal aunt*					
	20–29	30–39	40–49	50–59	60–69	70–79
29	.018	.017	.016	.014	.011	.009
39	.061	.058	.053	.046	.039	.031
49	.147	.139	.128	.112	.094	.076
59	.262	.249	.229	.203	.172	.140
69	.367	.350	.323	.287	.246	.204
79	.433	.414	.383	.343	.296	.248
lifetime risk	1 in 2–3	1 in 2–3	1 in 2–3	1 in 3	1 in 3	1 in 4

Age of onset of mother

40–49

Age of woman	Age of onset of maternal aunt*					
	20–29	30–39	40–49	50–59	60–69	70–79
29	.017	.015	.013	.011	.009	.006
39	.057	.052	.046	.038	.030	.022
49	.137	.125	.110	.092	.073	.056
59	.245	.225	.199	.167	.134	.106
69	.344	.317	.282	.240	.196	.158
79	.407	.377	.338	.289	.239	.196
lifetime risk	1 in 2–3	1 in 2–3	1 in 3	1 in 3	1 in 4	1 in 5

50–59

Age of woman	Age of onset of maternal aunt*					
	20–29	30–39	40–49	50–59	60–69	70–79
29	.015	.013	.011	.008	.006	.004
39	.051	.044	.036	.028	.021	.016
49	.122	.107	.089	.070	.053	.040
59	.220	.194	.162	.130	.101	.078
69	.311	.275	.233	.190	.151	.121
79	.369	.329	.281	.233	.188	.154
lifetime risk	1 in 2–3	1 in 3	1 in 3	1 in 4	1 in 5	1 in 7

Claus Table 4 continued

	Age of onset of mother											
	60-69						70-79					
	Age of onset of maternal aunt*											
	20-29	30-39	40-49	50-59	60-69	70-79	20-29	30-39	40-49	50-59	60-69	70-79
29	.013	.010	.008	.006	.004	.003	.010	.008	.006	.004	.003	.002
39	.043	.035	.027	.020	.015	.011	.034	.026	.019	.014	.010	.008
49	.104	.086	.067	.051	.038	.029	.082	.065	.049	.036	.027	.021
59	.187	.157	.125	.096	.075	.059	.151	.121	.093	.071	.056	.046
69	.267	.226	.183	.145	.116	.094	.218	.178	.141	.111	.090	.077
79	.320	.274	.225	.182	.148	.124	.264	.219	.177	.143	.120	.105
lifetime risk	1 in 3	1 in 3-4	1 in 4-5	1 in 5	1 in 7	1 in 8	1 in 4	1 in 4-5	1 in 6	1 in 7	1 in 8	1 in 10

* maternal aunt ≈ maternal grandmother

Claus Table 5 Predicted cumulative probability of breast cancer for a woman who has a mother and paternal aunt* affected with breast cancer, by age of onset of the affected relatives

Age of woman	Age of onset of mother											
	20–29						30–39					
	Age of onset of paternal aunt*											
	20–29	30–39	40–49	50–59	60–69	70–79	20–29	30–39	40–49	50–59	60–69	70–79
29	.010	.009	.008	.008	.007	.007	.008	.007	.006	.005	.005	.005
39	.033	.030	.028	.026	.025	.025	.026	.023	.021	.019	.018	.018
49	.080	.073	.068	.065	.063	.062	.064	.057	.052	.048	.046	.045
59	.148	.136	.127	.121	.117	.115	.119	.108	.097	.092	.089	.086
69	.214	.198	.186	.178	.173	.170	.176	.160	.148	.140	.134	.131
79	.260	.241	.228	.219	.214	.210	.257	.185	.180	.176	.170	.166
lifetime risk	1 in 4	1 in 4	1 in 4–5	1 in 5	1 in 5	1 in 5	1 in 4	1 in 6	1 in 6	1 in 6	1 in 6	1 in 6

Age of woman	Age of onset of mother											
	40–49						50–59					
	Age of onset of paternal aunt*											
	20–29	30–39	40–49	50–59	60–69	70–79	20–29	30–39	40–49	50–59	60–69	70–79
29	.006	.005	.004	.004	.004	.003	.005	.004	.003	.003	.002	.002
39	.021	.018	.016	.014	.013	.012	.018	.014	.012	.010	.009	.009
49	.053	.045	.040	.036	.034	.032	.045	.037	.032	.028	.026	.024
59	.100	.087	.078	.071	.068	.065	.087	.074	.064	.058	.054	.051
69	.150	.132	.120	.111	.106	.102	.132	.114	.101	.093	.087	.084
79	.216	.197	.154	.144	.138	.134	.187	.167	.152	.123	.116	.113
lifetime risk	1 in 5	1 in 5	1 in 6–7	1 in 7	1 in 7	1 in 8	1 in 5	1 in 6–7	1 in 7	1 in 8	1 in 9	1 in 9

Claus Table 5 continued

	Age of onset of mother											
	60–69						70–79					
	Age of onset of paternal aunt*											
	20–29	30–39	40–49	50–59	60–69	70–79	20–29	30–39	40–49	50–59	60–69	70–79
29	.004	.003	.003	.002	.002	.002	.004	.003	.002	.002	.001	.001
39	.016	.012	.010	.008	.007	.007	.015	.011	.009	.007	.006	.005
49	.041	.033	.027	.023	.021	.019	.038	.030	.024	.020	.018	.016
59	.079	.065	.055	.049	.042	.042	.074	.060	.050	.044	.039	.037
69	.121	.103	.090	.081	.076	.072	.116	.097	.083	.074	.068	.065
79	.168	.147	.132	.122	.103	.100	.148	.127	.112	.101	.095	.092
lifetime risk	1 in 6–7	1 in 7	1 in 7–8	1 in 8	1 in 10	1 in 10	1 in 7	1 in 7–8	1 in 9	1 in 10	1 in 10	1 in 11

*paternal aunt ≈ paternal grandmother

Claus Table 6 Predicted cumulative probability of breast cancer for a woman who has one maternal and one paternal second-degree relative (SDR) affected with breast cancer, by age of onset of the affected relatives

Age of woman	Age of onset of first relative										
	20-29						**30-39**				
	Age of onset of second relative										
	20-29	30-39	40-49	50-59	60-69	70-79	30-39	40-49	50-59	60-69	70-79
29	.007	.006	.005	.004	.004	.004	.005	.004	.003	.003	.003
39	.023	.020	.017	.016	.015	.014	.016	.014	.012	.011	.010
49	.057	.050	.044	.040	.038	.037	.042	.036	.032	.030	.029
59	.108	.095	.085	.079	.075	.073	.081	.071	.065	.061	.058
69	.160	.143	.130	.121	.116	.113	.124	.111	.102	.097	.094
79	.199	.179	.164	.155	.149	.145	.179	.144	.134	.128	.124
lifetime risk	1 in 5	1 in 6	1 in 6–7	1 in 7	1 in 7	1 in 7	1 in 6	1 in 7	1 in 8	1 in 8	1 in 8

Age of woman	Age of onset of first relative							
	40-49				**50-59**			**70-79**
	Age of onset of second relative							
	40-49	50-59	60-69	70-79	50-59	60-69	70-79	70-79
29	.003	.003	.002	.002	.002	.002	.001	.001
39	.011	.010	.009	.008	.008	.007	.005	.005
49	.030	.026	.024	.023	.022	.020	.016	.015
59	.061	.055	.050	.048	.048	.044	.037	.034
69	.098	.089	.083	.080	.080	.074	.065	.062
79	.128	.118	.112	.108	.108	.102	.091	.087
lifetime risk	1 in 8	1 in 8	1 in 9	1 in 9	1 in 9	1 in 10	1 in 11	1 in 11

Claus Table 7 Predicted cumulative probability of breast cancer for a woman who has two second-degree relatives (SDR), both paternal, affected with breast cancer, by age of onset of the affected relatives

Age of woman	Age of onset of first relative										
	20–29						30–39				
	Age of onset of second relative										
	20–29	30–39	40–49	50–59	60–69	70–79	30–39	40–49	50–59	60–69	70–79
29	.010	.009	.009	.008	.007	.006	.009	.008	.007	.006	.005
39	.033	.032	.030	.028	.025	.021	.030	.028	.025	.021	.017
49	.081	.079	.075	.069	.062	.054	.075	.069	.061	.052	.043
59	.149	.145	.138	.129	.116	.102	.138	.128	.115	.099	.084
69	.216	.210	.201	.188	.171	.152	.201	.188	.170	.149	.128
79	.262	.256	.245	.231	.211	.189	.245	.230	.200	.186	.162
lifetime risk	1 in 4	1 in 4	1 in 4	1 in 4–5	1 in 5	1 in 5	1 in 4	1 in 4–5	1 in 5	1 in 5–6	1 in 6

Age of woman	Age of onset of first relative									
	40–49				50–59			60–69		70–79
	Age of onset of second relative									
	40–49	50–59	60–69	70–79	50–59	60–69	70–79	60–69	70–79	70–79
29	.007	.006	.005	.004	.005	.003	.003	.002	.002	.001
39	.024	.020	.016	.013	.016	.012	.010	.009	.007	.006
49	.061	.052	.042	.034	.052	.042	.033	.026	.020	.017
59	.114	.098	.082	.067	.081	.066	.054	.053	.044	.038
69	.169	.147	.124	.105	.124	.104	.088	.087	.075	.067
79	.209	.184	.159	.137	.158	.135	.117	.116	.103	.094
lifetime risk	1 in 5	1 in 5–6	1 in 6	1 in 7	1 in 6	1 in 7	1 in 8	1 in 8	1 in 10	1 in 10

References

1 Haybittle J. Womens risk of dying of heart disease is always greater than their risk of dying of breast cancer. *BMJ* 1999; **318**:539.

2 Newman B, Austin M, Lee M, King M-C. Inheritance of human breast cancer: evidence for autosomal dominant transmission in high-risk families. *Proc Natl Acad Sci USA* 1988; **85**:3044–3048.

3 Claus EB, Risch N, Thompson WD. Autosomal dominant inheritance of early-onset breast cancer; implications for risk prediction. *Ca* 1994; **73**:643–651.

4 Beral V. Breast cancer and hormone-replacement therapy in the Million Women Study. *Lancet* 2003; **362**:419–427.

5 MacMahon B, Cole P, Brown J. Etiology of breast cancer: a review. *J Natl Cancer Inst* 1973; **50**:21–42.

6 Evans DG, Lalloo F. Risk assessment and management of high risk familial breast cancer. *J Med Genet* 2002; **39**:865–871.

7 Jernstrom H, Lerman C, Ghadirian P, Lynch HT, Weber B, Garber J, *et al.* Pregnancy and risk of early breast cancer in carriers of BRCA1 and BRCA2. *Lancet* 1999; **354**:1846–1850.

8 Jacobs TW, Byrne C, Colditz GA, Connolly JL, Schnitt S. Radial scars in benign breast-biopsy specimens and the risk of breast cancer. *New Eng J Med* 1999; **340**:430–436.

9 Ford D, Easton DF, Bishop DT, Narod SA, Goldgar DE. Risks of cancer in BRCA1-mutation carriers. *Lancet* 1994; **343**:692–695.

10 Ford D, Easton DF, Stratton M, Narod S, Goldgar D, Devilee P, *et al.* Genetic heterogeneity and penetrance analysis of the BRCA1 and BRCA2 genes in breast cancer families. *Am J Hum Genet* 1998; **62**:676–689.

11 Gail MH, Brinton LA, Byar DP, Corle DK, Green SB, Schairer C, *et al.* Projecting individualised probabilities of developing breast cancer for white females who are being examined annually. *J Natl Cancer Inst* 1989; **81**:1879–1886.

12 Berry DA, Iversen ES, Jr, Gudbjartsson DF, Hiller EH, Garber JE, Peshkin BN, *et al.* BRCAPRO validation, sensitivity of genetic testing of BRCA1/BRCA2, and prevalence of other breast cancer susceptibility genes. *J Clin Oncol* 2002; **20**:2701–2712.

13 McTiernan A, Kuniyuki A, Yasui Y, Bowen D, Burke W, Culver JB, *et al.* Comparisons of two breast cancer risk estimates in women with a family history of breast cancer. *Cancer Epidemiol Biomarkers Prev* 2001; **10**:333–338.

14 Tischkowitz M, Wheeler D, France E, Chapman C, Lucassen A, Sampson J, *et al.* A comparison of methods currently used in clinical practice to estimate familial breast cancer risks. *Ann Oncol* 2000; **11**:451–454.

15 Amir E, Evans DG, Shenton A, Lalloo F, Moran A, Boggis C, *et al.* Evaluation of breast cancer risk assessment packages in the family history evaluation and screening programme. *J Med Genet* 2003; **40**:807–814.

16 Cancer risks in BRCA2 mutation carriers. The Breast Cancer Linkage Consortium. *J Natl Cancer Inst* 1999; **91**:1310–1316.

17 Lalloo F, Cochrane S, Bulman B, Varley J, Elles R, Howell A, *et al.* An evaluation of common breast cancer gene mutations in a population of Ashkenazi Jews. *J Med Genet* 1998; **35**:10–12.

Chapter 6

Risk estimation in colorectal cancer

Fiona Lalloo

Introduction

Colorectal cancer (CRC) is the second most common cause of death from malignant disease in Western countries. In England and Wales there are approximately 30 000 new cases each year resulting in 17 000 deaths. Colorectal cancers commonly occur in the seventh decade and about 50 per cent are in the sigmoid colon and rectum. The pathology of CRC is usually adenocarcinoma, most of which develop from adenomas. However, only 5 per cent of adenomas will become malignant.

The prognosis of CRC depends on the stage of the disease, which correlates with Dukes classification of bowel cancer (1) –

A   cancer confined to the bowel wall

B   cancer extending beyond the outer limit of the muscularis propria

C   cases showing involvement of the regional lymph nodes.

Whilst approximately 15 per cent of bowel cancer overall is familial, in many cases the underlying genetic mechanism is unknown. The lifetime risk of bowel cancer is 1 in 25 for men and 1 in 30 for women within the north west of England (2). As with breast cancer, the risk to an individual increases with the number of relatives affected and decreasing age of diagnosis. Unlike breast cancer, there is no large data set for estimation of empiric risks for bowel cancer. However, there are distinct syndromes predisposing to bowel cancer, which are straightforward to diagnose using a combination of pedigree analysis and pathology data. These include familial adenomatous polyposis (FAP) and hereditary non-polyposis colorectal cancer (HNPCC) (Table 6.1).

The inheritance of bowel cancer can be summarized as:

- lifetime risk ≈ 1 in 25 for men;
- lifetime risk ≈ 1 in 30 for women;
- approximately 15–20 per cent of CRC are familial;
- approximately 10 per cent are due to a primary genetic factor;
- screening by colonoscopy is recommended when an individual's lifetime risk of CRC is ≥1 in 10.

As with all risk assessments, a three-generation pedigree should be obtained along with medical records to confirm the malignancies. The pathology of bowel polyps is

Table 6.1 Types of polyps associated with specific conditions

Disease	Type of colorectal lesion	Gene
Familial adenomatous polyposis	Adenomatous polyps (>100) Adenocarcinoma	*APC*
Hereditary non-polyposis colorectal cancer	Adenomatous polyps (few) Adenocarcinoma	*MLH1, MSH2 MSH6, PMS2*
Juvenile polyposis	Juvenile polyps Hamartomatous polyps Adenocarcinoma	*SMAD4*
Cowdens disease (allelic with Bannayan–Zonana syndrome)	Hamartomas	*PTEN*
Peutz–Jeghers syndrome	Hamartomas Adenocarcinoma	*STK11/LKB1*
Hereditary colorectal adenoma and carcinoma sequence	Adenomatous polyps Serrated adenoma Carcinoma	*CRAC1*
Hereditary mixed polyposis syndrome	Juvenile polyps Hyperplastic polyps Adenomatous polyps Mixed polyps Adenocarcinoma	Localized to unknown 6q
Hyperplastic polyposis	Serrated adenomas Hyperplastic polyps Mixed polyp	unknown

particularly important, as, for example, hamartomas imply conditions such as Peutz–Jeghers syndrome, Cowdens syndrome or tuberous sclerosis as opposed to FAP or HNPCC (Table 6.1). It is also important to consider other predisposing causes of malignancy such as inflammatory bowel disease. The risk of CRC is greater with ulcerative colitis and increases with the severity of the disease and the length of time diagnosed (3).

Epidemiological data

Most of the epidemiological data is based on studies of adenocarcinoma and adenomas. A recent meta-analysis of familial bowel cancer (4) studied 27 case–control and cohort studies to obtain pooled estimates of risks for various family histories. Relative risks (RR) were as follows:

One first-degree relative with CRC: RR 2.25

Greater than one relative with CRC: RR 4.25

One relative with CRC <45 years: RR 3.87

This is consistent with risk estimates from empirical data from Hodgson and Maher (5) (Table 6.2).

Table 6.2 Lifetime risk of bowel cancer associated with differing family history (S Hodgson and E Maher, *A Practical Guide to Human Cancer Genetics*, Cambridge University Press, Cambridge, 1999)

Age of diagnosis in relative/s	Lifetime risk
1 first-degree relative >45	1/17
1 first-degree relative <45	1/10
2 relatives[a] average age <60	1/6
2 relatives[a] average age >70	<1/10
3 FDR/SDR not fulfilling Amsterdam criteria	1 in 3–5
Amsterdam criteria or MMR mutation in FDR	30–40%

[a] 2 first-degree relatives (FDR) or 1 first-degree relative and 1 second-degree relative (SDR) who are first-degree relatives of each other.
MMR = mismatch repair gene.

The site of the malignancy is also of relevance to risk estimation. A genetic predisposition is more likely with right-sided tumours. Approximately 70 per cent of sporadic tumours occur in the rectum, with only 10 per cent at the caecum, whilst in HNPCC a higher proportion are proximally placed (6). The relative risk for a first-degree relative with colon cancer is 2.82 vs. 1.89 for a relative with rectal cancer (4).

As when assessing the age of diagnosis and site of CRC, it is important to take into account the number and distribution of adenomatous polyps. Polyps occur within the general population and the incidence increases with age, with 34 per cent of those over the age of 50 having a single colonic polyp (6).

Pathology

Adenomatous polyps within a relative increase the risk of bowel cancer. The relative risk associated with adenomas varies markedly with age, although a composite risk is as follows:

One first-degree relative with adenoma   1.99

Hyperplastic (metaplastic) polyps have traditionally been thought to be benign lesions with little significance for a cancer risk. However, CRC can develop in individuals with large or multiple hyperplastic polyps. Serrated adenomas are probably part of a spectrum including hyperplastic polyps and mixed hyperplastic/ adenoma polyps (7, 8). However, if these types of polyps are seen within a family, they are unlikely to be related to FAP or HNPCC.

Specific syndromes associated with bowel cancer

Familial adenomatous polyposis

Diagnosis is largely clinical, with the classical type being diagnosed with large numbers (>100) adenomatous polyps within the large bowel or rectum, either at colectomy or at endoscopy (9). Other features may be seen in FAP, including congenital hypertrophy of the retinal epithelium (CHRPE), jaw osteomas, supernumerary teeth, subcutaneous cysts and desmoid tumours (10–12). FAP is caused by germline mutations in the *APC* gene (13). For a fuller discussion of FAP see Chapter 9.

Hereditary non-polyposis colorectal cancer

Hereditary non-polyposis colorectal cancer is an autosomal dominant condition predisposing to bowel polyps, early-onset colorectal cancer, endometrial cancer, ovarian cancer, transitional cell carcinoma of the ureter and upper gastrointestinal cancers (14–16). HNPCC may be diagnosed clinically using diagnostic criteria. The original criteria, the Amsterdam criteria (15) (Box 6.1), were used to collect families for linkage analysis and are felt to be too stringent for clinical use. These criteria were therefore modified to include pathology other than CRC (17) (Box 6.2).

HNPCC is caused by mutations in a mismatch repair gene, with the majority of families having mutations in *MLH1* or *MSH2* (18). Tumours with these mutations typically exhibit microsatellite instability (MSI), which may then be used as a marker for the disease (19, 20). The Bethesda guidelines (Box 6.3) were constructed to determine which tumours should be studied for MSI. Chapter 10 deals with HNPCC in greater detail.

Box 6.1 Amsterdam criteria for the diagnosis of HNPCC

- At least three relatives should have histologically verified colorectal cancer; one of them should be a first-degree relative of the other two. Familial adenomatous polyposis should be excluded.
- At least two successive generations should be affected.
- One of the relatives should be below 50 years of age when the colorectal cancer is diagnosed.

Box 6.2 Modified (Amsterdam 2) criteria for the diagnosis of HNPCC

- There should be at least three relatives with an HNPCC-associated cancer (colorectal cancer, endometrial, small bowel, ureter or renal pelvis malignancy).
- One affected relative should be a first-degree relative of the other two.
- At least two successive generations should be affected.
- At least one malignancy should be diagnosed before age 50 years.
- FAP should be excluded in the colorectal cancer case(s).
- Tumours should be verified by pathological examination.

> ## Box 6.3   Bethesda criteria for MSI studies
>
> ◆ Subjects with cancer in families that fulfil Amsterdam criteria.
>
> ◆ Subjects with two HNPCC related cancers, including synchronous and metachronous CRCs or associated extracolonic cancers.
>
> ◆ Subjects with CRC and a first-degree relative with colorectal cancer and/or HNPCC-related extracolonic cancer and/or colorectal adenoma; one of the cancers diagnosed at age <45 years and the adenoma diagnosed at age <45 years.
>
> ◆ Subjects with CRC or endometrial cancer diagnosed at age <45 years.
>
> ◆ Subjects with right-sided CRC with an undifferentiated pattern (solid/cribriform) on histopathology diagnosed at age <45 years.
>
> ◆ Subjects with signet ring cell type CRC diagnosed at age<45 years.
>
> ◆ Subjects with adenomas diagnosed at age <40 years.

MYH polyposis

Homozygous mutations in *MYH* have recently been described in cases of adenomatous polyposis (21, 22). This is a recessive condition, although clinically these patients appear to have a similar picture to classical FAP or attenuated FAP with a similar CRC risk (23). They should be managed in the same way. *MYH*-associated polyposis is discussed further in Chapter 9.

There are a number of other syndromes that predispose to CRC (Table 6.1) and that are further discussed in Chapter 9. It is important to keep these conditions in mind when taking a family history or examining patients.

Importance of confirmation

The accuracy of recall of cancer diagnosis in relatives is not good for colorectal cancer, particularly beyond first-degree relatives (24, 25). A recent study has shown that affected individuals substantially under reported colorectal cancer even among first-degree relatives (26). This can substantially change the management strategy in families. The issue of polyps is also a particularly problematic one. Individuals are often referred with a diagnosis of "polyposis" in their family, but on obtaining pathology it often transpires that the relative had only minimal or hyperplastic polyps. Obtaining pathology reports is, therefore, of great importance in establishing the site and multiplicity of CRC and the number and type of polyps. Confirmation of other abdominal malignancies is important as endometrial, ovarian, gastric, small intestinal and biliary tree cancers, as well as transitional cell carcinoma of the ureter or renal pelvis, can substantially increase the chances of an MMR gene defect.

Approach to risk assessment

Risk assessment for CRC should include the following elements:

◆ Take a three-generation pedigree.

◆ Confirm the diagnosis of CRC and associated cancers in the family.

◆ Check pathology for type and number of polyps.

◆ If possible, examine affected individuals for other stigmata of disease such as skin lesions, (FAP, Muire–Torre), buccal pigmentation (Peutz–Jeghers syndrome) or macrocephaly (Cowdens syndrome).

◆ Assess whether the family tree fulfils diagnostic criteria for FAP or HNPCC. If these criteria are fulfilled, counsel and manage appropriately. If possible, obtain DNA from an affected family member for mutation screening of either *APC* or mismatch repair genes.

◆ If criteria are not fulfilled, undertake risk assessment using Table 6.2 and organize appropriate screening.

◆ If diagnostic criteria are not fulfilled for HNPCC, but the history is still suspicious, undertake MSI testing of tumours (using Bethesda criteria, Box 6.3) as a guide. If MSI is high, proceed to mismatch repair gene mutations screening. The risk estimation may then need to be increased, with associated change in management policy.

Example 1 – mother diagnosed with bowel cancer at 51 years of age and maternal aunt at 53 years (Fig. 6.1).

Step 1: Obtain confirmations.

Step 2: Pathology confirms rectal Dukes B in mother without other polyps and descending colon Dukes A in aunt with one other adenomatous polyp.

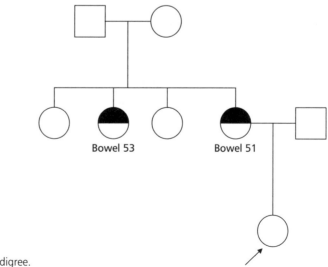

Bowel 53   Bowel 51

Fig. 6.1 Example 1 pedigree.

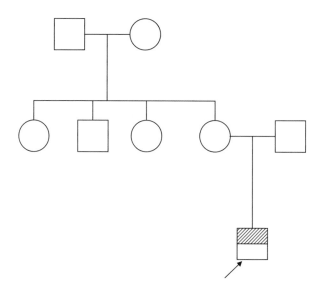

Fig. 6.2 Example 2 pedigree.

Step 3: Using Table 6.2, risk to proband is 1 in 6.

Step 4: Refer for screening.

Step 5: Discuss screening of other family members.

Example 2 – proband referred by surgeon with multiple adenomatous polyps at 30 years of age (Fig. 6.2).

Step 1: Obtain three-generation pedigree.

Step 2: Obtain notes and pathology.

Step 3: Pathology notes 20–25 polyps, biopsies show flat and villous adenomas.

Step 4: Risk assessment could either be FAP or *MYH*—associated polyposis, rarely HNPCC or other as yet unidentified predisposing gene.

Step 5: Obtain DNA for mutation screening; consider MSI on polyps if negative for *APC/ MYH1*.

Step 6: Offer screening to first-degree relatives.

References

1 Dukes CE. The classification of cancer of the rectum. *J Pathol Bacteriol* 1932; **35**:323–332.

2 Shah S, Evans DGR, Blair V. Assessment of relative risk of second primary tumours after ovarian cancer and the usefulness of double primary cases as a source if material for genetic studies with a cancer registry. *Ca* 1993; **72**:819–827.

3 Farrell RJ, Peppercorn MA. Ulcerative colitis. *Lancet* 2002; **359**:331–340.

4 Johns LE, Houlston RS. A systematic review and metaanalysis of familial colorectal cancer risk. *Am J Gastroenterol* 2001; **10**:2992–3003.

5 Hodgson S, Maher ER. *A practical guide to human cancer genetics*, 1st edn, 1999. Cambridge: Cambridge University Press.

6 Lanspa SJ, Lynch HT, Smyrk TC, Strayhorn P, Watson P, Lynch JF, *et al.* Colorectal adenomas in the Lynch syndromes. Results of a colonoscopy screening program. *Gastroenterology* 1990; **98**:1117–1122.

7 Jass JR. Familial colorectal cancer: pathology and molecular characteristics. *Lancet Oncol* 2000; **1**:220–226.

8 Leggett BA, Devereaux B, Biden K, Searle J, Young J, Jass J. Hyperplastic polyposis: association with colorectal cancer. *Am J Surg Pathol* 2001; **25**:177–184.

9 Bussey HJR. *Familial polyposis coli*, 1975. Baltimore: John Hopkins University Press,.

10 Gardener EJ, Richards RC. Multiple cutaneous and subcutaneous lesions occurring simultaneously with hereditary polyposis and osteomatosis. *Am J Hum Genet* 1953; **5**:139–147.

11 Jarvinen HJ. Desmoid disease as a part of familial adenomatous polyposis coli. *Acta Chir Scand* 1987; **153**:379–383.

12 Burn J, Chapman P, Delhanty J, Wood C, Lalloo F, Cachon-Gonzalez C, *et al.* The UK northern region genetic register for familial adenomatous polyposis coli; use of age of onset, congenital hypertrophy of retinal pigment epithelium and DNA markers in risk calculation. *J Med Genet* 1990; **28**:289–296.

13 Groden J, Thiliveris A, Samowitz W, Carlsen M, Gelbert L, Albertson H, *et al.* Identification and characterization of familial adenomatous polyposis coli gene. *Cell* 1991; **66**:589–600.

14 Lynch HT, Lanspa SJ, Bonan BM, Smyrk T, Watson P, Lynch JF, *et al.* Hereditary non-polyposis colorectal cancer–Lynch syndromes I and II. *Gastroenterol Clin North Am* 1988; **17**:679–712.

15 Vasen HFA, Mecklin JP, Khan PM, Lynch HT. The International Collaborative Group on Hereditary Non-Polyposis Colorectal Cancer (ICG-HNPCC). *Dis Colon Rectum* 1995; **34**:424–425.

16 Dunlop MG, Farrington SM, Carothers AD, Wyllie A, Sharp L, Burn J, *et al.* Cancer risk associated with germline DNA mismatch repair gene mutations. *Hum Mol Genet* 1997; **6**:105–110.

17 Vasen HFA, Watson P, Mecklin J-P, Lynch HT, ICG-HNPCC. New clinical criteria for hereditary nonpolyposis colorectal cancer (HNPCC, Lynch syndrome) proposed by the international collaborative group on HNPCC. *Gastroenterology* 1999; **116**:1453–1456.

18 Farrington SM, Lin-Goerke J, Ling J, *et al.* Systematic analysis of *hMSH2* and *hMLH1* in young colon cancer patients and controls. *Am J Hum Genet* 1998; **63**:749–759.

19 Brassett C, Joyce JA, Froggatt NJ, Williams G, Furmoss D, Walsh S, *et al.* Microsatellite instability in early onset and familial colorectal cancer. *J Med Genet* 1996; **33**:9481–985.

20 Jass JR, Cottier DS, Jeevaratnam P, *et al.* Diagnostic use of microsatellite instability in hereditary non-polyposis colorectal cancer. *Lancet* 1995; **346**:1200–1201.

21 Sampson JR, Dolwani S, Jones S, Eccles D, Ellis A, Evans DG, *et al.* Autosomal recessive colorectal adenomatous polyposis due to inherited mutations of MYH. *Lancet* 2003; **362**:39–41.

22 Al Tassan N, Chmiel NH, Maynard J, Fleming N, Livingston AL, Williams GT, *et al.* Inherited variants of MYH associated with somatic G:C–> T:A mutations in colorectal tumors. *Nat Genet* 2002; **30**:227–232.

23 Sieber OM, Lipton L, Crabtree M, Heinimann K, Fidalgo P, Phillips RK, *et al.* Multiple colorectal adenomas, classic adenomatous polyposis, and germ-line mutations in MYH. *N Engl J Med* 2003; **348**:791–799.

24 Douglas FS, O'Dair LC, Robinson M, Evans DG, Lynch SA. The accuracy of diagnoses as reported in families with cancer: a retrospective study. *J Med Genet* 1999; **36**:309–312.

25 Evans DGR, Walsh S, Jeacock J, Robinson C, Hadfield L, Davies DR, *et al.* Incidence of hereditary non polyposis colorectal cancer in a population-based study of 1137 consecutive cases of colorectal cancer. *Br J Surg* 1997; **84**:1281–1285.

26 Mitchell RJ, Brewster D, Campbell H, Porteous ME, Wyllie AH, Bird CC, *et al.* Accuracy of reporting of family history of colorectal cancer. *Gut* 2004; **53**:291–295.

Chapter 7

Risk estimation in ovarian cancer

D. Gareth R. Evans

Introduction

Ovarian cancer is the most common gynaecological cancer, affecting approximately 1 in 70 of the general female population. Ovarian cancer generally presents late and the overall 5-year survival for ovarian cancer is only 28 per cent. If diagnosed with stage I–II ovarian cancer, the prognosis is much improved with a 5-year survival of up to 84 per cent (1).

It has been estimated that 5 to 10 per cent of cases are due to autosomal dominantly inherited genes (2). It is hoped that identification and screening of this high-risk group will reduce the mortality from ovarian cancer. A number of inherited cancer syndromes have been identified in which ovarian cancer is a part. In hereditary non-polyposis colorectal cancer (HNPCC), ovarian cancer is associated with endometrial, bowel, uro-epithelial and other gastrointestinal malignancies. Breast cancer does not appear to be a major part of this phenotype. The majority of these families are caused by mutations in the DNA mismatch repair genes *MSH2* on chromosome 2p or *MLH1* on chromosome 3 (3).

The largest proportion of hereditary ovarian cancer cases originate from families with significant family histories – either of ovarian, breast or both cancers. The majority of these families are due to mutations in *BRCA1* (BReast CAncer 1 gene).

Effect of histology and age on risk estimation

Accurate risk estimation in ovarian cancer families requires confirmation of tumour histology (Table 7.1). It is important to distinguish between epithelial ovarian cancer and the rarer germ cell tumours of the ovary, in which there is no clear association with an increased risk of either ovarian cancer or of other malignancy in the proband or close relatives. There is also evidence to suggest that only certain types of epithelial ovarian cancer that confer an increased risk. Mucinous cancers are not associated with *BRCA1* or *BRCA2* mutations (4), and do not appear to increase risk in case–control studies for either breast or ovarian cancer (5). Borderline tumours of the ovary are also not associated with a mutations in either *BRCA1* or *BRCA2* (4, 6) and do not appear to increase substantially the risk of invasive ovarian cancer in relatives (6). Papillary

Table 7.1 Effect of tumour histology on ovarian cancer risk as part of breast/ovarian family history

Increased risk	No increased risk
Epithelial ovarian	Mucinous epithelial (but part of HNPCC)
Papillary serous	Germ cell
Fallopian tube	Borderline

serous peritoneal primary tumours and fallopian tube cancers should probably be treated as ovarian cancers for the purposes of risk estimation as both are part of the *BRCA1/2* cancer risk pattern.

When assessing risk in a family, therefore, strenuous attempts should be made to confirm not only the ovarian cancer diagnosis, but also the actual histology. Attempts to obtain the histology report should be made if this does not appear on the death certificate (if the relative is deceased) or in the cancer registry. Consent from the affected individual will be required if she is still living. Indeed, a living affected relative many years after a reported diagnosis should be an indication that the pathology may be of the more curable non-epithelial or non-invasive types, which would not confer much in the way of increased risks, or of a different diagnosis altogether. As many as 20 per cent of reported diagnoses of ovarian cancer in second-degree or more distant relatives turn out to be inaccurate (7). Equally, a reported history of "stomach" or "womb" cancer in relatives in a family with a history of breast and ovarian cancer should raise the suspicion that this could have been ovarian.

Whilst earlier age at diagnosis is an additional risk factor (8), it is not as great as for breast cancer. This may be partly due to the fact that ovarian cancer is rare before 40 years of age in *BRCA1* mutation carriers and 50 years in *BRCA2* and appears to occur at an almost equal frequency in *BRCA1/2* carriers from those ages (9). Indeed, for all familial ovarian cancer there appears to be a heterogeneity in age of onset (8).

Epidemiological studies

A number of studies have highlighted the increased risk of epithelial ovarian cancer in first-degree relatives of individuals affected with epithelial ovarian cancer (10) (Table 7.2.). Before using these figures in a family with only one or two cases of ovarian cancer, however, it is important to confirm ethnicity. In a family of Ashkenazi Jewish origin, the risks will be increased (Table 7.4.)

BRCA1 and *BRCA2*

Linkage studies have shown that of families containing at least two cases of epithelial ovarian carcinoma and no male breast cancer, 92 per cent (95 per cent CI 76–100 per cent) are due to *BRCA1* mutations (11). Numerous different *BRCA1*

Table 7.2 Effect of one and two first-degree relative with ovarian cancer on lifetime risk

Average age of diagnosis of ovarian cancer	Risk
One relative	
<50	1 in 15
50–60	1 in 20 to1 in 25
>60	1 in 35
Two relatives	
<60	1 in 5
>60	1 in 10

mutations have been reported throughout the gene. There are, however, some founder mutations, which occur with higher frequency within specific populations (see below), such as 185delAG mutation in exon 2 amongst the Ashkenazi Jewish population.

It may well be that so-called site-specific ovarian cancer families are in fact virtually all caused by *BRCA1/2* mutations. Supportive evidence for this comes from the long-term follow-up of apparently site specific families (12), new cancers in families from the UKCCCR familial ovarian cancer study (13), linkage (14) and mutation analysis in the families (15).

Ovarian cancer risks associated with *BRCA1* and *BRCA2*

Women with germline *BRCA1* or *BRCA2* (*BRCA1/2*) mutations have a substantially increased risk of breast and ovarian cancer as compared with the general population (9, 16–18). Controversy still exists over the true lifetime risk associated with mutations in *BRCA1*, with population studies apparently showing risks as low as 40 per cent (17). More recent, large-scale studies are in keeping with high levels of risk for both genes (9). A reasonable approach, using the available data from these studies, would be to quote a range of ovarian cancer risks of 30 to 60 per cent for *BRCA1* and 10 to 30 per cent for *BRCA2*.

A woman's risk within this range will depend on the ascertainment of the family and the mutation position (19, 20). A woman with six relatives with ovarian cancer, including a mother and sister, will frankly not believe you if you quote a risk of 30 per cent for her if she carries a *BRCA1* mutation in exon 11, the risk obtained from population-based studies (17). Indeed, her risk, based on her own family history, may be closer to 80 per cent. Equally, it would be wrong to quote a risk of 60 per cent to an Ashkenazi Jewish woman who carries the 5382insC mutation in *BRCA1* and whose only family history is a mother with breast cancer aged 45 years.

Although counselling on the basis of the ovarian cancer cluster region (OCCR, between nucleotides 3035 and 6639) in *BRCA2* is controversial, it would be reasonable

Table 7.3 Breast Cancer Linkage Consortium (BCLC) criteria

- At least four cases of breast or ovarian cancer in the family.
- The breast cancer cases should be diagnosed under the age of 60 years.
- Male breast cancer may be diagnosed at any age.
- Epithelial ovarian cancer may be diagnosed at any age.

---

to quote a risk nearer 20 to 30 per cent in a family with a *BRCA2* mutation in the OCCR and in which ovarian cancer has already occurred.

Risk determination when mutation status unknown

Accurate risk determination in families concerned about ovarian cancer is a multistep process:

- Confirm diagnosis in all abdominal malignancy.
- Confirm histology of ovarian tumours.
- Determine ethnicity and whether a founder mutation is relevant.
- For single ovarian cancers only, and not Ashkenazi Jewish, use Table 7.2.
- Determine whether the family meets BCLC criteria using Table 7.3. If so, use *BRCA1/2* risks and position in pedigree.
- If the family does not meet BCLC criteria, use Table 7.4.
- If suggestive of HNPCC, use 10% risk for cancer.
- Risk can be modified using non-genetic risk factors, Table 7.5.

If a family fulfils criteria for the Breast Cancer Linkage Consortium (BCLC) (Table 7.3), the risks to affected individuals and relatives can be based on published data from these families (18). Families fulfilling these criteria have a high probability of having a mutation in *BRCA1/2* and risks can be derived from known mutation risks and family position.

Example 1 – An affected individual with breast cancer, 40 years of age, in a family with two other breast cancers <60 years and an ovarian cancer, has a high probability of a genetic cancer.

Method 1: The maximum risk for ovarian cancer would occur if the mutation was in *BRCA1*, so the risk is 30 to 60 per cent.

Method 2: Consider the relative risks that the mutation is in *BRCA1* or *BRCA2*. In families fulfilling BCLC criteria, with a single case of ovarian cancer there is a 70 to 80 per cent chance of a *BRCA1* mutation and a 15 to 25 per cent chance of a mutation in *BRCA2* (18). Using mid-range risks for each gene, her ovarian cancer risks would therefore be 80 per cent of 40 per cent (32 per cent *BRCA1* risk) and 20 per cent of

Table 7.4 Probability of a *BRCA1* or *BRCA2* mutation for a given family history

Family history	Chance of *BRCA1/2* mutation (%)	Lifetime risk of ovarian cancer to FDRs (%)	Lifetime risk of breast cancer to female FDRs (%)
OC <50 non-AJ	10	6–7	12–15
OC >50 non-AJ	3	4	10–12
OC <50 AJ	60	10	26–30
OC >50 AJ	30	7	18–20
1 OC + 1 BC <50 or double primary	33	8	20–24
1 OC + 2 BC <60	60	13	30–33
2 OC (av. <60)	40	20	24–26
2 OC (av. >60)	20	10	16–18
2OC + 1BC <60	80	25	30–40
3 OC	90	30	25–35
>3 OC	100	40	30–40

OC = ovarian cancer; BC = breast cancer; FDR = first-degree relative; AJ = Ashkenazi Jewish.

20 per cent (4 per cent *BRCA2* attributable risk) making a total of 36 per cent. This could be given as a lifetime risk of 1 in 3 of ovarian cancer.

Families not fulfilling BCLC criteria can be assessed for *BRCA1/2* risks using a number of computerized programmes (21–24). Equally there are risk assessment packages which allow assessment of ovarian cancer risk in these families based on a likelihood of being a heterozygote *BRCA1/2* mutation carrier. For ease of assessment, Table 7.4 provides estimates for the risk of *BRCA1/2* combined (i.e. a mutation in either gene).

From Table 7.4, it can be seen which family histories convey a high risk for ovarian cancer (lifetime risk 10 per cent or more). A second-degree relative may also be at high risk if the intervening relative is a male, the intervening relative is a female less than 40 years, or who has died unaffected less than 50 years. Second-degree relatives will also be at increased risk in families fulfilling BCLC criteria.

Founder mutations

Populations with founder mutations may have a much higher chance of there being a *BRCA1* or *BRCA2* mutation to account for an aggregation of breast and ovarian cancer. Up to 60 per cent of ovarian cancer and 30 per cent of early onset breast cancer in the Ashkenazi Jewish population is due to one of just three mutations (25): 185delAG 5382insC in *BRCA1* and 6174delT in *BRCA2*. Approximately 1 in 40 Ashkenazi Jews are mutation carriers (25, 26). In the UK, all of the predicted genetic risk within the Ashkenazi Jewish population is accounted for by these three mutations (27).

Other genes predisposing to ovarian malignancy

Other genes which predispose to ovarian cancer include *MSH2* and *MLH1*, but these genes only confer around a 12 per cent lifetime risk of ovarian cancer (3, 28). The risk of ovarian cancer appears to be higher for *MSH2* and in particular for an exon 5 splice site mutation, which appears to substantially increase the risk of early-onset ovarian cancer (29). Indeed, ovarian cancer diagnosed at age <30 years of age may be more likely to be due to HNPCC mutations than *BRCA1/2*, with 2 per cent of 101 invasive ovarian cancers having a *MLH1* mutation, but no mutations being detected in *BRCA1/2* (6). Lifetime risks of ovarian cancer associated with HNPCC vary between 9 and 12 per cent (28, 30). Although it is still possible that other genes predisposing to ovarian cancer exist, the great majority of high-risk families are accounted for by *BRCA1*, *BRCA2*, *MSH2* and *MLH1*.

Ovarian malignancy and other syndromes

A number of inherited conditions have been linked to an increased risk of "ovarian cancer", but in reality these links are to non-epithelial tumours. Sex cord tumours are increased in both Peutz–Jeghers (30) and testicular feminization syndrome (31), but the outcome of sex cord and germ cell tumours in general is much better than for epithelial tumours. Gorlin syndrome (naevoid basal cell carcinoma syndrome (NBCCS)) is said to have an increased risk of ovarian cancer; however, only one report of malignancy has been made (32). Although ovarian fibromas are common in Gorlin syndrome they are of low malignant potential (33).

Non-genetic risk factors

A number of adverse and protective factors have been identified for ovarian cancer risk (Table 7.5). Pregnancy, use of the combined oral contraceptive (COC) and an early menopause reduce the risk of ovarian cancer (34). Unlike in breast cancer, the age at time of the pregnancy is not so important. While some of these factors work by reducing the number of ovulations, the effect of pregnancy far exceeds that predicted by 9 months

Table7.5 Risk factors for ovarian cancer

Adverse factors	Protective factors
Nulliparity	Pregnancy
Late menopause	Early menopause
Family history	COC use
Obesity	Tubal ligation
Ionizing radiation	Oophorectomy
Early menarche?	Late menarche?

COC = combined oral contraceptive

anovulation. Interestingly, these factors do not appear to be protective for mucinous ovarian cancer, confirming that this is almost certainly a different entity (35).

The COC appears to be the most effective modifiable risk factor with 10 years or more of use halving the risk in those with a family history (36) as well as in *BRCA1* mutation carriers (37). Other, more controversial, potential risk factors are fertility drugs, which stimulate ovulation. While some studies have suggested an increased risk from fertility drugs, possibly through hyperovulation (38), other studies have refuted this and a pooled analysis of case–control studies shows no significant effect (39).

It is possible to modify the estimate of a woman's risk from genetic factors using her hormonal and reproductive data. Thus a woman who is at 40 per cent risk by carrying a pathogenic mutation in *BRCA1* should be quoted a risk of <20 per cent if she has taken the oral contraceptive for more than 10 years and successfully become pregnant.

Management of increased risk of ovarian cancer

Screening

There is limited evidence for the efficacy of ovarian screening. This is available in some countries through research trials or *ad hoc* screening programmes. Transvaginal ultrasound examination with Doppler and annual, or more frequent, CA125 blood tests are the most frequently utilized methods of screening, although other biomarkers are under investigation. There are some concerns as to the reliability of detecting ovarian cancer at an early stage, particularly when ovarian ultrasound is used.

Prophylactic oophorectomy

The data on risk reduction for ovarian cancer after oophorectomy was limited until recently. Moreover, papillary serous peritoneal cancers (PSPC), which arise from the same cell lineage as ovarian cancer and are clinically indistinguishable from stage III ovarian cancer, have been reported in high-risk women who have undergone the procedure (40). Struewing *et al.* (41) reported the result of prophylactic oophorectomy on 12 large families with a strong history of breast and ovarian cancer, but without information on *BRCA1/2* mutation status. Two cases of intra-abdominal carcinomatosis were noted after prophylactic oophorectomy in 28 women (460 women years of follow-up) who were first-degree relatives of ovarian cancer cases, compared with eight ovarian cancers in 346 first-degree relatives of cases (1600 women years of follow-up) who had not undergone oophorectomy. Although these results are suggestive of ovarian cancer risk reduction (from a 24-fold increased risk to 13-fold risk) following prophylactic oophorectomy, the sample size was not large enough to demonstrate a statistically significant effect.

Combined data on *BRCA1/2* mutation carriers from a number of US and European centres recently indicated that bilateral prophylactic oophorectomy reduces the risk of ovarian cancer by 96 percent and the risk of breast cancer by 49 per cent (42). Taking the upper level of the 95 per cent confidence interval of the hazard ratio as a conservative estimate, prophylactic oophorectomy reduces the risk of ovarian cancer by nearly 90 per cent and the risk of breast cancer by almost 30 per cent. However, using other studies, prophylactic oophorectomy reduces breast cancer risk by 50 per cent in *BRCA1* mutation carriers and genetically uncharacterized women (43–45).

The timing of prophylactic oophorectomy relative to childbearing years is important. The overall mean age at diagnosis of ovarian cancer in the Rebbeck *et al.* (42) data set was 50.8 years (range: 30 to 73 years), which supports the practice of prophylactic oophorectomy in *BRCA1/2* mutation carriers as soon as feasible after childbearing is completed.

Tubal ligation

Tubal ligation may also reduce ovarian cancer risk in *BRCA1* (but not *BRCA2)* mutation carriers (46), but its reported efficacy (60 per cent reduction) is not nearly as great as prophylactic oophorectomy.

References

1 Young RC, Walton LA, Ellenberg SS, Homesley HD, Willbanks GD, Decker DG, *et al.* Adjuvant therapy in stage I and stage II epithelial ovarian cancers – results of two prospective randomised trials. *N Engl J Med* 1990; **322**:1021–1027.

2 Hildreth NG, Kelsey JL, LiVolsi VA, Fischer DB, Holford TR, Mostow ED, *et al.* An epidemiologic study of epithelial carcinoma of the ovary. *Am J Epidemiol* 1981; **114**:398–405.

3 Liu B, Parsons R, Papodopoulos N, Nicolaides NC, Lynch HT, Watson P, *et al.* Analysis of mismatch repair genes in hereditary nonpolyposis colorectal cancer. *Nature Med* 1996; **2**:169–174.

4 Werness BA, Ramus SJ, DiCioccio RA, Whittemore AS, Garlinghouse-Jones K, Oakley-Girvan I, *et al.* Histopathology, FIGO stage, and BRCA mutation status of ovarian cancers from the Gilda Radner familial ovarian cancer registry. *Int J Gynecol Pathol* 2004; **23**:29–34.

5 Shah S, Evans DGR, Blair V. Assessment of relative risk of second primary tumours after ovarian cancer and the usefulness of double primary cases as a source if material for genetic studies with a cancer registry. *Ca* 1993; **72**:819–827.

6 Stratton JF, Thompson D, Bobrow L, Dalal N, Gore M, Bishop DT, *et al.* The genetic epidemiology of early-onset epithelial ovarian cancer: a population-based study. *Am J Hum Genet* 1999; **65**:1725–1732.

7 Douglas FS, O'Dair LC, Robinson M, Evans DG, Lynch SA. The accuracy of diagnoses as reported in families with cancer: a retrospective study. *J Med Genet* 1999; **36**:309–312.

8 Ponder BAJ, Easton DF, Peto J. Risk of ovarian cancer associated with a family history: preliminary report of the OPCS study. In: **Sharp F, Mason WP, Leake RE, eds.** *Ovarian Cancer: Biological and therepeutic challenges*, 1990, pp. 3–6. Cambridge: Chapman Hall.

9 Antoniou A, Pharoah PD, Narod S, Risch HA, Eyfjord JE, Hopper JL, *et al.* Average risks of breast and ovarian cancer associated with BRCA1 or BRCA2 mutations detected in case Series unselected for family history: a combined analysis of 22 studies. *Am J Hum Genet* 2003; **72**:1117–1130.

10 Schildkraut JM, Thompson WD. Familial ovarian cancer: a population-based case–control study. *Am J Epidemiol* 1988; **128**:456–466.

11 Narod SA, Ford D, Deville P, Barkardottir RB, Lynch HT, Smith SA, *et al.* An evaluation of genetic heterogeneity in 145 breast-ovarian cancer families. *Am J Hum Genet* 1995; **56**:254–264.

12 Evans DG, Ribiero G, Warrell D, Donnai D. Ovarian cancer family and prophylactic choices. *J Med Genet* 1992; **29**:416–418.

13 Sutcliffe S, Pharoah PDP, Easton DF, Ponder BAJ, UKCCCR Familial Ovarian Cancer Study Group. Ovarian and breast cancer risks to women in families with two or more cases of ovarian cancer. *Int J Cancer* 2000; **87**:110–117.

14 Steichen-Gesdorf E, Gallion HH, Ford D, Girodet C, Easton DF, DiCioccio RA, *et al.* Familial site-specific ovarian cancer is linked to BRCA1 on 17q12–21. *Am J Hum Genet* 1994; **55**:870–875.

15 Risch HA, McLaughlin JR, Cole DE, Rosen B, Bradley L, Kwan E, *et al.* Prevalence and penetrance of germline BRCA1 and BRCA2 mutations in a population series of 649 women with ovarian cancer. *Am J Hum Genet* 2001; **68**:700–710.

16 Easton DF, Bishop DT, Ford D, Crockford GP, Breast Cancer Linkage Consortium. Genetic linkage analysis in familial breast and ovarian cancer: results from 214 families. *Am J Hum Genet* 1993; **52**:678–701.

17 Struewing JP, Hartge P, Wacholder S, Baker SM, Berlin M, McAdams M, *et al.* The risk of cancer associated with specific mutations of BRCA1 and BRCA2 among Ashkenazi Jews. *N Engl J Med* 1997; **336**:1401–1408.

18 Ford D, Easton DF, Stratton M, Narod S, Goldgar D, Devilee P, *et al.* Genetic heterogeneity and penetrance analysis of the BRCA1 and BRCA2 genes in breast cancer families. *Am J Hum Genet* 1998; **62**:676–689.

19 Gayther S, Warren W, Mazoyer S, *et al.* Germline mutations of the BRCA1 gene in breast and ovarian cancer families provide evidence for genotype–phenotype correlation. *Nature Genet* 1995; **11**:428–433.

20 Gayther SA, Mangion J, Russell P, Seal S, Barfoot S, Ponder BAJ, *et al.* Variation of risks of breast and ovarian cancer associated with different germline mutations of the BRCA2 gene. *Nature Genet* 1997; **15**:103–105.

21 Shattuck-Eidens D, Oliphant A, McClure M, McBride C, Gupte J, Rubano T, *et al.* BRCA1 sequence analysis in women at high risk for susceptibility mutations. Risk factor analysis and implications for genetic testing. *JAMA* 1997; **278**:1242–1250.

22 Couch FJ, Deshano ML, Blackwood MA, Galzone K, Stopper J, Campeau L, *et al.* BRCA1 mutations in women attending clinics that evaluate the risk of breast cancer. *N Engl J Med* 1997; **336**:1409–1415.

23 Frank TS, Manley SA, Olufunmilayo I, *et al.* Sequence analysis of BRCA1 and BRCA2: Correlations of mutations with family history and ovarian cancer risk. *J Clin Oncol* 1998; **16**:2417–2425.

24 Parmigiani G, Berry D, Aguilar O. Determining carrier probabilities for breast cancer-susceptibility genes BRCA1 and BRCA2. *Am J Hum Genet* 1998; **62**:145–158.

25 Abeliovich D, Kaduri L, Lerer I, Weinberg N, Amir G, Sagi M, *et al.* The founder mutations 185delAG and 5382insC in BRCA1 and 6174delT in BRCA2 appear in 60% of ovarian cancer and 30% of early-onset breast cancer patients among Ashkenazi women. *Am J Hum Genet* 1997; **60**:505–514.

26 Struewing JP, Abeliovich D, Peretz T, Avishai N, Kaback MM, Collins FS, *et al.* The carrier frequency of the BRCA1 185delAG mutation is approximately 1 percent in Ashkenazi Jewish individuals. *Nature Genet* 1995; **11**:198–200.

27 Lalloo F, Cochrane S, Bulman B, Varley J, Elles R, Howell A, *et al.* An evaluation of common breast cancer gene mutations in a population of Ashkenazi Jews. *J Med Genet* 1998; **35**:10–12.

28 Aarnio M, Mecklin J-P, Aaltonen LA, Nyström-Lahti M, Järvinen HJ. Lifetime risk of different cancers in the hereditary nonpolyposis colorectal cancer (HNPCC) syndrome. *Int J Cancer* 1995; **64**:430–433.

29 Froggatt NJ, Green J, Brassett C, Evans DG, Bishop DT, Kolodner R, *et al.* A common MSH2 mutation in English and North American HNPCC families: origin, phenotypic expression, and sex specific differences in colorectal cancer. *J Med Genet* 1999; **36**:97–102.

30 Swisher E. Hereditary cancers in obstetrics and gynecology. *Clin Obstet Gynecol* 2001; **44**:450–463.

31 Wysocka B, Serkies K, Debniak J, Jassem J, Limon J. Sertoli cell tumor in androgen insensitivity syndrome – a case report. *Gynecol Oncol* 1999; **75**:480–483.

32 Strong LC. Genetic and environmental interactions. *Ca* 1977; **40**:1861–1866.

33 Evans DG, Ladusans EJ, Rimmer S, Burnell LD, Thakker N, Farndon PA. Complications of the naevoid basal cell carcinoma syndrome: results of a population based study. *J Med Genet* 1993; **30**:460–464.

34 Riman T, Dickman PW, Nilsson S, Correia N, Nordlinder H, Magnusson CM, *et al.* Risk factors for invasive epithelial ovarian cancer: results from a Swedish case–control study. *Am J Epidemiol* 2002; **156**:363–373.

35 Riman T, Dickman PW, Nilsson S, Correia N, Nordlinder H, Magnusson CM, *et al.* Risk factors for invasive epithelial ovarian cancer: results from a Swedish case-control study. *Am J Epidemiol* 2002; **156**:363–373.

36 Walker GR, Schlesselman JJ, Ness RB. Family history of cancer, oral contraceptive use, and ovarian cancer risk. *Am J Obstet Gynecol* 2002; **186**:8–14.

37 Narod SA, Risch H, Moslehi R, Dorum A, Neuhausen S, Olsson H, *et al.* Oral contraceptives and the risk of hereditary ovarian cancer. Hereditary Ovarian Cancer Clinical Study Group. *N Engl J Med* 1998; **339**:424–428.

38 Shushan A, Paltiel O, Iscovich J, Elchalal U, Peretz T, Schenker JG. Human menopausal gonadotropin and the risk of epithelial ovarian cancer. *Fertil Steril* 1996; **65**:13–18.

39 Ness RB, Cramer DW, Goodman MT, Kjaer SK, Mallin K, Mosgaard BJ, *et al.* Infertility, fertility drugs, and ovarian cancer: a pooled analysis of case-control studies. *Am J Epidemiol* 2002; **155**:217–224.

40 Piver MS, Baker TR, Jishi M, Sandecki AM, Tsukada Y, Natarajan N, *et al.* Familial ovarian cancer: a report of 658 families from the Gilda Radner familial ovarian cancer registry 1981–1991. *Ca* 1993; **71**:582–588.

41 Struewing JP, Watson P, Easton DF, Ponder BA, Lynch HT, Tucker MA. Prophylactic oophorectomy in inherited breast/ovarian cancer families. *J Natl Cancer Inst Monogr* 1995; 33–35.

42 Rebbeck T, Lynch HT, Neuhausen S, Narod S, van't Veer L, Garber JE, *et al.* Prophylactic oophorectomy in carriers of *BRCA1* and *BRCA2* mutations. *N Engl J Med* 2002; **346**:1616–1622.

43 Meijer WJ, van Lindert AC. Prophylactic oophorectomy. *Eur J Obstet Gynecol Reprod Biol* 1992; **47**:59–65.

44 Parazzini F, Braga C, La Vecchia C, Negri E, Acerboni S, Franceschi S. Hysterectomy, oophorectomy in premenopause, and risk of breast cancer. *Obstet Gynecol* 1997; **90**:453–456.

45 Rebbeck TR, Levin AM, Eisen A, Snyder C, Watson P, Cannon-Albright L, *et al.* Breast cancer risk after bilateral prophylactic oophorectomy in BRCA1 mutation carriers. *J Natl Cancer Inst* 1999; **91**:1475–1479.

46 Narod SA, Sun P, Ghadirian P, Lynch H, Isaacs C, Garber J, *et al.* Tubal ligation and risk of ovarian cancer in carriers of BRCA1 or BRCA2 mutations: a case-control study. *Lancet* 2001; **357**:1467–1470.

Management of familial breast and breast–ovarian cancer in Europe

Pål Møller

Background

History

Paul Broca, in 1866, was the first to describe inherited breast–ovarian cancer (1). He demonstrated the transmission of the assumed underlying genetic defect, its expression, the age-related and sex-limited penetrance, and the possibilities of modifying environmental and genetic factors, but his work attracted limited attention. The concept of inherited breast cancer re-emerged a hundred years later, when it was subjected to formal segregation analyses, which also demonstrated an association with ovarian cancer (2). Efforts were undertaken to locate the genes, leading to description of the BReast CAncer 1 and 2 (*BRCA1* and *BRCA2*) genes. It emerged that in some families most women died of ovarian cancer:the genetic basis of inherited breast–ovarian cancer had been uncovered. *BRCA2* mutations also cause cancers in other organs. Mutations in a number of additional genes cause multiorgan cancer syndromes (*TP53, PTEN, ATM, CHEK2*). Thus, in contrast to the popular concept of 'inherited breast cancer', we are faced with the need for a multidisciplinary approach to a number of distinct multiorgan cancer syndromes.

Familial breast cancer

Some studies have demonstrated that not all dominantly inherited breast cancer is associated with mutations in *BRCA1* or *BRCA2* and suggested the existence of other dominant genes (3). Others disagree and conclude that the responsible genes may be recessive, have low penetrance or be multifactorially interacting, but not dominant with high penetrance (4). Thus 'familial breast cancer' includes both the inherited syndromes with known genetic defects and the more frequent familial clusters that remain unexplained. In keeping with common practice, this chapter deals with familial breast cancer including familial ovarian cancer, and not with the rare multiorgan cancer syndromes.

Sociology of health care

Health care is based on cultural structures. These include the autonomy of individual doctors and different groups of doctors, the roles of doctors versus other health care workers, administrative versus scientific arguments, new legislation giving patients consumer rights, privacy including insurance issues, patenting of genes, etc. The management of inherited breast cancer has become a test case for a number of these issues. In addition, it is associated with debate about female sexuality, childbearing, quality of life and women's rights. Local and national arrangements reflect different local traditions, incorporating these social and cultural differences. These differences are beyond the scope of this chapter – the aim here is to describe the agreed principles.

The Biomed2 Demonstration Program

In recognition of the sociological aspects if health care, the European Union funded a Biomed2 Demonstration Program to describe the situation and suggest recommendations for European activity. Scientific reports emerged, among them a full issue of a scientific journal containing 68 reports (5) and a collaborative textbook including 22 chapters (6). A significant part of the reports described the cultural basis, the problems addressed when implementing new genetic knowledge and the similarities and differences between countries. A consensus was reached (7), not through negotiations, but acknowledging that there actually was a consensus on current knowledge and on what was reasonable to recommend at the time. It may be considered a cultural consensus as well as scientific advice. It has the underlying assumption that equal health care provision should be given irrespective of social class. This shared European cultural factor may not be recognized to the same degree elsewhere. The reports contain detailed descriptions of the platform underlying the discussions in this chapter – they are not specifically referenced but are available for those interested in the details.

Referral, family history and genetic counselling

Referral

Patients may be self-referred or referred by physicians. Either requires education of both the public and medical practitioners.

Family history and storage of information

Collection of information on the family, validating the information obtained and storage and retrieval of the information, for both the single patient and for the whole kindred, is mandatory to achieving conclusions based on family history. In Europe, many countries have medical genetics departments collecting, validating and storing such information as a resource for the whole family. Access to information from such medical files is restricted by legislation in many countries. Informed consent from each family member is needed to reveal personal information to his or her relatives. Access to medical files of the deceased is subjected to informed consent by their living relatives. Although European countries in principle have the same legislation, the clinical practice may vary. These variations will diminish as health services are forced to comply with the legal framework as this is now being harmonized within the European Union.

The following principles underlie the documentation and interpretation of family history:

♦ Family history should be extended both on the maternal and the paternal side.

♦ All cancer diagnoses should be verified in medical files and/or cancer registries. Histopathological reports on tumour characteristics are relevant to risk estimates for the different causative mutations.

♦ Informed consent from all living relatives and from living relatives of all deceased should be filed prior to looking up their medical files.

♦ Probability calculations using information from the family history should be carried out to assess risk for given individuals. (Referral criteria are indications to initiate a family history; risk levels should be calculated when the family history has been completed.)

♦ Affected carriers should be identified to be selected for mutation testing.

♦ Blood samples from all living affecteds should be stored to prepare for mutation testing.

♦ Exclusion/demonstration of the possibility that more than one mutation may segregate in the family should be carried out.

♦ When a mutation is found, verification that all relevant cancer cases have the mutation should be carried out, again to exclude that more than one mutation is segregating in the family and/or to identify phenocopies and adjust risk levels for their relatives.

The value of national cancer registries cannot be overestimated. Such registers contain validated diagnoses of deceased family members, and this information may be retrieved with the permission of the living relatives.

Efficacy and ethics

One particular aspect of referrals has gained attention: should we be allowed to actively seek out patients at risk? If so, should we be restricted by the usual codes on confidentiality (never inform a third party of a patient's health problems without his/her consent)? It was argued some years ago that we might throw away the old rules for the sake of 'doing good'.

In Norway, the approach was to suggest to patients that they contact their relatives so that they may contact the genetics services. Now this country has one of the highest compliance rates reported for the uptake of genetic testing in kindreds with demonstrated *BRCA1* mutations (8).

Most mutation-carrying kindreds have lived with their mutations for hundreds of years. They may need a few years to be identified, to relate to the new situation and to reflect on it and they may need to see the proof that we can actually prevent and cure. Some are concerned about insurance issues, and they may not tolerate any discussion on violating confidentiality rules. We have seen arguments that genetic counselling and genetic testing may disturb the quality of life (including the right not to know). There is, however, no evidence that this is so (9). The dilemma of possibly harming those we want to help has not been demonstrated to be true. In most European centres, clinical activity conforms to established medical ethics, and it has been demonstrated that such activity is efficient and does not inflict harm on the families. In conclusion, it is not necessary to abandon traditional medical ethics to inform and help these families.

Informed consent

Informed consent to predictive testing

Informed, written consent is mandatory prior to predictive genetic testing. It is implicit that "informed" consent is not obtainable without proper genetic counselling, and proper genetic counselling implies an extended and validated family history. Genetic counselling implies information on the consequences of the disorder, the probability of developing or transmitting it, and the ways in which this may be prevented, avoided or ameliorated (10).

Informed consent to diagnostic testing

Until now, mutation testing of patients with cancers has been undertaken after the demonstration of a family history indicating inherited cancer, which means that it has been done in the setting of genetic counselling for assumed inherited cancer. Initially, genetic testing was by linkage and other means as part of research to identify the genes involved. Currently, the most common technique is sequencing of BRCA1 and BRCA2 to identify mutations. In areas where there is a high frequency of particular mutations, a high capacity for testing for these prior to sequencing has been developed.

The laboratory testing capacity would now permit screening for frequent local mutations in all incident breast or ovarian cancers. However, there is insufficient capacity for genetic counselling for all newly diagnosed cancer patients; genetic testing at the time of a cancer diagnosis may not be appropriate and exploring the family history should not be done unless the patient wishes. The suggestion of a diagnostic genetic test, as well as obtaining the written informed consent, could be done by the treating physician. The written information and the consent should include an offer of referral for genetic counselling if a genetic cause is demonstrated.

Informed consent is a contract

Informed consent and genetic counselling, as described in this chapter, are impossible without a multidisciplinary team having agreed on, and established routines for, the health care the patients may need. Informed consent may be considered an agreement between the health care system and each patient. The written, as well as the verbal, information given through the counselling process is part of the consent. The standardization and documentation of the content of the counselling process have legal aspects, and the counsellor cannot make this contract without an agreement with the multidisciplinary team that the health offers in question are actually available to the patient.

Informed consent to research

Informed consent to research should always be separate from consent to health care. It should be explicitly stated that access to health care is independent from collaboration for research and that permission may be withdrawn without any explanation and at any time.

Mutation testing

In general, mutation testing, when available, is free or a small contribution from the patient is required. The laboratory standards differ widely. Full sequencing of both BRCA1 and BRCA2 is not obtainable for a significant part of the populations at high risk. Full mutation testing, including large rearrangements, promoter variations, etc., is not routinely implemented anywhere. Functional assays to determine the effects of missense mutations are not available. Even the best laboratories provide false negative answers, and the negative predictive value of a test is unknown.

This situation will remain in the foreseeable future. As a consequence, a number of families will remain dependent on health care offered on the basis of family history alone. However, high-capacity testing for locally frequent (founder) mutations is a cost-effective way to identify women at risk, and possibly the only way to identify those who have few female relatives and consequently do not have a family history of breast cancer (11–13). It is foreseeable that any women may soon claim access to testing for locally frequent mutations. This will be a logical next step when testing of all incident cancers has been undertaken (see discussion above). It can be done quickly and cheaply and without false positives and uncertain test results.

Familial ovarian cancer

Inherited ovarian cancer is caused by mutations in BRCA1, BRCA2 or by mutations in mismatch repair genes (MSH2 and MLH1). Familial ovarian cancer apart from these inherited syndromes has not been verified. Familial ovarian cancer associated with breast cancer can be discussed as part of the BRCA1 and BRCA2 syndromes.

Familial breast cancer

BRCA1-associated breast cancer is, as a group, different from all other breast cancers (14, 15, 16). Other inherited syndromes including breast cancer may present biologically different cancers as well, but this is less well described. BRCA2-associated breast cancer has younger onset but is otherwise similar to sporadic breast cancer (15). Some familial clusters of breast cancer obviously are due to chance, occurring as a function of the high prevalence of breast cancer in the population.

Chemoprevention

There is no consensus in Europe on chemoprevention. Trials and research continue. Whether or not the trials have indicated beneficial effects is controversial, and that is where we are today – discussing the results of trials. We all agree that oestrogen-receptor-positive breast cancer may be prevented by oestrogen receptor blocking agents and by blocking oestrogen production (aromatase inhibitors). There is evidence that this is true, but to what extent, with what side-effects, and which compounds to advocate, are debated.

Correspondingly, we may believe that oestrogens (oral contraceptives and hormone replacement therapy – HRT) may induce breast cancer, and there is evidence that this is so. In contrast, we may believe that hormones should not induce receptor-negative cancers, and it does not fit our way of thinking that the opposite seems true. Oophorectomy reduces the risk (17), tamoxifen reduces the risk (18) and oral contraceptives increase the risk (19) for breast cancer in *BRCA1* carriers.

The majority of chemoprevention trials have not been properly stratified on mutation status, and it is not straightforward to interpret the results with respect to the different genetic subgroups of inherited breast cancers. In summary, the conclusion is that oestrogen receptor blockers and aromatase inhibitors are assumed to prevent receptor-positive tumours. Theoretically, these substances may not prevent receptor-negative tumours, but the empirical data does not completely support this.

Oral contraceptives earlier in life may reduce ovarian cancer risk in *BRCA1* mutation carriers (20). They may also increase breast cancer risk (19). Oral contraceptives are not advocated as chemoprevention against ovarian cancer, and there is no strong argument against using oral contraceptives if otherwise indicated.

Management of inherited ovarian cancer

BRCA1 mutation carriers are at risk for ovarian cancer from 40 years of age and *BRCA2* carriers about 10 years later. As the time in the preclinically detectable stage may be substantial, preventive measures may be instituted at least 5 years prior to these ages. There is no evidence for intrafamilial association of age at onset of disease: the frequent advice to start preventive measures 5 year prior to the youngest affected in the family has not been properly validated.

Annual screening with ultrasound and for serum CA 125 has no documented effect on morbidity or mortality: the majority of cases prospectively detected within early detection trials have spread at diagnosis and are assumed to have poor prognosis. One series of such prospectively detected ovarian cancers demonstrated a 5-year survival of no more than 59 per cent (21). In addition, at prophylactic oophorectomy, cancers with spread have frequently been found in women with no sign of disease. As discussed above, oral contraceptives are not advocated to prevent ovarian cancers.

Prophylactic oophorectomy at the end of childbearing reportedly prevents 96 per cent of ovarian cancers in *BRCA1* carriers (17). Following oophorectomy, HRT may be instituted without increasing breast cancer risk, but this is not properly documented. The suggestion that prophylactic oophorectomy should not be discussed prior to 35 years of age has become generally accepted (22).

Management of familial breast cancer

Follow-up and prevention should include:

- *BRCA1* mutation carriers (by testing or assumed by family history):
  - Annual mammography and MRI (if available) from 30 years on. For demonstrated mutation carriers there should be no upper age limit. Healthy, at-risk women based on family history alone will have low probability for being mutation carriers past 70 years of age.
  - Prophylactic mastectomy should be presented as an option.
  - Prophylactic oophorectomy past 35 years of age when family is completed.
- *BRCA2* mutation carriers (by testing or assumed by family history):
  - As for *BRCA1* mutation carriers, but oophorectomy may not be indicated before 40 years of age.
  - There is no consensus on practical use, but antioestrogens may prevent oestrogen-receptor-positive tumours.
- Familial breast cancer (high breast cancer risk according to family history):
  - Annual mammography from 30 years on. Mammography every second year (population screening) may be sufficient past 60 years. MRI assumed to be beneficial if available.
  - There is no consensus on practical use, but antioestrogens may prevent oestrogen-receptor-positive tumours.

BRCA1-associated breast cancer

Age-related risk

BRCA1 mutation carriers are at risk for breast cancer from 30 years of age. After 35 years of age, the annual incidence in healthy female *BRCA1* carriers is 2 to 4 per cent per year. Initial reports included selection artefacts and variations related to small numbers, but recent reports on penetrance from family-based series as well as incident cancers show similar results (23, 24). Mutation carriers need preventive health care from 30 years of age and for the rest of their life. As discussed for ovarian cancer, above, there is no proof of intrafamilial association for age at onset.

Mammography and MRI

BRCA1 mutation carriers are at risk for high grade, oestrogen-receptor-negative breast cancers with an assumed poor prognosis (14, 15). The diagnosis may be even worse than predicted by the bad prognostic characteristics (25). Retrospective series demonstrated a 5-year survival as low as 63 per cent (26). In addition, the tumours may be not be detectable by mammography (27), making them unavailable for early diagnosis and treatment by mammography. Early reports on the effect of early diagnosis by mammography were optimistic because most *BRCA1* cancers were detected before spread. Survival analyses, however, demonstrated that the 5-year survival was actually 63 per cent (14).

European *BRCA1* mutation carrying women today know that we believe that MRI is superior to mammography – we are obliged to tell them at genetic counselling when disclosing the test result. At present, we are awaiting the outcome of large-scale research studies using MRI for early diagnosis in *BRCA1* mutation carriers. *BRCA1* mutation carriers should be offered annual clinical mammography, and probably MRI, from 30 years of age, because it is agreed that mammography alone is not good enough (27, 28). All European centres do not have equal capacity to offer MRI. Within a short time, we need to know whether or not MRI alone may substitute for mammography and thereby reduce workload for follow-up on these women.

Surgery

Surgical treatment
When *BRCA1*-associated breast cancer is diagnosed, it is treated according to stage and prognostic markers. It may seem a paradox that this may lead to an affected women being offered breast conserving surgical therapy, while her healthy sister may be offered prophylactic surgery, but that does happen. Some consider this situation an obvious mistake to be corrected; others argue that we have no empirical evidence that breast-conserving surgery is less effective for survival.

Surgical prevention
Prophylactic oophorectomy reduces the risk of breast cancer in *BRCA1* mutation carriers (17). As mentioned above, HRT may be used after oophorectomy. We would, however, like to see more studies confirming the latter conclusion, especially if the uterus is preserved and combined oestrogen/progesterone HRT utilized.

Prophylactic mastectomy substantially reduces the risk for breast cancer. Different centres have adopted different strategies. Some have argued that we have to gain knowledge and we cannot advise prophylactic surgery without knowing the outcome of other measures others feel obliged to discuss risk-reducing mastectomy (28–30). There is no agreement on which surgical procedure to advocate. Reconstructive surgery after prophylactic mastectomy is, in most centres, considered an obligation. Again, there is no general agreement on how the reconstruction should be performed. A detailed discussion on surgical techniques, their benefit, disadvantages and impact on risk for cancer later in life, is outside the scope of this chapter. In general, the more complete the breast tissue removal, the less the remaining risk for breast cancer would be, and the greater the side-effects. A discussion on whether or not prophylactic mastectomy should be actively advocated may await more information on the effect of MRI screening.

Antioestrogens and chemotherapy

Treatment

As the tumours are oestrogen receptor negative, the *BRCA1* mutation carriers are, as a group, treated differently with respect to oestrogen blocking agents compared to *BRCA1* mutation non-carriers. The emerging picture of biological differences between *BRCA1*-associated and other breast cancers may lead to similar differences with respect to chemotherapy in the future.

Chemoprevention

BRCA1 breast cancers are oestrogen receptor negative and not supposed to be prevented by oestrogen blocking agents. As discussed above, however, not all observations fit this paradigm.

Randomized trials

Prophylactic mastectomy and oophorectomy are considered personal choices and are not suitable for randomized trials. As it is generally accepted that mammography is inferior to MRI, it is ethically impossible to suggest a randomized trial to prove it. Irrespective of all ethical arguments, a randomized trial would not be achievable. A putative group randomized to the non-MRI arm would be expected to privately buy what the health care system would not give them. It is available, and many can afford it.

Summary

BRCA1 mutation carriers should be offered annual clinical mammography and MRI (if available) from 30 years of age. A discussion on whether or not prophylactic mastectomy should be actively advocated may await knowledge on the effect of MRI. Those who want prophylactic mastectomy should be able to obtain it, but there are wide variations in how this offer is presented, and there is no agreement on how the surgical procedure should be performed. An option that may not have been given enough attention is oophorectomy at end of childbearing age – this may reduce both the morbidity and mortality in *BRCA1* carriers to as low as 25 per cent of the initial level by taking most of the ovarian cancer risk away and simultaneously possibly halving the breast cancer risk. The combined effect of MRI and oophorectomy is an alternative to prophylactic mastectomy, but we have no prospective empirical data on efficacy.

BRCA2-associated breast cancer

The annual incidence of breast cancer is somewhat lower than for *BRCA1* mutation carriers, the tumours are often low or medium grade, and they are often oestrogen receptor positive (15). Preventive and curative treatment is the same as for *BRCA1* carriers as discussed above, apart from the treatment modalities dependent on the characteristics of the tumours. Any women at high risk for young-onset breast cancer may benefit from the preventive modalities advocated for *BRCA1* mutation carriers, and it is the impression that *BRCA2* mutation carriers are included without discussing cost/benefit. *BRCA2* mutation carriers may benefit from chemoprevention blocking the oestrogen receptors or lowering the oestrogen levels because their tumours may demonstrate oestrogen receptors.

Familial breast cancer

Women in breast cancer kindreds without ovarian cancer may be at high risk for breast cancer. Prospective series of such women have demonstrated that they, in contrast to *BRCA1* carriers, may be diagnosed with precancers or infiltrating cancers at early stages, and that the prognosis when diagnosed in follow-up programmes with annual clinical mammography is in accordance with the favourable stages at detection. The Biomed2 study indicated cure for those diagnosed with precancer and a 91 per cent 5-year survival for *BRCA1/2*-negative infiltrating cancers with or without spread (14). Whether or not to suggest annual MRI for this group as well is a question of capacity. In most countries, resources do not allow it at the moment, and we obviously have to serve the demonstrated *BRCA1* mutation carriers firstly. Within a short time, however, it is foreseeable that this group as well will be satisfied with nothing but the best, and additional MRI is better than mammography alone. One may, actually, argue that this group should be given the highest priority for MRI because we have empirical evidence that early diagnosis and treatment may cure these women.

Conclusions

Management of familial breast and ovarian cancers includes obtaining a complete family history and a thorough knowledge of the different genetic syndromes causing a high risk of breast cancer. Conditional probability calculations to assess risk for individuals within the kindreds, and proper counselling based on the combined information can then be carried out. The counselling session should include an offer of genetic testing when appropriate. This requires the availability of laboratory resources, including both techniques to uncover different types of mutations and the capacity to perform testing within a reasonable time. Sisters and daughters of affected individuals in breast/ovarian cancer mutation-negative kindreds should be offered the same health care as demonstrated mutation carriers. All information should be stored appropriately and it should, by informed consent from each individual registered, be available to all members of the kindred who need it. For this to be achieved, the storing system must have appropriate retrieval functions. With regard to third parties, the files should keep the highest level of confidentiality. The files should be available for quality control (validation of the activity) and for research.

   The conclusion from the analysis of a family history and any testing should be disclosed in a genetic counselling session where the available health care options and their effects are discussed, and the patient enabled to make her choice. Information on these issues should also be obligatory prior to genetic testing as a basis for the written informed consent filed prior to testing.

Women at high risk for familial breast cancer should be offered annual clinical mammography from 30 years of age. Proven *BRCA1/2* mutation carriers, at least, should be offered additional MRI, if available. Prophylactic mastectomy should be available for those high-risk women who request it. *BRCA1* mutation carriers may not benefit from antioestrogen chemoprevention, but data are conflicting. The other groups may benefit.

Familial ovarian cancer in breast cancer kindreds is restricted to the *BRCA1* and *BRCA2* syndromes. Oophorectomy at the end of childbearing ages may be advocated. Oophorectomy will reduce both ovarian cancer and breast cancer risk. HRT may be used until the expected menopause, but the empirical data underlying the latter recommendation is insufficient.

References

1 Broca P. *Traite des tumeurs*, 1866, pp.150–155. Paris.

2 Iselius L, Littler M, Morton N. Transmission of breast cancer – a controversy resolved. *Clin Genet* 1992; **41**:211–217.

3 Møller P, Borg A, Heimdal K, *et al.* The *BRCA1* syndrome and other inherited breast or breast-ovarian cancers in a Norwegian prospective series. *Europ J Cancer* 2001; **37**:1027–32.

4 Antoniou A, Pharoah PD, McJullan G, *et al.* A comprehensive model for familial breast cancer incorporating BRCA 1, *BRCA2* and other genes. *Europ J Cancer* 2002; **86**:76–83.

5 Steel M, ed. *Dis Markers* 1999; **15**:1–211.

6 Morrison PJ, Hodgson SY, Haites NE, eds. *Familial breast and ovarian cancer. Genetics, screening and management*, 2002. Cambridge: Cambridge University Press.

7 Møller P, Evans G, Haites N, *et al.* Guidelines for follow-up of women at high risk for inherited breast cancer: consensus statement from the Biomed 2 Demonstration Programme on Inherited Breast Cancer. *Dis Markers* 1999; **15**:207–211.

8 Bodd TL, Reichelt J, Heimdal K, Møller P. Uptake of *BRCA1* genetic testing in adult sisters and daughters of known mutation carriers in Norway. *J Genet Counselling* 2003; **12**:405–417.

9 Broadstock M, Michie S, Marteau T. Psychological consequences of predictive genetic testing: a systematic review. *Eur J Hum Genet* 2000; **8**:731–738.

10 Harper PS. *Practical genetic counselling*, 1994, p.3. Oxford: Butterworth-Heinemann.

11 Heimdal K, Maehle L, Møller P. Costs and benefits of diagnosing familial breast cancer. *Dis Markers* 1999; **15**:167–173.

12 Møller P, Heimdal K, Apold J, *et al.* Genetic epidemiology of *BRCA1* mutations in Norway. *Europ J Cancer* 2001; **37**:2428–2434.

13 Scottish–Northern Irish *BRCA1/BRCA2* Consortium. *BRCA1* and *BRCA2* mutations in Scotland Northern Ireland. *Brit J Cancer* 2003; **88**:1256–1262.

14 Møller P, Borg A, Evans OD, *et al.* Survival in prospectively ascertained familial breast cancer: analysis of a series stratified by tumour characteristic, BRCA mutations and oophorectomy. *Int J Cancer* 2002; **101**:555–559.

15 Lakhani SR, van de Vijver MJ, Jacquemier J, *et al.* The pathology of familial breast cancer: predictive value of immunohistochemical markers oestrogen receptor, progesterone receptor, HER-2, and p53 in patients with mutations in *BRCA1* and *BRCA2*. *J Clin Oncol* 2002; **20**:1310–1318.

16 Eccles DM, Evans OD, Mackay J. Guidelines for a genetic risk based approach to advising women with a family history of breast cancer. UK Cancer Family Study Group (UKCFSG). *J Med Genet* 2000; **37**:203–209.

17 Rebbeck TR, Lynch HT, Neuhausen SL, *et al.* Prophylactic oophorectomy in carriers of *BRCA1* or *BRCA2* mutations. *N Engl J Med* 2002; **346**:1616–1622.

18 Narod SA, Brunet JS, Ghadirian P, *et al.* Tamoxifen and risk of contralateral hereditary breast cancer clinical study group. *Lancet* 2000; **356**:1876–1881.

19 Narod SA, Dube MP, Klijn J, *et al.* Oral contraceptives and the risk of breast cancer in *BRCA1* and *BRCA2* mutation carriers. *J Natl Cancer Inst* 2002; **94**:1773–1779.

20 Narod SA, Risch H, Moslehi R, *et al.* Oral contraceptives and the risk of hereditary ovarian cancer. Hereditary ovarian cancer clinical study group. *N Engl J Med* 1998; **339**:424–428.

21 Maehle L, Apold J, Heimdal K, Møller P. Survival in prospectively detected inherited ovarian cancer. In: **Benites J, Devilee P, Goldgar D, Eccles D**, eds. *The Breast Cancer Linkage Consortium (BCLC) and the International Collaborative Group on Familial Breast and Ovarian Cancer (ICG- FBOC) 14th general meeting. Madrid, June 2nd–4th 2003.* Book of abstracts, p 70.

22 Eisinger F, Alby N, Bremond A, *et al.* INSERM-FNCLCC collective expertise. Recommendations for medical management of women with genetic risk of developing breast and/or ovarian cancer. *Ann Genet* 1999; **42**:51–64.

23 Antoniou A, Pharoah PDP, Narod S, *et al.* Average risks of breast and ovarian cancer associated with *BRCA1* or *BRCA2* mutations detected in case series unselected for family history: a combined analysis of 22 studies. *Am J Hum Genet* 2003; **72**:1117–1130.

24 Heimdal K, Mæhle L, Apold J, Pedersen JC, Møller P. The Norwegian founder mutations in BRCA 1: high penetrance confirmed in an incident cancer series and differences observed in the risk of ovarian cancer. *Europ J Cancer* 2003; **39**:2205–2213.

25 Foulkes WD, Chappuis PQ, Wong N, *et al.* Primary node negative breast cancer in BRCA1 mutation carriers has a poor outcome. *Ann Oncol* 2000; **11**:307–313.

26 Verhoog LC, Brekelmans CT, Seynaeve C, *et al.* Survival and tumour characteristics of breast-cancer patients with germline mutations of BRCA 1. *Lancet* 1998; **351**:316–321.

27 Kuhl CK, Schmutzler RK, Leutner CC, *et al.* Breast MR imaging screening in 192 women proved or suspected to be carriers of a breast cancer susceptibility gene: preliminary results. *Radiology* 2000; **215**:267–279.

28 Evans D, Lalloo F, Shenton A, Boggis C, Howell A. Uptake of screening and prevention in women at very high risk of breast cancer. *Lancet* 2001; **358**:889–890.

29 Julian-Rainier CM, Bouchard LJ, Evans DO, *et al.* Women's attitudes toward presymptomatic DNA testing and prophylactic surgery in families with a *BRCA1* or *BRCA2* mutation. *Lancet* 2001; **355**:2015–2020.

30 Meijers-Heijboer EJ, Verhoog LC, Brekeimans CT, *et al.* Preventive strategies for hereditary breast or ovarian carcinoma differ from one country to another: differences among English, French and Canadian women. *Cancer* 2000; **92**:959–968.

Management of familial breast and ovarian cancer in North America

Barbara C. McGillivray

Introduction

Women identified to have either a *BRCA1* or *BRCA2* mutation have an increased lifetime risk of breast cancer of 50 to 85 per cent. Having a *BRCA1* mutation also confers a lifetime risk of 15 to 45 per cent for ovarian cancer. The ovarian cancer risk associated with a *BRCA2* mutation has been estimated to be as high as 20 per cent (1).

With the advent of hereditary cancer programmes, a number of screening recommendations have been made for women who have been shown to carry such mutations or who are judged to be at high risk because of their family history even though no *BRCA1* or *2* mutation has been identified. Most of these recommendations were initially made on the basis of expert opinion and consensus, but evidence-based options are now becoming available (2–5). In addition, mathematical models have been used to estimate survival benefits utilizing various surveillance methodologies (2). Such analyses have demonstrated that presymptomatic care provides additional life years over no care, with the greatest increase in survival occurring in women with identified mutations. Timely entry into screening with regular examinations, imaging and the use of risk-reducing surgeries (mastectomy and oophorectomy) is associated with improved survival.

Most hereditary cancer programmes have established recommendations for ongoing surveillance of women identified to be *BRCA1* or *2* mutation carriers or whose family histories fulfil testing criteria (Box 8.1). Families of the latter description may have uninformative results or no living members to initiate testing or may simply have chosen not to have molecular testing.

Cancer surveillance for such women includes monthly breast self-examination, twice yearly clinical breast examination and yearly mammography (Table 8.1). Mammography should begin at an age 5 to 10 years younger than the earliest presentation of breast cancer in the family, but not prior to age 25. The option of risk-reducing mastectomy may also be considered. Ovarian screening is discussed for mutation-positive families and those with a family history of ovarian cancer. Risk-reducing salpingo-oophorectomy after completion of childbearing is recommended for at-risk women in such families because of the limitations of currently available modalities for ovarian cancer screening.

Box 8.1 **Criteria for genetic testing**

- Family member with a confirmed *BRCA* mutation.
- Personal history of breast cancer diagnosed prior to age 35.
- Personal history of epithelial ovarian cancer prior to age 60.
- Breast and/or ovarian cancer in Ashkenazi Jewish family.
- Family history of multiple cases of breast and/or ovarian cancer:

  - individual with both breast and ovarian cancer;
  - personal history of more than one primary breast cancer, with one prior to age 50;
  - one case of breast cancer plus one case of ovarian cancer in close family relatives;
  - one case of male breast cancer and another family member with either breast or ovarian cancer;
  - two cases of breast cancer, premenopausal or prior to age 50;
  - two or more cases of ovarian cancer at any age;
  - three or more cases of breast cancer, with one prior to 50.

      B.C. Cancer Agency Hereditary Cancer Program recommendations, 2004

Table 8.1 Breast and ovarian cancer screening guidelines for high risk women in a family fulfilling testing criteria or with a known mutation (BC Cancer Agency high risk clinic screening recommendations, 2004)

Modality	Frequency	Onset
Breast self examination	Monthly	
Clinical breast/ regional lymph node examination	Every 6 months	
Mammography	Yearly	5–10 years prior to earliest diagnosis of breast cancer; but not before age 25
Other: ultrasound examination, MRI	As per radiologist	
Pelvic examination[a]	Every 6 months	
Transvaginal pelvic ultrasound examination[a]	Yearly	
Serum CA-125 tumour marker[a]	Every 6 months	

[a] all have limitations with unclear efficacy. Risk reducing salpingo-oophorectomy should be considered after completion of childbearing.

MRI = magnetic resonance imaging.

Breast screening

Breast examination

Both self-examination and clinical examination of breast tissue are recommended to high-risk women and mutation carriers. Some tumours may not be evident on mammography and may be picked up on palpation alone. The Canadian National Breast Screening Study (6) was a randomized trial to evaluate mammography, over and above both self-examination and clinical breast examination, in 50 to 59-year-old women. A greater number of breast cancers was detected in women receiving both breast examination and mammography (in itself an important finding), and some 6 per cent of tumours were detected by physical examination even though they were not obvious on the mammogram. Such data suggest that a combination of methods is preferable to reliance on mammography alone. There are not yet data available with similar comparisons in younger women or those at genetic high risk. If women are encouraged to practice monthly breast self-examinations, increasing the frequency of clinical breast examination to twice yearly may enhance and encourage their screening behaviour.

Breast imaging

Mammography is routinely recommended on a yearly basis as a screening modality to women over 50 years of age, but mammography is recommended at much younger ages for women with mutations in *BRCA1/2* or *TP53* or a significant family history. A number of randomized studies have shown that such screening in women over age 50 reduces mortality by 25 to 30 per cent, a reduction recently confirmed by the Swedish randomized trials (7). Similarly, in Holland, a national breast cancer screening programme was at least initially associated with a three-fold increase in the breast cancer detection rate among women in the 50- to 69-year age group (8). There is no consensus yet regarding the efficacy of mammography among women less than 50 years of age.

The frequency of mammography or other breast imaging techniques, such as ultrasound examination or magnetic resonance imaging (MRI), has been questioned for *BRCA1* carriers, who are more likely to develop highly proliferative tumours. When histological phenotypes of breast cancers from women less than 40 years of age were compared, tumours from *BRCA1*-positive women were more likely to be high grade or atypical medullary carcinoma (9). As well, both *BRCA1* carriers and women under 40 with newly diagnosed breast cancer are more likely to have node-positive disease. The Rotterdam Family Cancer Clinic observed an overall rate of 35 per cent node-positive tumours among high-risk women (both known mutation carriers and high risk by family history alone), but the rate averaged 60 per cent for known carriers and those under 40 years (10). In a recent review (11), six of thirteen *BRCA1* or *2* mutation carriers who chose surveillance over risk-reducing surgery developed interval malignant disease in less than a year. All had clinical breast examination and mammography at baseline. The suggestion that high-risk women have more frequent imaging is handled in some clinics by staggering ultrasound examination and mammography on a 6-monthly basis. Such a schedule is not yet evidence based.

MRI of breast tissue is offered by some programmes as studies suggest there may be an increased sensitivity over standard mammography. The Dutch National MRI study suggests that MRI is more sensitive within the high-risk group, resulting in the detection of malignancies at an earlier stage (12).

Risk-reducing mastectomy

The utility of risk-reducing mastectomy for increased breast cancer risk has been questioned, although recommendations for such surgeries have been part of high risk programmes for some years. Women considering risk-reducing mastectomy must weigh the benefits of prevention of breast cancer and alleviation of anxiety regarding screening against the diminished quality of life and increased anxiety around the decision to have surgery. Hartmann *et al.* (13) conducted a retrospective study of women choosing risk-reducing mastectomy because of a family history of breast cancer. The risks were defined as high or moderate, with high-risk families suggesting autosomal dominant inheritance (similar to criteria for offering mutation analysis) and moderate-risk having a less striking family history. High-risk women had an at least 90 per cent reduction in the incidence of breast cancer; moderate risk women were found to have a reduction of 89.5 per cent.

Meijers-Heijboer *et al.* (14) conducted a prospective study of 139 unaffected *BRCA1/2* positive women. Fifty-five percent chose to have risk-reducing mastectomy, with the remainder having regular surveillance. In a 3-year follow-up, none of the women who had surgery developed breast cancer, while eight breast cancers (about the number expected) occurred in the women who had surveillance only. Rebbeck *et al.* (15) observed a 90 per cent reduction of breast cancer risk in a similar prospective study of *BRCA1* or *2* positive women followed for 5.5 years. The postmastectomy cancers all occurred in women who had subcutaneous mastectomies.

Hoogerbrugge *et al.* (16) have described pathological lesions seen in tissue from women with a 30 to 85 per cent lifetime risk of breast cancer undergoing risk-reducing mastectomy. Over half of the specimens had high-risk histopathological lesions, including atypical lobular or ductal hyperplasia, lobular carcinoma *in situ* or ductal carcinoma *in situ*. None of these lesions was detected by mammography. The authors suggest that the findings support early risk-reducing surgery.

Chemoprevention of breast cancer

The use of selective oestrogen receptor modulators to prevent breast cancer recurrence is well established. The Breast Cancer Prevention Trial randomized over 13 000 women at increased risk for breast cancer because of either age over 60 years, age between 35 and 60 with a 5-year predicted increased risk or a history of lobular carcinoma *in situ* (17).

Women received either tamoxifen or placebo and were followed for 5 years. Women in the tamoxifen arm of the study demonstrated a 50 per cent overall reduction in breast cancer occurrence. Subgroup analysis documented reduction of breast cancer in *BRCA2*, but not *BRCA1*, mutation-positive women. These findings probably reflect the much higher incidence of oestrogen-receptor-negative tumours in women carrying *BRCA1* mutations.

A more recent, retrospective, matched, case–control study (18) of mutation (*BRCA1* or *2*) positive women with either unilateral or bilateral breast cancer found a 75 per cent reduction in the risk for contralateral breast cancer among those treated with tamoxifen for 2 to 4 years. Reduction in risk was also associated with oophorectomy or previous chemotherapy. The authors felt that the tamoxifen-associated risk reduction was independent of that seen with oophorectomy.

As tamoxifen treatment is also associated with increased risks of endometrial cancer, thromboembolic disease and cataracts, its use in young, unaffected women needs to be balanced against the benefits. A second selective oestrogen receptor modulator, raloxifene, was noted to reduce breast cancer risk in a placebo-controlled trial designed to assess efficacy for prevention and treatment of osteoporosis (19). Trials are ongoing at present to compare tamoxifen and raloxifene treatment in postmenopausal women. The use of selective oestrogen receptor modulators for chemoprevention in high-risk women should continue to be under the auspices of a clinical trial for the time being.

Ovarian screening

BRCA1 mutations confer an increased risk for invasive epithelial ovarian cancer as well as related cancers involving the peritoneum and fallopian tubes. Available surveillance methods include pelvic examination, transvaginal ultrasound examination and serum CA 125 measurement. However, none of these methods is of proven efficacy, and both false positive and false negative results often occur. As well, ovarian malignancy is frequently at an advanced stage when diagnosed. For these reasons, risk-reducing oophorectomy has been recommended for high-risk women to reduce the risk of both gynaecological cancers and breast cancer.

Oophorectomy

In a retrospective review (20), four of 33 women at 25 per cent risk or greater of carrying a germline *BRCA1* or *2* mutation who underwent risk-reducing oophorectomy were found to have microscopic or small tumours on histopathological examination of the surgical specimen. Significantly, most of these women had had normal transvaginal ultrasound examinations within 6 months prior to surgery.

Kauff *et al.* prospectively followed 170 *BRCA1* or *2* positive women for 2 years (21). Of 98 women who chose risk-reducing salpingo-oophorectomy, three developed breast cancer and one, peritoneal cancer. Of the 72 women who declined surgery but underwent surveillance, eight developed breast cancer, four, ovarian cancers and one, peritoneal cancer. It is too early to tell whether these results will translate into increased survival.

Similar results were noted by Rebbeck *et al.* in a retrospective analysis of mutation-positive women followed for up to 8 years (22). Almost 20 per cent of women undergoing surveillance only were diagnosed with ovarian cancer, and 2.3 per cent of the women who had risk-reducing surgery were found to have stage I ovarian cancer at the time of operation. Only two (0.8 per cent) of the women who had undergone risk-reducing oophorectomy subsequently developed primary peritoneal cancer (0.8 per cent). The incidence of breast cancer was also halved in the women who had risk reducing oophorectomy. An editorial accompanying these reports concluded that risk-reducing surgery could be supported for such high-risk women (23). Of further note, oophorectomy can be delayed until completion of childbearing, as the mean age at time of diagnosis of ovarian cancer among these patients was 51 years.

A recent study of risk-reducing surgery, in a group of Dutch women who were either mutation positive or determined to be at high risk, compared simple oophorectomy with salpingo-oophorectomy (24). In the latter group, five (9 per cent) of 58 *BRCA1*-positive women had tumours diagnosed on histopathological examination of the surgical specimens, with three involving the fallopian tube. Of the 38 women undergoing simple oophorectomy, three subsequently developed primary peritoneal cancer. These data support risk-reducing salpingo-oophorectomy rather than oophorectomy alone for women at high risk of developing ovarian cancer.

A question has been raised regarding whether complete hysterectomy should be performed for risk-reducing oophorectomy, rather than salpingo-oophorectomy alone. At this point, it is not clear whether mutation-positive women are also at increased risk of endometrial malignancy. In women who are also considering chemoprevention with tamoxifen, a complete hysterectomy would remove the treatment-related increased risk for endometrial cancer. Another rationale for total hysterectomy is complete removal of the fallopian tube, but almost all fallopian tube tumours occur in the distal two-thirds of the tube.

Although risk-reducing oophorectomy appears to be a more acceptable surgical option for most women than risk-reducing mastectomy, quality of life issues are important. Women choosing risk-reducing oophorectomy at the completion of childbearing will experience an immediate surgical menopause and will be at increased risk of osteoporosis. The possible use of hormone replacement therapy must be weighed against a possible increased risk for breast cancer. For these women, results of the chemoprevention trials with selective oestrogen receptor modulators may be of special interest.

Adherence to surveillance recommendations

The provision of clear screening recommendations and/or a high risk surveillance clinic for women is part of the assessment and counselling agenda covered in most hereditary cancer clinics. However, the adherence of patients to screening recommendations may vary. Although initial results suggested a perception of either a low or very high risk for malignancy might decrease screening uptake, Botkin *et al.* (25) found that over 80 per cent of *BRCA1* carriers did follow recommendations regarding breast self-examination, clinical breast examination and a yearly mammogram. Fewer than 30 per cent of these women maintained regular ovarian screening, although nearly half had had a risk-reducing oophorectomy within 2 years. Other authors (26, 27) have observed increased anxiety and poor uptake of screening among high-risk women but improvement after the provision of risk figures and risk management options. As well, physicians' attitudes regarding screening and risk-reducing surgery influence uptake (28). These attitudes may be personal or reflect certain cultural perceptions. Such data confirm the importance of education of both health professionals and patients, as well as follow-up of women seen in high-risk clinics.

References

1 Struewing JP, Hartge P, Wacholder S, Baker SM, Berlin M, McAdams M, *et al.* The risk of cancer associated with specific mutations of BRCA1 and BRCA2 among Ashkenazi Jews. *N Engl J Med* 1997; **336**:1401–1408.

2 Griffith GL, Edwards RT, Gray J, Wilkinson C, Turner J, France B, *et al.* Estimating the survival benefits gained from providing national cancer genetic services to women with a family history of breast cancer. *Br J Cancer* 2004; **90**:1912–1919.

3 DeMichele A, Weber BL. Risk management in BRCA1 and BRCA2 mutation carriers: lessons learned, challenges posed. *J Clin Oncol* 2002; **20**:1164–1166.

4 Pichert G, Bolliger B, Buser K, Pagani O. Evidence-based management options for women at increased breast/ovarian cancer risk. *Ann Oncol* 2003; **14**:9–19.

5 Burke W, Daly M, Garber J, Botkin J, Kahn MJ, Lynch P, *et al.* Recommendations for follow-up care of individuals with an inherited predisposition to cancer. II. BRCA1 and BRCA2. Cancer Genetics Studies Consortium. *JAMA* 1997; **277**:997–1003.

6 Miller AB, To T, Baines CJ, Wall C. Canadian National Breast Screening Study-2: 13-year results of a randomized trial in women aged 50–59 years. *J Natl Cancer Inst* 2000; **92**:1490–1499.

7 Nystrom L, Andersson I, Bjurstam N, Frisell J, Nordenskjold B, Rutqvist LE. Long-term effects of mammography screening: updated overview of the Swedish randomised trials. *Lancet* 2002; **359**:909–919.

8 Fracheboud J, Otto SJ, Van Dijck JA, Broeders MJ, Verbeek AL, de Koning HJ. Decreased rates of advanced breast cancer due to mammography screening in The Netherlands. *Br J Cancer* 2004; **91**:861–867.

9 Armes JE, Egan AJ, Southey MC, Dite GS, McCredie MR, Giles GG, *et al.* The histologic phenotypes of breast carcinoma occurring before age 40 years in women with and without BRCA1 or BRCA2 germline mutations: a population-based study. *Ca* 1998; **83**:2335–2345.

10 Brekelmans CT, Seynaeve C, Bartels CC, Tilanus-Linthorst MM, Meijers-Heijboer EJ, Crepin CM, *et al.* Effectiveness of breast cancer surveillance in BRCA1/2 gene mutation carriers and women with high familial risk. *J Clin Oncol* 2001; **19**:924–930.

11 Komenaka IK, Ditkoff BA, Joseph KA, Russo D, Gorroochurn P, Ward M, *et al.* The development of interval breast malignancies in patients with BRCA mutations. *Ca* 2004; **100**:2079–2083.

12 Kriege M, Brekelmans CT, Boetes C, Besnard PE, Zonderland HM, Obdeijn IM, *et al.* Efficacy of MRI and mammography for breast-cancer screening in women with a familial or genetic predisposition. *N Engl J Med* 2004; **351**:427–437.

13 Hartmann LC, Schaid DJ, Woods JE, Crotty TP, Myers JL, Arnold PG, *et al.* Efficacy of bilateral prophylactic mastectomy in women with a family history of breast cancer. *N Engl J Med* 1999; **340**:77–84.

14 Meijers-Heijboer H, van Geel B, van Putten WL, Henzen-Logmans SC, Seynaeve C, Menke-Pluymers MB, *et al.* Breast cancer after prophylactic bilateral mastectomy in women with a BRCA1 or BRCA2 mutation. *N Engl J Med* 2001; **345**:159–164.

15 Rebbeck TR, Friebel T, Lynch HT, Neuhausen SL, van ', V, Garber JE, *et al.* Bilateral prophylactic mastectomy reduces breast cancer risk in BRCA1 and BRCA2 mutation carriers: the PROSE Study Group. *J Clin Oncol* 2004; **22**:1055–1062.

16 Hoogerbrugge N, Bult P, Widt-Levert LM, Beex LV, Kiemeney LA, Ligtenberg MJ, *et al.* High prevalence of premalignant lesions in prophylactically removed breasts from women at hereditary risk for breast cancer. *J Clin Oncol* 2003; **21**:41–45.

17 Fisher B, Costantino JP, Wickerham DL, Redmond CK, Kavanah M, Cronin WM, *et al.* Tamoxifen for prevention of breast cancer: report of the National Surgical Adjuvant Breast and Bowel Project P-1 Study. *J Natl Cancer Inst* 1998; **90**:1371–1388.

18 Narod SA, Brunet JS, Ghadirian P, Robson M, Heimdal K, Neuhausen SL, *et al.* Tamoxifen and risk of contralateral breast cancer in BRCA1 and BRCA2 mutation carriers: a case-control study. Hereditary Breast Cancer Clinical Study Group. *Lancet* 2000; **356**:1876–1881.

19 Cummings SR, Eckert S, Krueger KA, Grady D, Powles TJ, Cauley JA, *et al.* The effect of raloxifene on risk of breast cancer in postmenopausal women: results from the MORE randomized trial. Multiple Outcomes of Raloxifene Evaluation. *JAMA* 1999; **281**:2189–2197.

20 Lu KH, Garber JE, Cramer DW, Welch WR, Niloff J, Schrag D, *et al.* Occult ovarian tumors in women with BRCA1 or BRCA2 mutations undergoing prophylactic oophorectomy. *J Clin Oncol* 2000; **18**:2728–2732.

21 Kauff ND, Satagopan JM, Robson ME, Scheuer L, Hensley M, Hudis CA, *et al.* Risk-reducing salpingo-oophorectomy in women with a BRCA1 or BRCA2 mutation. *N Engl J Med* 2002; **346**:1609–1615.

22 Rebbeck T, Lynch HT, Neuhausen S, Narod S, van't Veer L, Garber JE, *et al.* Prophylactic oophorectomy in carriers of *BRCA1* and *BRCA2* mutations. *N Engl J Med* 2002; **346**:1616–1622.

23 Haber D. Prophylactic oophorectomy to reduce the risk of ovarian and breast cancer in carriers of BRCA mutations. *N Engl J Med* 2002; **346**:1660–1662.

24 Olivier RI, van Beurden M, Lubsen MA, Rookus MA, Mooij TM, van de Vijver MJ, *et al.* Clinical outcome of prophylactic oophorectomy in BRCA1/BRCA2 mutation carriers and events during follow-up. *Br J Cancer* 2004; **90**:1492–1497.

25 Botkin JR, Smith KR, Croyle RT, Baty BJ, Wylie JE, Dutson D, *et al.* Genetic testing for a BRCA1 mutation: prophylactic surgery and screening behavior in women 2 years post testing. *Am J Med Genet* 2003; **118A**:201–209.

26 Lerman C, Rimer B, Trock B, Balshem A, Engstrom PF. Factors associated with repeat adherence to breast cancer screening. *Prev Med* 1990; **19**:279–290.

27 Gil F, Mendez I, Sirgo A, Llort G, Blanco I, Cortes-Funes H. Perception of breast cancer risk and surveillance behaviours of women with family history of breast cancer: a brief report on a Spanish cohort. *Psychooncology* 2003; **12**:821–827.

28 Eisinger F, Stoppa-Lyonnet D, Lasset C, Vennin P, Chabal F, Nogues C, *et al.* Comparison of physicians' and cancer prone women's attitudes about breast/ovarian prophylactic surgery. Results from two national surveys. *Fam Cancer* 2001; **1**:157–162.

Chapter 9

Management of familial adenomatous polyposis and other inherited polyposis syndromes

E. Sheridan and R. S. Houlston

Introduction

Colorectal polyps can be grouped according to their histology. The most important subgroups are adenomatous polyps and hamartomatous polyps. Adenomatous polyps account for around 30 to 50 per cent of all polyps and are premalignant lesions. They are detectable in around 15 to 20 per cent of the population by age 50, the risk increasing with age (Fig. 9.1). Autopsy series suggest that the incidence is even higher, with 60 per cent of men having a polyp by age 50 compared with only 40 per cent of women.

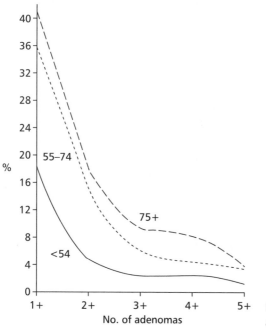

Fig. 9.1 Risks of polyps with age (1).

Table 9.1 Inherited polyposis syndromes

Syndrome	Acronym	Type of polyp	OMIM reference number	Gene involved	Inheritance
Familial adenomatous polyposis	FAP	Adenomatous	175100	*APC*	Dominant
Hereditary non-polyposis colorectal cancer	HNPCC	Adenomatous	120435	*MLH1* *MSH2* *MSH3* *PMS1*	Dominant
Peutz–Jeghers syndrome	PJS	Hamartomatous	175200	*STK11*	Dominant
Cowden's disease	CD	Hamartomatous	158350	*PTEN*	Dominant
Bannayan–Riley–Ruvalcaba syndrome	BRRS	Hamartomatous	153480	*PTEN*	Dominant
Juvenile polyposis	JPS	Hamartomatous	174900	*BMP2R* *SMAD4*	Dominant
MYH polyposis	MyHP	Adenomatous		*MYH*	Recessive

Data are limited but prevalence has been reported to be as high as 15.6 per cent for polyps of >1 cm by age 75 (1).

Adenomatous polyps are therefore common and their presence alone does not necessarily imply that an individual suffers from one of the colorectal cancer predisposition syndromes, all of which have colonic polyposis as a feature. These conditions are characterized by other features which, on the whole, make them easily distinguishable. The major adenomatous syndromes are familial adenomatous polyposis (FAP), hereditary non-polyposis colorectal cancer (HNPCC) and MYH polyposis.

Hamartomatous polyps are uncommon but confer a considerable malignancy risk. The syndromes associated with hamartomatous polyposis include juvenile polyposis syndrome (JPS) and Peutz–Jeghers syndrome (PJS).

Hyperplastic polyps (10–30 per cent of all polyps) confer a much lower risk of malignancy. Simple mucosal tags tend to be small (<0.5 cm), distal and of little clinical consequence. There are also a variety of other, rarer, types of polyp such as lipomas.

This chapter considers the inherited polyposis syndromes listed in Table 9.1.

Familial adenomatous polyposis (FAP)

FAP is the best known of the colorectal polyposes. It was first described by Harrison-Cripps and Skilfasowski in the 1880s in independent publications. A series of classic papers by Lockhart-Mummery in the 1920s established the familial nature of FAP and led to the establishment of the first register for this disease.

Clinical features

Multiple colonic polyps in early adulthood or adolescence are the hallmark of FAP (Fig. 9.2). The mean age at presentation with polyps is 16 years (range 7–36 years). Penetrance is almost 100 per cent by age 40 with colorectal cancer developing in the vast majority of untreated mutation carriers with a mean age at diagnosis of 39 (2) (Fig. 9.3). FAP is not rare, affecting between 1 in 14 000 to 1 in 8 000 of the population. In the Yorkshire region of the UK, with a population of 3.5 million, there are 125 families diagnosed with FAP.

Variants of familial adenomatous polyposis

In 1951, Gardner drew attention to the presence of osteomas, fibromas and epidermal or sebaceous cysts in FAP sufferers. Gardner's syndrome is a variant of FAP with these features; odontomas and desmoid tumours are also regarded as part of the Gardner's

Fig. 9.2 Resection specimen from patient with FAP showing carpeting of the mucosa with polyps. See also colour plate section.

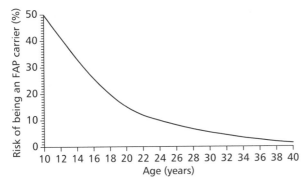

Fig. 9.3 Offspring risk of being an FAP carrier given negative bowel examination by age (2).

phenotype. In fact most FAP patients, and some sporadic CRC patients, will have features of Gardner's syndrome, so clinicians now use the term only rarely.

Attenuated FAP (AFAP) is a milder form of FAP characterized by the presence of fewer adenomas and often with later onset. Sometimes, colorectal cancer only presents in the sixth decade.

Extracolonic manifestations (ECMs)

FAP is a multisystem disorder. Characteristic ECMs include those seen in Gardner's syndrome. In addition, congenital hypertrophy of the retinal pigment epithelium (CHRPE), dentiginous cysts and fundic gland polyps of the stomach are features of the condition. These latter are all benign and of little clinical consequence other than being markers for FAP.

Malignant ECMs are also common in FAP. There is a clear excess of adrenal, brain and hepatobiliary cancers. Primary hepatoblastoma is well recorded and papillary thyroid cancer is 160 times more common in FAP than in the general population. Medulloblastoma is the commonest type of brain tumour seen in FAP, although astrocytoma is also seen. Whilst the relative risks for these tumours may be high, the absolute risk remains low even in FAP families.

Duodenal cancer is also seen at relatively high frequency in FAP (lifetime risk is 4–10 per cent) (3, 4). It is the leading cause of death in patients who have had a prophylactic colectomy (5). Duodenal adenomatosis is regarded as a precursor lesion for duodenal cancer.

Molecular genetics of FAP

FAP results in the main from germline mutations in the *APC* gene transmitted in an autosomal dominant fashion. A variable proportion of patients who manifest a very similar phenotype have recessive mutations in the *MYH* gene (see below).

The *APC* gene is located on chromosome 5q21. The cDNA is 8535 bp long, coding for a protein consisting of 2843 amino acids. There are 15 exons, the last exon comprises some 75 per cent of the coding sequence. The APC protein has a central role in cell adhesion and cellular transcription. The key tumour suppressor function of APC depends on its ability to regulate the stability and localization of β-catenin, an essential component of the Wnt pathway. Stabilized β-catenin translocates to the nucleus and binds with members of the Lef/Tcf family of transcription factors. The vast majority of *APC* mutations are nonsense or frameshifts, which produce a truncated product unable to bind β-catenin, which then accumulates to high levels in the nucleus.

There are three common *APC* mutations – a 5 bp deletion at codon 1061, another at codon 1309, and a deletion of the whole gene. These sequence changes account for about 25 per cent of all germline pathogenic mutations. A tiny proportion of cytogenetically visible deletions have been reported. These tend to be associated with developmental delay and a characteristic appearance of long face, abnormal ears and downslanting palpebral fissures (6).

Genotype/phenotype correlation in FAP

FAP characterized by hundreds to thousands of adenomas is classically seen in association with mutations between codons 160 and 1600. The highest CRC risk appears to be associated with mutations around codon 1300, including the common 1309 deletion. In contrast, attenuated polyposis (AFAP) is associated with mutations in the extreme 5′ and 3′ ends of the gene as well as the alternatively spliced regions of exon 9.

Desmoid tumours tend to be associated with mutations distal to codon 1444. In one series of patients, 60 per cent with mutations within codons 1445–1580 developed desmoid tumours (7). Mutations between codons 447 and 1444 are associated with the development of CHRPE. Loss of the wild type allele in tumours tends to accompany germline mutations between codons 1194 and 1392. Germline mutations outside of this region tend to be accompanied by mutations in the somatic mutation cluster region (MCR) between codons 1286 and 1513. Duodenal adenomatosis has been reported more frequently with mutations between codons 976 and 1067 (8).

The *APC* variant I1307K in Ashkenazis results in a doubling of risk for adenomas and colorectal cancer and may also result in AFAP-like phenotype (9). The E1317Q variant seen in Caucasians and in about 1 per cent of Ashkenazis may result in a multiple adenoma/colorectal cancer phenotype but the overall penetrance is unclear (10). The pathogenicity of E1317Q remains in doubt. It is in linkage disequilibrium with a nonsense change at the extreme 5′ end of the gene that may the true causative mutation (10).

Clinical management and treatment of FAP

Family history and confirmation of diagnosis

A detailed family tree taking note of any extracolonic manifestations, particularly unusual skin findings, is essential. Since malignancy is common, a history of weight loss, bleeding per rectum, passage of mucus or abnormality of bowel habit should be sought. Examination should include a survey of the skin. Further investigations may help to clarify the diagnosis. Formal examination for CHRPE may be useful as is an orthopantogram to identify dentiginous cysts.

Pathology should always be obtained, with the characteristic gross pathology findings in FAP being of hundreds of polyps (but remember AFAP). Microscopy may reveal the presence of the classic crypt adenomata. These are not seen in HNPCC, but are seen in both FAP and in association with mutations in the MYH gene.

Eye examinations

The classic CHRPE seen in FAP is described with a halo of depigmentation. It occurs in multiple quadrants and may be referred to as bear tracking (Fig. 9.4). However, FAP is not the only cause of this type of lesion and up to 3 per cent of controls in the study performed by the Northern FAP register had up to three CHRPE. Eighty-eight percent of *APC* mutation carriers had *four or more* lesions.

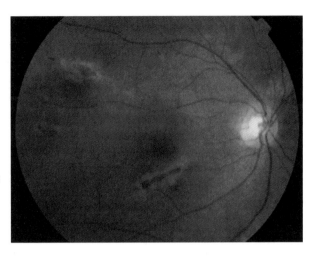

Fig. 9.4 Classic cigar-shaped congenital hypertrophy of the retinal pigment epithelium of FAP showing the surrounding pale halo. See also colour plate section.

Mutation analysis

Families with FAP should always undergo mutation analysis, and modern techniques will identify the mutation in up to 90 per cent of cases (11). Knowledge of the mutation may inform decisions about definitive treatment (12).

In dominant families where no mutation can be identified, linkage can be used to identify the high risk allele and allow appropriate advice to be given. In new cases with no previous family history, mutation analysis is valuable in providing advice to offspring; the common 1061 and 1309 mutations are often seen in these cases. Although up to one-third of all FAP cases result from new mutations, the possibility of MYH should be borne in mind.

Surveillance

Half of *APC* mutation carriers will have polyps by age 16 although cancer by this age is rare. The object of surveillance in FAP is to document the natural history of the disorder and identify the point at which individuals with polyps require surgery. Surveillance should be offered to at-risk individuals from age 11 or 12 (Box 9.1). There is little data on how adolescents cope with bowel surveillance, but a limited survey from the Northern Registry indicated that compliance and coping were better when surveillance was instituted early rather than in the late teens. Once polyps develop the risk of malignancy rises rapidly, and there is only a very limited place for polypectomy. Most mutation carriers (but not those with AFAP) will have rectal polyps, so sigmoidoscopy may be the first line of surveillance. Rectal sparing is well described even in classic FAP, so more extensive screening by colonoscopy should be part of any regime, although not necessarily on as regular a basis.

Although cancers of the thyroid (papillary), adrenals, brain and liver (hepatoblastoma) are well described in FAP, no rational screening policies are available for these lesions.

> Box 9.1 **Screening protocol in FAP**
>
> ◆ Annual sigmoidoscopy from age 11–12.
>
> ◆ Colonoscopies at age 15, 18, 21 and later if no polyps are identified although 90 per cent of mutation carriers will have polyps by age 20.
>
> ◆ In at-risk individuals whose genetic status cannot be determined by linkage or mutation analysis, screening may be discontinued at age 40.

AFAP

These policies are not appropriate for AFAP families. In these cases 2 to 3-yearly colonoscopy from midteens should be initiated.

Definitive management

Surgical intervention ultimately means some form of colectomy. This is commonly performed between the ages of 16 and 30 years. Colectomy with ileorectal anastamosis and subsequent survey of the rectal stump is a reasonable option. The risk of cancer in the rectal stump continues to rise with age, and rectal surveillance needs to be continued. By midlife, excision of the remaining colon with ileoanal pouch formation will be necessary.

Management of desmoid disease in FAP

The frequency of desmoid disease remains unclear. Overall, about 10 per cent of FAP sufferers develop clinically significant desmoids; however both the large German and Italian registers recorded a total incidence of intra and extra-abdominal desmoids of >20 per cent (8, 12). Furthermore, whilst there is a clear tendency to increased desmoid risks with mutations between codons 1445 and 1580, they have been seen in association with mutations in all exons. Intra-abdominal desmoids are difficult to operate on, and complete excision may be very difficult. They may encroach upon intra-abdominal structures, and sometimes heroic surgery is required to deal with them; they are still a cause of death in FAP patients. Chemotherapy has shown some success, but there is no place for irradiation.

There is a view that desmoids can be induced by surgery and many would discourage elective surgery in patients with desmoids. Once apparent they may be monitored by MRI, although there is little place for this investigation as a screening tool in asymptomatic patients.

Management of upper GI polyposis in FAP

Virtually all patients with *APC* mutations will develop fundic gland polyps; however, these are of little real significance (13). In the West, the frequency of gastric adenomas in FAP is 2 to 6 per cent, but there is no elevation in gastric cancer risk. In Japan the situation is different – here there is a significant risk of gastric cancer and adenomas are seen in 40 to 50 per cent of FAP patients (13). As adenoma risk is associated with *H. pylori* infection, it has been suggested that *H. pylori* infection should be sought in FAP patients and treated by triple therapy (14).

Although duodenal adenomatosis is pretty much universal in FAP patients, the lifetime risk of duodenal cancer is 4 to 10 per cent (4). Duodenal adenomatosis can be graded using the Spigelman classification (15). Cancer risk seems to be highest with advanced-stage adenomatosis. Endoscopic surveillance of the duodenum is commonly recommended but its efficacy remains unproven. Surgical resection may be considered in those with advanced stage adenomatosis, but a review of 56 patients with advanced adenomatosis revealed both very high rates of small bowel recurrence, with most treatments, and high morbidity (4). Interestingly, decision analysis suggests that life expectancy is increased by only 7 months if pancreaticoduodenectomy is performed in the presence of advanced stage adenomatosis (16). There is still no proven approach to the management of these lesions.

MYH polyposis

Mutations in the *MYH* gene cause a recessive colorectal cancer predisposition syndrome (17). Phenotypically this is associated with multiple colonic polyps and the colonic phenotype may be indistinguishable from AFAP or classical FAP.

Whilst *APC* mutations have been identified in only a minority of cases of classical AFAP with <100 adenomas, early data indicate that biallelic germline *MYH* mutations may account for 25 per cent of such cases. In the series reported by Sampson *et al.*, eight of 107 cases with classical FAP (>100 adenomas) had *MYH* mutations (18). The disorder tends to present later than classical FAP. In the two major series, the mean ages at presentation were 46 and 51.3 with a range of 13 to 70 (18, 19). The presenting feature was cancer in about 50 per cent of cases in the two series. Confusion with FAP is furthered by the fact that colorectal microadenomata and duodenal adenomata, previously considered hallmarks of FAP, have been reported in this condition, as has CHRPE.

To date, six truncating mutations, four missense, one in frame insertion and two putative splice site mutations have been reported. Y165C (53 per cent of all mutations) and G382D (32 per cent) are the commonest mutations in Caucasians. E466X is the only mutation reported in eight unrelated Indians from Gujarat, and Y90X was found in the only Pakistani patient reported so far.

Hereditary non-polyposis colorectal cancer (HNPCC)

The management of HNPCC is described in Chapter 10.

Hamartomatous polyposis syndromes

Introduction

Hamartomas represent an overgrowth of cells or tissues native to the area in which they normally reside, typically involving mesenchymal or stromal elements. Hamartomatous polyps of the gastrointestinal tract, either as isolated lesions or as part of inherited syndromes, are rare. Hamartomas of the gastrointestinal tract were originally not considered to have malignant potential; however, this is not the case and several hamartomas syndromes are associated with substantially increased risks of both intestinal and extraintestinal malignancies. The syndromes associated with hamartomatous polyposis include juvenile polyposis syndrome (JPS), Peutz–Jeghers syndrome (PJS), Cowden's disease (CD), and Bannayan–Riley–Ruvalcaba syndrome (BRRS). All of these syndromes are dominantly inherited with variable penetrance. The spectrum and magnitude of the cancer risk, both intestinal and extragastrointestinal, varies between the syndromes.

Juvenile polyposis syndrome

Clinical features

Juvenile polyposis (JPS) is probably the most common of the hamartomatous syndromes. Between 20 and 50 per cent of affected individuals have a family history of the disease and birth defects are seen in about 15 per cent of cases (20, 21). The most commonly associated birth defects include malrotation of the midgut, genitourinary defects and cardiac defects. The majority of individuals with congenital defects appear to have sporadic disease, inviting speculation that such cases are a consequence of new mutations.

In infancy, JPS patients present with gastrointestinal bleeding, either acute or chronic, intussusception, rectal prolapse, or protein-losing enteropathy (22). In adulthood, patients tend not to have a protein-losing enteropathy, more commonly presenting with gastrointestinal blood loss, either acute or chronic. Such patients typically have fewer than 200 polyps, most commonly affecting the rectosigmoid.

There are no universally accepted criteria for a diagnosis of JPS, however, the scheme proposed by Giardiello et al. (23) represents a clinically useful definition – three or more juvenile polyps within the colon, polyposis involving the entire gastrointestinal tract or any number of polyps in a proband with a family history of juvenile polyps.

Histological features of JPS

Histologically, the typical gastrointestinal JPS polyp is unilobulated and smooth (Fig. 9.5). There is a gross infiltration of the lamina propria by chronic inflammatory

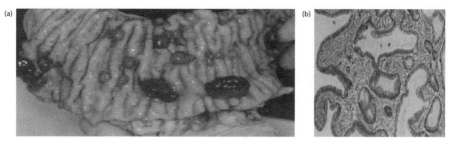

Fig. 9.5 (a) Colon with multiple juvenile polyps; (b) histology of a juvenile polyp. See also colour plate section.

cells. Cystic dilation of glandular type structures lined by a normal-appearing columnar epithelium is pathognomonic.

Cancer risk associated with juvenile polyposis

The cancer risk associated with juvenile polyposis syndrome has, until recently, been debated – however, it is now well established that the risk is substantially increased. In a large retrospective review of patients from St Mark's Polyposis Registry published in 1988 (24), 18 of 80 patients (22 per cent) developed colorectal cancer. The mean age at diagnosis of cancer was 34 years. Coburn *et al.* (25) studied the cancer incidence in 218 patients with JPS. Thirty-six of the patients (17 per cent) developed gastrointestinal cancers, most commonly of the colorectum but also upper gastrointestinal malignancies. The mean age at diagnosis of cancer was 33 years. Desai *et al.* (22) subsequently revaluated the data from the St Mark's Polyposis Registry, estimating the risk of colorectal cancer by the age of 60 to be around 70 per cent.

Molecular genetics of juvenile polyposis

Juvenile polyposis was originally thought to be associated with germline mutations in the *PTEN* (*p*hosphatase with *ten*sin homology) gene on chromosome 10q22–23 (26). Mutations in *PTEN* were subsequently shown to cause Cowden's disease and BRRS (27, 28). It is now generally thought that the original kindred in which a *PTEN* mutation was identified probably represented a case of Cowden's rather than JPS. Recently, it has been shown that germline mutations in the *SMAD4* gene located at chromosome 18q21 account for around 50 per cent of JPS cases (29).

The *SMAD4* gene encodes a cytoplasmic mediator involved in the transforming growth factor-beta (TGFß) signal transduction pathway (Fig. 9.6). Activation at the receptor level leads to second messenger signalling through serine and threonine kinases. This leads to the formation of heteromeric complexes between SMAD4 and other members of the SMAD family of proteins. Transportation to the nucleus and interaction with cellular DNA leads to growth inhibition. Mutations in the *SMAD4* gene probably lead to a loss of heteromeric complex formation and resultant growth

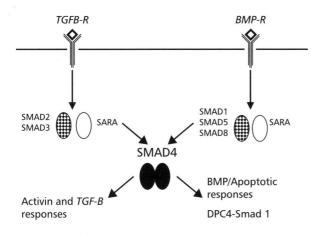

Fig. 9.6 TGFβ–SMAD signal transduction pathway. TGFβ = transforming growth factor-beta;

inhibition and neoplastic progression. Recent studies indicate that mutations in *BMPR1A* provide an alternative mechanism to *SMAD4* for causing the disease.

How overgrowth of stromal elements within a PJS hamartoma leads to cancer is unclear. Kinzler and Vogelstein postulated that production of a microenvironment "landscapes" the epithelial element of the hamartoma (30). With growth of the mesenchymal component, this results in epithelial dysplasia that eventually progresses to cancer. This theory is supported by the fact that as hamartomatous polyps enlarge and the mesenchymal component expands, they take on a serrated or villous-type configuration which is associated with epithelial dysplasia.

Management and surveillance of juvenile polyposis

The management and surveillance of patients with JPS and at-risk relatives is dictated by the increased risk of upper and lower gastrointestinal malignancies associated with the disease. It is also influenced by clinical symptoms and the degree of polyposis. Both affected and at-risk individuals should be screened, probably starting in the late teenage life by upper and lower gastrointestinal endoscopy. If an initial screen is negative, endoscopy should ideally be carried out every 3 years and thence afterwards, provided findings are negative. If a screen is positive, management will depend on the extent of polyposis and the feasibility of endoscopic excision of the polyps. Diffuse polyposis may require colectomy or gastrectomy. Screening should subsequently be carried out annually until the patient is free of disease, after which the interval between screenings can then be extended to every 3 years. Colorectal adenocarcinoma should be treated by total abdominal colectomy with ileorectal anastomosis or restorative proctocolectomy. Identification of germline mutations in *SMAD4* or *BMPR1A* within a family opens up the possibility of presymptomatic gene testing of unaffected family members and obviates the need for endoscopic surveillance in non-carriers.

Peutz–Jeghers syndrome (PJS)

Clinical features

Peutz–Jeghers syndrome (PJS) is the second most common hamartomatous syndrome. It is a characterized by hamartomatous polyposis of the gastrointestinal tract and melanin pigmentation of the orofacial region (Fig. 9.7). Although PJS polyps are seen most commonly in the small bowel they can occur throughout the gastrointestinal tract and at other extraintestinal sites such as the kidney, ureter, gallbladder, bronchus and nasal passage. Melanin deposition occurs most commonly in the perioral region or buccal mucosa, but can also occur in the genital region or on the hands and feet. Approximately 75 per cent of PJS cases are familial, the remainder presumably resulting from new mutations or possibly low penetrance variants (31).

The initial presentation of PJS occurs most commonly with abdominal pain secondary to obstruction or impending obstruction with polyp intussusception or gastrointestinal blood loss. Patients can also present with gastrointestinal malignancy as their primary presentation.

Histological features of PJS

The typical PJS polyp is different histologically from a JPS polyp. Instead of a dense inflammatory response, hypertrophy or hyperplasia of the smooth muscle layer occurs extending in a tree-like fashion into the superficial epithelial layer. The extensive dilation

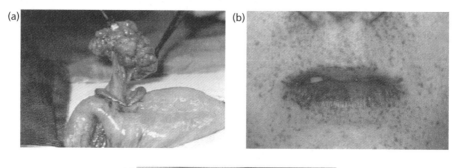

Fig. 9.7 Clinical features of Peutz–Jeghers syndrome: (a) Peutz–Jeghers polyp within the small bowel; (b) perioral mucocutaneous pigmentation; and (c) melanin deposition of the digits. See also colour plate section.

of cystic-filled spaces, pathognomonic for the JPS polyp, are not seen. As smooth muscle extends upward toward the epithelial layer, invagination of the epithelium leads to epithelial cells becoming trapped within the underlying smooth muscle, giving the appearance of penetration through the basement membrane. This resembles local invasion by malignant cells – therefore a diagnosis of early cancer requires identification of an elevated mitotic rate or cellular atypia (32).

Cancer risk associated with Peutz–Jeghers syndrome

An increased risk of gastrointestinal and extragastrointestinal cancer is well recognized in PJS. Extraintestinal malignancies associated with PJS include pancreatic, breast, ovarian and testicular carcinomas, and adenoma malignum of the uterine cervix. In addition, testicular sex cord and Sertoli-cell tumours can occur in prepubertal boys affected with PJS, leading to sexual precocity and gynaecomastia. The production of oestrogen in ovarian tumours in girls with PJS has also been reported, causing sexual precocity (32).

To clarify the cancer risk associated with PJS, a meta-analysis of published studies has recently been reported by Giardello *et al.* (33). The relative risk (RR) of cancer in patients with PJS compared with the general population was based on 210 individuals described in six publications. For patients with PJS, the RR for all cancers was 15. A statistically significant increased risk was noted for oesophagus, stomach, small intestine, colon, pancreas, lung, breast, uterus and ovary, but not testicular or cervical malignancies. The cumulative risk for all cancer was 93 per cent by age 64.

Molecular genetics of Peutz–Jeghers syndrome

Germline mutations in the serine/threonine kinase gene *STK11* on chromosome 19p13.3 account for about 50 per cent of PJS (31, 34). This *STK11* gene encodes for a multifunctional serine–threonine kinase that is an important second messenger in signal transduction. Many of the cancers reported in association with PJS develop from hamartomas in which *STK11* functions as a tumour suppressor. *STK11*, however, also plays a role in a number of pathways involved in controlling cell growth and apoptosis (Fig. 9.8). Therefore it is likely that the tumourigenic potential of these mutations is mediated through alternative mechanisms in many tissues, especially those in which hamartoma development is not a feature.

The genesis of polyposis, as well as associated clinical features and malignancies, is likely to be more complex. Alterations in particular genes, along with modifying environmental and epigenetic influences, are probably important to a greater or lesser degree, depending on the syndrome and whether sporadic or familial variants are being considered. Around 50 per cent of PJS patients have no detectable *STK11* mutation and families with PJS unlinked to chromosome 19p13.3 have been reported, implying genetic heterogeneity (34). Furthermore, a second disease locus on chromosome 19q13.4 has been proposed on the basis of genetic linkage (35).

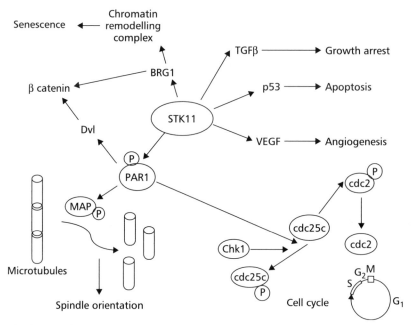

Fig. 9.8 STK11 pathway.

Management and surveillance of Peutz–Jeghers syndrome

The substantial cancer risk associated with PJS supports the need for surveillance in patients with the disease for the early detection of tumours. A number of guidelines for screening have been proposed from different of clinical centres. Most advocate upper and lower endoscopy, breast examination and some form of surveillance for pancreatic (transabdominal and endoscopic ultrasound examination, abdominal computerized tomography, CA-19-9) and gynaecological malignancies (ultrasound, cervical cytology and CA125). The optimal surveillance strategy for cancer detection is unknown and current schemes for screening differ widely in terms of when to start, screening intervals and procedures used to detect cancer (34). Recommendations from the St Marks's Polyposis Registry are summarized in Table 9.2. Current surveillance guidelines have been based upon risk estimates from retrospective cohort studies without taking into account the mutation status of the patients that may influence the cancer risk associated with the disease.

Management of gastrointestinal polyposis is dictated according to symptoms and abnormalities detected on surveillance examination. Polyps that are symptomatic, greater than 1.5 cm in size or have features suggestive of frank malignancy should be treated by exploratory celiotomy or enteroscopic polypectomy. Patients so affected should undergo complete intraoperative enteroscopic examination of the small bowel and polypectomy.

Table 9.2 Screening and surveillance program advocated by the St Mark's Polyposis Registry for patients with Peutz–Jeghers syndrome

Procedure	Interval
Both sexes	
Endoscopy – Gastroscopy and colonoscopy every year	1-yearly
Laparotomy and preoperative enteroscopy for small bowel polyps	
Small bowel X-ray	2-yearly
Females	
Mammography from age 25–35	5-yearly
Mammography from age 35–38	2-yearly
Mammography from age 50	1-yearly
Cervical smears	3-yearly
Males	
Testicular ultrasound if feminizing features	

Cowden's disease

Clinical features

Cowden's disease (CD) is unique among the hamartomatous syndromes because polyps arise more commonly from ectodermal and/or endodermal elements. Hamartomas involve the skin, intestine, breast and thyroid gland (36). Eighty percent of patients present with dermatologic manifestations, the most common being trichilemmoma, benign tumours of the hair shaft. The second most common organ involved is the central nervous system. Cowden's disease associated with cerebellar gangliocytomatosis is referred to as the Lhermitte–Duclos syndrome. Approximately 40 per cent of CD patients have macrocephaly, but only around a third of CD patients have evidence of gastrointestinal polyposis (37).

Cancer risk associated with Cowden's disease

The majority of patients with CD will develop some form of benign thyroid or breast disease (36). In addition, the projected lifetime risk of thyroid and breast cancers are 10 per cent and 30 to 50 per cent respectively (38–40). To date, there has been no reported increase in risk of gastrointestinal malignancy associated with CD.

Molecular genetics of Cowden's disease

Most patients with CD harbour germ line mutations in the *PTEN* gene located at chromosome 10q22 (41). PTEN is a tumour suppressor. Biologically, PTEN acts as a negative regulator of PI3-kinase signalling by catalysing the dephosphorylation of PIP3. Overexpression of the gene leads to reduced cell and organ size, and conversely cells mutant for PTEN are larger than wild type.

Management and surveillance of Cowden's disease

Although no increased risk of colorectal cancer has been reported, the syndrome is rare and a small increase in risk may go undocumented. Gastrointestinal polyposis associated with CD should be managed by endoscopic surveillance. Surveillance for breast malignancies should include mammography/ultrasound implemented from age 25. Although no specific recommendations for thyroid surveillance have been agreed, it is probably prudent that annual clinical examination is started from the late teen years, supported by thyroid ultrasound every 1 to 2 years.

Bannayan–Riley–Ruvalcaba (Ruvalcaba–Myhre–Smith) syndrome

Clinical features

Bannayan–Riley–Ruvalcaba syndrome (BBRS) has only recently been recognized. Besides hamartomatous polyps of the gastrointestinal tract, BRRS is characterized by macrocephaly, mental retardation, delayed psychomotor development, lipid storage myopathy and Hashimoto's thyroiditis. Hyperpigmentation of the skin of the penis is seen in the most patients.

Cancer risk in Bannayan–Riley–Ruvalcaba syndrome

To date, there has been no increased risk of colorectal carcinoma, other gastrointestinal malignancies or extraintestinal malignancy documented in patients with BRRS. However, on the basis that mutations in *PTEN* cause the disease, it is probable that the risk profile will in part parallel CD

Molecular genetics of Bannayan–Riley–Ruvalcaba syndrome

Bannayan–Riley–Ruvalcaba syndrome, like CD, is primarily caused by germline mutations in the *PTEN* gene (42). A failure to identify mutations in a number of sporadic cases suggests that other loci may also cause the disorder (43).

Management and surveillance of Bannayan–Riley–Ruvalcaba syndorme

Although no increased risk of cancer has been documented in patients with BRRS there is some controversy as to whether or not this syndrome represents a distinct clinical entity or merely a variant of CD. Clinically, macrocephaly, delayed psychomotor development, and hyperpigmentation of the skin of the penis can be seen in patients with CD. Moreover, the same genetic mutations have been recognized in CD. Therefore, careful consideration of other hamartomatous syndromes should be given. The diagnosis of BBRS syndrome should be one of exclusion.

Summary of hamartomatous polyposes

The hamartomatous polyposes are rare, accounting for 1 per cent or less of the annual incidence of colorectal cancer. At least initially, they are characterized by an *overgrowth* of cells and tissues native to the area in which they normally occur. However, patients are at an increased lifetime risk of both intestinal and extraintestinal malignancies. The molecular genetics of these rare syndromes have only recently been elucidated; there appears to be still undefined genetic heterogeneity. Appropriate screening and surveillance will be predicated on clinical presentation and knowledge of the biology of each disorder. Although surveillance strategies in these syndromes have not been rigorously evaluated, highly targeted surveillance is warranted on the basis of the associated cancer risks.

References

1 Williams AR, Balasooriya BA, Day DW. Polyps and cancer of the large bowel: a necropsy study in Liverpool. *Gut* 1982; **23**:835–842.

2 Burn J, Chapman P, Delhanty J, *et al.* The UK Northern region genetic register for familial adenomatous polyposis coli: use of age of onset, congenital hypertrophy of the retinal pigment epithelium, and DNA markers in risk calculations. *J Med Genet* 1991; **28**:289–296.

3 Bjork J, Akerbrant H, Iselius L, *et al.* Periampullary adenomas and adenocarcinomas in familial adenomatous polyposis: cumulative risks and APC gene mutations. *Gastroenterology* 2001; **121**:1127–1135.

4 de Vos tot Nederveen Cappel WH, Jarvinen HJ, Bjork J, Berk T, Griffioen G, Vasen HF. Worldwide survey among polyposis registries of surgical management of severe duodenal adenomatosis in familial adenomatous polyposis. *Br J Surg* 2003; **90**:705–710.

5 Nugent KP, Phillips RK. Rectal cancer risk in older patients with familial adenomatous polyposis and an ileorectal anastomosis: a cause for concern. *Br J Surg* 1992; **79**:1204–1206.

6 Cross I, Delhanty J, Chapman P, *et al.* An intrachromosomal insertion causing 5q22 deletion and familial adenomatous polyposis coli in two generations. *J Med Genet* 1992; **29**:175–179.

7 Kadmon M, Tandara A, Herfarth C. Duodenal adenomatosis in familial adenomatous polyposis coli. A review of the literature and results from the Heidelberg Polyposis Register. *Int J Colorectal Dis* 2001; **16**:63–75.

8 Bertario L, Russo A, Sala P, *et al.* Multiple approach to the exploration of genotype-phenotype correlations in familial adenomatous polyposis. *J Clin Oncol* 2003; **21**:1698–1707.

9 Sieber O, Lipton L, Heinimann K, Tomlinson I. Colorectal tumourigenesis in carriers of the APC I1307K variant: lone gunman or conspiracy? *J Pathol* 2003; **199**:137–139.

10 Hahnloser D, Petersen GM, Rabe K, *et al.* The APC E1317Q variant in adenomatous polyps and colorectal cancers. *Cancer Epidemiol Biomarkers Prev* 2003; **12**:1023–1028.

11 Giardiello FM, Brensinger JD, Petersen GM. AGA technical review on hereditary colorectal cancer and genetic testing. *Gastroenterology* 2001; **121**:198–213.

12 Friedl W, Caspari R, Sengteller M, *et al.* Can APC mutation analysis contribute to therapeutic decisions in familial adenomatous polyposis? Experience from 680 FAP families. *Gut* 2001; **48**:515–521.

13 Kashiwagi H, Spigelman AD. Gastroduodenal lesions in familial adenomatous polyposis. *Surg Today* 2000; **30**:675–682.

14 Leggett B. FAP: another indication to treat H pylori. *Gut* 2002; **51**:463–464.

15 Groves CJ, Saunders BP, Spigelman AD, Phillips RK. Duodenal cancer in patients with familial adenomatous polyposis (FAP): results of a 10 year prospective study. *Gut* 2002; **50**:636–641.

16 Vasen HF, Bulow S, Myrhoj T, *et al.* Decision analysis in the management of duodenal adenomatosis in familial adenomatous polyposis. *Gut* 1997; **40**:716–719.

17 Al Tassan N, Chmiel NH, Maynard J, *et al.* Inherited variants of MYH associated with somatic G:C–>T:A mutations in colorectal tumors. *Nat Genet* 2002; **30**:227–232.

18 Sampson JR, Dolwani S, Jones S, *et al.* Autosomal recessive colorectal adenomatous polyposis due to inherited mutations of MYH. *Lancet* 2003; **362**:39–41.

19 Sieber OM, Lipton L, Crabtree M, *et al.* Multiple colorectal adenomas, classic adenomatous polyposis, and germ-line mutations in MYH. *N Engl J Med* 2003; **348**:791–799.

20 Haggitt RC, Reid BJ. Hereditary gastrointestinal polyposis syndromes. *Am J Surg Pathol* 1986; **10**:871–87.

21 Sachatello CR, Hahn IS, Carrington CB. Juvenile gastrointestinal polyposis in a female infant: Report of a case and review of the literature of a recently recognized syndrome. *Surgery* 1974; **75**:107–114.

22 Desai DC, Neale KF, Talbot IC, Hodgson SV, Phillips RKS. Juvenile polyposis. *Br J Surg* 1995; **82**:14–17.

23 Giardiello FM, Hamilton SR, Kern SE. Colorectal neoplasia in juvenile polyposis or juvenile polyposis. *Arch Dis Child* 1991; **66**:971–975.

24 Jass JR, Williams CB, Bussay HJR, Morson BC. Juvenile polyposis – a precancerous condition. *Histopathology* 1988; **13**:619–630.

25 Coburn MC, Pricolo VE, DeLuca FG, Bland KI. Malignant potential in intestinal juvenile polyposis syndromes. *Ann Surg Oncol* 1995; **2**:386–391.

26 Olschwang S, Serova-Sinilnikova OM, Lenoir GM, Gilles T. PTEN germ-line mutations in juvenile polyposis coli. *Nat Genet* 1998; **18**:12–14.

27 Liaw D, Marsh DJ, Li J, *et al.* Germ-line mutations of the PTEN gene in Cowden's disease, an inherited breast and thyroid cancer syndrome. *Nat Genet* 1997; **16**:64–67.

28 Marsh DJ, Dahia PLM, Coulon V, *et al.* Germ-line mutations in PTEN are present in Bannayan-Zonana syndrome. *Nat Genet* 1997; **16**:333–334.

29 Howe JR, Roth S, Ringold JC, *et al.* Mutations in the SMAD4/DPC4 gene in juvenile polyposis. *Science* 1998; **280**:1086–1088.

30 Kinzler KW, Vogelstein B. Landscaping the cancer terrain. *Science* 1998; **280**:1036–1037.

31 Hemminki A, Markie D, Tomlinson I, *et al.* A Serine/threonine kinase gene defective in Peutz–Jeghers syndrome. *Nature* 1998; **391**:184–187.

32 Tomlinson IPM, Houlston RS. Peutz–Jeghers syndrome. *J Med Genetics* 1997; **34**:1007–1011.

33 Giardello FM, Brensinger JD, Tersmette AC, *et al.* Very high risk of cancer in familial Peutz–Jeghers syndrome. *Gastroenterology* 2000; **119**:1447–1453.

34 Lim W, Hearle N, Shah B, Murday V, *et al.* Further observations on LKB1/STK11 status and cancer risk in Peutz–Jegher syndrome. *Br J Cancer* 2003; **89**:308–313.

35 Mehenni H, Gehrig C, Nezu J, *et al.* Loss of LKB1 kinase activity in Peutz–Jeghers syndrome and evidence for allelic and locus heterogeneity. *Am J Hum Genet* 1998; **63**:1641–1650.

36 Eng C. Cowden syndrome. *J Genet Counseling* 1997; **6**:181–191.

37 Marsh DJ, Kum JB, Lunetta KL, *et al.* PTEN mutation spectrum and genotype-phenotype correlations in Bannayan-Riley-Ruvalcaba syndrome suggest a single entity with Cowden syndrome. *Hum Mol Genet* 1999; **8**:1461–1472.

38 Hanssen AMN, Fryns JP. Cowden syndrome. *J Med Genet* 1995; **32**:117–119.

39 Starink TM, van der Veen JPW, Arwert F, *et al.* The Cowden syndrome. A clinical and genetic study in 21 patients. *Clin Genet* 1986; **29**:222–233.

40 Longy M, Lacombe D. Cowden disease. Report of a family and review. *Ann Genet* 1996; **39**:35–42.

41 Nelen MR, Padberg GW, Peeters EAJ, *et al.* Localization of the gen for Cowden disease to chromosome 10q22–23. *Nat Genet* 1996; **13**:114–116.

42 Zigman AF, Lavine JE, Jones MC, Boland CR, Carethers JM. Localization of the Bannayan-Riley-Ruvalcaba syndrome gene to chromosome 10q23. *Gastroenterology* 1997; **113**:1433–1437.

43 Carethers JM, Furnari FB, Zigman AF, *et al.* Absence of PTEN/MMAC1 germline mutations in sporadic Bannayan-Riley-Ruvalcaba syndrome. *Cancer Res* 1998; **58**:2724–2726.

Chapter 10

Management of hereditary non-polyposis colorectal cancer

H. F. A. Vasen, J. Burn, E. Sheridan, R. S. Houlston and F. Douglas

Introduction

Bowel cancer affects approximately 3 per cent of the population and most occurs by chance or due to environmental risk. Approximately 10 to 15 per cent of patients with colorectal cancer (CRC) have a family history of CRC, and 5 per cent of patients have early-onset (<45 years) CRC. A combination of genetic and environmental factors is likely to play a role in the aetiology of CRC in these cases.

In a small fraction of cases, genetic factors play a dominant role. These inherited conditions causing multiple polyposis, such as familial adenomatous polyposis (FAP), were the first inherited predisposition syndromes to be identified due to a relatively obvious phenotype. An American physician, Aldred Warthin, suspected a predisposition to hereditary bowel cancer without multiple polyposis at the beginning of the twentieth century. In 1913, he published data on a family (family G) in which there was a clear excess of endometrial and gastric cancers. When the family was reinvestigated by Lynch and Krush in 1971, the tumour spectrum included mainly colorectal and endometrial cancers, and the predisposition appeared to be inherited in an autosomal dominant manner (1). The syndrome was named Lynch syndrome or hereditary non-polyposis colorectal cancer (HNPCC).

In the early 1990s, the genes responsible for HNPCC were identified. These genes, referred to as mismatch repair (MMR) genes, play a role in the correction of mismatches that arise during DNA replication. Lack of mismatch repair function is associated with the presence of microsatellite instability in tumours, the hallmark of HNPCC. Estimates of the frequency of the syndrome vary. Originally it was thought that 5 to 10 per cent of all CRC would occur in the context of HNPCC. Direct estimates indicate that 1 to 2 per cent of all CRC occurs in MMR mutation carriers (2, 3).

Diagnostic criteria

Most families with HNPCC are identified by the presence of multiple cases of bowel cancer over several generations in the absence of the florid polyposis seen in most cases

Box 10.1 **Clinical criteria of HNPCC**

I. Amsterdam criteria (all criteria must be met)

- One member diagnosed with colorectal cancer before age 50 years
- Two affected generations
- Three affected relatives, one of them a first-degree relative of the other two
- FAP should be excluded
- Tumours should be verified by pathologic examination

II. Amsterdam criteria II (all criteria must be met)

- There should be at least three relatives with an HNPCC-associated cancer (colorectal cancer or cancer of the endometrium, small bowel, ureter, or renal pelvis)
- One should be a first-degree relative of the other two
- At least two successive generations should be affected
- At least one should be diagnosed before age 50 years
- FAP should be excluded in the colorectal cancer cases
- Tumours should be verified by pathologic examination

Bethesda guidelines (meeting features listed under any of the criteria is sufficient)

- Individuals with cancer in families that meet the Amsterdam criteria
- Individuals with two HNPCC-related cancers, including synchronous and metachronous colorectal cancers or associated extracolonic cancers (note: endometrial, ovarian, gastric, hepatobiliary, or small bowel cancer or transitional cell carcinoma of the renal pelvis or ureter)
- Individuals with colorectal cancer and a first-degree relative with colorectal cancer and/or HNPCC-related extracolonic cancer and/or a colorectal adenoma; one of the cancers diagnosed at age younger than 45 years, and the adenoma diagnosed at age younger than 40 years
- Individuals with colorectal cancer or endometrial cancer diagnosed at age younger than 45 years
- Individuals with right-sided colorectal cancer with an undifferentiated pattern (solid/cribriform) on histopathology diagnosed at age younger than 45 years (note: solid/cribriform defined as poorly differentiated or undifferentiated carcinoma composed of irregular, solid sheets of large eosinophilic cells and containing small gland-like spaces)

> - Individuals with signet-ring cell type colorectal cancer diagnosed at age younger than 45 years
> - Individuals with adenomas diagnosed at age younger than 40 years
>
> ### Revised Bethesda guidelines
>
> - Colorectal cancer diagnosed in a patient who is less than 50 years of age
> - Presence of synchronous, metachronous colorectal, or other HNPCC-associated tumours[1], regardless of age
> - Colorectal cancer with the MSI-H histology diagnosed in a patient who is less than 60 years of age
> - Colorectal cancer diagnosed with one or more first-degree relatives with an HNPCC-related tumour, with one of the cancers being diagnosed under age 50 years
> - Colorectal cancer diagnosed with two or more first- or second degree relatives with HNPCC-related tumours, regardless of age.
>
> [1] HNPCC-related tumours include colorectal, endometrial, stomach, ovarian, pancreas, ureter and renal pelvis, biliary tract, and brain (usually glioblastoma) tumours, sebaceous gland adenomas and keratoacanthomas, and carcinoma of the small bowel.

of FAP. The diagnosis is essentially an operational one; the chief clinical criteria are shown in Box 10.1. It is probably true to say that the original Amsterdam criteria (ACI) are still the most widely used for the identification of families (4). The revised Amsterdam criteria (ACII) were developed in response to concerns that ACI did not take into account the presence of highly suggestive extracolonic malignancies (5). Both ACI and ACII were designed to identify families suitable for research purposes. The Bethesda criteria were designed to identify families where analysis of tumours was more likely to reveal microsatellite instability (6). Recently, these criteria have been revised (7). None of the criteria are perfect; they are not intended to exclude suspected families from genetic counselling and mutation analysis. There are schools of thought that would now define HNPCC simply in terms of the presence of MMR mutations; however, since mutation analysis is neither universally available nor absolutely accurate, this is not a tenable position at present.

HNPCC tumours

A number of different cancers are now recognized as being part of HNPCC. Cancer of the large bowel (colorectal) accounts for most of the cancer burden. There appears to be a right-sided preponderance regarding the site of bowel cancer in most studies (8). Endometrial cancer is the second most common tumour and, in women, some studies have shown this to be the most common, affecting approximately 40 per cent of female gene carriers (9).

Table 10.1 Lifetime cancer risk in HNPCC

Cancer	Lifetime risk (%)
Colorectal (men)	65–80
Colorectal (women)	30–70
Endometrial	40–60
Ovarian	4–12
Gastric	2–13
Urinary tract	4–6
Renal cell	3
Bile duct/gallbladder	2
Small bowel	4–7

Gastric cancer has become less frequent in individuals with mismatch repair gene mutations in line with its decrease in the wider population. This decrease in gastric cancer is thought to reflect both improved living conditions, and hence a decrease in the prevalence of *Helicobacter pylori*, and also the widespread use of refrigeration leading to a decrease in other methods of food preservation, namely salting, pickling, smoking and soaking in spirit alcohol (10). The observation that incidence of gastric cancer in HNPCC has also fallen may imply that there is a gene–environment interaction, which may have great significance in the development of strategies to reduce the likelihood of cancers in those with mismatch repair gene defects.

Overall penetrance figures vary between studies (Table 10.1) (11–13). The combination of endometrial cancer and ovarian cancer confers a higher risk in women than does CRC in all studies. A variety of other tumours are seen, especially brain, renal pelvis, ureter and bile duct tumours. All have a frequency of <5 per cent in mutation carriers. Small bowel tumours are seen in 4 to 7 per cent of HNPCC cases. They are so rare in the general population that a good argument can be made for regarding small bowel tumours as features of HNPCC until proven otherwise.

The issue of breast cancer in HNPCC is contentious; however, there is little epidemiological data to show an excess in mutation carriers (14). One case in an HNPCC family showed loss of heterozygosity at the appropriate MMR locus in the breast cancer of a female family member, but the same group were unable to replicate the finding in a larger cohort (15).

HNPCC variants

Muir–Torre syndrome (MTS)

MTS is the combination of characteristic skin lesions with HNPCC. Suggestive skin lesions are sebaceous tumours, including adenomas, epitheliomas and carcinomas, and keratoacanthomas. Sebaceous tumours are rare and are a good marker for HNPCC (16).

Careful review of skin histology may be required to achieve or refute a diagnosis in these cases.

Turcot syndrome

Turcot's original observations were on sib pairs with brain tumours and colorectal cancers. The designation Turcot syndrome now tends to be used clinically to describe families in which this constellation of tumours is seen (17). The combination of medulloblastoma and colorectal cancer is seen chiefly in FAP (see above) and is dominant. Cases of Turcot syndrome have been described with classical dominant mutations in the HNPCC genes, but a recessive syndrome due to MMR mutations with a Turcot-like phenotype is being increasingly recognized (see below).

Pathology of HNPCC

Features of CRC associated with HNPCC include an increased proportion of mucinous tumours, poorly differentiated tumours and tumours with marked host lymphocytic infiltration and lymphoid aggregation at the tumour margin (18). However, the absence of such features does not rule out HNPCC. The majority of endometrial tumours associated with HNPCC are of the endometrioid type (19). Certain histopathological features, such as mucinous differentiation, solid-cribriform growth pattern, a high grade and possible necrosis, might suggest that a tumour is due to a mismatch repair defect.

Molecular genetics

The major cause of HNPCC is mutations in DNA mismatch repair genes. The major function of the MMR pathway is the elimination of base–base mismatches and insertion–deletion loops. The latter affect repetitive DNA and result in losses and gains of microsatellite repeat units. The pathway requires at least six different MMR proteins in humans. MSH2 complexes with MSH6 to form the hMutSα heterodimer, which is crucial to the recognition of base–base mismatches. A corresponding MutSβ heterodimer, comprising MSH2 and MSH3, is involved in insertion–deletion loop recognition. MLH1 and PMS2 complex to form the hMutLα heterodimer. This co-ordinates the interplay between the mismatch recognition complex and the other members of the MMR pathway (20).

Dominant germline mutations in the genes that encode members of the MMR pathways are the cause of the majority of HNPCC. *MLH1* (3p22.3) and *MSH2* (2p21) account for about 50 per cent and 40 per cent respectively of all HNPCC (21). Ten per cent of cases are due to mutations in *MSH6* and to date over 300 mutations in these three genes have been recorded. Mutations in a very small number of families have been recorded in *PMS2*. There is strong evidence to suggest that mutations in *PMS1* do not result in HNPCC. Mutations in *EXO1*, *MLH3* and *TGFβRII* have been recorded as the cause of HNPCC in isolated families. However, additional studies did not support a major causative role of these genes in HNPCC (22–24).

Genotype/phenotype correlations

There are reports indicating that mutations in *MSH2* confer a higher risk for extra-colonic cancers, especially cancer of the urinary tract, as compared to *MLH1* mutations. *MSH6* mutations may be associated with a higher risk of endometrial cancer and a lower risk of colorectal cancer in females (25).

Recently, a syndrome was identified in which children with biallelic DNA-MMR gene mutations in *MLH1*, *MSH2*, *MSH6* or *PMS2* develop clinical signs of neurofibromatosis type 1, in particular café-au-lait spots and early-onset neoplasia (26). The pattern of malignancies is characteristic with brain tumours, haematological malignancies in the first decade and colorectal cancer in the second decade.

A few families have been reported with mono or biallelic *PMS2* mutations (27). In such families, heterozygotes do not appear to have an HNPCC phenotype, and there is real doubt that *PMS2* mutations cause classical dominant HNPCC.

Microsatellite instability (MSI)

MSI is the hallmark of HNPCC; it is defined as the presence of extra alleles at a microsatellite when compared with normal DNA from the same individual. It was first recognized in yeast and identified in humans when loss of heterozygosity was investigated at the HNPCC candidate loci identified by linkage (Fig. 10.1). MSI results from frameshift mutations at repeats; however, the likelihood that any microsatellite will show instability when MMR is abrogated depends on the tumour type and the sequence context of the microsatellite. Mononucleotide repeats are more likely to show

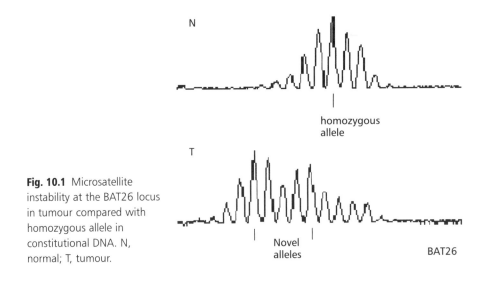

Fig. 10.1 Microsatellite instability at the BAT26 locus in tumour compared with homozygous allele in constitutional DNA. N, normal; T, tumour.

instability than dinucleotide repeats. It is possible that if enough markers are studied then all tumours will show some level of MSI.

A panel of five markers was approved for the identification of MSI in colorectal tumours at a meeting at the National Cancer Institute in 1997. MSI was classified into MSI high (MSI-H), where two or more of the panel showed instability, MSI low (MSI-L), where one marker showed instability and MSI stable (MSS) where none of the markers showed instability (28).

Overall 15 to 20 per cent of sporadic colon cancers demonstrate MSI; the figure is even higher in early-onset sporadic colon malignancy. This is usually due to hypermethylation of the *MLH1* promotors, thus MSI alone in colon cancer is a poor predictor of HNPCC (29). MSI in sporadic rectal cancers, however, is rare and is a good marker of HNPCC. A large study of apparently sporadic adenomas has shown that 1.6 per cent have a MSI-H phenotype (30). Five of the six patients with a MSI-H adenoma were found to carry a MMR mutation. Another recent study showed that about 75 per cent of adenomas detected in HNPCC families showed MSI as well as loss of MMR protein (31). MSI is also seen in extracolonic malignancies in HNPCC and about 15 per cent of sporadic endometrial and gastric cancers show MSI.

Immunohistochemistry

The protein expression of the MMR genes might be analysed by using antibodies against the MLH1, MSH2 and MSH6-proteins. Immunohistochemical (IHC) staining can be performed on formalin-fixed, paraffin-embedded tissue sections. When analysing MLH1, MSH2 and MSH6 expression, tissue stroma and normal epithelium are used as internal controls. Only if there is no nuclear staining of the tumour for one of the antibodies and at the same time normal staining of the internal control tissue, can it be concluded that there is loss of expression of the involved MMR protein.

Most studies so far have used antibodies against MLH1, MSH2 and MSH6. Because the PMS2 protein forms a heterodimer with the MLH1 protein, it has been hypothesized that absence of the MLH1 protein due to a germline mutation also leads to loss of PMS2 protein caused by abrogation of the total protein complex. Indeed, using antibodies against PMS2 in a large series of tumours from carriers of a *MLH1* mutation, loss of both proteins was frequently observed and by adding PMS2 antibodies significantly more *MLH1* mutation carriers were identified (32). IHC analysis might also be performed in adenomas. We found loss of protein expression in most (74 per cent) of the adenomas detected in *MSH2* or *MLH1* mutation carriers. As adenomas in MMR mutation carriers are usually larger than sporadic adenomas and a higher proportion have villous components and/or high grade dysplasia, IHC analysis of adenomas might be considered in young patients (<50 years) if the adenomas are large (>7 mm), show high-grade dysplasia and/or have a villous component (33).

Genetic testing

It is regarded as current standard practice to undertake mutation testing in those families that include a living affected relative with an HNPCC-related cancer and to test this individual. Once a mutation is identified in such an affected family member it becomes possible to offer predictive testing to other family members. Both mutation testing and predictive testing should, where possible, be undertaken by those with experience in genetic testing to ensure that issues of confidentiality and information sharing are explained within the consent process.

Due to the heterogeneity of the mutation spectrum in MMR genes, screening for mutations is both time-consuming and expensive. The mutation detection rate in families meeting the Amsterdam criteria I/II is approximately 50 per cent. However, in families with a low suspicion of HNPCC, the detection rate is much lower (<25 per cent). In contrast to other hereditary cancers, in familial CRC, relatively cheap tests, that is MSI and IHC analysis, are available that can be used to identify families which have a high predicted probability of carrying a mutation. IHC analysis can also predict which gene has been mutated. It has been recommended to perform MSI analysis in all tumours from patients that meet the Bethesda criteria (Box 10.1). Various studies have shown that these criteria are appropriate to identify HNPCC families.

We have recently performed MSI analysis in 631 families suspected of HNPCC. The proportion of MSI-H /MSI-L tumours was highest in families that met the Amsterdam criteria (59 per cent) and in patients with multiple HNPCC-associated cancers (44 per cent). In patients with early-onset CRC (<45 years), the proportion of MSI-H/L tumours was 29 per cent (32).

Although our studies indicated that when using antibodies raised against the four MMR proteins, the sensitivity of IHC is approximately the same as that for MSI, IHC cannot completely replace MSI analysis as long as the role of other putative MMR gene in hereditary CRC has not been elucidated. For this reason, we prefer MSI analysis as first step in families suspected of HNPCC, but not fulfilling the Amsterdam criteria (34). In these cases, the probability of detecting a mutation is relatively low (<25 per cent). In the total group of Amsterdam-negative families, MSI analysis will provide global information on loss of MMR function, including alterations in MMR genes other than the known genes. In MSI-H and MSI-L cases, IHC should be performed as a second step. In the cases of MSS, IHC for MSH6 might be considered, as one study had shown that tumours from MSH6 carriers might be stable (MSS) (35). On the other hand, in families fulfilling the revised Amsterdam criteria in which the probability of detecting a mutation is relatively high (>50 per cent), we recommend IHC as first diagnostic step because the result might indicate which MMR gene is mutated. If a negative staining pattern is found, mutation analysis of the respective gene is the next step. In case of doubtful interpretation or positive staining of all MMR proteins, MSI analysis should be

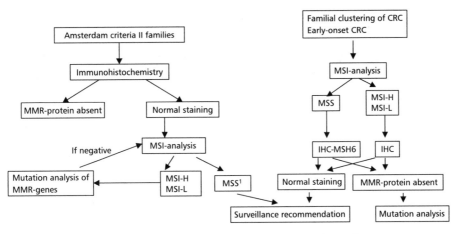

Fig. 10.2 Approach for families with clustering of non-polyposis colorectal cancer (CRC).

[1] Consider in a higly suspicious family analysis of a second tumour. MSI, microsatellite instability; MSS, MSI stable; IHC, immunohistochemistry; MMR, mismatch repair gene.

performed. In case of the absence of MSI, the analysis of a second tumour from the same family is recommended to exclude the presence of phenocopies. Figure 10.2 summarizes our current approach.

Surveillance

Colon screening

Surveillance is the mainstay of HNPCC treatment. It is offered to mutation carriers, and those at 50 per cent risk on the basis of the pedigree. Three-yearly colonoscopy reduced the risk of CRC by half and the risk of death from CRC by 65 per cent in HNPCC families (36). Colorectal surveillance is generally offered from age 20–25. There is good evidence that polyps in HNPCC progress more quickly and that longer surveillance intervals are associated with a higher risk of interval cancers (37). Therefore, the interval between colonoscopy should be 1 to 2-yearly and polyps should be removed when seen. For those individuals in which colonoscopy is technically difficult or who have multiple polyps, consideration should be given to colectomy. In Table 10.2 we summarize the recommendations for surveillance in families with clustering of CRC categorized according to the clinical criteria and the results of MSI and IHC analysis.

The 10-year risk of metachronous second CRC in the Dutch HNPCC registry was 15.7 per cent with a mean age at first cancer of 45 (38). These data stress the need for follow-up after surgery. Clearly, if a mutation carrier develops CRC, then consideration should be given to surgical treatment. Carriers with a partial colectomy

Table 10.2 Consequences of test results on clinical management of families that comply with the Bethesda or Amsterdam criteria

Clinical criteria	MSI analysis	IHC analysis	Mutation analysis	Clinical management
Amsterdam II	MSI-H	Loss of protein expression	Mutation identified	According to HNPCC guidelines[1]
Amsterdam II	Two MSS tumours	Normal protein expression in 2 tumours	Not indicated	Colonoscopy 3 yearly from 5–10 years before first diagnosis CRC in family
Revised Bethesda	MSI-H/L	Loss of protein expression	No mutation identified	According to HNPCC guidelines[1]
Revised Bethesda	MSS	Normal expression	Not performed	Colonoscopy 3–6 yearly from 5–10 years before first diagnosis CRC in family

[1] surveillance by colonoscopy every 2 years from age 20–25 years, annual surveillance of endometrium from age 30 years; consider subtotal colectomy and ileorectal anastomosis in patients who present with CRC.

have a high risk of subsequent CRC. In the Dutch series, the 10-year risk of second CRC after subtotal colectomy was only 3.4 per cent. Prophylactic colectomy at the time of first diagnosis of CRC may be a sensible treatment option (39). In contrast, prophylactic colectomy in unaffected mutation carriers has not found favour in Europe.

Extracolonic screening

Clearly, for females there is a considerable risk of endometrial cancer and a moderate risk for ovarian cancer. There is no proven surveillance regime for either (40). However, transvaginal ultrasound scan and direct visualization of the uterine cavity can be performed on an out-patient basis together. A study has shown that this is well-tolerated and early stage, asymptomatic endometrial cancers have been detected using this approach (41). Hysterectomy and bilateral salpingo-oophorectomy may be considered after menopause in carriers of an *MSH6* mutation. Bilateral salpingo-oophorectomy might be considered in *MSH2* and *MLH1* mutation carriers after completion of childbearing if there is clustering of ovarian cancer in the family.

The risk of gastric cancer in HNPCC in Western countries is low. Screening by means of endoscopy has been suggested but is unproven. Gastric surveillance should only be discussed in those families that have a high incidence of this tumour. In countries such as Japan and Korea, where the risk of gastric cancer is much higher, screening has been suggested.

Screening of the uroepithelial tract is debatable. There is no association with a specific genotype and a pragmatic approach is to offer it only to families in whom these cancers have been recorded. In such cases yearly urinalysis, urine cytology and renal ultrasound scan from age 40 has been used.

Chemotherapy for colon cancers due to a mismatch repair mutation

Most chemotherapy achieves its effect by DNA damage. Normal cells with intact repair mechanisms and regulated growth are less susceptible to chemotherapeutic agents than many cancer cells, hence the possibility of treatment. However, until recently, this has been a blunt weapon. As molecular understanding of the differences between tumour and normal cells has advanced, more attention has been devoted to targeting tumour cells specifically and to tailoring a person's chemotherapy to maximize efficacy against their particular tumour. Fluorouracil-based regimes represent the current gold standard in adjuvant chemotherapy for bowel cancer. Recent *in vitro* studies have shown that MMR-proficient cells treated with 5-FU grow more slowly than MMR-deficient cells (42). This suggests that a competent MMR system is a critical condition for selective 5-FU cytotoxity. Clinical studies on the efficacy of 5-FU in MSI-H colon cancer are contradictory. On the one hand it has been postulated that MSI is a predictive factor for a positive response to 5-FU chemotherapy (43). On the other hand recent studies suggested that patients with MSI-H tumours receiving 5-FU based chemotherapy have a trend toward a worse outcome compared to those not receiving treatment (44, 45). Although this may seem a negative step for those with such tumours, it represents the beginning of a process in which only effective drugs will be used against a particular tumour.

Chemoprevention

There is tantalizing evidence that HNPCC may be susceptible to environmental manipulation, as demonstrated by the decrease in the incidence of gastric cancer and perhaps also by the apparent differences in penetrance between men and women.

There is interest at the moment regarding the role of aspirin in bowel cancer prevention. Several large studies have demonstrated that aspirin reduces the risk of bowel cancer in the general population. There is separate evidence suggesting that resistant starch (an isomer of starch) may also play a role in reducing bowel cancer risk. At the moment, there is a large international study attempting to answer questions regarding such interventions in HNPCC and whether either aspirin or starch or both could have sufficient benefit to be recommended as preventative treatment.

Summary

HNPCC is a multisystem disorder; the diagnosis is still essentially clinical. Although a variety of molecular tests are available to assist in or confirm the diagnosis, the mainstay of diagnosis remains an accurate family history. MSI testing and IHC are valuable adjuncts to diagnosis and are of use in guiding molecular analysis. However, a variable proportion of HNPCC families remain undefined at a molecular level. Improvements in mutation analysis may change this.

Treatment is chiefly by means of screening and regimens vary with local resources. The screening programmes are lifelong once started. To promote maximal compliance with the recommended surveillance protocols, careful education and counselling about all details of the disease are essential. Experience has shown that individual specialists cannot adequately guarantee long-term surveillance of high-risk families, and this can lead to considerable morbidity and mortality. In several countries, these problems have inspired specialists to establish national and regional registries that monitor the continuity of the surveillance programmes by periodic assessment of the screening results. The registries also ensure that the same protocol is offered to various branches of the families that are followed-up by different specialists. Hereditary cancer registries also have a role in the assessment of the results of long-term surveillance. This is important as the value of most suggested protocols is as yet unknown.

References

1 Lynch HT, Krush AJ. Cancer family "G" revisited: 1895–1970. *Cancer* 1971; **27**:1505–1511.

2 Dunlop MG, Farrington SM, Nicholl I, Aaltonen L, Petersen G, Porteous M, Carothers A. Population carrier frequency of hMSH2 and hMLH1 mutations. *Br J Cancer* 2000; **83**:1643–1645.

3 Salovaara R, Loukola A, Kristo P, Kaariainen H, Ahtola H, Eskelinen M, Harkonen N, Julkunen R, Kangas E, Ojala S, Tulikoura J, Valkamo E, Jarvinen H, Mecklin JP, Aaltonen LA, de la Chapelle A. Population-based molecular detection of hereditary nonpolyposis colorectal cancer. *J Clin Oncol* 2000; **18**:2193–2200.

4 Vasen HF, Mecklin JP, Khan PM, Lynch HT. The International Collaborative Group on Hereditary Non-Polyposis Colorectal Cancer (ICG-HNPCC). *Dis Colon Rectum* 1991; **34**:424–425.

5 Vasen HF, Watson P, Mecklin JP, Lynch HT. New clinical criteria for hereditary nonpolyposis colorectal cancer (HNPCC, Lynch syndrome) proposed by the International Collaborative group on HNPCC. *Gastroenterology* 1999; **116**:1453–1456.

6 Rodriguez-Bigas MA, Boland CR, Hamilton SR, Henson DE, Jass JR, Khan PM, Lynch H, Perucho M, Smyrk T, Sobin L, Srivastava S. A national cancer institute workshop on hereditary nonpolyposis colorectal cancer syndrome: meeting highlights and Bethesda guidelines. *J Natl Cancer Inst* 1997; **89**:1758–1762.

7 Umar A, Boland CR, Terdiman JP, Syngal S, de la Chapelle A, Ruschoff J, Fishel R, Lindor NM, Burgart LJ, Hamelin R, Hamilton SR, Hiatt RA, Jass J, Lindblom A, Lynch HT, Peltomaki P, Ramsey SD, Rodriguez-Bigas MA, Vasen HF, Hawk ET, Barrett JC, Freedman AN, Srivastava S. Revised Bethesda guidelines for hereditary nonpolyposis colorectal cancer (Lynch syndrome) and microsatellite instability. *J Natl Cancer Inst* 2004; **96**:261–268.

8 Vasen HF, Offerhaus GJ, Hartog Jager FC, Menko FH, Nagengast FM, Griffioen G, van Hogezand RB, Heintz AP. The tumour spectrum in hereditary non-polyposis colorectal cancer: a study of 24 kindreds in the Netherlands. *Int J Cancer* 1990; **46**:31–34.

9 Dunlop MG, Farrington SM, Carothers AD, Wyllie AH, Sharp L, Burn J, Liu B, Kinzler KW, Vogelstein B. Cancer risk associated with germline DNA mismatch repair gene mutations. *Hum Mol Genet* 1997; **6**:105–110.

10 Palli D. Epidemiology of gastric cancer: an evaluation of available evidence. *J Gastroenterol* 2000; **35** Suppl **12**:84–89.

11 Aarnio M, Mecklin JP, Aaltonen LA, Nystrom-Lahti M, Jarvinen HJ. Life-time risk of different cancers in hereditary non-polyposis colorectal cancer (HNPCC) syndrome. *Int J Cancer* 1995; **64**:430–433.

12 Aarnio M, Sankila R, Pukkala E, Salovaara R, Aaltonen LA, de la Chapelle A, Peltomaki P, Mecklin JP, Jarvinen HJ. Cancer risk in mutation carriers of DNA-mismatch-repair genes. *Int J Cancer* 1999; **81**:214–218.

13 Vasen HF, Stormorken A, Menko FH, Nagengast FM, Kleibeuker JH, Griffioen G, Taal BG, Moller P, Wijnen JT. MSH2 mutation carriers are at higher risk of cancer than MLH1 mutation carriers: a study of hereditary nonpolyposis colorectal cancer families. *J Clin Oncol* 2001; **19**:4074–4080.

14 Vasen HF, Morreau H, Nortier JW. Is breast cancer part of the tumour spectrum of hereditary nonpolyposis colorectal cancer? *Am J Hum Genet* 2001; **68**:1533–1535.

15 Risinger JI, Barrett JC, Watson P, Lynch HT, Boyd J. Molecular genetic evidence of the occurrence of breast cancer as an integral tumour in patients with the hereditary nonpolyposis colorectal carcinoma syndrome. *Cancer* 1996; **77**:1836–1843.

16 Rutten A, Burgdorf W, Hugel H, Kutzner H, Hosseiny-Malayeri HR, Friedl W, Propping P, Kruse R. Cystic sebaceous tumours as marker lesions for the Muir-Torre syndrome: a histopathologic and molecular genetic study. *Am J Dermatopathol* 1999; **21**:405–413.

17 Hamilton SR, Liu B, Parsons RE, Papadopoulos N, Jen J, Powell SM, Krush AJ, Berk T, Cohen Z, Tetu B. The molecular basis of Turcot's syndrome. *N Engl J Med* 1995; **332**:839–847.

18 Shashidharan M, Smyrk T, Lin KM, Ternent CA, Thorson AG, Blatchford GJ, Christensen MA, Lynch HT. Histologic comparison of hereditary nonpolyposis colorectal cancer associated with MSH2 and MLH1 and colorectal cancer from the general population. *Dis Colon Rectum* 1999; **42**:722–726.

19 de Leeuw WJ, Dierssen J, Vasen HF, Wijnen JT, Kenter GG, Meijers-Heijboer H, Brocker-Vriends A, Stormorken A, Moller P, Menko F, Cornelisse CJ, Morreau H. Prediction of a mismatch repair gene defect by microsatellite instability and immunohistochemical analysis in endometrial tumours from HNPCC patients. *J Pathol* 2000; **192**:328–335.

20 Harfe BD, Jinks-Robertson S. DNA mismatch repair and genetic instability. *Annu Rev Genet* 2000; **34**:359–399.

21 Peltomaki P. Role of DNA mismatch repair defects in the pathogenesis of human cancer. *J Clin Oncol* 2003; **21**:1174–1179.

22 Jagmohan-Changur S, Poikonen T, Vilkki S, Launonen V, Wikman F, Orntoft TF, Moller P, Vasen H, Tops C, Kolodner RD, Mecklin JP, Jarvinen H, Bevan S, Houlston RS, Aaltonen LA, Fodde R, Wijnen J, Karhu A. EXO1 variants occur commonly in normal population: evidence against a role in hereditary nonpolyposis colorectal cancer. *Cancer Res* 2003; **63**:154–158.

23 Hienonen T, Laiho P, Salovaara R, Mecklin JP, Jarvinen H, Sistonen P, Peltomaki P, Lehtonen R, Nupponen NN, Launonen V, Karhu A, Aaltonen LA. Little evidence for involvement of MLH3 in colorectal cancer predisposition. *Int J Cancer* 2003; **106**:292–296.

24 Shin KH, Park YJ, Park JG. Mutational analysis of the transforming growth factor beta receptor type II gene in hereditary nonpolyposis colorectal cancer and early-onset colorectal cancer patients. *Clin Cancer Res* 2000; **6**:536–540.

25 Wijnen J, De Leeuw W, Vasen H, van der Klift H, Moller P, Stormorken A, Meijers-Heijboer H, Lindhout D, Menko F, Vossen S, Moslein G, Tops C, Brocker-Vriends A, Wu Y, Hofstra R, Sijmons R, Cornelisse C, Morreau H, Fodde R. Familial endometrial cancer in female carriers of MSH6 germline mutations. *Nat Genet* 1999; **23**:142–144.

26 Trimbath JD, Petersen GM, Erdman SH, Ferre M, Luce MC, Giardiello FM. Cafe-au-lait spots and early onset colorectal neoplasia: a variant of HNPCC? *Fam Cancer* 2001; **1**:101–105.

27 De Rosa M, Fasano C, Panariello L, Scarano MI, Belli G, Iannelli A, Ciciliano F, Izzo P. Evidence for a recessive inheritance of Turcot's syndrome caused by compound heterozygous mutations within the PMS2 gene. *Oncogene* 2000; **19**:1719–1723.

28 Boland CR, Thibodeau SN, Hamilton SR, Sidransky D, Eshleman JR, Burt RW, Meltzer SJ, Rodriguez-Bigas MA, Fodde R, Ranzani GN, Srivastava S. A National Cancer Institute workshop on microsatellite instability for cancer detection and familial predisposition: development of international criteria for the determination of microsatellite instability in colorectal cancer. *Cancer Res* 1998; **58**:5248–5257.

29 Cunningham JM, Christensen ER, Tester DJ, Kim CY, Roche PC, Burgart LJ, Thibodeau SN. Hypermethylation of the hMLH1 promoter in colon cancer with microsatellite instability. *Cancer Res* 1998; **58**:3455–3460.

30 Loukola A, Salovaara R, Kristo P, Moisio AL, Kaariainen H, Ahtola H, Eskelinen M, Harkonen N, Julkunen R, Kangas E, Ojala S, Tulikoura J, Valkamo E, Jarvinen H, Mecklin JP, de la Chapelle A, Aaltonen LA. Microsatellite instability in adenomas as a marker for hereditary nonpolyposis colorectal cancer. *Am J Pathol* 1999; **155**:1849–1853.

31 Iino H, Simms L, Young J, Arnold J, Winship IM, Webb SI, Furlong KL, Leggett B, Jass JR. DNA microsatellite instability and mismatch repair protein loss in adenomas presenting in hereditary non-polyposis colorectal cancer. *Gut* 2000; **47**:37–42.

32 de Jong AE, van Puijenbroek M, Hendriks Y, Tops C, Wijnen J, Ausems MG, Meijers-Heijboer H, Wagner A, van Os TA, Brocker-Vriends AH, Vasen HF, Morreau H. Microsatellite instability, immunohistochemistry, and additional PMS2 staining in suspected hereditary nonpolyposis colorectal cancer. *Clin Cancer Res* 2004; **10**:972–980.

33 de Jong AE, Morreau H, van Puijenbroek M, Eilers PH, Wijnen J, Nagengast FM, Griffioen G, Cats A, Menko FH, Kleibeuker JH, Vasen HF. The role of mismatch repair gene defects in the development of adenomas in patients with HNPCC. *Gastroenterology* 2004; **126**:42–48.

34 Hendriks Y, Franken P, Dierssen JW, De Leeuw W, Wijnen J, Dreef E, Tops C, Breuning M, Brocker-Vriends A, Vasen H, Fodde R, Morreau H. Conventional and tissue microarray immunohistochemical expression analysis of mismatch repair in hereditary colorectal tumours. *Am J Pathol* 2003; **162**:469–477.

35 Berends MJ, Wu Y, Sijmons RH, Mensink RG, van der Sluis T, Hordijk-Hos JM, de Vries EG, Hollema H, Karrenbeld A, Buys CH, van der Zee AG, Hofstra RM, Kleibeuker JH. Molecular and clinical characteristics of MSH6 variants: an analysis of 25 index carriers of a germline variant. *Am J Hum Genet* 2002; **70**:26–37.

36 Jarvinen HJ, Aarnio M, Mustonen H, Aktan-Collan K, Aaltonen LA, Peltomaki P, de la Chapelle A, Mecklin JP. Controlled 15-year trial on screening for colorectal cancer in families with hereditary nonpolyposis colorectal cancer. *Gastroenterology* 2000; **118**:829–834.

37 Vasen HF, Nagengast FM, Khan PM. Interval cancers in hereditary non-polyposis colorectal cancer (Lynch syndrome). *Lancet* 1995; **345**:1183–1184.

38 de Vos tot Nederveen Cappel WH, Nagengast FM, Griffioen G, Menko FH, Taal BG, Kleibeuker JH, Vasen HF. Surveillance for hereditary nonpolyposis colorectal cancer: a long-term study on 114 families. *Dis Colon Rectum* 2002; **45**:1588–1594.

39 de Vos tot Nederveen Cappel WH, Buskens E, van Duijvendijk P, Cats A, Menko FH, Griffioen G, Slors JF, Nagengast FM, Kleibeuker JH, Vasen HF. Decision analysis in the surgical treatment of colorectal cancer due to a mismatch repair gene defect. *Gut* 2003; **52**:1752–1755.

40 Dove-Edwin I, Boks D, Goff S, Kenter GG, Carpenter R, Vasen HF, Thomas HJ. The outcome of endometrial carcinoma surveillance by ultrasound scan in women at risk of hereditary nonpolyposis colorectal carcinoma and familial colorectal carcinoma. *Cancer* 2002; **94**:1708–1712.

41 Baxter NP, Duffy SR, Sheridan E. Endometrial abnormalities in three sisters from a family with hereditary non-polyposis colorectal cancer syndrome. *Br J Obstet Gynaecol* 2002; **109**:1076–1078.

42 Carethers JM, Chauhan DP, Fink D, Nebel S, Bresalier RS, Howell SB, Boland CR. Mismatch repair proficiency and *in vitro* response to 5-fluorouracil. *Gastroenterology* 1999; **117**:123–131.

43 Elsaleh H, Joseph D, Grieu F, Zeps N, Spry N, Iacopetta B. Association of tumour site and sex with survival benefit from adjuvant chemotherapy in colorectal cancer. *Lancet* 2000; **355**:1745–1750.

44 Ribic CM, Sargent DJ, Moore MJ, Thibodeau SN, French AJ, Goldberg RM, Hamilton SR, Laurent-Puig P, Gryfe R, Shepherd LE, Tu D, Redston M, Gallinger S. Tumour microsatellite-instability status as a predictor of benefit from fluorouracil-based adjuvant chemotherapy for colon cancer. *N Engl J Med* 2003; **349**:247–257.

45 de Vos tot Nederveen Cappel WH, Meulenbeld HJ, Kleibeuker JH, Nagengast FM, Menko FH, Griffioen G, Cats A, Morreau H, Gelderblom H, Vasen HF. Survival after adjuvant 5-FU treatment for stage III colon cancer in hereditary nonpolyposis colorectal cancer. *Int J Cancer* 2004; **109**:468–471.

Chapter 11

Management and risk assessment of less common familial cancers

Sameer Jhavar and Rosalind Eeles

Introduction

Genetic predisposition to cancer is becoming a well-recognized phenomenon. It has been well described for common cancers. It may now be a fact in other cancers as well, the evidence for which is considered in this chapter.

Prostate cancer

Prostate cancer is the commonest cancer diagnosed in men in the UK, excluding non-melanoma skin cancer. The lifetime risk of being diagnosed with prostate cancer for men in the UK is 1 in 14 (1), with risks as high as 1 in 8 being quoted in the US. The mortality rates due to prostate cancer have not increased in concordance with the increase in the incidence rates over the last years. This may be attributable to rise in the numbers of prostate cancer cases detected at screening. The factors that may increase the risk of developing prostate cancer are given in Box 11.1.

Evidence for familial prostate cancer risk and risk assessment

Up to 42 per cent of prostate cancer risk was found to be attributable to genetic factors from a Scandinavian study which estimated cancer risk among monozygotic versus dizygotic twins. Examining registry data from 44 000 twins, the authors found that prostate cancer had the largest genetic component of all cancers (2).

Men with a first-degree relative (brother, father or son) with prostate cancer have a higher risk compared with those without such a family history. In a multiethnic study of Whites, Blacks and Asians in the United States, a positive family history was associated with a two to three-fold increase in risk (3). Screen-detected prostate cancer was diagnosed in 264 out of 6930 men (4.13 per cent), between the ages of 50 and 80 years, in a study by Narod *et al.* (4). There was a higher prevalence of prostate cancer in the group of men with a first-degree relative affected compared with the group without such a family history and most of the increase in relative risk was contributed by affected brothers (prevalence = 10.2 per cent; relative risk = 2.62; P = 0.0002). A study by Steinberg *et al.* (5) found a trend of increasing risk of prostate cancer with

---

Box 11.1 **Risk factors for prostate cancer**

- ◆ Demographic factors:
  - increasing age
  - place of residence at birth
  - genetic factors
  - family history of prostate cancer
  - family history of breast cancer
  - ethnicity – Black
- ◆ Dietary factors:
  - high animal fat consumption (controversial)
  - low selenium intake (controversial)
  - low lycopene intake (controversial)
- ◆ Occupational factors:
  - cadmium exposure
  - radiation exposure
  - farming

---

increasing number of affected family members, such that men with two or three first-degree relatives affected had a 5-11-fold increased risk of developing prostate cancer, respectively.

Early onset of disease in the proband was found to be another important determinant of risk in 691 prostate cancer families (6). Using complex segregation analysis, the familial clustering was best explained by autosomal dominant inheritance of a rare high-risk allele predisposing to early onset prostate cancer. The estimated cumulative risk of prostate cancer for carriers showed that the allele was highly penetrant. By age 85, 88 per cent of carriers were projected to be affected with prostate cancer compared to only 5 per cent of non-carriers. In a recent study (7), up to 2 per cent of young onset prostate cancer patients were found to have mutations in the BRCA2 gene.

A Finnish prostate cancer screening trial evaluated the impact of family history on screening for prostate cancer in 32 000 men. Only 105 (11 per cent) of 964 participants who had positive family history had positive results on screening. Additionally, a total of 29 tumours were finally diagnosed, corresponding to a detection rate of 3.0 per cent and positive predictive value of 24 per cent. However, the risk associated with positive family history was not significantly increased as compared to those without a family history. Their findings do not support selective screening amongst men with affected relatives (8).

Nieder *et al.* (9) suggested that major risk factors for developing prostate cancer, including positive family history and African–American ethnicity, could be quantified for genetic counselling. Factors increasing familial risk for prostate cancer are closer degree of kinship, number of affected relatives, and early age of onset (under 50 years) among the affected relatives. Even in the absence of genetic testing, African–American men and men with a strong family history of prostate cancer may opt to initiate screening by prostate-specific antigen and digital rectal examination at age 40 years.

Most studies have suggested that there is no significant difference in survival of familial prostate cancer patients compared with those of sporadic cases (10).

Management

Early detection

Every attempt should be made to identify men with an increased risk for prostate cancer based on the risk factors listed in Box 11.1. Those found at higher risk could be offered screening strategies based on the combination of periodic Prostate Specific Antigen (PSA) testing, digital rectal examination and supplementing abnormal results with transrectal ultrasound-guided biopsy. The sensitivity and specificity of these tests can be significantly improved by using age-standardized PSA reference ranges, measuring percentage of free PSA, as well as using PSA velocity and density; however, controversy exists over the use of these latter parameters. McWhorter *et al.*'s (11) study on targeted screening has shown the importance of thorough screening in first-degree relatives of prostate cancer patients.

Chemoprevention

A recent prostate prevention study using finasteride (12) concluded that finasteride prevents or delays the appearance of prostate cancer, but this possible benefit should be weighed against the increased risk of sexual dysfunction and the fact that a higher number of high-grade prostate cancers occurred in the group treated with finasteride. It is not entirely clear whether the increased numbers of higher-grade tumours in the finasteride treated group was a treatment effect on the histology or a true reflection of the biological behaviour. Several studies have shown an increase in risk of prostate cancer with increase in dietary intake of animal fat. It is suggested that increased intake of fat, specifically animal fat, red meat and alpha linoelic acid, is associated with an increased risk of developing advanced disease (13). Recently, Fradet *et al.* (14) have found that survival is inversely associated with saturated fat intake.

There are convincing data to show the protective effects of soy proteins, carotenoid, lycopene (found in tomatoes), selenium and vitamin D on prostate cancer risk. However, data on the protective effects of vitamin E on reducing prostate cancer risk need further evaluation. The studies on dietary intake and prostate cancer risk are also controversial.

Gastric cancer

The highest incidence of stomach cancer is seen in Japan, South America and Eastern Europe. Cancer of the stomach is the fifth and sixth most common cancer diagnosed in males and females, respectively, in the UK. In the UK, the overall lifetime risk for developing stomach cancer is 1 in 44 for males and 1 in 86 for females (1). The incidence and mortality of stomach cancer have shown a slowly decreasing trend in the UK.

Adenocarcinoma, which is mainly sporadic in nature, is the predominant histopathological type of gastric cancer, accounting for 95 per cent of the cases. It is further divided in two histopathological subtypes – the intestinal type (exophytic or expansive and gland forming, often ulcerated) or the diffuse type (poorly differentiated and infiltrative causing thickening of the stomach) (15). These two subtypes are seen to arise in different settings and have distinct biological behaviour. The intestinal type predominates in high-risk geographic areas, arises on the background of precursor lesions (i.e. chronic atrophic gastritis or intestinal metaplasia), occurs more distally in the stomach and later in life (usually after the sixth decade), and spreads predominantly to the liver via the blood stream. In contrast, the diffuse type is seen to occur early in life without identifiable precursor lesions, spreads more diffusely in the stomach and spreads predominantly contiguously into the peritoneum.

The various risk factors for gastric cancer are shown in Box 11.2 and the precursor lesions that increase the risk for development of gastric cancer are shown in Box 11.3 (16).

Box 11.2 Risk factors for gastric cancer

- ◆ Acquired factors:
  - nutritional – high salt intake, high nitrate consumption, low dietary vitamin A and C, poor food preparation (smoked and salt cured), lack of refrigeration, poor drinking water (well water)
  - occupational – rubber workers, coal workers
  - habits – cigarette smoking
  - infections – *Helicobacter pylori* infection (5–6 fold increased risk), Epstein–Barr virus infection
  - environmental – radiation exposure
  - treatment related – prior gastric surgery for benign gastric ulcer disease.
- ◆ Genetic factors:
  - type A blood group
  - pernicious anaemia
  - family history of gastric cancer
  - hereditary non-polyposis colon cancer
  - Li–Fraumeni syndrome.

> ## Box 11.3 Precursor lesions increasing the risk of gastric cancer (16)
>
> ◆ Adenomatous gastric polyps
>
> ◆ Chronic atrophic gastritis
>
> ◆ Dysplasia
>
> ◆ Intestinal metaplasia
>
> ◆ Menetrier's disease

Evidence for inherited predisposition to gastric cancer and risk assessment

Kindreds exhibiting site-specific gastric cancer predilection have been reported. The patients in such families developed cancers which were more often of the undifferentiated type, frequently in the gastric cardia and with peritoneal and liver metastasis (17–20). La Vecchia *et al.* (21) and Zanghieri *et al.* (22) demonstrated familial clustering in 10 per cent of the gastric cancer cases. Epidemiological studies have shown the risk of gastric cancer in the first-degree relatives is increased to two to three fold (23). A recent Swedish family cancer database study showed familial risk of over 3.0 for signet ring cell gastric cancer (24).

In a retrospective clinicopathological correlation study of 548 pathologically confirmed gastric cancer cases, 74 (13.5 per cent) were found to have a positive family history of cancers in the first or second-degree relatives. In this study, the patients with a positive family history had bigger tumours and more often required a total gastrectomy than those without family history. The tumours in the patients with positive family history also had higher rate of *TP53* over expression, but the survival rates of these patients were similar to those without a family history. However, in this study, a family history of site specific stomach cancer was demonstrated in only 39 per cent (29/74) of cases (25).

A Japanese study (26) of 662 patients who died of stomach cancer demonstrated that cases with a family history of stomach cancer had an increased risk of death from the disease after controlling for age, number of siblings and all other risk factors for the disease. This was not gender specific. Additionally, in the subanalysis stratified by age, the association between positive family history and stomach cancer mortality was found to be stronger in the age group of 40 to 59 as compared to the age group 60 to 79 years. When two or more family members were affected the increment in risk was greater, especially in women. Other interesting findings of this study were that, in men, the increased risk of death from stomach cancer was seen only with history of stomach cancer in the father, whereas in women, the increased risk of death was maintained with history of stomach cancer in father, mother, or sister as well as in both parents combined. Environmental factors, for example infection by *H. pylori*, has been proposed as a cause for familial clustering of gastric cancer (27).

Familial site-specific gastric cancer

Definitions of hereditary diffuse gastric cancer (HDGC) and familial intestinal gastric cancer (FIGC) are shown in Box 11.4 (28).

Gastric cancer within inherited cancer syndromes

Hereditary non-polyposis colon cancer (HNPCC) is well recognized as predisposing to gastric malignancy (29). In the first report of this syndrome, cancer of the stomach was actually diagnosed more often than colorectal neoplasms (30). There is a four-fold increased risk of gastric cancer in addition to a high risk of colorectal cancer in the carriers of mutations in *MLH1* and *MSH2* (31, 32). Microsatellite instability (MSI) (see Chapter 10) is significantly associated with distal (antral) gastric tumours and a positive family history of gastric cancer (33).

Familial adenomatous polyposis (FAP) can involve the stomach in the form of fundic gland polyps. These hyperplastic lesions are seen in up to 75 per cent of individuals with FAP and in the past have been considered to be exclusively benign lesions. Hsieh and Huang *et al.* (34) suggested, from their study on primary gastric cancers, that the *APC* gene, which is a cause of FAP, might be involved in a subset of differentiated gastric cancers. The frequent associations of premalignant lesions, such as gastric

---

Box 11.4 Definitions of familial gastric cancer (28)

- Hereditary diffuse gastric cancer:
  - two or more documented cases of diffuse gastric cancer in the first or second-degree relatives with at least one cancer diagnosed before the age of 50
  - three or more cases of diffuse gastric cancer in the first or second-degree relatives independent of the age of onset.
- Familial intestinal gastric cancer in high-incidence countries (Japan, Portugal):
  - three or more relatives with intestinal gastric cancer, one being a first-degree relative of the others
  - intestinal gastric cancer in at least two successive generations
  - diagnosis before 50 in at least one individual.
- Familial intestinal gastric cancer in low-incidence countries:
  - two first or second-degree relatives affected, with one diagnosed before the age of 50
  - three or more affected relatives with IGC at any age.

polyps, in other inherited cancer predisposition syndromes, such as Cowden's syndrome and Peutz–Jeghers syndrome (PJS), implicates the role of *PTEN* and *STK11* genes respectively, although their role is small. Gastric cancer could also occur as a component of the cancer spectrum in Li–Fraumeni syndrome families.

Whilst gastric cancer is not a common feature of families with either *BRCA1* or *BRCA2* mutations, there is a significant excess of gastric malignancy associated with *BRCA2* mutations (RR 2.6, 95 per cent CI 1.5–4.6) (35). Pathological confirmation of the cases was not available in most families. No similar effect was seen for *BRCA1* (36).

Familial gastric cancer gene

In 1998, Guildford *et al.* demonstrated germ line mutations in the E-cadherin gene (*CDH1* located on chromosome 16q22) in affected members of three Maori New Zealand families with early-onset, poorly differentiated and high-grade diffuse gastric cancer (37). Most deaths from these gastric cancers cases occurred under the age of 40 years. This finding was confirmed and extended to a proportion of non-Maori European gastric cancer families (38, 39). However, mutations in *CDH1* contribute little to the overall burden of gastric malignancy. In a review on inherited risk of gastric cancer, Bevan and Houlston *et al.* concluded that several genes might be associated with the risk of gastric cancer (40).

Management

Caldas *et al.* suggested mutation screening of the E-cadherin gene in gastric cancer families meeting criteria for HDGC (41). They also noted that since five individuals below the age of 18 had developed diffuse gastric carcinoma, testing of minors might be justified.

Individuals with early-onset, intestinal-type gastric cancer should be evaluated for a family history of HNPCC-related cancers, and, in selected cases, MSI or immunohisto-chemical analysis of *MLH1/MSH2* should be offered.

Recent data have suggested that fundic polyps, which are a manifestation of FAP in the stomach, may not always behave in a benign fashion (42). Therefore, it seems prudent to offer regular upper gastrointestinal endoscopy and duodenoscopy to all individuals with FAP.

Mass screening in countries with low incidence of gastric cancer is not economically or practically feasible but early gastric cancer may be detected by heightened awareness of suggestive symptoms and the use of aggressive radiological and endoscopic methods. Endoscopic surveillance of patients undergoing partial gastrectomy for benign disease should be performed if dysplasia is found on biopsy. Individuals at high risk of stomach cancer could be offered surveillance by upper gastrointestinal endoscopies, but there are no data to support this management choice (43). Treatment of *H. pylori*-positive patients using antibiotics is recommended only in those with proven ulcer disease or in those with non-ulcer disease in whom other measures have failed (16).

Pancreatic cancer

Pancreatic cancer is the seventh most common cancer diagnosed in the UK (1). The overall lifetime risk for developing pancreatic cancer is 1 in 96 for males and 1 in 95 for females (1). Risk factors for pancreatic cancer are given in Box 11.5. Table 11.1 shows the various inherited syndromes that may increase the risk of developing pancreatic cancer.

Evidence for inherited predisposition to pancreatic cancer and risk assessment

There is no formally agreed definition for familial pancreatic cancer. However, Hruban *et al.* proposed that families that contained two or more first-degree relatives with pancreatic cancer constituted those with familial pancreatic cancer (44). Evidence suggests that ≥10 per cent pancreatic cancers could be inherited as an autosomal dominant trait. The primary characteristics of such families includes early age at onset (median age 43 years) and high penetrance (more than 80 per cent) of pancreatic cancer. Some family members developed pancreatic insufficiency before the onset of cancer (45–47).

An estimated increase in risk for pancreatic cancer of approximately two-fold has been found in association with diabetes mellitus, and this risk was found to be significantly elevated if the history of diabetes mellitus preceded the diagnosis of pancreatic cancer by more than 5 years (48, 49).

The cumulative incidence of pancreatic cancer, to age 70 years, is 40 per cent in patients with hereditary pancreatic cancer resulting from gain-of-function mutations in the protease serine-1 gene (*PRSS1*), which causes hereditary pancreatitis (50).

Mutation in the *p16* gene (*CDKN2*) can cause pancreatic adenocarcinoma and can result in pancreatic cancer in association with melanoma. Further evidence of the role of *CDKN2* in pancreatic tumourigenesis was provided by Whelan *et al.* (51), who described a kindred with an increased risk of pancreatic cancers, melanomas and

---

Box 11.5 Risk factors for pancreatic cancer

- Cigarette smoking (accounts for up to 30 per cent of the cases)
- Coffee consumption (conflicting evidence)
- Alcohol consumption (conflicting evidence)
- Familial predisposition (5–8 per cent)
- Chronic pancreatitis: hereditary and non-hereditary (magnitude of risk controversial, probably up to 5 per cent of all pancreatic cancer cases)
- Diabetes mellitus (exact relationship not understood well)

Table 11.1 Syndromes associated with an increased risk of pancreatic cancer

Syndrome	Inheritance	Clinical features	Component cancers
Hereditary pancreatitis	AD	Abdominal pain due to pancreatitis and its complications, increased amylase, portal and splenic thrombosis	Pancreatic carcinoma
Inherited breast/ovarian cancer syndrome particularly in those with *BRCA2* mutations	AD	Early onset of component cancers, bilaterality of cancers	Breast cancer, ovarian cancer, prostate cancer, pancreatic cancer, and melanoma
Familial melanoma	AD	Malignant melanoma, dysplastic nevi	Melanoma, pancreatic cancer
Hereditary non-polyposis colorectal cancer	AD	Early age of onset of component tumours, bilateral and multifocal	Colon cancer, endometrial cancer, stomach cancer, ovarian cancer, hepatobiliary cancer, kidney cancer, breast cancer and pancreatic cancer
Peutz–Jeghers syndrome	AD	Melanin spots on lips, buccal mucosa and digits; pigmented macules within pre-existing psoriatic plaques. Nasal, bronchial, ureteral, bladder, and multiple intestinal polyps; intussusception; gastrointestinal bleeding; gynaecomastia	Rare malignant transformation of small intestinal polyps, increased risk for breast and pancreatic cancers, benign ovarian tumours, testicular tumours
Multiple endocrine neoplasia type I (Werner syndrome)	AD	Skin rash, peptic ulcer, ulcerative gastritis, diarrhoea, steatorrhoea, hypoglycaemia, hyperglycaemia, glucose intolerance, Cushing's syndrome, bone pain	Islet cell tumours, pituitary adenomas, parathyroid adenomas, adrenocortical adenomas, bronchial carcinoids, duodenal carcinoids

Table 11.1 (Continued)

Syndrome	Inheritance	Clinical features	Component cancers
Von Hippel–Lindau syndrome	AD	Neurological symptoms due to cerebellar and spinal haemangioblastomas, visual disturbances due to retinal angiomas, haematuria due to renal cell carcinoma, hypertension due to phaeochromocytoma, testicular mass due to epididymal cystadenoma	Phaeochromocytoma, cerebellar and spinal haemangioma, renal cell carcinoma, retinal angioma, pancreatic, liver and renal cysts, pancreatic carcinoma
Li-Fraumeni syndrome	AD	Early onset of cancers and multiple cancers within individuals	Rhabdomyosarcoma, soft tissue sarcoma, breast cancer, brain tumour, osteosarcoma, leukaemia, adrenocortical carcinoma, lung adenocarcinoma
Dyskeratosis congenita	XLR	Cutaneous pigmentation, dystrophy of the nails, oral leukoplakia, atresia of the lacrimal ducts, testicular atrophy, anaemia and others	Skin cancer, oesophageal cancer, pancreatic adenocarcinoma
Phaeochromocytoma–islet cell tumour syndrome	AD	Sweating, hypertensive retinopathy, tachycardia, congestive heart failure, episodic hypertension, proteinuria, hypercalcaemia	Phaeochromocytoma (usually bilateral), pancreatic islet cell tumour

AD = autosomal dominant; AR = autosomal recessive; XLR = X-linked recessive.

possibly additional types of tumours (squamous cell cancer of the pancreas, squamous cell cancer of the tongue) cosegregating with a *CDKN2* mutation.

A recent segregation analysis of 287 pedigrees, ascertained through an index case with pancreatic cancer, provided evidence for a major gene involved in the aetiology of pancreatic cancer and suggested that this gene behaved in an autosomal dominant fashion (52).

Two recent studies have shown that germ line mutations in the *BRCA2* gene (found in 17–19 per cent of familial pancreatic cancers analysed) are one of the most common inherited genetic alterations in familial pancreatic cancers (53, 54).

Management

All attempts should be made to identify individuals at risk for developing pancreatic cancer based on the risk factors mentioned above. Management of individuals documented to be at an increased risk for developing pancreatic cancer is controversial at present. Options range from close observation to aggressive surgical intervention. High-resolution spiral CT scan and endoscopic retrograde cholangiopancreatography (ERCP) are very important tools in this setting and are being studied.

The European Registry Of Hereditary Pancreatitis and Familial Pancreatic Cancer (EUROPAC), is a Europe-wide register for patients and families with pancreatic cancer. It exemplifies one such initiative, which attempts to: (1) develop a clear understanding of the genetic relationship between hereditary pancreatitis and pancreatic cancer; and (2) develop screening protocols for high-risk individuals. Further information can be obtained from their website http://www.liv.ac.uk/surgery/europac.html.

Lung cancer

Lung cancer is the second most common cancer diagnosed in males and the third most common cancer in females in the UK. The overall lifetime risk for developing lung cancer is 1 in 13 and 1 in 23 for males and females, respectively (1). Lung cancers fall into two main categories: small cell lung cancer and non-small cell lung cancer. There are very rare instances of other types such as sarcoma, carcinoid, lymphoma and mucous gland tumours. The non-small cell types are commoner and are comprised of adenocarcinoma, epidermoid cancer and the large cell variety. The small cell (oat cell) type accounts for 20 per cent of lung cancers, is of neuroendocrine origin, and has the highest response rates to systemic chemotherapy. The risk factors are given in Box 11.6.

Evidence for inherited predisposition to lung cancer and risk assessment

Wu *et al.* summarized the findings of their multicentre study on lifetime non-smokers in the US, which included 646 female lung cancer patients and 1252 population controls (55). A 30 per cent increased risk was associated with a history of respiratory tract

---

Box 11.6 **Risk factors for lung cancer**

- Tobacco smoking
- Exposure to other carcinogens, e.g. asbestos, polyaromatic hydrocarbons, chromium, nickel, inorganic arsenic compounds
- Genetic susceptibility

---

cancer in parents or siblings, after adjustment for exposure to environmental tobacco smoke in adult life. Lung cancer, which represented approximately two-thirds of the respiratory tract cancers, occurred more frequently in first-degree relatives of lung cancer patients than in comparable relatives of population controls. A significant three-fold increased risk for lung cancer was associated with lung cancer diagnosed in mothers and sisters. An increased risk in relation to family history of lung cancer among parents and siblings who were smokers, as well as in those who were non-smokers, was also observed in this study. The association with family history of lung cancer was strengthened when the analysis was restricted to adenocarcinoma of the lung. However, the authors pointed out that there was no association between family history of other cancers and risk of lung cancer in non-smokers.

Amongst more than 600 patients with lung cancer who were either life-time non-smokers or exsmokers who had stopped smoking 15 years prior to their diagnosis, a slightly increased risk of lung cancer was seen with five or more relatives affected with any cancer (56).

Hwang *et al.* assessed the incidence of lung and smoking-related cancers in 33 carriers of germ line *TP53* mutations and in 1230 non-carriers from 97 families ascertained through childhood soft tissue sarcoma patients (57). An increased risk of a variety of histological types of lung cancer was observed in the carriers of *TP53* mutations. Mutation carriers who smoked had a 3.16-fold (95 per cent CI = 1.48–6.78) higher risk for lung cancer than the mutation carriers who did not smoke.

Inherited predisposition, in the form of genetic differences in the DNA repair capacity across smokers, could play a role in lung cancer because not all smokers develop lung cancer. A higher risk for developing non-small cell lung cancer has been found in one study in smokers with low activity of one of the DNA repair enzymes, 8-oxyguanine DNA N-glycosylase (58).

Lung cancer is seen as a part of various inherited cancer syndromes listed in Table 11.2.

Management

Wherever possible, an attempt should be made to identify individuals at higher risk for developing lung cancer on the basis of history of exposure to the environmental risk factors mentioned above and assessment for any cancer predisposing conditions.

Table 11.2 Inherited cancer syndromes predisposing to lung cancer

Syndrome	Inheritance	Component tumours
Multiple endocrine neoplasia I (Werner syndrome)	AD	Pancreatic tumours, pituitary adenomas, parathyroid adenoma, bronchial carcinoid
Familial alveolar carcinomas	unknown	Alveolar cell lung cancers
Li–Fraumeni syndrome	AD	Rhabdomyosarcoma, bone and soft tissue sarcoma, breast cancer, brain tumour, leukaemia, adrenocortical carcinomas, lung adenocarcinomas
Waldenstrom's macroglobinaemia	AD	Lung adenocarcinoma, other lymphoproliferative diseases
Malignant mesothelioma	Possibly AD	Malignant mesothelioma
Pulmonary fibrosis, familial (fibrocystic pulmonary dysplasia)	AD	Alveolar cell lung carcinoma

A study by Lee *et al.* did not support the case for retinoid-based (β-carotene, α-tocopherol and isotretinoin) chemoprevention for lung cancer in patients with high risk for lung cancer (59). Interestingly, another study showed that the incidence of lung cancer was actually higher in the group randomized to receive β-carotene (60). A recent study by Pastorino *et al.* showed that combined use of low-dose spiral CT and PET scanning in selective cases could effectively detect lung cancer early in high-risk cases (age ≥50 years and smoking history of ≥20 pack years) (61).

Cessation of smoking has roughly halved the lung cancer mortality in the UK. Stopping smoking is undoubtedly the key to preventing lung cancer; if smoking is stopped by middle age, even in those who have smoked for many years, then: (a) most of the subsequent risk of lung cancer is avoided; and (b) 90 per cent of risk attributable to tobacco is avoided (62).

Testicular tumours

Testicular cancer is the most common malignancy in men between the ages of 15–40 years. Germ cell tumours of the testis, the predominant histological type, are either seminomas, arising from the cells lining the seminiferous tubules, or non-seminomatous. Teratomas are the predominant tumours in the non-seminomatous category. Risk factors are listed in Box 11.7.

Evidence for familial testicular cancer and risk assessment

Families with multiple cases of testicular cancers are rare. The report on familial testicular cancers by Raghavan *et al.* illustrates the dominant inheritance and bilaterality of hereditary testicular tumours, suggesting that the sons (and other first-degree relatives) of men with bilateral tumours are at particular risk (63). In an epidemiological study

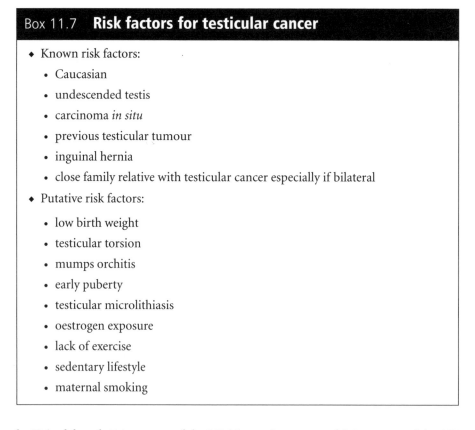

Box 11.7 Risk factors for testicular cancer

- ◆ Known risk factors:
  - Caucasian
  - undescended testis
  - carcinoma *in situ*
  - previous testicular tumour
  - inguinal hernia
  - close family relative with testicular cancer especially if bilateral
- ◆ Putative risk factors:
  - low birth weight
  - testicular torsion
  - mumps orchitis
  - early puberty
  - testicular microlithiasis
  - oestrogen exposure
  - lack of exercise
  - sedentary lifestyle
  - maternal smoking

by Heimdal *et al.*, 5.4 per cent of the 922 Norwegian cases and 2.1 per cent of the 237 Swedish cases with testicular cancer had a relative with confirmed testicular cancer; 57 per cent of these were first-degree relatives (64). The standardized incidence ratios were found to be higher for brothers compared with that for fathers or sons. Patients with familial testicular cancer had bilateral tumours more often than sporadic cases (9.8 per cent bilaterality in familial vs. 2.8 per cent in sporadic cases; P = 0.02). For patients with seminoma, age of onset was lower in familial than in sporadic cases (32.9 vs. 37.6 years; P = 0.06). The prevalence of undescended testis did not seem to be higher in familial than in sporadic testicular cancer in this study. However, a further segregation analysis of 978 Scandinavian patients with testicular tumours was suggestive of an autosomal recessive model of inheritance with an estimated gene frequency of 3.8 per cent and a lifetime penetrance for homozygotes of 43 per cent (65).

From an epidemiological study of 42 families with two or more testicular cancers from the UK, it was found that brothers of patients had an eight to ten-fold increase in risk and fathers of patients had a four-fold increase in risk, implying a recessive genetic model (66).

Approximately 5 per cent of the 500 patients with unilateral testicular germ cell cancer studied by Von der Masse had a screening-biopsy-confirmed contralateral testicular

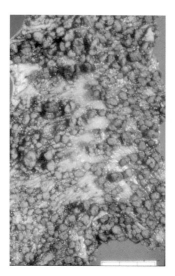

Fig. 9.2 Resection specimen from patient with FAP showing carpeting of the mucosa with polyps.

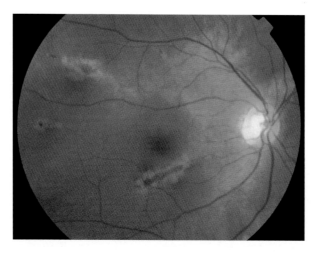

Fig. 9.4 Classic cigar-shaped congenital hypertrophy of the retinal pigment epithelium of FAP showing the surrounding pale halo.

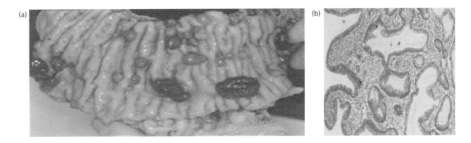

Fig. 9.5 (a) Colon with multiple juvenile polyps; (b) histology of a juvenile polyp.

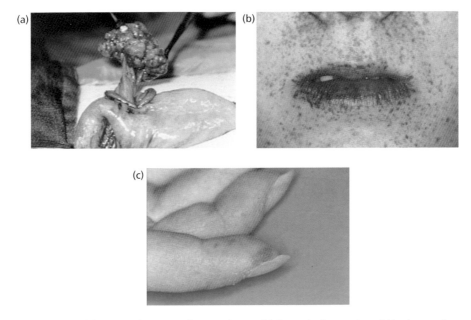

Fig. 9.7 Clinical features of Peutz–Jeghers syndrome: (a) Peutz–Jeghers polyp within the small bowel; (b) perioral mucocutaneous pigmentation; and (c) melanin deposition of the digits.

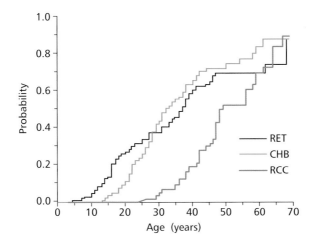

Fig. 13.1 Age-related risk of three major VHL complications (RET = retinal angioma; CHB = cerebellar haemangioblastoma, RCC = clear cell renal cell carcinoma). In most cases diagnosis was symptomatic, rather than presymptomatic. From Maher *et al.* 1990 (3).

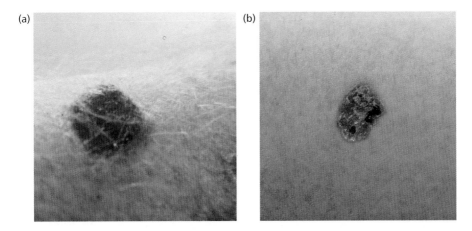

Fig. 15.1 (a) Pink/orange and raised basal cell naevus and (b) crusting and bleeding basal cell carcinoma in a patient with Gorlin syndrome.

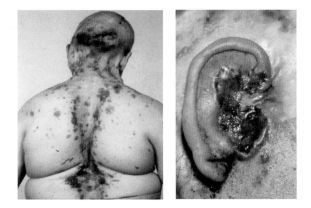

Fig. 15.6 Gorlin syndrome patient 25 years post craniospinal irradiation for medulloblastoma.

carcinoma *in situ,* with an estimated risk of progression to invasive cancer of 50 per cent by 5 years (67). The issue of routine biopsy of the contralateral testis in patients diagnosed with unilateral testicular germ cell tumour is controversial. This could be of value if there are signs suggesting atrophy of the contralateral testis.

Huddart *et al.* questioned whether the familial predisposition of testicular tumours extends to female germ cell tumours, as well as male germ cell tumours, as they identified three families with at least one case of ovarian germ cell tumour in each, suggesting this possibility (68). None of the families reported by Huddart *et al.* had any features suggesting Li–Fraumeni syndrome or any other familial cancer syndrome.

Management

Attempts should be made to identify any of the above risk factors for developing testicular cancer. Options for early detection of testicular cancer include regular physical examination and ultrasound of suspicious masses. Regular tumour marker measurements are not currently advisable in this setting.

Cryptorchidism is also associated with an increased risk for testicular cancer. Most data suggest that orchiopexy performed before puberty decreases the risk of developing a germ cell tumour in that testis. If the testis is inguinal, hormonally functioning and can be easily examined, then surveillance is advised. If the testis is difficult to examine adequately or is not amenable to surgery, then orchidectomy is advisable.

Bladder cancer

Excluding non-melanoma skin cancers, bladder cancer is the fifth most common cancer diagnosed in the UK, accounting for approximately 5 per cent of all cancers (1). The estimated lifetime risk of developing bladder cancer is 1 in 30 for men and 1 in 79 for women in the England and Wales (1). A number of risk factors have been identified (Box 11.8).

Evidence for inherited predisposition to bladder cancer and risk assessment

Kantor *et al.* found a higher relative risk for developing bladder cancer in individuals with a family history of bladder cancer in an analysis of more than 2000 bladder

---

Box 11.8 Risk factors for bladder cancer

- Cigarette smoking
- Occupational exposure to rubber and rubber products, dyes, cables and leather
- Drug exposure, e.g. cyclophosphamide, phenacetin
- Parasitic infection, e.g. *Schistosoma haematobium*

cancer cases and more than 5000 controls (69). In a recent familial bladder cancer study from the National Swedish Family Cancer Database (70), familial risk was found to be higher in daughters as compared to sons and sibling risk was higher as compared to offspring risk. Patient's age at onset modified familial risk and the highest familial risk of approximately seven-fold (95 per cent CI = 2.61–14.24) was observed in brothers of bladder cancer probands diagnosed before the age of 45 years.

The slow N-acetylation genotype (*NAT2*) has been demonstrated to be a susceptibility factor in occupational and smoking-related bladder cancer (71). Most bladder cancer patients without identified exposure to aryl amines also had a higher proportion of slow acetylators when compared to the non-malignant controls.

With the possible exception of hereditary retinoblastoma (72) and hereditary non-polyposis colon cancer (HNPCC), bladder cancer is not a component in hereditary cancer syndromes.

Management

It is important to look for occupational exposures in familial bladder cancer cases. Screening for at-risk individuals can be done by annual urine cytology, supplemented by cystoscopy if abnormal. Other methods of diagnosing bladder cancer such as detecting minichromosome maintenance 5 (Mcm5) proteins in urinary sediments look promising (73); however, these haven't reached the bedside at the time of writing.

Oesophageal cancer

Oesophageal cancer is the seventh most common cancer diagnosed in the UK and is predominantly a cancer of old age. The overall lifetime risk for developing oesophageal cancer is 1 in 75 for males and 1 in 95 for females. Once diagnosed, the survival is very poor (1). Oesophageal cancer has a very high incidence in the Caspian littoral parts of northern Iran, the southern republics of former Soviet Union and in the northern parts of China. A number of risk factors have been identified, some more important for adenocarcinoma (Box 11.9).

Evidence for inherited predisposition to oesophageal cancer and risk assessment

A survey of pedigrees of 225 patients affected by oesophageal cancer in Yangquan, Shanxi Province of northern China, suggested a mendelian autosomal recessive inheritance of a gene that influences susceptibility to oesophageal cancer (74). The maximum penetrance of oesophageal cancer among males with the disease genotype was 100 per cent, but among females it was 63.5 per cent. The mean age at onset for both men and

---

Box 11.9 **Risk factors for oesophageal cancer**

- Tobacco consumption
- Ethanol consumption
- Chronic gastro-oesophageal reflux disease/Barrett's oesophagus (adenocarcinoma)
- Obesity (adenocarcinoma)
- Weekly reflux symptoms
- Achalasia cardia
- History of head and neck cancer
- History of breast cancer treated with radiotherapy
- Low intake of fruits and vegetables
- Dietary deficiencies of β-carotene, vitamin E, selenium
- Dietary practices (hot beverages, fermented vegetables)
- Environmental carcinogens (asbestos, perchloroethylene, combustion products)

---

women was 62 years. The age-dependent penetrance for males with the disease genotype by the ages of 60 and 80 years was 41.6 per cent and 95.2 per cent respectively, whereas for females it was 26.4 per cent and 60.5 per cent respectively. Inclusion of environmental risk factors – such as cigarette smoking, pipe smoking, alcohol drinking, eating hot food and eating pickled vegetables – into the models did not provide significant improvement of the fit of the models to these data.

Oesophageal cancer within syndromes (hereditary and non-hereditary)

Tylosis

Palmoplantar keratoderma (PPK) is an autosomal dominantly inherited syndrome that has been classified into diffuse, punctate and focal forms according to the pattern of hyperkeratosis on the palms and soles (75). The diffuse type can be further sub-divided into epidermolytic PPK (EPPK) and non-epidermolytic PPK (NEPPK or tylosis) by the presence or absence of epidermolysis on histopathology, respectively. Whilst oesophageal malignancy has been reported in three kindreds with EPPK (76, 77), the most widely recognized association is with NEPPK – tylosis.

Ellis *et al.* (78) reviewed the largest of the Liverpool families of tylosis and oesophageal cancer. Tylosis had been diagnosed in 89 of 345 persons and 57 of the 89 were still alive. Of the 32 tylotic members of the family who had died, 21 succumbed to cancer of the oesophagus and 11 from other causes. In this family, tylosis had a late onset and was inherited as an autosomal dominant trait with complete penetrance by puberty, and involved other anatomic sites including oral leukoplakia and follicular changes. The epidermis, from biopsies of the skin of the soles, showed gross acanthosis, hyperkeratosis (without parakeratosis) and hypergranulosis, but there was no spongiosis and no evidence of intracellular oedema or lysis of any keratinocytes. It should be remembered that there are other forms of tylosis not associated with oesophageal carcinoma.

Other conditions

There is an approximately 10 per cent risk of developing oesophageal adenocarcinoma in patients with Barrett's oesophagus, a precancerous condition that features chronic gastro-oesophageal reflux disease. Risk factors for Barratt's oesophagus listed in Box 11.10 (79).

Plummer–Vinson/Paterson–Kelly syndrome is characterized by iron-deficiency anaemia, glossitis, kelosis, brittle fingernails, splenomegaly and oesophageal webs. Approximately 10 per cent of individuals with Plummer–Vinson/Paterson–Kelly syndrome develop hypopharyngeal or oesophageal squamous cell carcinomas.

Oesophageal cancer also features in dyskeratosis congenita, a condition in which there is cutaneous pigmentation, dystrophy of the nails, oral leukoplakia, lacrimal duct aplasia, testicular atrophy and anaemia, amongst others.

Oesophageal cancer has been seen in association with achalasia of the cardia (16–30 fold increased risk), prior aerodigestive tract malignancies, Human Papilloma Virus (HPV) infection (especially in high risk areas) and *H. pylori* gastritis (an inverse association).

Management

Wherever possible, risk factors and inherited clinical conditions predisposing to oesophageal cancer should be identified. Individuals at a higher risk for development

---

Box 11.10 Risk factors for Barratt's oesophagus (79)

- Caucasian
- Male
- >45 years
- Obesity
- Smoking
- Family history of gastric malignancy
- Exposure to drugs such as nitrates, benzodiazepines, anticholinergics, theophyllines
- Chronic (>10 years) gastro-oesophageal reflux disease (>3 × week)
- 8 cm of mucosa affected by Barrett's metaplasia and ulceration or stricture in the region of mucosa affected with Barrett's metaplasia without evidence of *H. pylori* infection

of oesophageal cancers can be best managed by offering periodic screening using upper gastrointestinal endoscopies supplemented by tissue diagnosis of suspicious lesions. Population screening programmes based on oesophageal cytology and confirmation by endoscopies have shown great promise in the high-risk areas of northern China.

Head and neck cancer

Head and neck cancer (excluding oesophageal and lung cancer) is the seventh most common cancer diagnosed in the UK. It is the sixth most common cancer in males in the UK(1). The risk factors are given in Box 11.11.

Evidence for genetic predisposition for head and neck cancer and risk assessment

A family history of squamous cell carcinoma of the head and neck (SCCHN) in first-degree relatives results in an increase in relative risk (between 3.0 and 4.0) of SCCHN (80, 81). This finding, along with evidence from epidemiological studies that patients with multiple primary tumours are more likely to have a family history of SCCHN, as compared to those with only a single primary tumour, suggests that genetic factors have a role in this disease (82).

Although the predominant cause of SCCHN is exposure to tobacco and alcohol, there is a clear disparity between the number of people who develop tumours and the total number exposed. Inherited differences in carcinogen metabolism and DNA repair due to genetic polymorphisms have been suggested as a possible cause for this variation in susceptibility.

Box 11.11 **Risk factors for head and neck cancer**

- Tobacco consumption
- Alcohol consumption
- Diet high in smoked foods
- Poor oral hygiene
- Chronic laryngitis and voice abuse (laryngeal cancers)
- Acid reflux disease
- Nutritional vitamin deficiencies (particularly vitamin A)
- Human papilloma virus and Epstein–Barr virus infection
- Exposure to wood dust, asbestos, nitrogen mustard
- Inherited cancer predisposing conditions/syndromes
- Family history of head and neck cancer in first-degree relatives/family history of relatives having multiple primary tumours

Table 11.3 Features of various inherited cancer syndromes in which head and neck cancer occurs

Syndrome	Inheritance	Component cancers	Clinical features
Familial adenomatous polyposis (FAP, Gardener syndrome)	AD	Colorectal cancer, periampullary carcinomas, hepatoblastoma, bile duct carcinoma, osteosarcoma, adrenal carcinoma, thyroid carcinoma, mandibular osteomas	Multiple colon polyps, multiple duodenal polyps, desmoids, epidermoid cysts, sebaceous cysts, congenital hypertrophy of retinal pigment epithelium, mesenteric fibromatosis
Bloom's syndrome	AR (predominantly seen in those with Jewish ancestry)	Leukaemia, lymphomas, gastrointestinal tumours, laryngeal and cervical cancers	Short thin stature, delicate features, long thin face, growth deficiency, telangiectasia, photosensitivity, medial deviation of fingers (clinodactyly), immune deficiency causing multiple infections, other skin abnormalities, e.g. acanthosis nigrans, icthyosis, hypertrichosis, café au lait spots
Muir–Torre (variant of HNPCC)	AD	Sebaceous skin tumours, colon cancer, small bowel cancer, stomach cancer, cancer of the endometrium, kidney, ovaries, bladder, breast, larynx	Basal cell carcinomas, keratoacanthomas, colonic diverticulas
Xeroderma pigmentosum	AR	Early-onset basal cell carcinomas, squamous cell skin cancers, especially lip cancers, malignant melanomas, keratoacanthomas, angiomas, sarcomas and adenocarcinomas	Photophobia and conjunctivitis in childhood, skin photosensitivity, skin erythema and blistering, progression to poikiloderma (atopic skin changes), actinic keratoses, early-onset skin neoplasm, ectropion, low IQ, mental deterioration, deafness, neurological abnormalities
Familial melanoma	AD	Malignant melanomas, pancreatic cancers, SCCHN	Malignant melanoma, dysplastic naevi
Hereditary breast/ovarian cancer syndrome (mainly in those with *BRCA2* mutations)	AD	Breast cancer, ovarian cancer, colon cancer, prostate cancer, laryngeal cancer, pharyngeal cancer and oral cavity cancer	Frequent bilateral disease, early age of onset
Li–Fraumeni syndrome	AD	Soft tissue sarcomas, breast cancers, brain tumours, osteosarcomas, leukaemia, adrenocortical carcinomas, laryngeal cancers	Early age of onset and multiple primary cancers

AD = autosomal dominant; AR = autosomal recessive; SCCHN = squamous cell carcinoma of the head and neck.

Polymorphisms in genes coding for carcinogen detoxifying enzymes

Extensive research has been done to study the association of polymorphisms in genes coding for carcinogen detoxifying enzymes, especially the glutathione S transferase (GST), cytochrome P 450 and N-acetyl transferase family of genes, and susceptibility to precancerous and cancerous lesions in the head and neck region. The hypothesis is that individuals with an inherited tendency to inadequately detoxify carcinogens in tobacco and alcohol may have increased risk of developing SCCHN.

A recent review of all the case–control studies to date on the GST family of genes has shown that, although the findings are inconsistent, most large studies have demonstrated an elevated risk of an upper aero-digestive tract cancer with null genotype for *GSTM1* or *GSTT1* (83). The inconsistent findings could be due to the differences in the frequency of null genotype in a particular ethnic group (84), the site of cancer (85), different carcinogen exposures, the GST (GSTT1, GSTM1 or GSTP1) being studied (86) or the sample size and the methodology used.

Current knowledge of the role of NAT and CYP 450 polymorphisms in head and neck cancer susceptibility is inconsistent and this reflects the polymorphism frequency differences within different ethnic groups and sites of cancer studied.

Head and neck cancer occurs as a part of various inherited cancer syndromes (Table 11.3).

Management

Wherever possible examination should be performed for the presence of an inherited cancer predisposing syndrome. At the moment, offering routine panendoscopy as a means of surveillance for high-risk cases is controversial in the context of its low yield. There should be a low threshold for ENT (ear nose and throat) assessment in high-risk cases that develop any of the following suspicious symptoms:

- mouth sore/ ulcer that fails to heal or that bleeds easily;
- persisting white (leucoplakia) or red (erythroplakia) patch in the mouth;
- a lump or thickening in the mouth, throat, tongue, neck;
- difficulty in chewing or swallowing food;
- new and persistent pain in the head and/or neck region.

Smoking and alcohol consumption should be discouraged while counselling high-risk individuals.

Brain tumours

Gliomas are central nervous system neoplasms derived from glial cells and comprise astrocytomas, glioblastoma multiforme, oligodendrogliomas and ependymomas. The

Table 11.4 Brain tumours within inherited cancer syndromes

Cancer syndrome	Mode of inheritance	Locus	Brain tumour
Neurofibromatosis 1 (NF1)	AD	17q11.2 (*NF1*)	Gliomas, sarcomas
Neurofibromatosis 2 (NF2)	AD	22q12.2 (*NF2*)	Schwannomas (acoustic neuromas), meningiomas and gliomas
Von Hippel–Lindau (VHL)	AD	3p25–p26 (*VHL*)	Haemangioblastomas
FAP	AD	*APC*	Glioblastomas, medulloblastomas
HNPCC	AD	PMs2, *MIH1*	Glioblastomas, medulloblastomas
Turcot syndrome	AR	unknown	Astrocytoma
Tuberous sclerosis type I and II	AD	9q32–34 (*TSC1*) 16p13.3 (*TSC2*)	Subependymal giant cell, astrocytomas
Li–Fraumeni syndrome	AD	17p13.1 (*Tp53*)	Gliomas, PNETs
Basal nevus (Gorlin's)	AD	9q31 (*PTCH*)	Medulloblastomas
Melanoma–astrocytoma syndrome	AD	*P16*	Gliomas

AD = autosomal dominant; AR = autosomal recessive; PNET = primitive neuroectodermal tumours.

estimated lifetime risk for developing tumours in the brain and the central nervous system (CNS) is 1 in 147 for males and 1 in 207 for females (1).

Brain tumours within cancer syndromes and risk assessment

Brain tumours and the cancer syndromes within which they are known to occur are shown in Table 11.4. Of these, Turcot syndrome must be considered when there is a family history of polyposis, although there is controversy over this description. Brain tumours have been described with both *APC* and mismatch repair gene mutations. There may, however, be a recessive form of polyposis associated with brain tumours. Familial clustering of gliomas, however, often occurs in the absence of these tumour syndromes. On the basis of segregation analyses in families with multiple glioma patients, autosomal recessive and multifactorial mendelian models have been suggested (87–89). First-degree relatives of patients who were diagnosed with primary brain tumours between 1958 and 1997 from the Swedish Cancer Registry were found to have a two to three-fold higher risk of developing a primary brain tumour of the same histopathology as that of the patient (89).

Management

Wherever suspected, clinical examination and relevant tests should be performed to see if any clinical features suggestive of a relevant cancer syndrome are present. The typical features of the various syndromes are listed in Table 11.5.

Table 11.5 Clinical features of various cancer syndromes predisposing to brain tumours

Cancer syndrome	Clinical features
Neurofibromatosis 1	Neurofibromatosis, café au lait spots (6 spots each more than 1.5 cm in diameter), axillary freckling, Lisch nodules, macrocephaly, kyphoscoliosis, pseudoarthosis, renal artery stenosis
Neurofibromatosis 2	NF2 plaques (i.e. raised pigmented skin lesions with excess hair), café au lait spots as lesser feature, subcutaneous tumours on peripheral nerves, papillary skin neurofibroma, posterior subcapsular or nuclear cataract, macular hamartoma, hearing loss, tinnitus
Von Hippel–Lindau	Headaches, vomiting and neurological symptoms due to cerebellar lesions, retinal neurological symptoms due to spinal haemangioblastomas, visual disturbances due to angiomas, haematuria due to renal cell carcinomas, hypertension due to phaeochromocytoma, testicular mass due to epididymal cystadenoma
Turcot syndrome	Colon polyps, café au lait spots, hepatic nodular hyperplasia
Tuberous sclerosis type I and II	Mental retardation, seizures, brain and retinal hamartomas, adenoma sebaceum (facial angiofibroma), shagreen patch, ungal fibromas, white (hypopigmented) skin macules (ash-leaf shaped evident only under Wood's light), multiple enamel pits, bilateral renal angiomyolipoma, subependymal glial nodule/ tubers (on CT or MRI scan)
Li–Fraumeni syndrome	Families with multiple cases of sarcomas and other cancers, notably breast cancer, early age of onset of component tumours and multiple primaries within individuals
Gorlin syndrome (basal nevus)	Pits on the palms and soles, odontogenic keratocysts of the jaw, hypertelorism, lamellar calcification of the falx cerebri, bridging of the sella tursica, abnormal cervical vertebrae, rib anomalies, epidermal cysts of the skin
Melanoma–astrocytoma syndrome	Astrocytomas and other CNS tumours

References

1 Cancer Research UK. *CancerStats*. 2002.

2 **Lichtenstein P, Holm NV, Verkasalo PK, Iliadou A, Kaprio J, Koskenvuo M, *et al.*** Environmental and heritable factors in the causation of cancer – analyses of cohorts of twins from Sweden, Denmark, and Finland [see comments]. *N Engl J Med* 2000; **343**:78–85.

3 **Whittemore AS, Wu AH, Kolonel LN, John EM, Gallagher RP, Howe GR, *et al.*** Family history and prostate cancer risk in black, white, and Asian men in the United States and Canada. *Am J Epidemiol* 1995; **141**:732–740.

4 **Narod SA, Dupont A, Cusan L, Diamond P, Gomez JL, Suburu R, *et al.*** The impact of family history on early detection of prostate cancer. *Nat Med* 1995; **1**:99–101.

5 **Steinberg GD, Carter BS, Beaty TH, Childs B, Walsh PC.** Family history and the risk of prostate cancer. *Prostate* 1990; **17**:337–347.

6 **Carter BS, Beaty TH, Steinberg GD, Childs B, Walsh PC.** Mendelian inheritance of familial prostate cancer. *Proc Natl Acad Sci USA* 1992; **89**:3367–3371.

7 **Edwards SM, Kete-Javai Z, Meitz J, Hamoudi R, Hope Q, Osin P, *et al.*** Two percent of men with early-onset prostate cancer harbor germline mutations in the BRCA2 gene. *Am J Hum Genet* 2003; **72**:1–12.

8 Makinen T, Tammela TL, Stenman UH, Maattanen L, Rannikko S, Aro J, *et al.* Family history and prostate cancer screening with prostate-specific antigen. *J Clin Oncol* 2002; **20**:2658–2663.

9 Nieder AM, Taneja SS, Zeegers MP, Ostrer H. Genetic counseling for prostate cancer risk. *Clin Genet* 2003; **63**:169–176.

10 Bratt O, Damber JE, Emanuelsson M, Gronberg H. Hereditary prostate cancer: clinical characteristics and survival. *J Urol* 2002; **167**:2423–2426.

11 McWhorter WP, Hernandez AD, Meikle AW, Terreros DA, Smith JA Jr, Skolnick MH, *et al.* A screening study of prostate cancer in high risk families. *J Urol* 1992; **148**:826–828.

12 Thompson IM, Goodman PJ, Tangen CM, Lucia MS, Miller GJ, Ford LG, *et al.* The influence of finasteride on the development of prostate cancer. *N Engl J Med* 2003; **349**:215–224.

13 Giovannucci E, Rimm EB, Colditz GA, Stampfer MJ, Ascherio A, Chute CC, *et al.* A prospective study of dietary fat and risk of prostate cancer. *J Natl Cancer Inst* 1993; **85**:1571–1579.

14 Fradet Y, Meyer F, Bairati I, Shadmani R, Moore L. Dietary fat and prostate cancer progression and survival. *Eur Urol* 1999; **35**:388–391.

15 Lauren P. The two histological main types of gastric carcinoma: diffuse and so-called intestinal-type carcinoma. An attempt at histo-clinical classification. *Acta Path Microbiol Scand* 1965; **64**:31–49.

16 Karpeh MS, Kelsen DP, Tepper JE. Cancer of the stomach. In: DeVita VT Jr, Hellman S, Rosenberg SA, eds. *Cancer: principles and practice of oncology*, 2001, pp.1092–1126. Philadelphia, USA: Lippincott Williams and Wilkins.

17 Maimon SN, Zinninger MM. Familial gastric cancer. *Gastroenterology* 1953; **25**:139–152.

18 Woolf CM, Isaacson EA. An analysis of 5 "stomach cancer families" in the state of Utah. *Cancer* 1961; **14**:1005–1016.

19 Triantafillidis JK, Kosmidis P, Kottardis S. Genetic studies of gastric cancer in humans: An appraisal. *Cancer* 1958; **11**:957.

20 Kakiuchi H, Itoh F, Kusano M, Adachi Y, Mita H, Mihara M, *et al.* Familial gastric cancer in the Japanese population is frequently located at the cardiac region. *Tumour Biol* 1999; **20**:235–241.

21 La Vecchia C, Negri E, Franceschi S, Gentile A. Family history and the risk of stomach and colorectal cancer. *Cancer* 1992; **70**:50–55.

22 Zanghieri G, Di Gregorio C, Sacchetti C, Fante R, Sassatelli R, Cannizzo G, *et al.* Familial occurrence of gastric cancer in the 2-year experience of a population-based registry. *Cancer* 1990; **66**:2047–2051.

23 Goldgar DE, Easton DF, Cannon-Albright LA, Skolnick MH. Systematic population-based assessment of cancer risk in first-degree relatives of cancer probands. *J Natl Cancer Inst* 1994; **86**:1600–1608.

24 Hemminki K, Li X. Familial risk of cancer by site and histopathology. *Int J Cancer* 2003; **103**:105–109.

25 Lee WJ, Hong RL, Lai IR, Chen CN, Lee PH, Huang MT. Clinicopathologic characteristics and prognoses of gastric cancer in patients with a positive familial history of cancer. *J Clin Gastroenterol* 2003; **36**:30–33.

26 Yatsuya H, Toyoshima H, Mizoue T, Kondo T, Tamakoshi K, Hori Y, *et al.* Family history and the risk of stomach cancer death in Japan: differences by age and gender. *Int J Cancer* 2002; **97**:688–694.

27 Hemminki K, Jiang Y. Familial and second gastric carcinomas: a nationwide epidemiologic study from Sweden. *Cancer* 2002; **94**:1157–1165.

28 Caldas C, Carneiro F, Lynch HT, Yokota J, Wiesner GL, Powell SM, *et al.* Familial gastric cancer: overview and guidelines for management. *J Med Genet* 1999; **36**:873–880.

29 Lynch HT, Smyrk TC, Watson P, Lanspa SJ, Lynch JF, Lynch PM, *et al.* Genetics, natural history, tumor spectrum, and pathology of hereditary nonpolyposis colorectal cancer: an updated review. *Gastroenterology* 1993; **104**:1535–1549.

30 Warthin AS. Heredity with reference to carcinoma. *Arch Intern Med* 1913; **12**:546–555.

31 Lynch HT, Smyrk T. Hereditary nonpolyposis colorectal cancer (Lynch syndrome). An updated review. *Cancer* 1996; **78**:1149–1167.

32 Watson P, Lynch HT. Extracolonic cancer in hereditary nonpolyposis colorectal cancer. *Cancer* 1993; **71**:677–685.

33 Ottini L, Palli D, Falchetti M, D'Amico C, Amorosi A, Saieva C, *et al.* Microsatellite instability in gastric cancer is associated with tumor location and family history in a high-risk population from Tuscany. *Cancer Res* 1997; **57**:4523–4529.

34 Hsieh LL, Huang YC. Loss of heterozygosity of APC/MCC gene in differentiated and undifferentiated gastric carcinomas in Taiwan. *Cancer Lett* 1995; **96**:169–174.

35 The Breast Cancer Linkage Consortium. Cancer risks in BRCA2 mutation carriers. *J Natl Cancer Inst* 1999; **91**:1310–1316.

36 Ford D, Easton DF, Bishop DT, Narod SA, Goldgar DE. Risks of cancer in BRCA1-mutation carriers. Breast Cancer Linkage Consortium. *Lancet* 1994; **343**:692–695.

37 Guilford P, Hopkins J, Harraway J, McLeod M, McLeod N, Harawira P, *et al.* E-cadherin germline mutations in familial gastric cancer. *Nature* 1998; **392**:402–405.

38 Gayther SA, Gorringe KL, Ramus SJ, Huntsman D, Roviello F, Grehan N, *et al.* Identification of germ-line E-cadherin mutations in gastric cancer families of European origin. *Cancer Res* 1998; **58**:4086–4089.

39 Richards FM, McKee SA, Rajpar MH, Cole TR, Evans DG, Jankowski JA, *et al.* Germline E-cadherin gene (CDH1) mutations predispose to familial gastric cancer and colorectal cancer. *Hum Mol Genet* 1999; **8**:607–610.

40 Bevan S, Houlston RS. Genetic predisposition to gastric cancer. *Q J Med* 1999; **92**:5–10.

41 Caldas C, Carneiro F, Lynch HT, Yokota J, Wiesner GL, Powell SM, *et al.* Familial gastric cancer: overview and guidelines for management. *J Med Genet* 1999; **36**:873–880.

42 Zwick A, Munir M, Ryan CK, Gian J, Burt RW, Leppert M, *et al.* Gastric adenocarcinoma and dysplasia in fundic gland polyps of a patient with attenuated adenomatous polyposis coli. *Gastroenterology* 1997; **113**:659–663.

43 Foulkes WD, Lanke E, Jefferies S, Chappuis PO. Genetic susceptibility to carcinoma of the head and neck, stomach and pancreas. In: Eeles RA, Easton DF, Ponder BAJ, Eng C, eds. *Genetic predisposition to cancer*, 2004. UK: Arnold.

44 Hruban RH, Petersen GM, Ha PK, Kern SE. Genetics of pancreatic cancer. From genes to families. *Surg Oncol Clin N Am* 1998; **7**:1–23.

45 Banke MG, Mulvihill JJ, Aston CE. Inheritance of pancreatic cancer in pancreatic cancer-prone families. *Med Clin North Am* 2000; **84**:677–690, x–xi.

46 Brentnall TA, Bronner MP, Byrd DR, Haggitt RC, Kimmey MB. Early diagnosis and treatment of pancreatic dysplasia in patients with a family history of pancreatic cancer. *Ann Intern Med* 1999; **131**:247–255.

47 Meckler KA, Brentnall TA, Haggitt RC, Crispin D, Byrd DR, Kimmey MB, *et al.* Familial fibrocystic pancreatic atrophy with endocrine cell hyperplasia and pancreatic carcinoma. *Am J Surg Pathol* 2001; **25**:1047–1053.

48 Wideroff L, Gridley G, Mellemkjaer L, Chow WH, Linet M, Keehn S, *et al.* Cancer incidence in a population-based cohort of patients hospitalized with diabetes mellitus in Denmark. *J Natl Cancer Inst* 1997; **89**:1360–1365.

49 Everhart J, Wright D. Diabetes mellitus as a risk factor for pancreatic cancer. A meta-analysis. *JAMA* 1995; **273**:1605–1609.

50 Lowenfels AB, Maisonneuve P, DiMagno EP, Elitsur Y, Gates LK Jr, Perrault J, *et al.* Hereditary pancreatitis and the risk of pancreatic cancer. International Hereditary Pancreatitis Study Group. *J Natl Cancer Inst* 1997; **89**:442–446.

51 Whelan AJ, Bartsch D, Goodfellow PJ. Brief report: a familial syndrome of pancreatic cancer and melanoma with a mutation in the CDKN2 tumor-suppressor gene. *N Engl J Med* 1995; **333**:975–977.

52 Klein AP, Beaty TH, Bailey-Wilson JE, Brune KA, Hruban RH, Petersen GM. Evidence for a major gene influencing risk of pancreatic cancer. *Genet Epidemiol* 2002; **23**:133–149.

53 Murphy KM, Brune KA, Griffin C, Sollenberger JE, Petersen GM, Bansal R, *et al.* Evaluation of candidate genes MAP2K4, MADH4, ACVR1B, and BRCA2 in familial pancreatic cancer: deleterious BRCA2 mutations in 17%. *Cancer Res* 2002; **62**:3789–3793.

54 Hahn SA, Greenhalf B, Ellis I, Sina-Frey M, Rieder H, Korte B, *et al.* BRCA2 germline mutations in familial pancreatic carcinoma. *J Natl Cancer Inst* 2003; **95**:214–221.

55 Wu AH, Fontham ET, Reynolds P, Greenberg RS, Buffler P, Liff J, *et al.* Family history of cancer and risk of lung cancer among lifetime nonsmoking women in the United States. *Am J Epidemiol* 1996; **143**:535–542.

56 Brownson RC, Alavanja MC, Caporaso N, Berger E, Chang JC. Family history of cancer and risk of lung cancer in lifetime non-smokers and long-term ex-smokers. *Int J Epidemiol* 1997; **26**:256–263.

57 Hwang SJ, Cheng LS, Lozano G, Amos CI, Gu X, Strong LC. Lung cancer risk in germline p53 mutation carriers: association between an inherited cancer predisposition, cigarette smoking, and cancer risk. *Hum Genet* 2003; **113**:238–243.

58 Paz-Elizur T, Krupsky M, Blumenstein S, Elinger D, Schechtman E, Livneh Z. DNA repair activity for oxidative damage and risk of lung cancer. *J Natl Cancer Inst* 2003; **95**:1312–1319.

59 Lee JS, Lippman SM, Benner SE, Lee JJ, Ro JY, Lukeman JM, *et al.* Randomized placebo-controlled trial of isotretinoin in chemoprevention of bronchial squamous metaplasia. *J Clin Oncol* 1994; **12**:937–945.

60 The Alpha-Tocopherol, Beta Carotene Cancer Prevention Study Group. The effect of vitamin E and beta carotene on the incidence of lung cancer and other cancers in male smokers. *N Engl J Med* 1994; **330**:1029–1035.

61 Pastorino U, Bellomi M, Landoni C, De Fiori E, Arnaldi P, Picchio M, *et al.* Early lung-cancer detection with spiral CT and positron emission tomography in heavy smokers: 2-year results. *Lancet* 2003; **362**:593–597.

62 Cancer Research UK. *Lung cancer and smoking UK*, 2001; **27**.

63 Raghavan D, Jelihovsky T, Fox RM. Father–son testicular malignancy. Does genetic anticipation occur? *Cancer* 1980; **45**:1005–1009.

64 Heimdal K, Olsson H, Tretli S, Flodgren P, Borresen AL, Fossa SD. Risk of cancer in relatives of testicular cancer patients. *Br J Cancer* 1996; **73**:970–973.

65 Heimdal K, Olsson H, Tretli S, Fossa SD, Borresen AL, Bishop DT. A segregation analysis of testicular cancer based on Norwegian and Swedish families. *Br J Cancer* 1997; **75**:1084–1087.

66 Forman D, Oliver RT, Brett AR, Marsh SG, Moses JH, Bodmer JG, *et al.* Familial testicular cancer: a report of the UK family register, estimation of risk and an HLA class 1 sib-pair analysis. *Br J Cancer* 1992; **65**:255–262.

67 von der Maase H, Rorth M, Walbom-Jorgensen S, Sorensen BL, Christophersen IS, Hald T, *et al.* Carcinoma in situ of contralateral testis in patients with testicular germ cell cancer: study of 27 cases in 500 patients. *Br Med J* (Clin Res Ed) 1986; **293**:1398–1401.

68 Huddart RA, Thompson C, Houlston R, Huddart RA, Nicholls EJ, Horwich A. Familial predisposition to both male and female germ cell tumours? *J Med Genet* 1996; **33**:86.

69 Kantor AF, Hartge P, Hoover RN, Fraumeni JF Jr. Familial and environmental interactions in bladder cancer risk. *Int J Cancer* 1985; **35**:703–706.

70 Plna K, Hemminki K. Familial bladder cancer in the National Swedish Family Cancer Database. *J Urol* 2001; **166**:2129–2133.

71 Risch A, Wallace DM, Bathers S, Sim E. Slow N-acetylation genotype is a susceptibility factor in occupational and smoking related bladder cancer. *Hum Mol Genet* 1995; **4**:231–236.

72 Sanders BM, Jay M, Draper GJ, Roberts EM. Non-ocular cancer in relatives of retinoblastoma patients. *Br J Cancer* 1989; **60**:358–365.

73 Stoeber K, Swinn R, Prevost AT, Clive-Lowe P, Halsall I, Dilworth SM, *et al.* Diagnosis of genito-urinary tract cancer by detection of minichromosome maintenance 5 protein in urine sediments. *J Natl Cancer Inst* 2002; **94**:1071–1079.

74 Zhang W, Bailey-Wilson JE, Li W, Wang X, Zhang C, Mao X, *et al.* Segregation analysis of esophageal cancer in a moderately high-incidence area of northern China. *Am J Hum Genet* 2000; **67**:110–119.

75 Lucker GP, van de Kerkhof PC, Steijlen PM. The hereditary palmoplantar keratoses: an updated review and classification. *Br J Dermatol* 1994; **131**:1–14.

76 Clarke CA, McConnelL RB. Six cases of carcinoma of the oesophagus occurring in one family. *Br Med J* 1954; **4897**:1137–1138.

77 Howel-Evans W, McConnell RB, Clarke CA, Sheppard PM. Carcinoma of the oesophagus with keratosis palmaris et plantaris (tylosis): a study of two families. *Q J Med* 1958; **27**:413–429.

78 Ellis A, Field JK, Field EA, Friedmann PS, Fryer A, Howard P, *et al.* Tylosis associated with carcinoma of the oesophagus and oral leukoplakia in a large Liverpool family–a review of six generations. *Eur J Cancer B Oral Oncol* 1994; **30B**:102–112.

79 Jankowski JA, Harrison RF, Perry I, Balkwill F, Tselepis C. Barrett's metaplasia. *Lancet* 2000; **356**:2079–2085.

80 Copper MP, Jovanovic A, Nauta JJ, Braakhuis BJ, de Vries N, van dW, I, *et al.* Role of genetic factors in the aetiology of squamous cell carcinoma of the head and neck. *Arch Otolaryngol Head Neck Surg* 1995; **121**:157–160.

81 Foulkes WD, Brunet JS, Kowalski LP, Narod SA, Franco EL. Family history of cancer is a risk factor for squamous cell carcinoma of the head and neck in Brazil: a case-control study. *Int J Cancer* 1995; **63**:769–773.

82 Foulkes WD, Brunet JS, Sieh W, Black MJ, Shenouda G, Narod SA. Familial risks of squamous cell carcinoma of the head and neck: retrospective case-control study. *BMJ* 1996; **313**:716–721.

83 Geisler SA, Olshan AF. GSTM1, GSTT1, and the risk of squamous cell carcinoma of the head and neck: a mini-HuGE review. *Am J Epidemiol* 2001; **154**:95–105.

84 Nair UJ, Nair J, Mathew B, Bartsch H. Glutathione S-transferase M1 and T1 null genotypes as risk factors for oral leukoplakia in ethnic Indian betel quid/tobacco chewers. *Carcinogenesis* 1999; **20**:743–748.

85 Kihara M, Kihara M, Kubota A, Furukawa M, Kimura H. GSTM1 gene polymorphism as a possible marker for susceptibility to head and neck cancers among Japanese smokers. *Cancer Lett* 1997; **112**:257–262.

86 Jourenkova-Mironova N, Voho A, Bouchardy C, Wikman H, Dayer P, Benhamou S, *et al.* Glutathione S-transferase GSTM3 and GSTP1 genotypes and larynx cancer risk. *Cancer Epidemiol Biomarkers Prev* 1999; **8**:185–188.

87 de Andrade M, Barnholtz JS, Amos CI, Adatto P, Spencer C, Bondy ML. Segregation analysis of cancer in families of glioma patients. *Genet Epidemiol* 2001; **20**:258–270.

88 Malmer B, Iselius L, Holmberg E, Collins A, Henriksson R, Gronberg H. Genetic epidemiology of glioma. *Br J Cancer* 2001; **84**:429–434.

89 Malmer B, Henriksson R, Gronberg H. Familial brain tumours-genetics or environment? A nationwide cohort study of cancer risk in spouses and first-degree relatives of brain tumour patients. *Int J Cancer* 2003; **106**:260–263.

Part 3

Inherited cancer syndromes

Chapter 12

The neurofibromatoses

J. M. Friedman

Background

Three clinically and genetically distinct diseases are classified as neurofibromatoses: neurofibromatosis 1 (NF1), neurofibromatosis 2 (NF2) and schwannomatosis. The inclusion of these three conditions in a single group reflects the fact that they share certain clinical features, but it is important to distinguish each disease from the others because their natural history, complications and management differ. One form of neurofibromatosis does *not* evolve into one of the other forms during the course of the disease.

Neurofibromatosis 1

Introduction

NF1, which is also known as von Recklinghausen's disease or peripheral neurofibromatosis, is by far the most common form of neurofibromatosis. The disorder was first described in detail by von Recklinghausen in 1882 (1), and elegant clinical monographs on NF1 were written by Crowe, Schull and Neel in 1956 (2) and by Riccardi and Eichner in 1986 (3).

NF1 is characterized by multiple café au lait spots, axillary and inguinal freckling, multiple cutaneous neurofibromas and iris Lisch nodules. Learning disabilities are frequent. Less common, but potentially more serious, manifestations include plexiform neurofibromas, optic and other central nervous system gliomas, malignant peripheral nerve sheath tumours, vasculopathy and dystrophic osseous lesions of the spine, long bones (especially tibia) or sphenoid wing. The median age at death among NF1 patients is about 15 years earlier than expected in the general population, and about one-third of people with NF1 die before 45 years of age. Vasculopathy, malignant peripheral nerve sheath tumours and central nervous system tumours appear to be the most frequent causes of premature death in people with NF1.

NF1 is an autosomal dominant disease with virtually complete penetrance by adulthood. About half of all cases result from new mutations. Diagnosis of the disease, which is based on characteristic clinical findings, is sometimes difficult or impossible in small children because clinical features accumulate with age. Pathogenic mutations of the *NF1* gene can be demonstrated by molecular testing in about 95 per cent of NF1 patients, but such testing is usually not necessary for diagnosis. Prenatal diagnosis is often possible but is of limited prognostic value.

Prevalence

Estimates of the prevalence of NF1 range from 1/962 to 1/7800, with most clustering around 1/3000 (4). Reported population-based studies have identified people with NF1 in a variety of different ways, and this, along with the variable expressivity, age dependence of many features and increased mortality associated with NF1, probably accounts for the variability in prevalence estimates. There does not appear to be any difference in prevalence by gender. NF1 occurs in all ethnic groups that have been studied adequately, but it is not certain whether the prevalence varies among these groups.

The mutation rate at the *NF1* locus has been estimated to be 1/7800 to 1/23 000 gametes (4). This is one of the highest locus-specific mutation rates known in humans. Sporadic or founder cases may represent mosaicism for an NF1 mutation.

Diagnosis

The clinical diagnostic criteria for NF1, developed by an NIH Consensus Conference in 1987 (5) (Box 12.1), are both highly specific and highly sensitive in adults with NF1 (6). The sensitivity of the NIH criteria is much lower in very young children. Almost all children who have inherited NF1 from an affected parent can be identified within the first year of life because the diagnosis requires just one feature in addition to a positive family history. In contrast, only about half of patients with sporadic NF1 meet the

---

Box 12.1   NIH diagnostic criteria for NF1 (6, 11)

NF1 is diagnosed in an individual who has two or more of the following features:

- Six or more café au lait macules over 5 mm in greatest diameter in prepubertal individuals and over 15 mm in greatest diameter in postpubertal individuals
- Two or more neurofibromas of any type or one plexiform neurofibroma
- Freckling in the axillary or inguinal regions
- Optic glioma
- Two or more Lisch nodules (iris hamartomas)
- A distinctive osseous lesion such as sphenoid dysplasia or thinning of the long bone cortex with or without pseudoarthrosis
- A first-degree relative (parent, sib or child) with NF1 as defined by the above criteria.

NIH diagnostic criteria by 1 year of age (7). Almost all NF1 patients can be diagnosed clinically by 8 years of age (7–10).

A brief checklist of features frequently seen in NF1 is shown in Table 12.1 in the format used by the National Neurofibromatosis Foundation (NNFF) International Database (11). Multiple café au lait spots develop in infancy in more than 95 per cent of NF1 patients (7), and there are few other conditions that produce such spots in large numbers (see differential diagnosis, below). Both parents of young children with multiple café au lait spots but no other features of NF1 should be examined carefully for signs of NF1. If one parent is affected, NF1 can be diagnosed in the child. If neither parent is affected, and the child does not have features of another condition associated with multiple café au lait spots, the child should be strongly suspected of having NF1 and followed clinically in the same way as a child with a definite diagnosis. A definite diagnosis of NF1 can be made in most of these children by 4 years of age using the NIH diagnostic criteria (7).

A Noonan syndrome phenotype with ocular hypertelorism, down-slanting palpebral fissures, low-set ears and webbed neck occurs in some NF1 patients. The NF1– Noonan syndrome has a variety of causes, including the segregation of two different, relatively common, autosomal dominant traits in some families and segregation as a variant of NF1 in others (12).

Segmental NF1 is diagnosed in patients who have typical features that are restricted to one part of the body and whose parents are both unaffected (13). Segmental NF1 represents mosaicism for a somatic *NF1* mutation, at least in some instances (14), although most patients who have been reported with mosaicism for an *NF1* mutation have mild generalized neurofibromatosis (13).

Molecular genetic testing

Isolating the gene

The *NF1* locus was identified in 1990 (15–17), after it had been localized generally by linkage (18) and precisely by two unique chromosomal translocations that disrupted the locus (19, 20). *NF1* is a large gene, spanning some 350 kilobases of genomic DNA on chromosome 17q11.2 (21). The transcript is ubiquitously expressed. The gene contains 60 exons and exhibits a complex pattern of alternative splicing (22). Neurofibromin, the protein product of the *NF1* gene, acts as a negative regulator of the ras oncogene and probably has other functions as well (21). Neurofibromin functions as a tumour suppressor – "second hit" somatic *NF1* mutations have been demonstrated in a variety of benign and malignant tumours from NF1 patients (23).

Clinical testing

A pathogenic mutation of the *NF1* locus can be identified in >95 per cent of NF1 patients by a multistep mutation detection protocol that is available for clinical use (24). This protocol involves an optimized protein truncation test followed by sequencing of

Table 12.1 Features to look for in diagnosing NF1 – this form, from the NNFF International Database (12), lists the most common characteristic features of the disease

Feature	Observation							
Height/length	_ _ . _ _ cm							
Head circumference	_ _ . _ cm							
Number of café au lait spots (>5 mm before puberty; >15 mm after puberty)	None	1	2	3	4	5	6 or more	
Intertriginous freckling	Absent		Present					
Subcutaneous neurofibromas	None	1	2	3–9	10–50	>50		
Cutaneous neurofibromas	None	1	2	3–9	10–50	>50		
Plexiform neurofibroma –location (circle as many as apply)	None	Orbit	Face	Head/neck	Trunk	Dorsal trunk	Ventral arm	Leg
Paraspinal neurofibromas	Absent by scan	Absent clinically	Present by scan	Unknown				
Xanthogranulomas	Absent	Present						
Lisch nodules	Absent	Present on slit lamp exam	Possible	Unknown				
Proptosis	Absent	Unilateral	Bilateral					
Optic glioma	Absent by scan	Absent clinically						
	Present asymptomatic	Present symptomatic						
Seizures – type	None	Febrile only	Hypsarrhythmia					
	Generalized	Partial	Multiple types					
	Present – type unknown	Other						
Hydrocephalus	Absent clinically	Absent by scan						
	Aqueductal stenosis	Other non-communicating						
	Communicating	Present, type unknown						

Intellectual development	Normal	Mildly delayed	Significant delay
Learning problems	None		Specific learning problems
Hypertension	Absent	Present	Blood pressure: _/_
Congenital heart defect	Absent clinically		Absent by special testing
	Aortic stenosis	ASD	PDA
	Pulmonary stenosis	Tetralogy of Fallot	VSD
	Other type of CHD		Multiple types of CHD
	Possible CHD		
Vasculopathy	Absent clinically		Renal artery stenosis
	Arterial stenosis (non-renal)		Moya-moya
	Other		
Age puberty began	<10 years	10–15 years	>15 years
Dysmorphic features	No	Yes	Possible
Congenitally bowed tibia or pseudoarthrosis	Absent clinically	Absent radiographically	Present
Dysplastic vertebrae	Absent clinically	Absent radiographically	Present
Scoliosis	Absent clinically	Absent radiographically	Present
Dysplastic sphenoid wing	Absent clinically / Present bilateral	Absent radiographically / Present unilateral	
Neoplasm – type (circle as many as apply)	None	Glioma (non-optic)	Leukaemia
	Malignant peripheral nerve sheath tumour		Other sarcoma
	Carcinoma	Phaeochromocytoma	
	Malignancy, other type		Malignancy present, type unknown

CHD = congenital heart defect; VSD = ventricular septal defect; PDA = patent ductus arteriosus; ASD = atrial septal defect.

genomic DNA and cDNA if a truncated peptide is found. Fluorescent *in situ* hybridization (FISH) analysis for whole gene deletions, direct sequencing of the entire cDNA, long-range reverse transcriptase polymerase chain reaction (RT-PCR), Southern blot analysis and cytogenetic analysis are performed sequentially if a mutation is not found by the protein truncation test.

Molecular genetic testing is not used routinely for diagnosis of NF1 but may be indicated in certain unusual circumstances, for example, when a young child has an optic glioma or moya-moya that would be managed differently if NF1 were present. Molecular testing is also indicted when an adult has NF1 and wishes to have prenatal diagnosis in a subsequent pregnancy. Identification of a pathogenic mutation in the affected parent permits prenatal diagnosis to be performed on a foetal sample obtained by chorionic villous sampling or amniocentesis (25, 26). When prenatal diagnosis is being considered, it is important to complete molecular testing before the pregnancy is initiated because it sometimes takes several months to identify a pathogenic mutation, and occasionally (<5 per cent of cases), an *NF1* mutation cannot be identified despite exhaustive molecular analysis. In practice, few at-risk families choose to have prenatal diagnosis for NF1 because the test can only identify the presence or absence of the *NF1* mutation that is segregating in the family; the severity of disease manifestations usually cannot be determined prenatally.

Linkage
Prenatal diagnosis can also be performed by linkage in informative families (26–28).

Clinical progression
Many NF1 patients develop only cutaneous manifestations and Lisch nodules, but the frequency of more serious complications increases with age. Various manifestations of NF1 have different characteristic times of appearance (7, 10, 29). Tibial or sphenoid wing dysplasia may be apparent at birth. Café au lait spots are usually noticed early in infancy and may increase in number during the first few years of life. Axillary, inguinal and other skin fold freckling is usually not seen in infants but becomes apparent in early childhood. Diffuse plexiform neurofibromas of the face and neck rarely appear after 1 year of age, and diffuse plexiform neurofibromas of other parts of the body develop before adolescence. In contrast, deep nodular plexiform neurofibromas are rarely seen in early childhood and usually remain asymptomatic even in adults. Optic gliomas develop in the first few years of life, and the rapidly-progressive dysplastic form of scoliosis almost always develops between 6 and 10 years of age. Malignant peripheral nerve sheath tumours usually occur in adolescents and young adults.

Discrete cutaneous neurofibromas are not seen in infancy and are infrequent before puberty (29). The total number of cutaneous neurofibromas in adults with NF1 varies from a few to hundreds or thousands. Cutaneous neurofibromas continue to appear and to grow in size throughout life, although the rate may vary greatly from year to year.

Plexiform neurofibromas may be nodular or diffuse and superficial or deep. They may affect virtually any organ in the body (30, 31). Superficial nodular tumours below the skin are called subcutaneous neurofibromas. Like deep nodular plexiform neurofibromas, subcutaneous neurofibromas may appear discrete or extend along the course of a nerve, sometimes spanning the entire length of a limb. About 40 per cent of asymptomatic adults with NF1 have deep nodular plexiform neurofibromas on imaging studies (32, 33). Diffuse plexiform neurofibromas, which are thought to be congenital, may be superficial and confined to the skin, or they may invade adjacent tissues. It is often impossible to determine whether a diffuse neurofibroma that appears small on the surface of the body is superficial or extends into underlying tissues without an MRI of the affected area (30). Some congenital diffuse plexiform neurofibromas are very extensive, causing compression, distortion or hypertrophy of adjacent soft tissues and bone.

Cardiovascular disease is an important but often overlooked feature of NF1 (34). Vasculopathy of the renal arteries can cause hypertension, especially in children and young adults with NF1 (35). NF1 vasculopathy involving arteries of the heart or brain can have serious or even fatal consequences (34). Congenital heart defects are seen occasionally in people with NF1, and valvular pulmonary stenosis, in particular, appears to be unusually frequent (36).

Malignant peripheral nerve sheath tumours are the most common malignant neoplasms associated with NF1, occurring in about 10 per cent of patients (37, 38). The median age at diagnosis is 26 years, and 5-year survival after diagnosis is only 21 per cent (37). About 15 per cent of children with NF1 develop optic pathway gliomas (39). Other central nervous system gliomas may be seen in children with NF1 but are much less frequent; such non-optic gliomas may also develop later in life (40, 41). A variety of other neoplasms, including juvenile chronic myelogenous leukaemia and myelodysplastic syndromes, are infrequent among NF1 patients, although more common than in the general population (41, 42).

Patients with NF1 are usually somewhat shorter and have somewhat larger heads than unaffected people of the same age and gender (43). Pubertal development is usually normal but may be delayed or precocious (44). NF1 patients who have gliomas involving the optic chiasm are at particular risk for developing precocious puberty.

Although most pregnancies in women with NF1 are normal, serious complications can occur (45). Many women with NF1 experience a rapid increase in the number and size of their neurofibromas during pregnancy.

Most people with NF1 have normal intelligence, but about half have a learning disorder of one kind or another (46, 47). Attention deficit disorders are also more frequent than expected in children with NF1 (48).

Patients with NF1 appear to die about 15 years earlier than expected, on average (38, 49). Premature death is usually associated with vasculopathy, malignant peripheral nerve sheath tumour or brain tumour.

Management

Box 12.2 provides recommendations for an initial workup of individuals suspected of having NF1. A much more extensive routine evaluation is advocated by some authorities (50).

Recommendations for routine follow-up of NF1 patients are given in Box 12.3. Similar recommendations have been made for the initial evaluation and subsequent health supervision of patients with NF1 by others (6, 51, 52).

The value of performing routine head MRI scanning in patients with NF1 at the time of diagnosis is controversial (53–55). The clinical significance of the hyperintense lesions that can be visualized on T2-weighted MRI in many children with NF1 is uncertain. These so-called "unidentified bright objects" (UBOs) are usually not seen on T1-weighted MRI or on CT scan and show no evidence of a mass effect. Some studies suggest that the presence, number, volume or location of UBOs correlates with

---

Box 12.2   Recommended initial evaluation for individuals suspected of having NF1

- Personal medical history with particular attention to features of NF1
- Family history with particular attention to features of NF1
- Physical examination with particular attention to the skin, skeleton and neurological systems
- Ophthalmologic evaluation including slit lamp examination of the irides
- Developmental assessment in children
- Other studies only as indicated on the basis of clinically apparent signs or symptoms.

Box 12.3   Recommended routine follow-up of individuals with NF1

- Annual physical examination by a physician who is familiar with the patient and with the disease
- Annual ophthalmological examination in childhood, less frequent periodic examination in adults
- Regular developmental assessment by screening questionnaire (in childhood)
- Regular blood pressure monitoring
- Other studies as indicated on the basis of clinically apparent signs or symptoms.

learning disabilities in children with NF1, but the findings have not been consistent among investigations (47, 56).

Discrete cutaneous neurofibromas that are disfiguring or in inconvenient locations can be removed surgically. This is an important aspect of treatment because disfigurement caused by NF1 is the most distressing manifestation for many patients (57). Plexiform neurofibromas can cause disfigurement, compromise function or lead to the development of malignant peripheral nerve sheath tumours (58). Small superficial plexiform tumours can often be removed without difficulty, but surgical treatment of extensive plexiform neurofibromas is usually unsatisfactory because of their intimate involvement with nerves, their frequent infiltration of adjacent structures and their tendency to grow back at the site of removal (58). Clinical trials of medical treatments are being undertaken (59). Current information on the status of these trials is available over the Internet at http://www.ctf.org/clinical_trials/.

Patients with NF1 who have disease involving the eye, central or peripheral nervous system, spine or long bones should be referred to an appropriate specialist for treatment. Optic pathway gliomas in children with NF1 usually exhibit a completely benign course that contrasts with that seen in patients who do not have NF1 (39). A benign course is also typical of most other central nervous system gliomas that develop in children with NF1, although a more aggressive course is sometimes seen in adults (40, 41). Treatment of dystrophic scoliosis and tibial dysplasia in NF1 patients is difficult and often unsatisfactory (60, 61).

Differential diagnosis

A rare recessive genocopy of NF1 has been reported in several consanguineous families in which a child with clinical features of NF1 and early-onset cancer was found to be homozygous for a mutation in one of the genes involved in DNA mismatch repair (62, 63). The parents of each of these children did not have NF1 but did have a family history of hereditary non-polyposis colon cancer, as expected. The *NF1* locus appears to be a target for somatic mutation in individuals with constitutional deficiency of mismatch repair (64, 65).

More than 100 conditions have been described that include at least one of the clinical features seen in NF1. Most of these disorders are easily distinguished from NF1 by different associated manifestations. Some conditions that are most often confused with NF1 are listed in Box 12.4.

Neurofibromatosis 2

Introduction

Neurofibromatosis 2 (NF2), which is also called bilateral acoustic neurofibromatosis or central neurofibromatosis, is misnamed. This reflects its confusion with NF1 before the two conditions were distinguished clinically (66, 67) and by genetic linkage

---

Box 12.4   Conditions that are most often confused with NF1

◆ NF2 (bilateral vestibular schwannomas, other tumours of the central nervous system and cranial and spinal nerves)

◆ familial multiple café au lait spots (an autosomal dominant trait without other features of NF1)

◆ LEOPARD syndrome (multiple lentigines, ocular hypertelorism, deafness, congenital heart disease)

◆ Bannayan–Riley–Ruvalcaba syndrome (multiple lipomas and haemangiomas, macrocephaly, spotted pigmentation of the glans penis)

◆ piebaldism (white forelock and areas of cutaneous depigmentation; small hyperpigmented areas resembling café au lait spots may be seen in association with areas of hypopigmentation)

◆ juvenile hyaline fibromatosis (multiple subcutaneous tumours, gingival fibromatosis)

◆ congenital generalized fibromatosis (multiple tumours of the skin, subcutaneous tissues, skeletal muscle, bones and viscera)

◆ multiple lipomatosis (multiple cutaneous lipomas)

◆ proteus syndrome (regional overgrowth, hyperpigmentation, multiple lipomas)

---

studies (68, 69). NF2 predisposes to the development of multiple, benign peripheral nerve sheath tumours, but these are schwannomas in the overwhelming majority of instances; neurofibromas are an infrequent feature of NF2.

NF2 was first described by Wishart in 1822 (70), some 60 years before von Recklinghausen's classic description of NF1. The conflation of NF1 and NF2 is largely attributable to an influential monograph by Harvey Cushing (71). The inheritance of NF2 as an autosomal dominant trait was recognized early (72, 73) and, although the features are variable, concordance of age at onset and severity is often seen among affected members of a family (74, 75). Penetrance is nearly (but not quite) complete. About half of cases are inherited and half are sporadic, apparently representing new mutations. Among the latter, at least 20 per cent are mosaic for a somatic mutation (76, 77).

Most people with NF2 develop schwannomas of the vestibular branch of both eight cranial nerves. Schwannomas of other cranial nerves or spinal nerves are frequent (75, 78). Meningiomas are also common, and ependymomas or astrocytomas may occur. Affected patients may have many benign tumours, but malignancy is quite infrequent. Mononeuropathy is sometimes seen in affected children, and polyneuropathy may occur in adults. Most affected individuals have associated ocular abnormalities, of which juvenile cataracts are the most common. Retinal hamartomas and optic nerve meningiomas may also compromise vision. Patients with severe disease present in childhood and often die in their 20s or 30s. More mildly affected individuals usually have later onset and may have a normal or nearly normal life expectancy.

Prevalence

The prevalence of NF2 cases diagnosed by the 1987 NIH criteria (5) was about 1/210 000 in a population-based study from the United Kingdom (79). The prevalence of asymptomatic cases (i.e. heterozygous carriers of an *NF2* mutation who have not yet been diagnosed with the disease) and symptomatic cases combined was estimated to be about 1/120 000, and the incidence at birth of individuals who carry an *NF2* mutation was estimated to be 1/33 000 to 1/41 000 in this population. These figures may all be too low because the 1987 NIH criteria do not identify all patients who carry constitutional mutations of the *NF2* gene (80). The incidence of constitutional *NF2* mutations at birth was estimated to be about 1/87 000 in a Finnish population-based study (81) that required histological confirmation for diagnosis but employed the NNFF diagnostic criteria, which are somewhat more sensitive (80).

Diagnosis

NF2 is a clinical diagnosis. The presence of bilateral schwannomas of the eight cranial nerve is considered to be pathognomonic for NF2. However, the observation of individuals who develop bilateral vestibular schwannomas over 60 or even 70 years of age (80) and the relative frequency of unilateral vestibular schwannomas among people who are this old raise the possibility that bilateral eight cranial nerve tumours may be coincidental, rather than a manifestation of NF2 in rare instances. Most adults with NF2 present with hearing loss, tinnitus and/or balance dysfunction, that is, with symptoms of a vestibular schwannoma. Younger patients often present with symptoms of another tumour and may not develop bilateral vestibular schwannomas until later in the course of their disease (78, 82).

Four different sets of diagnostic criteria have been proposed for NF2, but the 1987 and 1991 NIH criteria are considered to be obsolete (see http://consensus.nih.gov/cons/064/064_statement.htm and http://consensus.nih.gov/cons/087/087_statement.htm). Both the NNFF (6) and Manchester (83) diagnostic criteria are widely used clinically. Neither set is highly sensitive in isolated children or adolescents with NF2 (80), although most affected individuals can be diagnosed in adulthood as bilateral vestibular schwannomas usually can be demonstrated on a high-quality MRI examination by 30 years of age. The Manchester criteria appear to be most sensitive early in the course of the disease (80).

NNFF criteria (6)

- Individuals with the following clinical features have confirmed (definite) NF2:
  - bilateral vestibular schwannomas (VS)

or

- family history of NF2 (first-degree family relative)

plus

- unilateral VS <30 years *or*
- lesions of any two of the following types: meningioma, glioma, other schwannoma, juvenile posterior subcapsular lenticular opacities/ juvenile cortical cataract.

◆ Individuals with the following clinical features should be evaluated for NF2 (presumptive or probable NF2):

- unilateral VS <30 years *plus* at least one of the following: meningioma, glioma, other schwannoma, juvenile posterior subcapsular lenticular opacities/juvenile cortical cataract

or

- multiple meningiomas (two or more) *plus* unilateral VS <30 years *or* one of the following: glioma, other schwannoma, and juvenile posterior subcapsular lenticular opacities/juvenile cortical cataract.

Manchester criteria (83)

◆ The diagnosis of NF2 can be made in a subject who presents in any one of the following ways:

- bilateral vestibular schwannomas (VS) *or* a family history of NF2 *plus* unilateral VS

or

- lesions of any two of the following types: meningioma, glioma, neurofibroma, other schwannoma, and posterior subcapsular lenticular opacities

or

- multiple meningiomas (>1) *plus* unilateral VS *or* at least two lesions of any of the following kinds: glioma, posterior subcapsular lenticular opacity, neurofibroma, other schwannoma

or

- unilateral VS *plus* at least two lesions of any of the following kinds: meningioma, glioma, posterior subcapsular lenticular opacity, neurofibroma, other schwannoma.

Table 12.2 provides a brief check-list of features that should be assessed in patients in whom a diagnosis of NF2 is being considered. Evaluation of both parents for clinical, ophthalmological and MRI signs of NF2 or molecular diagnostic testing may be useful in establishing a diagnosis in young people with some typical features who do not meet the standard diagnostic criteria. Molecular genetic testing is usually unnecessary for diagnostic purposes in other circumstances.

Table 12.2 Features to look for in patients suspected of having NF2

History/examination	Features
Medical History	
Neurological symptoms	Previous cranial nerve or peripheral nerve tumour
	Previous brain tumour
	Previous spinal tumour
	Previous mononeuropathy (usually involving facial nerve)
	Previous polyneuropathy
	Hearing loss – bilateral or unilateral (e.g. difficulty hearing on the telephone with one ear)
	Tinnitus
	Balance dysfunction
	Headache
	Seizures
	Weakness (localized or generalized)
	Muscle wasting (localized or generalized)
	Pain (usually not debilitating)
	Focal sensory loss
Ocular lesions	Previous cataract
	Visual loss (unilateral or bilateral)
	Amblyopia
Skin lesions	Skin tumours
Family history	Parent or sib diagnosed with NF2
	Parent or sib with deafness, central nervous system or peripheral nerve tumours
	Other family history suggestive of NF2
General physical examination	
	Subcutaneous peripheral nerve tumours
	No skeletal features of NF1
Neurological examination	Hearing loss – bilateral or unilateral
	Balance dysfunction
	Weakness (localized or generalized)
	Muscle wasting (localized or generalized)
	Focal sensory loss
	Areflexia
	Subcutaneous tumour
Examination of skin	Cutaneous schwannoma (intracutaneous, slightly raised, hyperpigmented plaque lesion, often with excess hair) – usually few in number
	Discrete nodular firm, often tender cutaneous tumour (usually schwannomas rather than neurofibromas) – usually few in number
	Café au lait spots *not* unusually numerous; no intertrigenous freckling
Ophthalmology examination (including slit lamp exam)	Cataract (usually juvenile posterior subcapsular or cortical wedge opacities of lens)
	Retinal hamartoma
	Juvenile amblyopia
	Strabismus
	Abnormality of extraocular movement

Table 12.2 (Continued)

History/examination	Features
MRI scans	
Head with and without gandolinium enhancement, including internal auditory canal protocol (*3 mm slice thickness on both axial and coronal views through internal auditory canals*)	Tumour of 8th cranial nerve (usually bilateral) Tumour of other cranial nerves Meningioma (may be multiple) Brain tumour (usually ependymomas or astrocytomas, may be multiple)
Complete spine with and without gandolinium enhancement	Spinal nerve root tumour (usually multiple) Meningioma (may be multiple) Intramedullary tumour (usually ependymomas or astrocytomas, may be multiple)
Other	
	Audiogram – hearing loss Brain stem auditory evoked response – prolonged latencies CT head scan (if indicated clinically) – may show erosion of bone or intracranial calcification) Review of previous pathology of previous cranial and peripheral nerve tumours (to distinguish schwannomas and neurofibromas, which may be confused)

Molecular genetic testing

Isolating the gene

The *NF2* gene was identified by positional cloning after its location was inferred by linkage and by cytogenetic and loss of heterozygosity studies in NF2-related tumours (84, 85). The *NF2* locus was identified by two different groups, one of whom named the protein product "merlin" and the other of whom called it "schwannomin". The gene, which is located on chromosome 22q12.2, spans 110 kb and encodes 17 alternatively-spliced exons (86). Merlin is widely expressed in many cell types but is most abundant in neurons and glia. Merlin is a member of the protein 4.1 cytoskeleton-associated family that appears to act as a tumour suppressor by inhibiting cellular proliferation, although the precise mechanisms involved are uncertain (87, 88).

Clinical testing

Molecular genetic testing has a limited role in initial diagnosis of NF2, but such testing is useful in the presymptomatic children of an affected parent. Distinguishing children who have and have not inherited the *NF2* mutation from an affected parent permits the avoidance of unnecessary screening for tumours and ocular abnormalities in half of the children and encourages compliance with such screening in the other half. Prenatal diagnosis of NF2 by molecular genetic methods is possible but rarely requested.

Clinical testing of the *NF2* gene usually involves exon scanning by a standard method such as single strand conformational polymorphism analysis or denaturing gel electrophoresis. Confirmation of a specific mutation is usually done by direct sequencing of the involved segment of the gene. Such testing detects a pathogenic mutation in the blood of one-half to two-thirds of NF2 patients (78, 89). Some patients have mutations that result from large deletions or chromosomal rearrangements that are not detected by exon screening methods (90). In addition, at least 20 per cent of patients with sporadic NF2 have somatic mosaicism for an *NF2* mutation (76, 77, 91). In such cases, the pathogenic mutation can often be identified within tumour tissue, and the finding of an identical *NF2* mutation in two different NF2-associated tumours in a person with sporadic disease and no detectable mutation in the blood can be used to establish the presence of mosaic NF2. There is no evidence for locus heterogeneity in NF2.

Linkage

Presymptomatic diagnosis of NF2 can also be done in the children of an affected parent by linkage. Use of linkage generally requires testing of the affected parent and another affected relative to determine the allele that carries the *NF2* mutation in a family. Linkage may provide misleading results if attempted on the child of the first affected family member because of the frequency of somatic mutations in NF2 (91).

Clinical progression

NF2 is a progressive condition, but the course is variable. Although onset of symptoms is usually in the late teens or early 20s, some patients become symptomatic before 10 years of age and others remain asymptomatic until age 40 or later (75, 78, 82). Patients with sporadic disease that is unusually mild are often mosaic for an *NF2* mutation.

Symptoms present at the time of diagnosis are usually related to vestibular schwannomas – unilateral or bilateral hearing loss, tinnitus or balance disturbance – but other features of the disease that occurred earlier in life may not have been recognized as manifestations of NF2, especially in sporadic cases. Ocular signs and symptoms (posterior subcapsular or cortical wedge cataracts, retinal hamartomas, epiretinal membranes, amblyopia or strabismus) often are noted in early childhood, and cutaneous schwannomas frequently develop before adulthood (82, 92). Mononeuropathy with weakness, most often involving the facial nerve but sometimes involving another cranial or spinal nerve, may be seen (78). In children born to a parent who is known to have NF2, presymptomatic MRI screening frequently reveals the presence of vestibular schwannomas, spinal tumours, or other tumours characteristic of NF2 many years before they become symptomatic (78).

Once a patient with NF2 becomes symptomatic, the course is typically one of progressive loss of hearing and other neurological functions as the tumour burden increases with age (75, 78). In many patients, multiple surgical procedures produce complications that may further contribute to neurological disability. Chronic pain may occur but usually is less of a problem than progressive neurological deterioration. There may be generalized muscle weakness and wasting in the late stages of the disease. Earlier suggestions that NF2 is more severe in women than in men appear not to be true (75, 78).

Disease severity is variable but tends to be similar in affected members of an individual family (75, 79, 82). This intrafamilial concordance is partly a result of an allele–phenotype correlation – NF2 patients with nonsense or frame-shift mutations tend to have severe disease, and those with missense mutations, small in-frame deletions or large deletions tend to have mild disease (82). Patients with somatic mosaicism for an *NF2* mutation and those with mutations that are not found on routine molecular genetic screening of the blood (most of whom probably have mosaicism) tend to have mild disease (77). Although the risk of NF2 in the child of an individual with *NF2* mosaicism is much less than the 50 per cent expected for a constitutional autosomal dominant mutation, affected children of a mosaic founder are often more severely affected than their parents (78).

In the population-based United Kingdom study, the mean age at death of people with NF2 was 62 years (83). The average survival after diagnosis was about 15 years but varied greatly from person to person. Early age at onset is strongly associated poorer survival (82, 93). Development of malignant tumours is very uncommon in patients with NF2 but has been reported, especially in areas of the body that were previously treated by radiotherapy (94).

Management

Affected individuals

Patients who have been diagnosed with NF2 should be managed in a specialty centre that has multidisciplinary expertise in the treatment of this condition (95–97). Evaluation and management, which should be tailored to the severity and manifestations of the disease in each patient, should generally include annual clinical assessment with neurological and ophthalmological examination, annual MRI of the head with internal auditory canal protocol and annual audiological evaluation (unless hearing has been lost completely) (6, 75, 78, 96). MRI of the full spine every 2 to 3 years is usually sufficient in patients who are known to have spinal tumours, which usually grow slowly and may remain asymptomatic for many years. NF2 patients should be warned against swimming alone because of the possibility of becoming disoriented underwater, and genetic counselling should be offered to the family of every person who has been diagnosed with NF2.

Vestibular schwannoma growth rates are highly variable in people with NF2, even within a single individual at different times in his or her life (98, 99). Patients with small vestibular schwannomas that are stable in size may benefit from watchful waiting rather than treatment (96). Microsurgery is the preferred method of treatment in most NF2 patients but is more successful if done before the tumour reaches 1.5 to 2.0 cm in diameter (6, 96). Surgical treatment of larger vestibular schwannomas may be limited to debulking because complete removal is not possible.

Stereotactic radiotherapy is also an option for treatment of vestibular schwannomas but poses a risk of inducing malignancy in patients with NF2 (100). Stereotactic radiotherapy is the treatment of choice for palliation in some NF2 patients who have life-threatening tumours and are too ill to tolerate surgery (96). The use of sterotactic radiotherapy in NF2 patients in other circumstances is controversial.

Amplification often is useful for NF2 patients whose hearing is compromised but not completely lost. Brain stem implants may benefit some NF2 patients who have become deaf. Less frequently, cochlear implants can be used. It is usually easier for NF2 patients to learn sign language and lip reading before their hearing is completely lost.

Most other intracranial and spinal tumours in NF2 patients are slow growing and do not require surgical treatment. However, these tumours must be monitored clinically and by periodic MRI examination because some do grow and become symptomatic.

Preservation of vision in NF2 patients is especially important because of the likelihood that hearing will be lost during the course of the disease. Regular ophthalmological evaluation is essential, and cataracts and other lesions should be treated as necessary.

Asymptomatic at-risk individuals

Each child of a person with non-mosaic NF2 has a 50 per cent chance of developing NF2 as well, and early detection of vestibular schwannomas and ocular manifestations in these individuals can improve clinical management (6, 78). Molecular genetic testing of at-risk individuals by linkage or *NF2* mutation detection enables children who have inherited an *NF2* mutation to be distinguished from those who have not. Clinical screening is *not* necessary in children who do not inherit the *NF2* mutation from their affected parent.

Clinical screening should begin in childhood in at-risk individuals who have been found to have inherited an *NF2* mutation from their affected parent or who have not yet undergone genetic testing (6, 78). Ocular manifestations of NF2 are usually apparent in childhood, and spinal, vestibular or facial nerve tumours may become symptomatic before puberty. Therefore, annual ophthalmological and neurological examination and audiological evaluation are indicated. MRI screening for vestibular schwannomas should generally begin about age 12, although it is reasonable to start imaging studies earlier in families with early onset and to defer initiation of such studies until later in families with late onset. If tumours are not found, repeating the MRI scan in 2 to 3 years seems reasonable. If tumours are found, the screening protocol outlined for affected individuals should be followed.

Differential diagnosis

The presence of bilateral vestibular schwannomas in association with schwannomas of other nerves and central nervous system tumours is highly characteristic of NF2, but diagnostic uncertainty may exist in patients who present prior to development of bilateral vestibular schwannomas.

Young patients with NF1 may also have multiple spinal nerve root tumours but can usually be distinguished by the presence of other cutaneous and ocular manifestations of NF1. Pathologically, the spinal nerve root tumours in NF1 are neurofibromas rather than the schwannomas that are typically found in NF2.

Schwannomatosis, which is discussed below, may also be confused with NF2. By definition, the presence of tumours of the eighth cranial nerves precludes the diagnosis of schwannomatosis in a patient with multiple schwannomas elsewhere. Patients with NF2 tend to present earlier than those with schwannomatosis, to have symptoms related to neurological dysfunction rather than pain and to have characteristic ocular findings. Meningiomas are infrequent in patients with schwannomatosis, and other central nervous system tumours are not a feature of that disease.

A condition has been described that is characterized by the occurrence of multiple meningiomas without schwannomas or the other kinds of tumours associated with NF2 (101). Multiple meningiomas may be transmitted as an autosomal dominant trait but are usually sporadic.

Schwannomatosis

Introduction

The existence of schwannomatosis as a distinct entity was first suggested 20 years ago (102, 103), but it was not until molecular genetic studies in a series of familial cases demonstrated a pattern of changes incompatible with NF2 (104) that schwannomatosis was generally accepted as a distinct disease. Its clinical spectrum, natural history and genetic basis are still incompletely understood.

Schwannomatosis is defined clinically as the occurrence of multiple schwannomas in an individual who does not have the bilateral vestibular tumours characteristic of NF2. People with schwannomatosis typically have pain, which may be severe and incapacitating, rather than neurological dysfunction, as occurs in NF2. Most cases of schwannomatosis are sporadic, although the condition is transmitted as a variable autosomal dominant trait in some families. The genetic basis of schwannomatosis has not yet been identified, but the disease does not result from an inherited mutation of the *NF2* locus. Many cases of sporadic schwannomatosis may result from somatic mosaicism.

Prevalence

No population-based estimate of the prevalence of schwannomatosis has been reported, but the annual incidence of newly-identified cases was estimated to be about 1/1 700 000 in a Finnish population-based study (81). This study also included an estimate of the annual incidence of newly-identified NF2 cases, which was similar in magnitude (1/2 000 000) but less than half that observed in a study done in the United Kingdom (79). The Finnish study required histological confirmation for diagnosis of schwannomatosis but included both definite and presumptive cases defined by the Jacoby criteria (105).

Diagnosis

Schwannomatosis is a clinical diagnosis. The disease is diagnosed when multiple spinal, peripheral nerve and/or cranial nerve schwannomas are identified in a patient who does not have bilateral schwannomas of the eighth cranial nerve. Schwannomatosis was originally described as a disease characterized by multiple cutaneous schwannomas (also called neurilemmomas) and distinguished from NF1, in which the cutaneous nerve sheath tumours are neurofibromas (103). However, most patients with multiple cutaneous schwannomas have NF2, and cutaneous schwannomas do not appear to be a frequent feature of schwannomatosis (106).

The diagnostic criteria proposed by Jacoby and associates in 1997 (105) were developed for research purposes and probably exclude some cases of schwannomatosis in which histological evidence is lacking. On the other hand, the presumptive category includes some cases that have a constitutional or mosaic *NF1* or *NF2* mutation (92, 105, 107–109) and others that may be somatic mosaics for the putative schwannomatosis mutation.

Diagnostic criteria for schwannomatosis

◆ Definite schwannomatosis:
- two or more pathologically proven schwannomas

plus
- lack of radiographic evidence of vestibular nerve tumour at age >18 years.

◆ Presumptive or probable schwannomatosis:
- two or more pathologically proven schwannomas without symptoms of eighth-nerve dysfunction at age >30 years

or
- two or more pathologically proven schwannomas in an anatomically limited distribution (single limb or segment of the spine) without symptoms of eighth-nerve dysfunction at any age.

Molecular genetic testing

Isolating the gene

A mutation that causes schwannomatosis has not yet been identified, although the condition is transmitted in some families as an autosomal trait with incomplete penetrance and variable expressivity (104, 105). Molecular genetic studies of the *NF2* locus in tumours and blood from schwannomatosis patients clearly demonstrate that the disease is not caused by constitutional *NF2* mutations (104, 105, 110, 111). It is possible that schwannomatosis results from a structural alteration of chromosome 22 that predisposes to genomic instability in the *NF2* region (104, 105). If this is true, a discrete *SCH* locus might not exist.

Clinical testing

Molecular genetic testing of the *NF2* locus in white blood cells can sometimes be used to establish a diagnosis of NF2 (and rule out schwannomatosis) in a young patient with multiple schwannomas and a negative family history who has not yet developed bilateral vestibular schwannomas. However, molecular testing is often unnecessary in this circumstance because the diagnosis of NF2 can made on the basis of typical ophthalmological, MRI or cutaneous features.

Molecular genetic testing of the *NF2* locus in tumour tissue can exclude the diagnosis of NF2 in a person with multiple schwannomas, but such studies are generally limited to research laboratories. The finding of no *NF2* mutation in non-tumour tissue and *NF2* loss of heterozygosity with *different NF2* mutations of the retained allele in two or more tumours is incompatible with a diagnosis of NF2 and characteristic of schwannomatosis (104, 105, 110, 111).

Linkage

Linkage studies in rare schwannomatosis families suggest that the putative locus for schwannomatosis (*SCH*) lies centromeric to the *NF2* locus on chromosome 22 (104).

Clinical progression

Schwannomatosis is infrequently seen in children and usually presents in the third or fourth decade of life (81, 106). The predominant symptom is pain, although neurological dysfunction may also occur from spinal cord compression or as a result of surgical treatment of a painful tumour. The disease is progressive over the course of many years, and the pain may become disabling. In contrast to NF2, schwannomatosis is rarely, if ever, a fatal disease.

The spectrum of clinical features associated with schwannomatosis has not been fully delineated (105, 106). Schwannomas usually involve peripheral nerves, spinal nerves or both. Cutaneous schwannomas may occur (112) but appear to be infrequent (106). Cranial nerves may be involved, but the presence of bilateral vestibular schwannomas excludes the diagnosis. It would be surprising if the vestibular nerves were never involved, especially in elderly patients, but the marked predilection for development of schwannomas of the eighth cranial nerve that characterizes NF2 is clearly *not* a feature of schwannomatosis. Even in affected family members who are identified through another affected relative and ought not reflect a bias in ascertainment, vestibular schwannomas have not been reported (109). Multiple meningiomas may occur in schwannomatosis but are much less common than in NF2 (81, 104). Epidymomas and gliomas have not been reported in schwannomatosis patients. Ocular abnormalities do not appear to be a feature of the disease.

Multiple schwannomas are limited to one anatomic region or limb in about one-third of patients with schwannomatosis (106). These cases may represent somatic mosaicism for a *SCH* mutation.

Management

A general approach to management of patients with schwannomatosis has not been established, but it seems likely that referral to a specialty centre that has multidisciplinary expertise in the treatment of patients with peripheral and cranial nerve tumours would be beneficial, as it is in NF2.

Initial assessment requires MRI examination of the head with internal auditory canal protocol to exclude a diagnosis of NF2. MRI examination of the full spine is also necessary because of the frequency of spinal involvement, and MRI of other regions known or suspected to harbour tumours is probably useful. Ophthalmological examination with slit lamp exam and auditory screening are probably useful initially to exclude NF1 and NF2. Careful physical examination with particular attention to the skin is required for the same reason, and complete neurological examination is essential.

Periodic follow-up is necessary because the disease is progressive, although the optimal frequency of clinical and MRI re-evaluation has not been determined.

Surgical removal of schwannomas is often effective in reducing pain, but the tumours may grow back (106). Surgical treatment may also be indicated for spinal tumours that are producing neurological dysfunction as a result of compression. However, surgical treatment, especially if repeated in one particular area, may lead to permanent neurological damage.

Pain is often the most debilitating symptom in patients with schwannomatosis, and referral to a pain specialist is often indicated. The best approach to managing pain associated with schwannomatosis has not been determined.

Differential diagnosis

NF1 can present with multiple spinal, cranial and peripheral nerve tumours but can almost always be distinguished from schwannomatosis by the presence of characteristic cutaneous and ocular features in NF1. Pathological examination of an excised or biopsied tumour by a neuropathologist should permit differentiation of the neurofibromas that occur in NF1 from the schwannomas that occur in schwannomatosis.

Patients with NF2 may have multiple spinal and cranial nerve tumours that are histologically indistinguishable from those that occur in schwannomatosis. However, adults with NF2 usually have bilateral vestibular schwannomas that can be demonstrated on MRI examination. By definition, the presence of such tumours excludes the diagnosis of schwannomatosis.

NF2 often presents with neurological dysfunction in children and adolescents, and schwannomatosis infrequently does, but the differential diagnosis in these younger patients can be difficult. If there is an older affected relative, the diagnosis can usually be established unequivocally. Most younger patients with NF2 have ocular manifestations that are very useful distinguishing features. The presence of cutaneous schwannomas or meningiomas would make NF2 more likely but probably would not exclude a diagnosis of schwannomatosis. *NF2* mutation testing may be useful in confirming a diagnosis of NF2 in some equivocal, sporadic cases in young people.

References

1 Von Recklinghausen F. *Über die multiplen Fibrome der Haut und ihre Beziehungen zu multiplen Neuromen*, 1882. Berlin: August Hirschwald.

2 Crowe F, Schull W, Neel J. *A clinical, pathological, and genetic study of multiple neurofibromatosis*, 1956. Springfield, Illinois: Charles C. Thomas.

3 Riccardi V, Eichner J. *Neurofibromatosis: Phenotype, natural history, and pathogenesis*, 1986. Baltimore: Johns Hopkins University Press.

4 Rasmussen SA, Friedman JM. NF1 gene and neurofibromatosis 1. *Am J Epidemiol* 2000; **151**:33–40.

5 Neurofibromatosis: Conference statement. National Institutes of Health Consensus Development Conference. *Arch Neurol* 1988; **45**:575–578.

6 Gutmann D, Aylsworth A, Carey J, Korf B, Marks J, Pyeritz R, *et al*. The diagnostic evaluation and multidisciplinary management of neurofibromatosis 1 and neurofibromatosis 2. *JAMA* 1997; **278**:51–57.

7 DeBella K, Szudek J, Friedman JM. Use of the National Institutes of Health criteria for diagnosis of neurofibromatosis 1 in children. *Pediatrics* 2000; **105**:608–614.

8 Friedman J, Birch P. Type 1 neurofibromatosis: A descriptive analysis of the disorder in 1,728 patients. *Am J Med Genet* 1997; **70**:138–143.

9 Wolkenstein P, Freche B, Zeller J, Revuz J. Usefulness of screening investigations in neurofibromatosis type 1. A study of 152 patients [see comments]. *Arch Dermatol* 1996; **132**:1333–1336.

10 Huson S. Neurofibromatosis 1: A clinical and genetic overview. In: Huson S, Hughes R, eds. *The neurofibromatoses: a pathogenic and clinical overview*, 1994, pp. 160–203. London: Chapman and Hall.

11 Friedman J, Greene C, Birch P, and the NNFF International Database P. National Neurofibromatosis Foundation International Database. *Am J Med Genet* 1993; **45**:88–91.

12 Carey J. Neurofibromatosis–Noonan syndrome. *Am J Med Genet* 1998; **75**:263–264.

13 Ruggieri M, Huson SM. The clinical and diagnostic implications of mosaicism in the neurofibromatoses. *Neurology* 2001; **56**:1433–1443.

14 Tinschert S, Naumann I, Stegmann E, Buske A, Kaufmann D, Thiel G, *et al*. Segmental neurofibromatosis is caused by somatic mutation of the neurofibromatosis type 1 (NF1) gene. *Eur J Hum Genet* 2000; **8**:455–459.

15 Viskochil D, Buchberg A, Xu G, Cawthon R, Stevens J, Wolff R, *et al*. Deletions and a translocation interrupt a cloned gene at the neurofibromatosis type 1 locus. *Cell* 1990; **62**:187–192.

16 Wallace M, Marchuk D, Andersen LB, Letcher R, Odeh H, Saulino A, Fountain J, *et al*. Type 1 neurofibromatosis gene: Identification of a large transcript disrupted in three NF1 patients. *Science* 1990; **249**:181–186.

17 Cawthon R, Weiss R, Xu G, Viskochil D, Culver M, Stevens J, Robertson M, *et al.* A major segment of the neurofibromatosis type 1 gene: cDNA sequence, genomic structure, and point mutations. *Cell* 1990; **62**:193–201.

18 Barker D, Wright E, Nguyen K, Cannon L, Fain P, Goldgar D, *et al.* Gene for von Recklinghausen neurofibromatosis is in the pericentromeric region of chromosome 17. *Science* 1987; **236**:1100–1102.

19 Fountain JW, Wallace MR, Bruce MA, Seizinger BR, Menon AG, Gusella JF, *et al.* Physical mapping of a translocation breakpoint in neurofibromatosis. *Science* 1989; **244**:1085–1087.

20 Ledbetter DH, Rich DC, O'Connell P, Leppert M, Carey JC. Precise localization of NF1 to 17q11.2 by balanced translocation. *Am J Hum Genet* 1989; **44**:20–24.

21 Viskochil D. The structure and function of the NF1 Gene: molecular pathophysiology. In: Friedman J, Gutmann D, MacCollin M, Riccardi V, eds. *Neurofibromatosis: phenotype, natural history, and pathogenesis*, 1999, pp. 119–141. Baltimore: Johns Hopkins University Press.

22 Vandenbroucke I, Callens T, De Paepe A, Messiaen L. Complex splicing pattern generates great diversity in human NF1 transcripts. BMC *Genomics* 2002; **3**:13.

23 Tucker T, Friedman JM. Pathogenesis of hereditary tumors: beyond the "two-hit" hypothesis. *Clin Genet* 2002; **62**:345–357.

24 Messiaen LM, Callens T, Mortier G, Beysen D, Vandenbroucke I, Van Roy N, *et al.* Exhaustive mutation analysis of the NF1 gene allows identification of 95% of mutations and reveals a high frequency of unusual splicing defects. *Hum Mutat* 2000; **15**:541–555.

25 Ars E, Kruyer H, Gaona A, Serra E, Lazaro C, Estivill X. Prenatal diagnosis of sporadic neurofibromatosis type 1 (NF1) by RNA and DNA analysis of a splicing mutation. *Prenat Diagn* 1999; **19**:739–742.

26 Origone P, Bonioli E, Panucci E, Costabel S, Ajmar F, Coviello DA. The Genoa experience of prenatal diagnosis in NF1. *Prenat Diagn* 2000; **20**:719–724.

27 Elyakim S, Lerer I, Zlotogora J, Sagi M, Gelman-Kohan Z, Merin S, *et al.* Neurofibromatosis type I (NFI) in Israeli families: linkage analysis as a diagnostic tool. *Am J Med Genet* 1994; **53**:325–334.

28 Upadhyaya M, Fryer A, MacMillan J, Broadhead W, Huson SM, Harper PS. Prenatal diagnosis and presymptomatic detection of neurofibromatosis type 1. *J Med Genet* 1992; **29**:180–183.

29 Friedman JM, Riccardi VM. Clinical and epidemiological features. In: Friedman JM, Gutmann DH, MacCollin M, Riccardi VM, eds. *Neurofibromatosis: phenotype, natural history, and pathogenesis*, 1999, pp. 29–86. Baltimore: Johns Hopkins University Press.

30 Friedrich RE, Korf B, Funsterer C, Mautner VF. Growth type of plexiform neurofibromas in NF1 determined on magnetic resonance images. *Anticancer Res* 2003; **23**:949–952.

31 Korf B. Neurofibromas and malignant tumors of the peripheral nerve sheath. In: Friedman J, Gutmann D, MacCollin M, Riccardi V, eds. *Neurofibromatosis: phenotype, natural history, and pathogenesis*, 1999, pp. 142–161. Baltimore: Johns Hopkins University Press.

32 Thakkar SD, Feigen U, Mautner VF. Spinal tumours in neurofibromatosis type 1: an MRI study of frequency, multiplicity and variety. *Neuroradiology* 1999; **41**:625–629.

33 Tonsgard J, Kwak S, Short M, Dachman A. CT imaging in adults with neurofibromatosis-1: Frequent asymptomatic plexiform lesions. *Neurology* 1998; **50**:1755–1760.

34 Friedman JM, Arbiser J, Epstein JA, *et al.* Cardiovascular disease in neurofibromatosis 1: report of the NF1 Cardiovascular Task Force. *Genet Med* 2002; **4**:105–111.

35 Fossali E, Signorini E, Intermite RC, *et al.* Renovascular disease and hypertension in children with neurofibromatosis. *Pediatr Nephrol* 2000; **14**:806–810.

36 Lin AE, Birch PH, Korf BR, *et al.* Cardiovascular malformations and other cardiovascular abnormalities in neurofibromatosis 1. *Am J Med Genet* 2000; **95**:108–117.

37 Evans DG, Baser ME, McGaughran J, Sharif S, Howard E, Moran A. Malignant peripheral nerve sheath tumours in neurofibromatosis 1. *J Med Genet* 2002; **39**:311–314.

38 Rasmussen SA, Yang Q, Friedman JM. Mortality in neurofibromatosis 1: an analysis using U.S. death certificates. *Am J Hum Genet* 2001; **68**:1110–1118.

39 Listernick R, Gutmann DH. Tumors of the optic pathway. In: Friedman JM, Gutmann DH, MacCollin M, Riccardi VM, eds. *Neurofibromatosis: phenotype, natural history, and pathogenesis*, 1999, pp. 203–230. Baltimore: Johns Hopkins University Press.

40 Gutmann DH, Rasmussen SA, Wolkenstein P, *et al.* Gliomas presenting after age 10 in individuals with neurofibromatosis type 1 (NF1). *Neurology* 2002; **59**:759–761.

41 Korf BR. Malignancy in neurofibromatosis type 1. *Oncologist* 2000; **5**:477–485.

42 Gutmann D, Gurney J. Other malignancies. In: Friedman JM, Gutmann DH, MacCollin M, Riccardi VM, eds. *Neurofibromatosis: phenotype, natural history, and pathogenesis*, 1999, pp. 231–249. Baltimore: Johns Hopkins University Press.

43 Szudek J, Birch P, Friedman JM, Participants NID. Growth in North American white children with neurofibromatosis 1 (NF1). *J Med Genet* 2000; **37**:933–938.

44 Virdis R, Street ME, Bandello MA, *et al.* Growth and pubertal disorders in neurofibromatosis type 1. *J Pediatr Endocrinol Metab* 2003; **16** Suppl 2:289–292.

45 Dugoff L, Sujansky E. Neurofibromatosis type 1 and pregnancy. *Am J Med Genet* 1996; **66**:7–10.

46 Kayl AE, Moore BD 3rd. Behavioral phenotype of neurofibromatosis, type 1. *Ment Retard Dev Disabil Res Rev* 2000; **6**:117–124.

47 North K, Riccardi V, Samango-Sprouse C, *et al.* Cognitive function and academic performance in neurofibromatosis 1: Consensus statement from the NF1 Cognitive Disorders Task Force. *Neurology* 1997; **48**:1121–1127.

48 Koth CW, Cutting LE, Denckla MB. The association of neurofibromatosis type 1 and attention deficit hyperactivity disorder. *Neuropsychol Dev Cogn Sect C Child Neuropsychol* 2000; **6**:185–194.

49 Zöller M, Rembeck B, Åkesson H, Angervall L. Life expectancy, mortality and prognostic factors in neurofibromatosis type 1: A twelve-year follow-up of an epidemiological study in Göteborg, Sweden. *Acta Derm Venerol* (Stockh) 1995; **75**:136–140.

50 Riccardi VM. Historical background and introduction. In: Friedman JM, Gutmann DH, MacCollin M, Riccardi VM, eds. *Neurofibromatosis: phenotype, natural history, and pathogenesis*, 1999, pp. 1–25. Baltimore: Johns Hopkins University Press.

51 Viskochil D. Neurofibromatosis Type I. In: Cassidy SB, Allanson JE, eds. *Management of genetic syndromes*, 2001. New York: Wiley and Sons.

52 Seashore M, Cho S, Deposito F, Sherman J, Wappner R, Wilson M. Health supervision for children with neurofibromatosis. *Pediatrics* 1995; **96**:368–372.

53 DeBella K, Poskitt K, Szudek J, Friedman JM. Use of unidentified bright objects on MRI for diagnosis of neurofibromatosis 1 in children. *Neurology* 2000; **54**:1646–1651.

54 Griffiths PD, Blaser S, Mukonoweshuro W, Armstrong D, Milo-Mason G, Cheung S. Neurofibromatosis bright objects in children with neurofibromatosis type 1: a proliferative potential? *Pediatrics* 1999; **104**:e49.

55 Menor F, Marti-Bonmati L, Arana E, Poyatos C, Cortina H. Neurofibromatosis type 1 in children: MR imaging and follow-up studies of central nervous system findings. *Eur J Radiol* 1998; **26**:121–131.

56 Hyman SL, Gill DS, Shores EA, *et al.* Natural history of cognitive deficits and their relationship to MRI T2-hyperintensities in NF1. *Neurology* 2003; **60**:1139–1145.

57 Wolkenstein P, Durand-Zaleski I, Moreno JC, Zeller J, Hemery F, Revuz J. Cost evaluation of the medical management of neurofibromatosis 1: a prospective study on 201 patients. *Br J Dermatol* 2000; **142**:1166–1170.

58 Rosser T, Packer RJ. Neurofibromas in children with neurofibromatosis 1. *J Child Neurol* 2002; **17**:585–91; discussion 602–604, 646–651.

59 Packer RJ, Rosser T. Therapy for plexiform neurofibromas in children with neurofibromatosis 1: an overview. *J Child Neurol* 2002; **17**:638–41; discussion 646–651.

60 Stevenson DA, Birch PH, Friedman JM, *et al*. Descriptive analysis of tibial pseudarthrosis in patients with neurofibromatosis 1. *Am J Med Genet* 1999; **84**:413–419.

61 Parisini P, Di Silvestre M, Greggi T, Paderni S, Cervellati S, Savini R. Surgical correction of dystrophic spinal curves in neurofibromatosis. A review of 56 patients. *Spine* 1999; **24**:2247–2253.

62 Wang Q, Lasset C, Desseigne F, *et al*. Neurofibromatosis and early onset of cancers in hMLH1-deficient children. *Cancer Res* 1999; **59**:294–297.

63 Ricciardone MD, Ozcelik T, Cevher B, *et al*. Human MLH1 deficiency predisposes to hematological malignancy and neurofibromatosis type 1. *Cancer Res* 1999; **59**:290–293.

64 Gutmann DH, Winkeler E, Kabbarah O, *et al*. Mlh1 deficiency accelerates myeloid leukemogenesis in neurofibromatosis 1 (Nf1) heterozygous mice. *Oncogene* 2003; **22**:4581–4585.

65 Wang Q, Montmain G, Ruano E, *et al*. Neurofibromatosis type 1 gene as a mutational target in a mismatch repair-deficient cell type. *Hum Genet* 2003; **112**:117–123.

66 Riccardi V. Neurofibromatosis: Clinical heterogeneity. *Curr Probl Cancer* 1982; **7**:1–34.

67 Riccardi V. The multiple forms of neurofibromatosis. *Pediatr Rev* 1982; **3**:292–298.

68 Seizinger BR, Rouleau GA, Ozelius LJ, *et al*. Genetic linkage of von Recklinghausen neurofibromatosis to the nerve growth factor receptor gene. *Cell* 1987; **49**:589–594.

69 Rouleau GA, Wertelecki W, Haines JL, *et al*. Genetic linkage of bilateral acoustic neurofibromatosis to a DNA marker on chromosome 22. *Nature* 1987; **329**:246–248.

70 Wishart JH. Case of tumours in the skull, dura mater, and brain. *Edinburgh Med Surg J* 1822; **18**:393–397.

71 Cushing H. *Tumors of the nervus acusticus and the syndrome of the cerebellopontile angle*, 1917, Philadelphia, London: W. B. Saunders company.

72 Gardner WJ, Frazier CH. Bilateral acoustic neurofibromas: a clinical study and field survey of a family of five generations with bilateral deafness in thirty eight members. *Arch Neurol Psychiatry* 1930; **23**:266–302.

73 Feiling A, Ward E. A familial form of acoustic tumours. *BMJ* 1920; **1**:496–497.

74 Zhao Y, Kumar RA, Baser ME, *et al*. Intrafamilial correlation of clinical manifestations in neurofibromatosis 2 (NF2). *Genet Epidemiol* 2002; **23**:245–259.

75 MacCollin M. Neurfibromatosis 2: Clinical aspects. In: Friedman JM, Gutmann DH, MacCollin M, Riccardi VM, eds. *Neurofibromatosis: phenotype, natural history, and pathogenesis*, 1999, pp. 299–326. Baltimore: Johns Hopkins University Press.

76 Kluwe L, Mautner VF. Mosaicism in sporadic neurofibromatosis 2 patients. *Hum Mol Genet* 1998; **7**:2051–2055.

77 Evans DG, Wallace AJ, Wu CL, Trueman L, Ramsden RT, Strachan T. Somatic mosaicism: a common cause of classic disease in tumor-prone syndromes? Lessons from type 2 neurofibromatosis. *Am J Hum Genet* 1998; **63**:727–736.

78 Evans DG, Sainio M, Baser ME. Neurofibromatosis type 2. *J Med Genet* 2000; **37**:897–904.

79 Evans DG, Huson SM, Donnai D, *et al*. A genetic study of type 2 neurofibromatosis in the United Kingdom. I. Prevalence, mutation rate, fitness, and confirmation of maternal transmission effect on severity. *J Med Genet* 1992; **29**:841–846.

80 Baser ME, Friedman JM, Wallace AJ, Ramsden RT, Joe H, Evans DG. Evaluation of clinical diagnostic criteria for neurofibromatosis 2. *Neurology* 2002; **59**:1759–1765.

81 Antinheimo J, Sankila R, Carpen O, Pukkala E, Sainio M, Jaaskelainen J. Population-based analysis of sporadic and type 2 neurofibromatosis-associated meningiomas and schwannomas. *Neurology* 2000; **54**:71–76.

82 Baser ME, Evans DG, Gutmann DH. Neurofibromatosis 2. *Curr Opin Neurol* 2003; **16**:27–33.

83 Evans DG, Huson SM, Donnai D, *et al*. A genetic study of type 2 neurofibromatosis in the United Kingdom. II. Guidelines for genetic counselling. *J Med Genet* 1992; **29**:847–852.

84 Rouleau GA, Merel P, Lutchman M, *et al*. Alteration in a new gene encoding a putative membrane-organizing protein causes neuro-fibromatosis type 2. *Nature* 1993; **363**:515–521.

85 Trofatter JA, MacCollin MM, Rutter JL, *et al*. A novel moesin-, ezrin-, radixin-like gene is a candidate for the neurofibromatosis 2 tumor suppressor. *Cell* 1993; **72**:791–800.

86 MacCollin M. Neurfibromatosis 2: Molecular biology. In: Friedman JM, Gutmann DH, MacCollin M, Riccardi VM, eds. *Neurofibromatosis: phenotype, natural history, and pathogenesis,* 1999, pp. 351–362. Baltimore: Johns Hopkins University Press.

87 Sun CX, Robb VA, Gutmann DH. Protein 4.1 tumor suppressors: getting a FERM grip on growth regulation. *J Cell Sci* 2002; **115**:3991–4000.

88 Xiao GH, Chernoff J, Testa JR. NF2: the wizardry of merlin. *Genes Chromosomes Cancer* 2003; **38**:389–399.

89 Parry DM, MacCollin MM, Kaiser-Kupfer MI, *et al*. Germ-line mutations in the neurofibromatosis 2 gene: correlations with disease severity and retinal abnormalities. *Am J Hum Genet* 1996; **59**:529–539.

90 Bruder CE, Hirvela C, Tapia-Paez I, *et al*. High resolution deletion analysis of constitutional DNA from neurofibromatosis type 2 (NF2) patients using microarray-CGH. *Hum Mol Genet* 2001; **10**:271–282.

91 Kluwe L, Mautner V, Heinrich B, *et al*. Molecular study of frequency of mosaicism in neurofibromatosis 2 patients with bilateral vestibular schwannomas. *J Med Genet* 2003; **40**:109–114.

92 Mautner VF, Lindenau M, Baser ME, *et al*. The neuroimaging and clinical spectrum of neurofibromatosis 2. *Neurosurgery* 1996; **38**:880–885; discussion 885–886.

93 Otsuka G, Saito K, Nagatani T, Yoshida J. Age at symptom onset and long-term survival in patients with neurofibromatosis Type 2. *J Neurosurg* 2003; **99**:480–483.

94 Baser M, Evans D, Jackler R, Sujansky E, Rubenstein A. Neurofibromatosis 2, radiosurgery and malignant nervous system tumours. *Br J Cancer* 2000; **82**:998.

95 Baser ME, Friedman JM, Aeschliman D, *et al*. Predictors of the risk of mortality in neurofibromatosis 2. *Am J Hum Genet* 2002; **71**:715–723.

96 Moffat DA, Quaranta N, Baguley DM, Hardy DG, Chang P. Management strategies in neurofibromatosis type 2. *Eur Arch Otorhinolaryngol* 2003; **260**:12–18.

97 Welling D, Slater P, Thomas R, McGregor J, Goodman J. The learning curve in vestibular schwannoma surgery. *Am J Otol* 1999; **20**:644–648.

98 Baser M, Makariou E, Parry D. Predictors of vestibular schwannoma growth in patients with neurofibromatosis Type 2. *J Neurosurg* 2002; **96**:217–222.

99 Mautner V, Baser M, Thakkar S, Feigen U, Friedman J, Kluwe L. Vestibular schwannoma growth in patients with neurofibromatosis Type 2: a longitudinal study. *J Neurosurg* 2002; **96**:223–228.

100 Bari M, Forster D, Kemeny A, Walton L, Hardy D, Anderson J. Malignancy in a vestibular schwannoma. Report of a case with central neurofibromatosis, treated by both stereotactic

radiosurgery and surgical excision, with a review of the literature. *Br J Neurosurg* 2002; **16**:284–289.

101 Maxwell M, Shih SD, Galanopoulos T, Hedley-Whyte ET, Cosgrove GR. Familial meningioma: analysis of expression of neurofibromatosis 2 protein Merlin. Report of two cases. *J Neurosurg* 1998; **88**:562–569.

102 Purcell SM, Dixon SL. Schwannomatosis. An unusual variant of neurofibromatosis or a distinct clinical entity? *Arch Dermatol* 1989; **125**:390–393.

103 Shishiba T, Niimura M, Ohtsuka F, Tsuru N. Multiple cutaneous neurilemmomas as a skin manifestation of neurilemmomatosis. *J Am Acad Dermatol* 1984; **10**:744–754.

104 MacCollin M, Willett C, Heinrich B, *et al*. Familial schwannomatosis: Exclusion of the NF2 locus as the germline event. *Neurology* 2003; **60**:1968–1974.

105 Jacoby LB, Jones D, Davis K, *et al*. Molecular analysis of the NF2 tumor-suppressor gene in schwannomatosis. *Am J Hum Genet* 1997; **61**:1293–1302.

106 MacCollin M, Woodfin W, Kronn D, Short MP. Schwannomatosis: a clinical and pathologic study. *Neurology* 1996; **46**:1072–1079.

107 Pulst SM, Riccardi V, Mautner V. Spinal schwannomatosis. *Neurology* 1997; **48**:787–788.

108 Evans DG, Mason S, Huson SM, Ponder M, Harding AE, Strachan T. Spinal and cutaneous schwannomatosis is a variant form of type 2 neurofibromatosis: a clinical and molecular study. *J Neurol Neurosurg Psychiatry* 1997; **62**:361–366.

109 Seppala MT, Sainio MA, Haltia MJ, Kinnunen JJ, Setala KH, Jaaskelainen JE. Multiple schwannomas: schwannomatosis or neurofibromatosis type 2? *J Neurosurg* 1998; **89**:36–41.

110 Kaufman DL, Heinrich BS, Willett C, *et al*. Somatic instability of the NF2 gene in schwannomatosis. *Arch Neurol* 2003; **60**:1317–1320.

111 Leverkus M, Kluwe L, Roll EM, *et al*. Multiple unilateral schwannomas: segmental neurofibromatosis type 2 or schwannomatosis? *Br J Dermatol* 2003; **148**:804–809.

112 Wolkenstein P, Benchikhi H, Zeller J, Wechsler J, Revuz J. Schwannomatosis: a clinical entity distinct from neurofibromatosis type 2. *Dermatology* 1997; **195**:228–231.

Chapter 13

von Hippel–Lindau disease

Eamonn R. Maher

Introduction

von Hippel–Lindau (VHL) disease is a dominantly inherited, multisystem disorder characterized by the development of retinal and central nervous haemangioblastomas, clear cell renal cell carcinoma (RCC), phaeochromocytoma, pancreatic endocrine tumours and endolymphatic sac tumours (ELSTs). In addition, renal, pancreatic and epididymal cysts are frequent.

VHL disease has an incidence of ~1 in 30 000. The condition is named after the German ophthalmologist Eugene von Hippel, who described the characteristic retinal features of the disease 100 years ago, and the Swedish pathologist Arvid Lindau who recognized the association between retinal and cerebellar lesions in 1926. Subsequently, renal cell carcinoma and phaeochromocytoma were recognized as integral features of the disorder (1), but the association with ELSTs was only defined within the past decade (2). The prognosis of VHL disease has been improved by the advent of routine surveillance of affected patients and asymptomatic gene carriers to detect complications at an early stage. In the future, effective antiangiogenic therapy (e.g. vascular endothelial growth factor antagonists) may improve management options for the treatment of CNS and retinal haemangioblastomas.

Clinical features of VHL

VHL disease is dominantly inherited with variable expression and age-dependent penetrance (Fig. 13.1). As can be seen in this figure, most cases present in the second and third decades, and non-penetrance at age 60 years is uncommon (3).

The major features of VHL disease are:

♦ retinal angiomatosis
♦ cerebellar and spinal haemangioblastomas
♦ clear cell renal cell carcinoma (RCC).

Penetrance is tumour-specific with, on average, an earlier onset for retinal angioma (mean 24.5 years at symptomatic diagnosis) and cerebellar haemangioblastoma (29 years) than for renal cell carcinoma (44 years). Nevertheless, by age 60 years the overall risk of retinal, cerebellar and renal tumours has been estimated at ~70 per cent for each

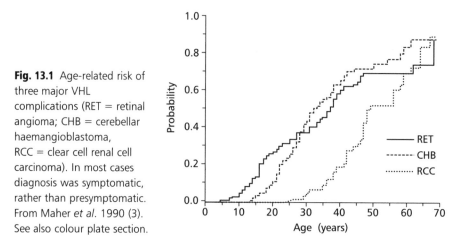

Fig. 13.1 Age-related risk of three major VHL complications (RET = retinal angioma; CHB = cerebellar haemangioblastoma, RCC = clear cell renal cell carcinoma). In most cases diagnosis was symptomatic, rather than presymptomatic. From Maher *et al.* 1990 (3). See also colour plate section.

tumour (3). The frequency of particular tumours within families is influenced by allelic heterogeneity (see later).

The most striking example of this is for phaeochromocytoma, which occurs in ~10 per cent of cases but is the most common feature of VHL disease in some kindreds and absent in others. VHL families without phaeochromocytoma are classified as Type 1 VHL disease and those with phaeochromocytoma as Type 2 (4). Type 2 is further subdivided into:

- those with renal cell carcinoma (RCC) and retinal and CNS haemangioblastomas (Type 2B)
- those with phaeochromocytoma and haemangioblastomas but not (or rarely) RCC (Type 2A)
- those with germline *VHL* mutations but with only phaeochromocytoma (Type 2C).

As with other familial cancer syndromes, patients with VHL disease not only have a greatly increased risk of RCC but, in addition, tumours develop at an early age and are frequently multiple (5, 6).

Frequency of VHL

The minimum birth incidence in the UK was estimated at ~3 per 100 000 persons and prevalences of ~2 per 100 000 and 2.5 per 100 000 were reported from the UK and Germany, respectively (7, 8). As these estimates preceded the advent of widespread molecular genetic diagnosis, they should be viewed as probable underestimates.

Diagnosis of VHL

A clinical diagnosis of VHL disease can be made by:

- The presence of a single VHL tumour (e.g. retinal or brain haemangioblastoma, clear cell renal cell carcinoma, phaeochromocytoma or ELST) in an individual with a close relative with VHL disease. The presence of multiple pancreatic, renal or epididymal cysts in a young at-risk relative is likely to indicate carrier status, but does not provide an unequivocal diagnosis.

◆ In isolated cases, the presence of two haemangioblastomas or a haemangioblastoma and another "VHL tumour".

As mutation analysis of the VHL gene will detect germline mutations in 95 per cent or more of non-mosaic cases, a clinical diagnosis should be confirmed by mutation analysis whenever possible. DNA diagnosis is particularly useful to identify VHL disease in isolated cases after the first tumour, or in those with an atypical presentation. For example, a germline VHL gene mutation may be detected in 4 per cent of sporadic cerebellar haemangioblastoma cases without clinical or radiological evidence of VHL disease and in up to 40 per cent of patients with apparently isolated familial phaeochromocytoma (9, 10).

Germline *SDHB* and *SDHD* mutations may be detected in familial phaeochromocytoma cases without *VHL* gene mutations. Other causes of familial clear cell RCC include chromosome 3 rearrangements and familial non-VHL clear cell RCC (11, 12).

Molecular genetic testing

The *VHL* gene was mapped to chromosome 3p25 in 1988 and identified 5 years later (13). The *VHL* coding sequence is contained within three exons and specifies two proteins, a full-length ~30 kDa 213 amino acid product and a shorter 19 kDa protein lacking the first 53 amino acids. $pVHL_{30}$ and $pVHL_{19}$ appear to have equivalent tumour suppressor activity and mutations within the first 53 amino acids are not seen in VHL patients (14). Germline deletions account for ~40 per cent of *VHL* gene mutations and the remainder are mostly accounted for (roughly equally) by missense substitutions and truncating mutations (4, 15). Most missense and truncating mutations are private, but recurrent mutations may occur at CpG dinucleotide hotspots (c.694 C > T, c.712 C > T, c.713 G > A) and a founder mutation (c.505 T > C) has been reported in families originating from the "Black Forest" region of southwest Germany (16).

VHL tumours appear to develop from a classical two hit mechanism with inactivation of the wild-type allele in tumour tissue (16, 17). However, VHL disease demonstrates complex genotype–phenotype correlations (Table 13.1). Thus the overwhelming majority of VHL families in which phaeochromocytoma have occurred (Type 2 phenotype) have a missense mutation. In contrast, deletions and truncating mutations predominate in families without phaeochromocytoma (Type 1 phenotype). Further heterogeneity may be seen in Type 2 kindreds. Thus most Type 2 families demonstrate susceptibility to phaeochromocytoma, RCC and phaeochromocytoma (Type 2B phenotype), but the c.505 T > C mutation is associated with a low risk of RCC (Type 2A phenotype) (16–18). Certain germline VHL mutations detected in patients with familial phaeochromocytoma (Type 2C phenotype) may be functionally distinct from those found in 2A and 2B kindreds, but in other cases the VHL mutation identified has

Table 13.1 Genotype–phenotype relationships in VHL disease

Lesion	Unselected UK series Type 1 and Type 2B[a]		Type 2A mutation (Tyr98His)[b]	Type 2B mutation (Arg167Trp)[b]
	Frequency (%)	Mean age at diagnosis (years)	Frequency (%)	Frequency (%)
Retinal angioma (haemangioblastoma)	59	25.4	47	71
Cerebellar haemangioblastoma	59	29	9	33
Spinal cord haemangioblastoma	13	33[c]		
Renal cell carcinoma	28	44	0	31
Phaeochromocytoma	7	30[c]	55	71

Comparison of frequency of major VHL manifestations in an unselected series from the UK (mainly Type 1 and Type 2B) and for two prototypic Type 2A and 2B mutations. Age at diagnosis was in most cases age at symptomatic diagnosis.

[a] Maher et al. 1990 (3);   [b] Chen et al. 1995 (20);   [c] Lonser et al. (19).

been reported previously in 2B kindreds (10). This latter finding provides important prognostic information and predicts that mutation carriers are at risk for RCC and haemangioblastomas in addition to phaeochromocytoma.

Protein function

The complex genotype–phenotype correlations observed in VHL disease suggest that the VHL protein (pVHL) will have multiple and tissue-specific functions (21). The VHL gene product has been implicated in a wide range of cellular processes including cell cycle control, fibronectin and extracellular matrix metabolism, apoptosis and microtubule function (22). However the best characterized function of pVHL is the regulation of proteolytic degradation of the μ subunits of the HIF-1 and HIF-2 transcription factors. Inactivation of the *VHL* tumour suppressor gene leads to upregulation of HIF-1 and HIF-2 expression (mimicking the effects of hypoxia), which activates expression of vascular endothelial growth factor (VEGF) and other molecules that promote angiogenesis (22–24).

Clinical testing

Molecular genetic testing is available in a number of service laboratories worldwide. A combination of direct sequencing and Southern analysis has a high detection rate, but whole-gene deletions may be missed by quantitative Southern analysis, and therefore fluorescence *in situ* hybridization (FISH) analysis may also be required (25, 26). Multiplex ligation-dependent probe amplification (MLPA) analysis appears to be an effective strategy to detect deletions and may replace Southern analysis for routine diagnostic use. The overall mutation detection rate should be 95 per cent or higher in non-mosaic cases. In families in which mutation analysis is not possible or unsuccessful, genetic linkage studies may be helpful as there is no evidence of linkage heterogeneity in VHL disease.

Surveillance and clinical management

The widespread adoption of a policy of proactively ascertaining affected individuals and their at-risk relatives, and then ensuring they are entered into systematic surveillance programmes, has improved the prognosis for families with VHL disease. Data on the age-related penetrance for individual tumour types (Fig. 13.1) provide a basis for developing surveillance programmes (3). Box 13.1 provides an example of a routine screening programme.

This protocol provides general guidelines for asymptomatic individuals. Symptomatic individuals should be investigated according to clinical indications. Genetic testing allows screening to be targeted to gene carriers in most families. Genetic testing in children is usually offered at 3–5 years. In view of the genotype–phenotype correlations observed in VHL disease, to a limited extent, screening programmes may be individualized, to take into account the specific mutation identified in the family (e.g. if phaeochromocytoma risk is predicted to be high more intensive screening may be indicated).

Box 13.1   von Hippel–Lindau disease surveillance protocols

Asymptomatic affected patient or gene carrier:

- annual physical examination by a physician familiar with VHL disease
- annual direct and indirect ophthalmoscopy (from age 5 years)
- MRI with gadolinium brain scan from age 15 years every 2–3 years to age 50 and every 3–5 years thereafter
- annual renal ultrasound or MRI scan (CT scan may be required if multiple renal or pancreatic cysts are present) from age 15 years (from age 11 years if at high risk for phaeochromocytoma)
- annual 24-hour urine collection for catecholamines from age 11 (from age 5 years if at high risk for phaeochromocytoma).

Asymptomatic at-risk relative of unknown or carrier status:

- as above but screening may be discontinued if no evidence of VHL disease by age 60 years.

N.B. Symptomatic patients should be investigated urgently

Organ-specific features of VHL disease

Retinal angiomas (histologically haemangioblastomas) are the most common presenting feature of VHL disease (mean age at symptomatic diagnosis 25 years) and are multiple in many cases. Retinal angiomas (mean 1.85 lesions) are found in almost 70 per cent of cases and the cumulative risk of visual loss has been estimated as 35 per cent in gene carriers, and 55 per cent in patients with retinal angiomas at age 50 years (27). Early detection and treatment of retinal angiomas by laser or cryosurgery reduces the risk of visual loss, although optic disc angiomas are very difficult to treat because of the dilemma of iatrogenic optic nerve damage.

Central nervous system haemangioblastomas are a cardinal feature in VHL disease. Cerebellar haemangioblastomas occur in ~70 per cent of cases and symptomatic spinal cord lesions in ~25 per cent. Supratentorial lesions are uncommon. Approximately 30 per cent of all patients with cerebellar haemangioblastoma have VHL disease and the mean age at diagnosis of those with VHL disease is considerably younger than in sporadic cases (mean 29 versus 48 years) (3, 5).

Haemangioblastomas are benign tumours and the results of surgery for single peripherally located cerebellar lesions are often excellent. However, multiple and recurrent tumours are common and sequential surgery may produce significant morbidity. The surgical treatment of brain stem and spinal tumours may be hazardous and result in disability. It is hoped that antiangiogenic therapy may offer a medical approach to the treatment of inoperable CNS and retinal haemangioblastomas, and preliminary clinical trials are in progress.

Renal cysts and tumours are major features of VHL disease. The frequency of renal cysts is age-related and renal cysts are present in most middle-aged patients. Cysts do not usually compromise renal function, but RCC may develop within a cyst, and such complex cysts require careful follow-up as the cystic component may involute while the solid tumour grows (28). However, most RCC do not develop from cysts and careful examination of the renal parenchyma from VHL patients often demonstrates microfoci of clear cell RCC (29) and sensitive immunostaining techniques may reveal numerous early neoplastic lesions (30). As early detection and treatment of RCC in VHL disease reduces morbidity and mortality, VHL patients and at-risk relatives should be offered annual renal imaging from age 16 years. Solid renal lesions do not necessarily need treatment when they are detected – they should be monitored until they reach 3 cm in size when conservative nephron-sparing surgery is performed. Following surgery there is a high risk of local recurrence (from new primary tumours) but the risk of distant metastasis is low (31), whereas 25 per cent of VHL patients with a tumour >3 cm develop metastatic disease (30, 32). Although experience with renal transplantation in VHL disease is limited, available information is reassuring, with no evidence of increased patient or graft morbidity or mortality (33).

Phaeochromocytoma only occurs in a minority (~10 per cent) of VHL cases but demonstrates marked interfamilial variability (6, 34, 35). Thus in many families, phaeochromocytoma is absent or rare, but in some, phaeochromocytoma is the most frequent feature and complex genotype–phenotype correlations are seen (see above). Phaeochromocytomas in VHL disease may be extra-adrenal and <5 per cent are malignant. Compared to sporadic cases, onset of phaeochromocytoma is earlier in VHL patients (~20 years). Conventionally, VHL patients and at-risk relatives are offered screening for phaeochromocytoma from age 10 years, but screening should be commenced earlier if there is a family history of phaeochromocytoma or a VHL Type 2 mutation is identified.

Pancreas cysts and tumours are both features of VHL disease. Multiple cysts are the most frequent pancreatic manifestation, but are rarely of clinical significance as impaired pancreatic function is uncommon. Pancreatic tumours occur in 5 to 10 per cent of cases and are usually non-secretory islet cell tumours. A high frequency of malignancy has been reported in VHL-associated islet cell tumours and surgery is indicated in tumours >3 cm while tumours <1 cm may be monitored (36, 37).

Endolymphatic sac tumours (ELST) can be detected by MRI in up to 11 per cent of cases (2), although only a minority are symptomatic, in which case they present with hearing loss, tinnitus and vertigo.

Epididymal cysts are very frequent in males (25–60 per cent) with VHL disease and can, if bilateral, impair fertility. However, epididymal cysts are not infrequent in the general population and their presence in an at-risk relative does not necessarily indicate carrier status.

Conclusions

VHL disease is a multisystem disorder, and so the effective management of families requires a co-ordinated multidisciplinary approach. It is crucial that responsibility for co-ordination of family ascertainment, screening and DNA testing is clearly assigned so that all at-risk relatives are contacted and offered surveillance and genetic testing as appropriate. For affected individuals and gene carriers, lifelong surveillance is required but increasing insights into the function of the *VHL* gene product may lead to the development of novel medical therapies.

References

1 Melmon KL, Rosen SW. Lindau's disease. Review of the literature and study of a large kindred. *Am J Med* 1964; **36**:595–617.

2 Manski TJ, Heffner DK, Glenn GM, Patronas NJ, Pikus AT, Katz D, *et al*. Endolymphatic sac tumors. A source of morbid hearing loss in von Hippel–Lindau disease. *JAMA* 1997; 277:1461–1466.

3 Maher ER, Yates JR, Harries R, Benjamin C, Harris R, Moore AT, *et al*. Clinical features and natural history of von Hippel–Lindau disease. *Q J Med* 1990; 77:1151–1163.

4 Zbar B, Kishida T, Chen F, Schmidt L, Maher ER, Richards FM, *et al*. Germline mutations in the Von Hippel–Lindau disease (VHL) gene in families from North America, Europe, and Japan. *Hum Mutat* 1996; **8**:348–357.

5 Maher ER, Yates JR, Ferguson-Smith MA. Statistical analysis of the two stage mutation model in von Hippel–Lindau disease, and in sporadic cerebellar haemangioblastoma and renal cell carcinoma. *J Med Genet* 1990; **27**:311–314.

6 Richard S, Beigelman C, Duclos JM, Fendler JP, Plauchu H, Plouin PF, *et al*. Phaeochromocytoma as the first manifestation of von Hippel–Lindau disease. *Surgery* 1994; **116**:1076–1081.

7 Maher ER, Iselius L, Yates JR, Littler M, Benjamin C, Harris R, *et al*. Von Hippel–Lindau disease: a genetic study. *J Med Genet* 1991; **28**:443–447.

8 Neumann HP, Wiestler OD. Clustering of features of von Hippel–Lindau syndrome: evidence for a complex genetic locus. *Lancet* 1991; **337**:1052–1054.

9 Hes FJ, McKee S, Taphoorn MJ, Rehal P, Der Luijt RB, McMahon R, *et al*. Cryptic von Hippel–Lindau disease: germline mutations in patients with haemangioblastoma only. *J Med Genet* 2000; **37**:939–943.

10 Woodward ER, Eng C, McMahon R, Voutilainen R, Affara NA, Ponder BA, *et al*. Genetic predisposition to phaeochromocytoma: analysis of candidate genes GDNF, RET and VHL. *Hum Mol Genet* 1997; **6**:1051–1056.

11 Teh BT, Giraud S, Sari NF, Hii SI, Bergerat JP, Larsson C, *et al*. Familial non-VHL non-papillary clear-cell renal cancer. *Lancet* 1997; **349**:848–849.

12 Woodward ER, Clifford SC, Astuti D, Affara NA, Maher ER. Familial clear cell renal cell carcinoma (FCRC): clinical features and mutation analysis of the VHL, MET, and CUL2 candidate genes. *J Med Genet* 2000; **37**:348–353.

13 Latif F, Tory K, Gnarra J, Yao M, Duh FM, Orcutt ML, *et al*. Identification of the von Hippel–Lindau disease tumor suppressor gene. *Science* 1993; **260**:1317–1320.

14 Iliopoulos O, Ohh M, Kaelin WG Jr. pVHL19 is a biologically active product of the von Hippel–Lindau gene arising from internal translation initiation. *Proc Natl Acad Sci USA* 1998; **95**:11661–11666.

15 Maher ER, Webster AR, Richards FM, Green JS, Crossey PA, Payne SJ, *et al*. Phenotypic expression in von Hippel–Lindau disease: correlations with germline VHL gene mutations. *J Med Genet* 1996; **33**:328–332.

16 Brauch H, Kishida T, Glavac D, Chen F, Pausch F, Hofler H, *et al*. Von Hippel–Lindau (VHL) disease with pheochromocytoma in the Black Forest region of Germany: evidence for a founder effect. *Hum Genet* 1995; **95**:551–556.

17 Prowse AH, Webster AR, Richards FM, Richard S, Olschwang S, Resche F, *et al*. Somatic inactivation of the VHL gene in Von Hippel–Lindau disease tumors. *Am J Hum Genet* 1997; **60**:765–771.

18 Bender BU, Eng C, Olschewski M, Berger DP, Laubenberger J, Altehofer C, *et al*. VHL c.505 T>C mutation confers a high age related penetrance but no increased overall mortality. *J Med Genet* 2001; **38**:508–514.

19 Lonser RR, Glenn GM, Walther M, Chew EY, Libutti SK, Linehan WM, *et al*. von Hippel–Lindau disease. *Lancet* 2003; **361**:2059–2067.

20 Chen F, Kishida T, Yao M, Hustad T, Glavac D, Dean M, *et al*. Germline mutations in the von Hippel–Lindau disease tumor suppressor gene: correlations with phenotype. *Hum Mutat* 1995; **5**:66–75.

21 Kaelin WG, Jr, Maher ER. The VHL tumour-suppressor gene paradigm. *Trends Genet* 1998; **14**:423–426.

22 Kaelin WG, Jr. Molecular basis of the VHL hereditary cancer syndrome. *Nat Rev Cancer* 2002; **2**:673–682.

23 Cockman ME, Masson N, Mole DR, Jaakkola P, Chang GW, Clifford SC, *et al*. Hypoxia inducible factor-alpha binding and ubiquitylation by the von Hippel–Lindau tumor suppressor protein. *J Biol Chem* 2000; **275**:25733–25741.

24 Maxwell PH, Wiesener MS, Chang GW, Clifford SC, Vaux EC, Cockman ME, *et al*. The tumour suppressor protein VHL targets hypoxia-inducible factors for oxygen-dependent proteolysis. *Nature* 1999; **399**:271–275.

25 Pack SD, Zbar B, Pak E, Ault DO, Humphrey JS, Pham T, *et al*. Constitutional von Hippel–Lindau (VHL) gene deletions detected in VHL families by fluorescence in situ hybridization. *Cancer Res* 1999; **59**:5560–5564.

26 Stolle C, Glenn G, Zbar B, Humphrey JS, Choyke P, Walther M, *et al*. Improved detection of germline mutations in the von Hippel–Lindau disease tumor suppressor gene. *Hum Mutat* 1998; **12**:417–423.

27 Webster AR, Maher ER, Moore AT. Clinical characteristics of ocular angiomatosis in von Hippel–Lindau disease and correlation with germline mutation. *Arch Ophthalmol* 1999; **117**:371–378.

28 Choyke PL, Glenn GM, Walther MM, Zbar B, Weiss GH, Alexander RB, *et al*. The natural history of renal lesions in von Hippel–Lindau disease: a serial CT study in 28 patients. *Am J Roentgenol* 1992; **159**:1229–1234.

29 Walther MM, Lubensky IA, Venzon D, Zbar B, Linehan WM. Prevalence of microscopic lesions in grossly normal renal parenchyma from patients with von Hippel–Lindau disease, sporadic renal cell carcinoma and no renal disease: clinical implications. *J Urol* 1995; **154**:2010–2014.

30 Mandriota SJ, Turner KJ, Davies DR, Murray PG, Morgan NV, Sowter HM, *et al*. HIF activation identifies early lesions in VHL kidneys: evidence for site-specific tumor suppressor function in the nephron. *Cancer Cell* 2002; **1**:459–468.

30 Steinbach F, Novick AC, Zincke H, Miller DP, Williams RD, Lund G, *et al*. Treatment of renal cell carcinoma in von Hippel–Lindau disease: a multicenter study. *J Urol* 1995; **153**:1812–1816.

32 Walther MM, Choyke PL, Glenn G, Lyne JC, Rayford W, Venzon D, *et al*. Renal cancer in families with hereditary renal cancer: prospective analysis of a tumor size threshold for renal parenchymal sparing surgery. *J Urol* 1999; **161**:1475–1479.

33 Goldfarb DA, Neumann HP, Penn I, Novick AC. Results of renal transplantation in patients with renal cell carcinoma and von Hippel–Lindau disease. *Transplantation* 1997; **64**:1726–1729.

34 Crossey PA, Eng C, Ginalska-Malinowska M, Lennard TW, Wheeler DC, Ponder BA, *et al*. Molecular genetic diagnosis of von Hippel–Lindau disease in familial phaeochromocytoma. *J Med Genet* 1995; **32**:885–886.

35 Maher ER, Eng C. The pressure rises: update on the genetics of phaeochromocytoma. *Hum Mol Genet* 2002; **11**:2347–2354.

36 Libutti SK, Choyke PL, Alexander HR, Glenn G, Bartlett DL, Zbar B, *et al*. Clinical and genetic analysis of patients with pancreatic neuroendocrine tumors associated with von Hippel–Lindau disease. *Surgery* 2000; **128**:1022–1027.

37 Libutti SK, Choyke PL, Bartlett DL, Vargas H, Walther M, Lubensky I, *et al*. Pancreatic neuroendocrine tumors associated with von Hippel Lindau disease: diagnostic and management recommendations. *Surgery* 1998; **124**:1153–1159.

Chapter 14

Multiple endocrine neoplasias

Fiona Lalloo

Introduction

The multiple endocrine neoplasias refer to inherited conditions predisposing to the development of tumours within more than one endocrine gland within the same patient. The term multiple endocrine adenopathy has been used in the past but the term multiple endocrine neoplasia (MEN) is now preferred.

There are two major types of MEN – MEN type 1 (also known as Wemer's syndrome (1)) and MEN type 2 (also known as Sipple's syndrome(2)). Each has specific endocrine glands involved in the syndrome (Table 14.1). Both are autosomal dominant, with the associated risks and implications for the wider family, and both require long-term follow-up and active management. The genes causing both types of MEN have been cloned and, in particular families, predictive testing is available. As a result of the long-term screening and management of affected and at-risk patients, and the early age of onset of problems and therefore screening, predictive testing for both conditions is offered in childhood.

Multiple endocrine neoplasia type 1

Post mortem studies have estimated the incidence of MEN1 to be 2.5 per thousand(3), although earlier studies suggested a prevalence of 0.01 per thousand.

Table 14.1 Tumour phenotype in multiple endocrine neoplasias

Tumour	MEN1	MEN2a	MEN2b	FMTC
Parathyroid	+	+	−	−
Pituitary	+	−	−	−
Pancreas	+	−	−	−
Phaeochromocytoma	−	+	+	−
MTC	−	+	+	+

MEN = multiple endocrine neoplasia; MTC = medullary thyroid carcinoma; FMTC = familial medullary thyroid carcinoma.

Consensus guidelines (4) suggest the following diagnostic criteria for MEN1:

♦ A case with two of three main MEN1-related endocrine tumours.

♦ Familial MEN1 if one case plus one first-degree relative with one of the tumours.

The age of onset of MEN1 is variable and ranges from 8 to 81 years with a penetrance of 50 per cent by 20 years and >90 per cent by 40 years (5).

Clinical features of MEN type 1

Tumours of the parathyroid gland, pancreas and anterior pituitary glands are characteristic of MEN type 1.

Parathyroid gland

♦ Most common tumour in MEN1.

♦ Occurs in 95 per cent patients with MEN1(6).

♦ Primary hyperparathyroidism is rare before 15 years but has been recorded at 4 years (7); usually occurs before 25 years.

♦ Primary hyperparathyroidism is usually the first clinical presentation of MEN1.

♦ May present with nephrocalcinosis, polyuria, polydipsia, constipation or malaise or may be asymptomatic.

♦ Biochemistry: hypercalcaemia with raised circulating parathyroid hormone (PTH).

♦ Tumours usually develop in three or four glands.

♦ Definitive treatment is total parathyroidectomy with life-long treatment with oral calcitrol but should be reserved for the symptomatic hypercalcaemic patient; total parathyroidectomy with a fresh parathyroid autograft to the forearm has been used (4); the asymptomatic patient should be observed.

♦ MEN1 accounts for between 2 and 4 per cent of cases of primary hyperparathyroidism (8).

Tumours of the pancreas

Pancreatic islet cell tumours are said to occur in between 30 and 80 per cent of patients with MEN1(6) and tend to result in the oversecretion of hormones. They occur at a younger age than sporadic islet cell tumours and are frequently multiple. As well as arising in the islet cells of the pancreas, these tumours may arise in the submucosa of the duodenum.

Gastrinomas

♦ Most common pancreatic tumour found in up to 40 to 50 per cent of MEN1 patients.

♦ Usually occurs after the age of 40 years.

♦ May be malignant with a proportion metastasizing prior to diagnosis.

- Results in Zollinger – Ellinson syndrome, which originally described a triad of islet cell tumours, gastric acid hypersecretion and severe peptic ulceration of the stomach and duodenum (9).

- Patients present with abdominal pain and gastrointestinal reflux; they may also develop diarrhoea and steatorrhoea.

- Gastrinomas in MEN are small, submucosal and multiple as opposed to sporadic tumours, which are usually large and solitary.

- Biochemistry: raised fasting serum gastrin concentration in association with an increased basal acid secretion.

- Treatment is difficult as the tumours are often multiple and surgical resection therefore not possible; symptoms of gastric acid secretion may be treated with a proton pump inhibitor (PPI); octreotide has been used to treat successfully.

- Of patients with Zollinger – Ellison syndrome, 16 to 38 per cent have MEN type1(3).

Insulinomas

- These account for a third of pancreatic tumours in MEN1.

- They may occur in association with gastrinomas in 10 per cent of patients.

- Insulinomas occur at a younger age in patients with MEN1, with a mean age of 29 years vs. 45 years in patients with sporadic tumours (6).

- Patients present with hypoglycaemic symptoms after fasting or exertion; this then improves with the ingestion of glucose.

- Biochemistry: raised plasma insulin concentrations in association with hypoglycaemia; raised levels of C-peptide and pro-insulin are useful indicators of the diagnosis.

- Treatment is surgical resection.

- Four per cent of patients presenting with insulinoma will have MEN1(10).

Glucagonoma

- Occurs in 3 per cent of patients with MEN1.

- Most cases present over the age of 40 years and tumours are usually large at presentation.

- Classically glucagonomas present with migratory necrolytic erythema, weight loss, anaemia and glucose intolerance. These symptoms are often absent in MEN1.

- Biochemistry: glucose intolerance and a raised fasting plasma glucagon level.

- Over 50 per cent of patients have metastatic disease at the time of diagnosis (10).

- Surgical resection is the treatment of choice, with octreotide and streptozotocin treatment in those with metastatic disease.

- Isolated glucagonomas are rarely due to MEN type1.

VIPomas

- Secrete vasoactive intestinal peptide (VIP) resulting in watery diarrhoea, hypokalaemia and hypochlorhydria.

- Most cases present over the age of 40 years and tumours are large.

- Usually located in the tail of the pancreas.

- VIPomas in children tend to be extrapancreatic and are not associated with MEN (3).

PPomas

- Oversecrete pancreatic polypeptide (PP) but without pathological sequelae (11).

- Found in a large number of patients with MEN.

- It is suggested that PP serum screening can be used as a marker for pancreatic disease (12).

Pituitary disease

- Incidence of pituitary disease in MEN 1 varies from 10 to 90 per cent depending on the series (3, 6).

- Age of onset of tumours, symptoms and signs are similar to non-MEN pituitary tumours (13).

- 60 per cent of tumours secrete prolactin, 25 per cent growth hormone (GH) and 5 per cent adrenocorticotrophin (ACTH); the remaining are non-functioning and present with a mass effect.

- Large pituitary tumours may cause compression of the optic chiasm and subsequent bitemporal homonomous hemianopia, or compression of the remaining pituitary tissue resulting in hypopituitarism.

- Other features are dependant upon the hormone secreted.

- Treatment is usually medical or transphenoidal hypophysectomy, if possible.

- Only 3 per cent of patients with anterior pituitary tumours have MEN type 1.

Other tumours in MEN type 1

A number of other tumours have been described in association with MEN type 1 including thyroid tumours, carcinoid, adrenal cortical tumours and lipomas (6).

Molecular genetics of MEN type 1

MEN type 1 is due to mutations of the *MENIN* gene (11q13). This gene, consisting of 10 exons, was cloned in 1997 (14, 15). The gene encodes a 610 amino acid protein. Mutations have been described in both familial and sporadic cases of MEN type1(16, 17). About 10 per cent of mutations arise *de novo*.

Mutations are described throughout the gene – there appears to be little genotype–phenotype correlation (unlike MEN type2). Most of the mutations are inactivating, suggesting a tumour suppressor function. Approximately 25 per cent are nonsense mutations, 45 per cent frameshift deletions or insertions, 10 per cent inframe deletions or insertions, 5 per cent splice-site mutations and the remainder missense mutations. As the mutations are spread throughout the coding region, mutation screening within any family is time consuming.

Management of MEN type 1

Families with a history consistent with that of MEN type 1 should be referred to a genetics centre for appropriate counselling regarding the condition. If possible, blood should be obtained from an affected member of the family for mutation screening.

At-risk and affected patients should be seen by an endocrinologist on an annual basis for biochemical screening and baseline imaging. This should start from early childhood, as the earliest tumour recorded was at 5 years (18).

If a familial mutation is detected, predictive testing becomes possible and should be offered, following the appropriate counselling, in childhood. If predictive testing for the family mutation is negative, children should be removed from the biochemical screening programme.

Multiple endocrine neoplasia type 2

MEN type 2 is an autosomal dominant condition predisposing to medullary thyroid carcinoma (MTC), parathyroid hyperplasia and phaeochromocytoma. All the subgroups have a high rate of MTC, with 90 per cent of carriers developing the condition (19, 20).

There are three subgroups of MEN type 2: MEN 2a, MEN2b and familial medullary thyroid carcinoma (FMTC).

Multiple endocrine neoplasia type 2a

- Accounts for 65 per cent of MEN2 families (21).
- MTC is present in 95 per cent of patients, which is bilateral and multifocal in 90 per cent of cases; average age of presentation of MTC is 38 years (22).
- MTC is usually the first manifestation of the disease.
- Phaeochromocytoma develops in 50 per cent of patients.
- Hyperparathyroidism develops in 5 to 20 per cent of patients (23); unlike in MEN type 1, this is usually non-recurrent.
- Mutation in the *RET* gene at codon 634 accounts for most families with MTC, phaeochromocytoma and hyperparathyroidism.
- In families without phaeochromocytoma, mutations in codons 609, 611, 618 and 620 of the *RET* gene are more common (24).

Multiple endocrine neoplasia type 2b

- Medullary thyroid carcinoma is very aggressive with an average age of diagnosis of 18 years (22).

- Phaeochromocytoma occurs in 50 per cent of cases at a younger age than MEN type 1.

- Parathyroid disease is usually absent.

- Patients have a characteristic facies, with thick lips, mucocutaneous nodules and marfanoid habitus; hyperplasia of the autonomic ganglia of the intestinal wall are also present (25, 26).

- Most patients have *RET* mutations at codon 918, although mutations at 883 and 922 have been described.

Familial medullary thyroid carcinoma

- Medullary thyroid carcinoma is the only manifestation.

- To avoid misclassifying small families, a kindred should only be described as FMTC if there are more than 10 carriers in the family, multiple carriers or cases in the family over the age of 50 years and adequate screening (4).

- Kindreds with *RET* mutations at codons 609, 611, 618, 620, 768, 791 and 891 have been identified (21).

Molecular genetics of MEN Type 2

Activating mutations in the *RET* proto-oncogene result in MEN type 2. *RET* (10q11.2) was identified as a candidate gene for MEN type 2 in 1993 and mutations were then described in this gene (27, 28). *RET* contains 21 exons and encodes for a tyrosine kinase receptor expressed in the C cell of the thyroid. A single activating mutation of one allele results in a neoplastic transformation (29). All mutations described in MEN type 2 result in gain of function.

There is a marked phenotype–genotype correlation as described above. Mutation screening is therefore easier, especially if the clinical picture is clear.

Management of MEN type 2

Given that mutation screening in MEN type 2 results in detection of mutations in 98 per cent of cases (30), new cases should have mutation screening. Predictive testing can then be offered to at-risk members of the family to determine management. Those patients in whom predictive testing is unavailable should be offered screening by basal and stimulated levels of calcitonin, serum calcium and PTH levels and 24-hour urinary catacholamines from 6 years of age.

Patients affected with, or mutation carriers of, MEN type 2 should be offered prophylactic thyroidectomy, either from the age of detection of the mutation if an adult or from childhood, depending upon the mutation. Patients with mutations resulting in MEN type 2b should have a prophylactic thyroidectomy within the first year of life. Those with mutations resulting from MEN type 2a should have surgery by the age of 5 years (4).

All patients should have screening for phaeochromocytoma using 24-hour urine collections for the measurement of catacholamines or metanephrines. For those patients with MEN type 2a, calcium levels and PTH levels should be undertaken. All patients should be referred to an endocrinologist for ongoing screening.

Young, isolated cases of MTC should be screened for *RET* mutations. If the routine mutation screening is negative, then sequencing (currently within research labs) of the remaining exons should be undertaken. With a negative mutation screen there is a 0.18 per cent chance of MEN 2 (4).

References

1 **Wermer P** Genetic aspects of adenomatosis of endocrine glands. *Am J Med* 1954; **16**:363–371.

2 **Sipple JH**. The association of phaeochromocytoma with carcinoma of the thyroid gland. *Am J Med* 1961; **31**: 163–166.

3 **Marx SJ**. Multiple endocrine neoplasia type 1. In: Vogelstein B, Kinzler KW, eds. *The genetic basis of human cancer*, 1998, pp. 489–506. New York: McGraw-Hill.

4 **Brandi ML, Gagel RF, Angeli A, Bilezikian JP, Beck-Peccoz P, Bordi C, et al.** Guidelines for diagnosis and therapy of MEN type 1 and type 2. *J Clin Endocrinol Metab* 2001; **86**:5658–5671.

5 **Giraud S, Zhang CX, Serova-Sinilnikova OM, Wautot V, Salandre J, Buisson N, et al.** Germ-line mutation analysis in patients with multiple endocrine neoplasia type 1 and related disorders. *Am J Hum Genet* 1998; **63**:455–467.

6 **Trump D, Farren B, Wooding C, Pang JT, Besser GM, Buchanan KD, et al.** Clinical studies of multiple endocrine neoplasia type 1 (MEN1). *Q J Med* 1996; **89**:653–669.

7 **Skogseid B, Eriksson B, Lundqvist G, Lorelius LE, Rastad J, Wide L, et al.** Multiple endocrine neoplasia type 1: a 10-year prospective screening study in four kindreds. *J Clin Endocrinol Metab* 1991; **73**:281–287.

8 **Uchino S, Noguchi S, Sato M, Yamashita H, Watanabe S, Murakami T, et al.** Screening of the Men1 gene and discovery of germ-line and somatic mutations in apparently sporadic parathyroid tumors. *Cancer Res* 2000; **60**:5553–5557.

9 **Zollinger RM, Ellison EH**. Primary peptic ulcerations of the jejunum associated with islet cell tumours of the pancreas. *Ann Surgery* 1955; **142**:709–728.

10 **Pannett AAJ, Thakker RV**. Multiple endocrine neoplasia type 1. *Endocrine-Related Cancer* 1999; **6**:449–473.

11 **Eckhauser FE, Cheung PS, Vinik AI, Strodel WE, Lloyd RV, Thompson NW**. Nonfunctioning malignant neuroendocrine tumors of the pancreas. *Surgery* 1986; **100**:978–988.

12 **Skogseid B, Oberg K**. Prospective screening in multiple endocrine neoplasia type 1. *Henry Ford Hosp Med J* 1992; **40**:167–170.

13 **Vasen HF, Lamers CB, Lips CJ**. Screening for the multiple endocrine neoplasia syndrome type I. A study of 11 kindreds in The Netherlands. *Arch Intern Med* 1989; **149**:2717–2722.

14 **Chandrasekharappa SC, Guru SC, Manickam P, Olufemi SE, Collins FS, Emmert-Buck MR, et al.** Positional cloning of the gene for multiple endocrine neoplasia-type 1. *Science* 1997; **276**:404–407.

15 Lemmens I, Van de Ven WJ, Kas K, Zhang CX, Giraud S, Wautot V, *et al.* Identification of the multiple endocrine neoplasia type 1 (MEN1) gene. The European Consortium on MEN1. *Hum Mol Genet* 1997; **6**:1177–1183.

16 Marx SJ, Agarwal SK, Kester MB, Heppner C, Kim YS, Emmert-Buck MR, *et al.* Germline and somatic mutation of the gene for multiple endocrine neoplasia type 1 (MEN1). *J Intern Med* 1998; **243**:447–453.

17 Agarwal SK, Kester MB, Debelenko LV, Heppner C, Emmert-Buck MR, Skarulis MC, *et al.* Germline mutations of the MEN1 gene in familial multiple endocrine neoplasia type 1 and related states. *Hum Mol Genet* 1997; **6**:1169–1175.

18 Stratakis CA, Schussheim DH, Freedman SM, Keil MF, Pack SD, Agarwal SK, *et al.* Pituitary macroadenoma in a 5-year-old: an early expression of multiple endocrine neoplasia type 1. *J Clin Endocrinol Metab* 2000; **85**:4776–4780.

19 Ponder BA, Ponder MA, Coffey R, Pembrey ME, Gagel RF, Telenius-Berg M, *et al.* Risk estimation and screening in families of patients with medullary thyroid carcinoma. *Lancet* 1988; **1**:397–401.

20 Easton DF, Ponder MA, Cummings T, Gagel RF, Hansen HH, Reichlin S, *et al.* The clinical and screening age-at-onset distribution for the MEN-2 syndrome. *Am J Hum Genet* 1989; **44**:208–215.

21 Eng C, Clayton D, Schuffenecker I, Lenoir G, Cote G, Gagel RF, *et al.* The relationship between specific RET proto-oncogene mutations and disease phenotype in multiple endocrine neoplasia type 2. International RET mutation consortium analysis. *JAMA* 1996; **276**:1575–1579.

22 Ponder BAJ. Multiple endocrine neoplasia type 2. In: Vogelstein B, Kinzler KW, eds. *The genetic basis of human cancer*, 1998, pp.475–487. New York: McGraw-Hill.

23 Schuffenecker I, Virally-Monod M, Brohet R, Goldgar D, Conte-Devolx B, Leclerc L, *et al.* Risk and penetrance of primary hyperparathyroidism in multiple endocrine neoplasia type 2A families with mutations at codon 634 of the RET proto-oncogene. Groupe D'etude des Tumeurs a Calcitonine. *J Clin Endocrinol Metab* 1998; **83**:487–491.

24 Mulligan LM, Eng C, Healey CS, Clayton D, Kwok JB, Gardner E, *et al.* Specific mutations of the RET proto-oncogene are related to disease phenotype in MEN 2A and FMTC. *Nat Genet* 1994; **6**:70–74.

25 Carney JA, Go VL, Sizemore GW, Hayles AB. Alimentary-tract ganglioneuromatosis. A major component of the syndrome of multiple endocrine neoplasia, type 2b. *N Engl J Med* 1976; **295**:1287–1291.

26 Williams ED, Pollock DJ. Multiple mucosal neuromata with endocrine tumours: a syndrome allied to von Recklinghausen's disease. *J Pathol Bacteriol* 1966; **91**:71–80.

27 Gardner E, Papi L, Easton DF, Cummings T, Jackson CE, Kaplan M, *et al.* Genetic linkage studies map the multiple endocrine neoplasia type 2 loci to a small interval on chromosome 10q11.2. *Hum Mol Genet* 1993; **2**:241–246.

28 Mulligan LM, Kwok JB, Healey CS, Elsdon MJ, Eng C, Gardner E, *et al.* Germ-line mutations of the RET proto-oncogene in multiple endocrine neoplasia type 2A. *Nature* 1993; **363**:458–460.

29 Santoro M, Carlomagno F, Romano A, Bottaro DP, Dathan NA, Grieco M, *et al.* Activation of RET as a dominant transforming gene by germline mutations of MEN2A and MEN2B. *Science* 1995; **267**:381–383.

30 Berndt I, Reuter M, Saller B, Frank-Raue K, Groth P, Grussendorf M, *et al.* A new hot spot for mutations in the ret protooncogene causing familial medullary thyroid carcinoma and multiple endocrine neoplasia type 2A. *J Clin Endocrinol Metab* 1998; **83**:770–774.

Chapter 15

Gorlin syndrome

D. Gareth R. Evans

Introduction

Gorlin syndrome, which is also widely known as basal cell naevus syndrome (BCNS) or nevoid basal cell carcinoma syndrome (NBCCS), was first fully delineated in 1960 (1). It is an autosomal dominant condition with high penetrance, although occasional patients may not have clear features on clinical assessment, even in adult life (2).

Over 100 clinical features have been associated with Gorlin syndrome, which are variable both within and between families (3). The condition is characterized by the development of multiple jaw (odontogenic) keratocysts in the second and third decades and basal cell carcinomas (BCCs) in the third decade onwards. Not every patient will develop both problems, with occasional patients with the condition developing neither into old age.

About 60 per cent of Gorlin syndrome patients have a recognizable clinical appearance with macrocephaly, bossing of the forehead, coarse facial features and facial milia. The shoulders slope downwards, often due to a Sprengel deformity of the scapula. Most individuals have skeletal anomalies such as bifid, splayed, or fused ribs and/or wedge-shaped vertebrae. These latter abnormalities, while usually being harmless, can lead to chest deformity with a pectus excavatum and abnormal chest shape, as well as scoliosis. Ectopic calcification, particularly in the falx cerebri, is present in over 90 per cent by 20 years of age, and this often appears in sheets (lammellar calcification). Congenital malformations are found in about 5 per cent.

Individuals with Gorlin syndrome are at risk of developing the childhood brain malignancy medulloblastoma, which occurs in 5 per cent of cases (2), and cardiac and ovarian fibromas (4, 5). Malignant transformation has been described rarely in the ovarian fibromas (6), but they usually remain benign. They can, however, reach a large size and are often calcified.

Prevalence

There have been very few studies of disease prevalence. The most quoted figure, 1 in 57 000, comes from a study of 4 million in north-west England (7). However, an increase in diagnosis has led to a revision of that figure to about 1 in 30 000. Indeed, the true figure may be somewhat larger due to lack of recognition of milder cases. A study in Australia gave a minimum prevalence of 1 in 164 000 (8), but probably also suffers from underdiagnosis. Although birth incidence could be higher, the near normal life expectancy means that birth incidence should be close to the true disease prevalence figure.

Diagnosis

A clinical diagnosis can be made when a patient fulfils the criteria in Table 15.1, and a checklist for diagnosis is shown in Table 15.2. There is a typical facial gestalt in Gorlin syndrome, but clinical examination must include the following, along with the following investigations:

- Measurement of head circumference for macrocephaly
- Careful examination of the skin for BCCs, naevi and milia
- Examination of hands and feet for plantar/ palmar pits
- AP and lateral radiographs of the skull
- An orthopantogram
- A chest radiograph
- A spinal radiograph.

Naevi and BCC

Characteristic features of the naevi and BCCs are shown in Fig. 15.1. The naevi can range in colour from brown through orange to pink and can usually be distinguished from moles. Features of local invasion that suggest an active BCC are a rolled edge, bleeding, crusting and a crater-like appearance. The pits are particularly useful and are

Table 15.1 Diagnostic criteria for Gorlin syndrome – a diagnosis can be made when two major and one minor or one major and three minor criteria are fulfilled (5)

Major criteria	Minor criteria
Lamellar (sheet-like) falx calcification or clear calcification <20 years	Childhood medulloblastoma – now often called primitive neuroectodermal tumour (PNET)
Jaw keratocyst	Lymphomesenteric or pleural cysts
Palmar/ plantar pits (2 or more)	Macrocephaly (OFC>97th centile)
First-degree relative with Gorlin syndrome	Cleft lip/palate
Multiple BCCs (2 or more) – careful thought needed for decreased BCC risk in dark-skinned people and increased risk for Caucasians in hot sunny climates	Vertebral anomalies Bifid/splayed/extra ribs Bifid vertebrae Polydactyly Ovarian and/or cardiac fibroma Ocular anomalies – cataract, developmental defects

OFC = occipito-frontal circumference.

Table 15.2 Features to aid diagnosis of Gorlin Syndrome

History/examination	Features
Clinical history	Any operations to remove "cysts" or skin lesions BCCs – often called "rodent ulcer" Any dental operation – especially for a bone cyst Childhood medulloblastoma Removal of cysts from unusual sites – bronchogenic/ lymphomesenteric Benign tumours of the ovaries/heart (fibromas)
Family history	Multiple BCCs/ jaw cysts/medulloblastoma or other features as above
Clinical examination of skin	Typical "rodent ulcers" BCCs Milia (milk spot lesions) particularly on forehead Brown/orange/pink naevi Punched out pits in the palms and soles
Dysmorphology	Head circumference >97th centile Frontal and parietal bossing Hypertelorism Sloping shoulders Course facial features Cleft lip and/or palate or high arched palate Extra fingers – polydactyly
Radiographs Chest	Bifid/splayed/ fused/missing ribs
Spine	Bifid/wedge-shaped vertebrae, scoliosis
Skull	Calcification in the falx cerebri
Orthopantogram (panorex)	Jaw keratocysts

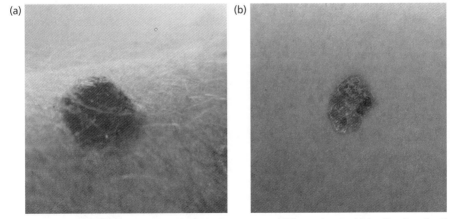

Fig. 15.1 (a) Pink/orange and raised basal cell naevus and (b) crusting and bleeding basal cell carcinoma in a patient with Gorlin syndrome. See also colour plate section.

more pronounced when the hands and feet are soaked in warm water. They may appear as white "punched out" or pink/red "pin prick" lesions.

Radiology

Typical features from radiological investigations are shown in Figs 15.2–15.5. If these investigations have already been undertaken, try to obtain the original films rather than repeating them, as patients with Gorlin syndrome are unusually susceptible to the adverse effects of X-irradiation. Bifid ribs or vertebrae and falx calcification are often not mentioned on routine X-ray reports, as these features are also found as normal variations in the general population.

There is no routine laboratory test to aid diagnosis and although chromosomal translocations or large cytogenetically detectable deletions on chromosome 9 can cause Gorlin syndrome, chromosome analysis is rarely helpful. However, fluorescence *in situ* hybridization (FISH) may help detect the 5 to 10 per cent of patients with large

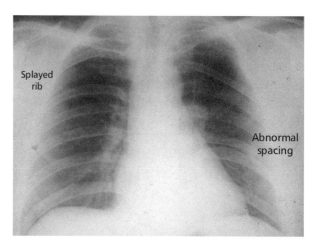

Fig. 15.2 Chest radiograph in Gorlin syndrome showing rib anomalies, demonstrated by abnormal spacing.

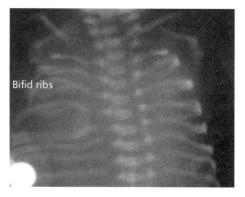

Fig. 15.3 Chest radiograph in a neonate with Gorlin syndrome showing severe rib anomalies.

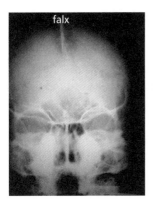
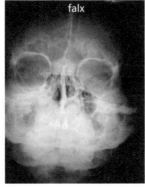

Fig. 15.4 Skull radiographs in Gorlin syndrome showing typical falx calcification.

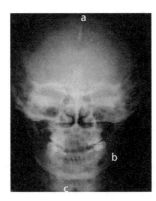

Fig. 15.5 Skull radiograph showing three major features of Gorlin syndrome: (a) falx calcification, (b) jaw cyst and (c) a bifid vertebrae.

deletions. Full mutation analysis is certainly helpful when identifying a clearly pathogenic mutation, but missense mutations can be difficult to interpret and a negative test does not rule out Gorlin syndrome in an equivocal case. This is because, as yet, no analysis is 100 per cent sensitive and mosaic cases in which the mutation is present in <10 per cent of lymphocytes are often missed.

Clinical progression of Gorlin syndrome

Macrocephaly

The first feature that is likely to be identified is macrocephaly. A large proportion of babies with Gorlin syndrome have to be born by Caesarean section due to the large head size. After birth the head growth chart often follows that of an arrested hydrocephalus pattern, but there is rarely true hydrocephalus. The head circumference increases above the 97th centile until 10 to 18 months and then drops back towards the 97th centile, maintaining that level into adult life. The large head size may also contribute to some delay in motor milestones, although as yet there is no psychometric evidence for more global delay.

Birth defects

Birth defects, such as cleft lip, palate or both (5 per cent), polydactyly and severe eye anomalies do occur. A range of eye problems from simple strabismus (squint) to microphthalmia, cataract and retinal changes have now been described (9). Severe skeletal defects due to multiple rib/ vertebral anomalies have also been reported (10). Open spina bifida is uncommon.

Medulloblastoma

During the first few years, the major concern is that of medulloblastoma, with about 5 per cent of patients with Gorlin syndrome developing this malignant tumour. The tumour tends to be of desmoplastic histology and has a favourable prognosis (2). Peak incidence of medulloblastoma in Gorlin syndrome is at about 2 years of age, compared to 7 years in its sporadic form (2, 7). Use of radiotherapy can lead to the development of thousands of BCCs in the radiation field (6, 7, 11) and should only be used, if necessary, through as few skin portholes as possible.

Jaw keratocysts

These can start at around 5 years of age, but the peak is in the teenage years. They present usually as swellings, which may be painless. Untreated they can lead to major tooth disruption and fracture of the jaw. Jaw cysts become less frequent after 30 years of age and it is unusual for keratocysts to occur *de novo* after this.

Naevi

Browny/pink/ orange naevi may occur in early childhood and if excised may have the histological appearance of BCC, which can create considerable alarm. Many naevi lie quiescent without evidence of aggressive behaviour, but active BCCs may grow from existing nevi (which can be very numerous). BCCs may, however, appear from virtually blemish-free skin as a typical rodent ulcer. They will usually crust, bleed and ulcerate, but can also present as a localized infection. It is not uncommon for BCCs to be treated with multiple courses of antibiotic and steroid cream in undiagnosed Gorlin syndrome patients. BCCs can occur in early childhood but in general do not present until late teenage/early adulthood. They become more frequent with age. They are most frequent in type 1 skin (white skin that burns but never tans – Celtic skin) and in those with excessive UV light exposure. BCCs are a particular problem in the radiation field following radiotherapy.

Other skin manifestations include milia, which can be very numerous over the facial area, and meibomian cysts in the eyelids. Sebaceous cysts are also common, especially around the knees. Skin tags (especially around the neck) often have the histological appearance of BCCs but do not act aggressively.

Table 15.3 Cumulative percentage risk of feature in lifetime or to a specified age

Disease feature	Frequency (%)	Age range
BCC <20 years	20	10 years upwards, unless exposed to excessive UV/radiation
BCC >20 years	80	
Odontogenic keratocysts <20 years of age	35	5 years onwards
Odontogenic keratocysts >20 years of age	70	
Macrocephaly (OFC >97th centile)	90	Birth onwards
Falx calcification <20 years	30–50	Age related, unusual <10 years unless irradiated
Falx calcification >20 years	>90	
Palmar and plantar pits	60–70	Birth onwards, but usually more prominent in adults
Rib anomalies	40–50	Birth
Vertebral anomalies	30–40	Birth
Ovarian fibroma	15–20	Puberty onwards in women
Ocular anomalies	20	Birth
Medulloblastoma	5	Birth to 7 years
Cleft lip/palate	3–5	Birth
Cardiac fibroma	2	Birth
Bronchogenic cysts	1–2	10–30 years
Lymphomesenteric cysts	1–2	10–40 years
Polydactyly	1–2	Birth
Lymphoma	1–2	Adulthood

Other features

There is no evidence that life expectancy in Gorlin syndrome is significantly different from average and the risk of other malignant tumours is not clearly increased, although lymphoma and meningioma have been reported. None occur at a frequency that warrants surveillance above that offered to members of the general population. The major problem is with cosmesis and the requirement for multiple skin and, usually to a lesser extent, jaw treatment. The risks of the various disease features are presented in Table 15.3.

Management of Gorlin syndrome

Gorlin syndrome is one of a number of autosomal dominant conditions that may benefit from a genetic register. It is important that each affected individual has a point of contact with an expert who is experienced with the condition. This may be an oral

Table 15.4 Treatments available for BCCs

Treatment	General population	Gorlin syndrome
Simple excision	Routine	Routine, but due to potential numbers may need to consider alternatives
Oral etretinate	Unusual	Has shown effectiveness, but side-effects common and should be avoided if pregnancy possible; may be poorly tolerated
Topical 5 fluorouracil (effudix)	Occasional	Can be effective with early lesions, but after initial control an aggressive lesion may require urgent attention
Laser treatment	Frequently used	May be useful for early, thin lesions and leaves less scarring than surgery
Radiotherapy	Routine treatment in 1950s to 90s, less frequent now	Should be avoided
Photodynamic therapy (PDT)	Not readily available	Showing initial good promise; not good with deep lesions although may improve with systemic treatment

surgeon, dermatologist, plastic surgeon, paediatrician or clinical geneticist. Awareness of the risk of medulloblastoma in the first years of life is important and may justify 6-monthly checks. However, there is no evidence for the efficacy of regular brain scans and frequent CT should be avoided. There is, nonetheless, probably justification for regular (12–18 monthly) jaw radiographs (orthopantograms) from around 8 years of age. Keratocysts identified early in life will usually need surgical excision.

The skin should also be checked at least annually and patients should be allowed easy access if they have skin problems in the meantime. The sheer number of lesions means that early treatment is essential to prevent long-term cosmetic problems, particularly facially. Surgical excision is now supplemented by a number of other options (Table 15.4). Strong advice about avoiding excessive sun exposure is important. Use of a complete sun block and covering the skin by using long sleeves, high collars and hats is important.

Radiotherapy should be avoided in the treatment of BCCs or other tumours in Gorlin syndrome unless absolutely vital. The long-term effects of radiotherapy can be devastating, particularly after craniospinal irradiation for medulloblastoma (Fig. 15.6). Indeed most paediatric oncologists would use chemotherapy now in the younger medulloblastoma patients.

Surveillance is probably not necessary for the other disease features. Birth defects of clinical significance will usually be apparent at birth (e.g. clefting). Although cardiac fibromas can cause serious problems in early life – these tumours are uncommon (2 per cent) and many are asymptomatic. Ovarian fibromas, although much more frequent (20 per cent), have a very low malignant potential and do not appear to affect the ability to become pregnant. If operative treatment is required, preservation of

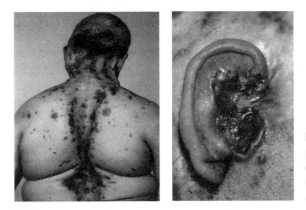

Fig. 15.6 Gorlin syndrome patient 25 years post craniospinal irradiation for medulloblastoma. See also colour plate section.

ovarian tissue is recommended, although there may be a risk of recurrence (12). Ovarian fibromas occasionally twist and can cause torsion of the ovary. Other features such as mesenteric and pleural cysts are rare and do not justify screening. The skeletal anomalies are rarely a cause of disability, and ocular abnormalities, although frequent, are again mostly found incidentally.

Molecular genetics

Gailani *et al* (13) found that 40 per cent of BCCs studied had deletions of the proximal region on the long arm of chromosome 9. The condition was linked to that region using affected families with no locus heterogeneity (14). The gene itself (*PTCH*) was identified as a homologue of the Drosophila gene *PATCHED* (15). As the mean age at onset of medulloblastoma in Gorlin patients is 2 years, compared to over 7 years in the general population, and there is loss of the normal allele in tumours (2), this confirms *PTCH* as a tumour suppressor gene in medulloblastoma as well as basal cell carcinoma. Loss of heterozygosity also appears to be the mechanism for the jaw cysts, whilst the congenital malformations are likely to be due to alterations in the concentration of the *PTCH* gene product in the exquisitely dosage-sensitive hedgehog signalling pathway (16).

The *PTCH* gene consists of 23 exons and encodes an integral membrane protein with 12 transmembrane regions, two extracellular loops, and a putative sterol-sensing domain. PTCH protein binds the secreted factor sonic hedgehog (SHH) and functions as the SHH receptor. PTCH represses the signalling activity of the coreceptor smoothened (SMOH) and, when in complex with SHH, this repression is inhibited and signalling ensues.

There are at least three forms of the PTCH protein in human cells (15). *PTCH2*, highly homologous to *PTCH1*, was isolated from chromosome 1p32.1–32.3 (17). Mutations were found in one sporadic medulloblastoma and one sporadic BCC. No mutations in *PTCH2* were found in 11 sporadic and 11 familial BCNS patients in whom *PTCH1* screening by single strand conformation polymorphism analysis (SSCP) had been negative.

There is currently no firm evidence for a genotype–phenotype correlation in Gorlin syndrome (18). There is sufficient variation in a single family to believe that chance, environmental exposure and possibly modifier genes could account for most of the variation.

Clinical molecular testing

Molecular genetic testing is available in a number of laboratories worldwide. Service testing is possible in the United Kingdom and through commercial labs in the US. The most sensitive technique is direct sequencing, but combinations of routine mutation scanning techniques such as SSCP, denaturing gel gradient electrophoresis (DGGE) and chemical cleavage have a high level of sensitivity. Combining these with a deletion strategy (FISH, Southern blotting, dosage PCR) detects over 90 per cent of gene aberrations in the second generation. Mutation detection may be less sensitive in the first affected individual in a family, probably because of mosaics. Mosaic Gorlin syndrome could be ascertained by testing DNA from tumours. An identical mutation found in two or more tumours but not present in lymphocyte DNA, or at a lower concentration, will strongly suggest mosaicism.

Identifying a pathogenic mutation (nonsense, frameshift, deletion/insertion, splice site) will confirm a clinical diagnosis. Due to technical limitations, a negative mutation screen cannot exclude Gorlin syndrome but will at least be partially reassuring in an individual falling short of clinical diagnostic criteria as long as a comprehensive analysis has been performed. Missense mutations are relatively common but may be difficult to interpret in an isolated patient falling short of diagnostic criteria.

Linkage

If a family mutation is not identified, linkage analysis may be helpful in determining whether equivocal individuals have the condition. In order to carry out linkage analysis, two affected patients need to be present in the family and preferably blood from both of these should be available. Care must be taken in the second generation as individuals may be falsely labelled as affected if the progenitor (first affected patient) is mosaic (19, 20), which could be suspected if they are more mildly affected.

Differential diagnosis of Gorlin syndrome

The differential diagnosis depends on the initial mode of presentation.

- In a baby with macrocephaly and other birth defects, a limited range of overgrowth syndromes such as Sotos and Beckwith–Wiedemann should be considered.
- Presentation with multiple BCCs or jaw keratocysts is usually Gorlin syndrome, with the diagnosis established by clinical examination and radiographs. However,

arsenic exposure may cause multiple BCCs in individuals who do not have Gorlin syndrome.

♦ A condition of trichoepitheliomas, milia and cylindromas presenting in the second and third decades is inherited as an autosomal dominant trait (21) (Online Mendelian Inheritance in Man database (OMIM) 601605). The milia are miniature trichoepitheliomas and appear only in sun-exposed areas. The trichoepitheliomas may degenerate into BCCs. Patients with this condition do not have the skeletal features of Gorlin syndrome.

♦ Multiple BCCs, follicular atrophoderma on the dorsum of hands and feet, decreased sweating and hypotrichosis are features of Bazex syndrome (22) (OMIM 301845). The pitting on the backs of the hands is reminiscent of orange peel and quite unlike the pits of Gorlin syndrome. The inheritance pattern is either autosomal or X-linked dominant.

♦ A dominantly inherited condition reminiscent of Bazex syndrome has been reported in a single family, Rombo syndrome (23) (OMIM 180730) is characterized by vermiculate atrophoderma, milia, hypotrichosis, trichoepitheliomas, BCCs and peripheral vasodilation with cyanosis. The skin is normal until later childhood, BCCs develop later and there is no reduction in sweating.

♦ A single family with another dominant syndrome (whether autosomal or X-linked could not be determined) of hypotrichosis, BCCs, milia and excessive sweating was reported by Oley *et al.* (24) (OMIM 109390).

♦ There appear to be families where BCCs in the absence of other features segregate in an autosomal dominant manner. These families do not appear to have mutations in *PTCH*.

References

1 **Gorlin RJ, Goltz RW**. Multiple nevoid basal-cell epithelioma, jaw cysts and bifid rib: a syndrome. *New Eng J Med* 1960; **262**:908–912.

2 **Cowan R, Hoban P, Kelsey A, Birch JM, Evans DGR**. The gene for the naevoid basal cell carcinoma (Gorlin) syndrome acts as a tumour suppressor gene in medulloblastoma. *Br J Cancer* 1997; **76**:141–145.

3 **Farndon PA, Gorlin RJ A**. Naevoid basal cell carcinoma syndrome. In: A Eeles R, Ponder B, Easton D, Horwich A, eds. *Genetic predisposition to cancer*, 1996, Vol. 1, pp.164–183. London: Chapman and Hall.

4 **Gorlin RJ**. Nevoid basal cell carcinoma syndrome. *Medicine* 1987; **66**:98–113.

5 **Evans DGR, Ladusans E, Rimmer S, Burnell LD, Thakker N, Farndon PA**. Complications of the naevoid basal cell carcinoma syndrome: results of a population based study. *J Med Genet* 1993; **30**:460–464.

6 **Strong LC**. Genetic and environmental interactions. *Cancer* 1977; **40**:1861–1866.

7 **Evans DGR, Farndon PA, Burnell LD, Gattameneni R, Birch J**. The incidence of Gorlin syndrome in 173 consecutive cases of medulloblastoma. *Br J Cancer* 1991; **64**:959–961.

8 **Shanley S, Ratcliffe J, Hockey A**, *et al.* Nevoid basal cell carcinoma syndrome: review of 118 affected individuals. *Am J Med Genet* 1994; **50**:282–290.

9 Black GC, Mazerolle CJ, Wang Y, *et al.* Abnormalities of the vitreoretinal interface caused by dysregulated Hedgehog signalling during retinal development. *Hum Mol Genet* 2003; **12**:3269–3276.

10 Evans DGR, Sims DG, Donnai D. Family implications of neonatal Gorlin syndrome. *Arch Dis Child* 1991; **66**:1162–1163.

11 Evans DGR, Birch J, Orton C. Brain tumours and the occurrence of severe invasive BCCs in first degree relatives with Gorlin syndrome. *Br J Neurosurg* 1991; **5**:643–646.

12 Seracchioli R, Bagnoli A, Colombo FM, Missiroli S, Venturoli S. Conservative treatment of recurrent ovarian fibromas in a young patient affected by Gorlin syndrome. *Hum Reproduction* 2001; **6**:1261–1263.

13 Gailani M, Leffell DJ, Bale AE. Evidence for a tumour suppressor gene on chromosome 9 in BCCs of the skin. *Am J Hum Genet* 1991; **49** suppl:454.

14 Farndon P, Delmastro RG, Evans DGR, Kilpatrick MW. Localisation of the gene for Gorlin (Naevoid basal cell carcinoma) syndrome on chromosome 9. *Lancet* 1992;. i:581–582.

15 Hahn H, Wicking C, Zaphiropoulous PG, *et al.* Mutations of the human homolog of Drosophila patched in the naevoid basal cell carcinoma syndrome. *Cell* 1996; **85**:841–851.

16 Villavicencio EH, Walterhouse DO, Iannaccone PM. The sonic hedgehog-patched-gli pathway in human development and disease. *Am J Hum Genet* 2000; **67**:1047–1054.

17 Smyth I, Narang MA, Evans T, *et al.* Isolation and characterization of human patched 2 (PTCH2), a putative tumour suppressor gene in basal cell carcinoma and medulloblastoma on chromosome 1p32. *Hum Mol Gen* 1999; **8**:291–297.

18 Wicking C, Shanley S, Smyth I, *et al.* Most germ-line mutations in the nevoid basal cell carcinoma syndrome lead to a premature termination of the PATCHED protein, and no genotype-phenotype correlations are evident. *Am J Hum Genet* 1997; **60**:21–26.

19 Evans DGR, Wallace AJ, Wu CL, Truman L, Ramsden RT, Strachan T. Somatic mosaicism: a common mechanism for sporadic disease in tumour prone syndromes? Lessons from type 2 neurofibromatosis. *Am J Hum Genet* 1998; **63**:727–736.

20 Moyhuddin A, Baser ME, Watson C, *et al.* Somatic mosaicism in neurofibromatosis 2: prevalence and risk of disease transmission to offspring. *J Med Genet* 2003; **40**:459–463.

21 Harada H, Hashimoto K, Ko MSH. The gene for multiple familial trichoepithelioma maps to chromosome 9p21. *J Invest Derm* 1996; **107**:41–43.

22 Bazex A, Dupre A, Christol B. Atrophodermic folliculaire, proliferations baso-cellulaires et hypotrichose. *Ann Derm Syph* 1966; **93**:241–254.

23 Michaelsson G, Olsson E, Westermark P. The Rombo syndrome: a familial disorder with vermiculate atrophoderma, milia, hypotrichosis, trichoepitheliomas, basal cell carcinomas and peripheral vasodilation with cyanosis. *Acta Derm Venerol* 1981; **61**:497–503.

24 Oley CA, Sharpe H, Chenevix-Trench G. Basal cell carcinomas, coarse sparse hair, and milia. *Am J Med Genet* 1992; **43**:799–804.

Chapter 16

Li–Fraumeni syndrome

J. M. Birch

Introduction

In 1969, Li and Fraumeni identified four families in which siblings or cousins were affected with soft tissue sarcoma during early childhood. There was a high incidence of cancers diagnosed at unusually early ages in the families of these children, including breast cancer, sarcomas and acute leukaemia. Li and Fraumeni concluded that these familial clusters of cancers were due to inherited predisposition (1, 2).

Subsequently, systematic epidemiological studies strongly supported the notion of genetic susceptibility and established that the main syndrome cancers were bone and soft tissue sarcoma, breast cancer, brain tumours, adrenocortical carcinoma (ACC) and acute leukaemia (3–7). Segregation analysis of families of children with soft tissue sarcoma demonstrated that the cancer distribution in the families was compatible with a rare autosomal dominant gene (gene frequency 0.00002), with a penetrance approaching 50 per cent by age 30 years and 90 per cent by age 60 (8, 9).

Li *et al.* proposed clinical criteria for the diagnosis of Li–Fraumeni syndrome (7) (Table 16.1). These criteria have been widely accepted, and such families are hereafter referred to as having classic Li–Fraumeni syndrome (LFS). An example of a family with classic LFS is shown in Fig. 16.1.

Table 16.1 Criteria for diagnosis of Li–Fraumeni or Li–Fraumeni like syndrome

Li–Fraumeni syndrome (7)	Li–Fraumeni-like syndrome (14)
Proband <45 years with a sarcoma	Proband <45 years with childhood tumour, sarcoma, brain tumour or adrenocortical tumour
Plus 1st degree relative <45 years with any cancer	Plus 1st or 2nd degree relative in the same lineage with typical LFS tumour at any age
Plus additional 1st or 2nd degree relative in the same lineage aged <45 years with any cancer or a sarcoma at any age	Plus another 1st or 2nd degree relative in the same lineage with any cancer <60 years

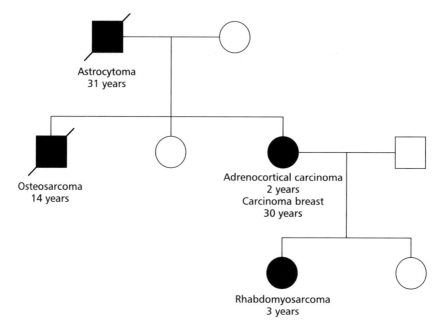

Fig. 16.1 A family with Li–Fraumeni syndrome.

The genetic basis of LFS

Malkin *et al.* adopted a candidate gene approach and analysed the *TP53* gene in five LFS families (10). Mutations in the *TP53* gene had been found in tumour tissue from sporadic sarcomas, brain tumours, leukaemias and carcinoma of the breast. In addition, mice with a constitutional *TP53* mutation had been shown to develop bone and soft tissue sarcomas, and other tumours, at an increased level (11). Germline mutations of *TP53* were found in all five families (10). Shortly after this report, a sixth LFS family with a germline *TP53* mutation was published (12). Subsequently, many groups throughout the world have reported such mutations in patients and families with clusters of LFS-associated cancers. To date there are nearly 300 published germline *TP53* mutations of confirmed or probable biological significance (13).

Germline *TP53* mutations in cancer families

It was apparent that germline *TP53* mutations were not confined to classic LFS families and that mutations in *TP53* could not be detected in all families. Three groups analysed series of LFS families and reported germline *TP53* mutations in 50 per cent (14–16). However, the methods used may have missed some mutations. With more comprehensive methods a rate of 75 per cent for mutations in LFS families was reported (17).

Many families who do not strictly conform to the LFS criteria have been found to carry *TP53* mutations. Birch *et al.* (14) defined these families as Li–Fraumeni-like (LFL) families (Table 16.1). In comprehensive analyses of 19 LFL families, germline *TP53* mutations were detected in nine (47 per cent) (17,18). In the literature, there are a further 28 LFL families with germline *TP53* mutations. Therefore these criteria appear to select families with a high likelihood of carrying such mutations.

Many groups have analysed the frequency of germline *TP53* mutations in patients with LFS-associated cancers. The selection criteria vary between studies with respect to age of onset of cancers, family history and presence of multiple tumours. Results can be summarized as follows:

Sarcomas: about 3 per cent of early onset osteosarcoma demonstrate germline mutations but mutations occur in up to 30 per cent of cases with a relevant family history or multiple primaries. In childhood rhabdomyosarcoma about 10 per cent are associated with mutations, but at very young ages, mutations may occur in more than 20 per cent (19–24).

Brain tumours: across all unselected series of brain tumours, about 5 per cent carried mutations but higher frequencies were seen with high grade gliomas, significant family histories or multiple tumours (25–31).

Breast cancers: collectively over 800 unselected breast cancer patients have been analysed and only two germline mutations were found: but amongst patients aged under 40 and under 30 years respectively, incidences of 1 per cent and 4 per cent respectively have been reported (32–37).

Adrenocortical carcinoma: four groups have analysed unselected series of childhood ACC. Wagner *et al.* (38) found mutations in three of six cases. Varley *et al.* (39), using comprehensive molecular methods, found germline *TP53* mutations in 11 of 14 (85 per cent) sporadic cases. Ribeiro *et al.* (40) analysed 36 childhood cases of ACC in Brazil, which has an incidence of ACC 10 to 15 times higher than most other countries (41). The same germline *TP53* mutation, a single base change at codon 337 (Arg to His), was found in 35 of these children. These observations were confirmed in an independent series of 37 adult and 18 childhood cases of ACC also from Brazil. The same codon 337 mutation was identified in 14 children and five adults (41). This may either be due to a founder effect or an environmental determinant present in the relevant area of Brazil resulting in *TP53* germline mutagenesis.

Multiple primaries: two series of patients with multiple primaries have been analysed (42–44). Combining the results, four of 64 were found to carry *TP53* mutations. It is noteworthy that in the four cases both the first and subsequent primaries were generally consistent with the LFS tumour spectrum.

Many of these studies analysed small series and used sub-optimal mutation detection methods. Therefore, the true mutation frequencies must be regarded as uncertain.

Distribution and frequency of germline *TP53* mutations

The *TP53* tumour suppressor gene encodes a multifunctional protein, which is involved in cell cycle control, apoptosis, differentiation and development, transcription, DNA replication, DNA repair and maintenance of genomic stability. The p53 protein is organized into five structural and functional regions, including a central sequence-specific DNA binding domain. The crystal structure of the core DNA binding domain consists of a large β-sandwich acting as a scaffold to two large loops and a loop–sheet–helix which together make all the interactions with DNA (45). Somatic *TP53* mutations are common in many human cancers. Unlike most tumour suppressor genes, in which deletions are the most frequent type of mutation, 87 per cent of somatic *TP53* mutations are single base substitutions. Just over 90 per cent of somatic mutations included in the International Agency for Research on Cancer (IARC) *TP53* database are located in the DNA binding domain. Certain hotspot codons have emerged which are far more frequently mutated than other residues. 24 per cent of somatic mutations are accounted for by alterations to five codons: 248, 273, 175, 245, 282 (46). These mutational hotspot residues play critical roles in the interaction of p53 protein with DNA, by directly contacting DNA (codons 248 and 273) or in stabilizing the DNA-binding surface (codons 175, 245, 282) (45).

The analyses presented below are based on families and patients in the published literature with mutations of confirmed or probable biological significance but exclude those of uncertain nature (47–49). The 54 cases of ACC from Brazil with identical mutations have also been excluded as these represent a distinct situation with a possible environmental aetiology (40, 41). Figure 16.2 represents the location and frequency distribution

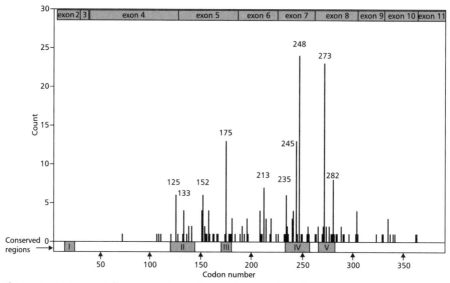

Fig. 16.2 Location and frequency of germline mutations within the *TP53* coding region.

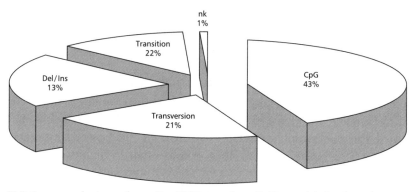

Fig. 16.3 Frequency by type of germline *TP53* mutations. Del/Ins = deletion/insertion; nk = not known; CpG = transition at CpG dinucleotide.

of 232 mutations within the coding region of *TP53* where the affected codons are specified. The figure also shows the exon delineation and the positions of the five evolutionary conserved domains (50). Whilst mutations occur from exon 4 to exon 10, 90 per cent are located in exons 5 to 8. The five "hotspot" codons for somatic mutations (175, 245, 248, 273 and 282) are also mutational "hotspots" in the germline. Mutations at these five codons account for 33 per cent of germline mutations. Codons 125,152, 213 and 235 have emerged as minor mutational hotspots but, except for codon 213, do not represent "hotspots" for somatic mutations. Figure 16.3 shows the distribution of mutation types.

The *TP53* phenotype and genotype–phenotype correlations

In the classic tumour suppressor model, malignant transformation follows the loss of both wild-type alleles, with retention of a single wild-type allele being sufficient to prevent malignant transformation. However, it has been demonstrated experimentally that some mutant forms of p53 protein confer a gain-of-function phenotype, as demonstrated by enhanced cell growth and increased tumourigenic potential and/or have the ability to inactivate the endogenous wild-type p53 protein in a dominant-negative fashion by forming a complex (51). Mutations at four of the main mutational hot-spot residues (codons 175, 245, 248 and 273) lead to proteins which display dominant-negative properties in experimental systems. These observations lead to the hypothesis that such gain-of-function/ dominant-negative mutations, if present in the germline, might lead to a more highly penetrant cancer phenotype within families.

To test this hypothesis, Birch *et al.* (17) compared cancer incidence among two groups of families – 12 with missense mutations in the DNA binding domain (Group A) and seven with any other type of mutation (Group B). It was demonstrated that Group A families showed a more penetrant phenotype characterized by a higher overall cancer incidence and earlier ages at diagnosis, especially of breast cancer and brain tumours. Hwang *et al.* (52) analysed cancer incidence among six families – three with protein-truncating mutations and three with missense mutations. No difference in cancer phenotype was found between the two groups. However, confirmed dominant-negative mutations contributed only 9 per cent of the individuals included in the analysis.

A recent analysis of 223 published families included in the IARC germline mutation database classified mutations into four structural groups according to the position of the affected residue within the p53 protein. Results showed that brain tumours were associated with missense mutations located in the DNA binding loops that contact the minor groove of DNA. ACCs, in contrast, were associated with missense mutations located in the loops opposing the protein–DNA contact surface. Loss of function mutations were associated with earlier-onset brain tumours, and the mean age for breast cancer was significantly younger for mutations in the DNA-binding sites. Therefore, there are variations in cancers depending on the effects of mutations on p53 protein structure (53).

A variety of cancers other than the principal LFS component cancers occur in some families. Kleihues *et al.* (54) and Nichols *et al.* (55) analysed frequencies of cancers in families and individuals published in the literature. This approach does not allow for methods of ascertainment of families, time periods of diagnosis, the degree of completeness of information and international variations in incidence. It was concluded that germline *TP53* mutations conferred an increased risk to a wide range of early-onset cancers, including lung, stomach, ovary, colon and rectum, prostate and cervix. However, the clinical criteria for LFS (Table 16.1) require at least two cancers diagnosed under the age of 45 years.

In order to overcome these problems, Birch *et al.* (56) carried out an analysis of 28 families with germline *TP53* mutations, selected according to standard criteria, and calculated the expected frequencies of cancers based on age, sex, morphology, site and calendar period-specific cancer incidence data for England and Wales. There were statistically significant excesses of carcinoma of the breast, soft tissue sarcomas, osteosarcoma, brain tumours, ACC, Wilms tumour, phyllodes tumour and carcinoma of the pancreas but risks for other common malignancies (e.g. colorectal, lung, bladder, prostate, ovary) were not increased in these families.

Estimation of cancer risks in *TP53* mutation carriers

Only one substantial study provides estimates of absolute cancer risks by age and sex. A method employing a maximum likelihood approach that takes account of, and corrects for, various sources of bias was developed (57). The method was applied to 13 families segregating a *TP53* mutation ascertained through a systematic study of more than 2500 children with cancer. Penetrances for all cancers combined, estimated to ages 16, 45 and 85 years, were 19 per cent, 41 per cent and 73 per cent respectively in males and 12 per cent, 84 per cent and 100 per cent in females. The difference in penetrance between males and females was almost entirely due to breast cancer, which represented 80 per cent of all female cancers in the 16 to 45 age class (16). Hwang *et al.* (52) also produced risk estimates which are broadly comparable. As discussed above, there may be variations in penetrance and cancer distribution depending on the class of mutation and this should be taken into account when counselling families on cancer risks.

Predictive genetic testing and clinical management of families with germline *TP53* mutations

Presymptomatic predictive testing should only be offered to at-risk individuals in families where a germline mutation has already been identified. It would be appropriate to search for a germline *TP53* mutation in families fulfilling the criteria for LFS (7) and LFL (14), pairs of first-degree relatives with typical LFS cancers (16) and patients with multiple primary LFS cancers. However, the frequency of germline *TP53* mutations may be low even among some apparently LF-like families (58).

The morphology, site, age and sex-specific incidence of cancer in mutation carriers is uncertain but the estimates discussed above provide a general framework for discussing cancer risks. The frequencies of the main cancers associated with germline *TP53* mutations in specific age groups relative to the expected population frequencies have been estimated (56). This provides a guide for counselling individual carriers about possible site-specific risks. However, the occurrence of cancers other than those for which a clear association has been demonstrated cannot be ruled out.

Childhood cancers are a common feature in LFS and LFL families but predictive tests in healthy children can only be justified if screening for early detection of such cancers confers a survival benefit or reduction in morbidity. There is recent evidence to suggest that screening for certain tumours in children at high risk may confer a survival benefit (59). Each request for predictive tests should be treated on its own merits, and testing in children may be appropriate in rare cases (60). In adult female mutation carriers, screening for early detection of breast cancer, the most common cancer in *TP53* mutation carriers, and chemoprevention, may be of benefit (61).

In conclusion, although the benefits of screening and chemoprevention in LFS/LFL remain controversial, it is essential that individuals have access to informed clinicians so that early symptoms may be investigated in a thorough and timely fashion. There are still many unresolved problems. These include choice of appropriate therapy for treating cancers in patients with germline *TP53* mutations, reliable estimates of cancer risks in carriers, clarification of genotype–phenotype variations in risk and the biological basis for the tissue specificity of cancers in *TP53* mutation carriers. Detailed statistical studies of large, well-documented cohorts of families and complementary molecular studies of mutant protein structure and function are required to resolve these problems.

References

1 **Li FP, Fraumeni JF Jr.** Soft-tissue sarcomas, breast cancer, and other neoplasms. A familial syndrome? *Ann Intern Med* 1969; **71**:747–752.

2 **Li FP, Fraumeni JF Jr.** Rhabdomyosarcoma in children: epidemiologic study and identification of a familial cancer syndrome. *J Natl Cancer Instit* 1969; **43**:1365–1373.

3 **Li FP, Fraumeni JF Jr.** Prospective study of a family cancer syndrome. *JAMA* 1982; **247**:2692–2694.

4 **Birch JM, Hartley AL, Marsden HB,** *et al.* Excess risk of breast cancer in the mothers of children with soft tissue sarcomas. *Br J Cancer* 1984; **49**:325–331.

5 **Strong LC, Stine M, Norsted TL.** Cancer in survivors of childhood soft tissue sarcoma and their relatives. *J Natl Cancer Inst* 1987; **79**:1213–1220.

6 **Birch JM, Hartley AL, Blair V,** *et al.* Cancer in the families of children with soft tissue sarcoma. *Cancer* 1990; **66**:2239–2248.

7 **Li FP, Fraumeni JF Jr, Mulvihill JJ,** *et al.* A cancer family syndrome in twenty-four kindreds. *Cancer Res* 1988; **48**:5358–5362.

8 **Williams WR, Strong LC.** Genetic epidemiology of soft tissue sarcomas in children. In: Muller H, W Weber, eds. Familial cancer. First international research conference on familial cancer, Basel, 1985, pp.151–153. Basel: Karger.

9 **Lustbader ED, Williams WR, Bondy ML,** *et al.* Segregation analysis of cancer in families of childhood soft-tissue-sarcoma patients. *Am J Hum Genet* 1992; **51**:344–356.

10 **Malkin D, Li FP, Strong LC,** *et al.* Germline p53 mutations in a familial syndrome of breast cancer, sarcomas and other neoplasms. *Science* 1990; **250**:1233–1238.

11 **Lavigueur A, Maltby V, Mock D,** *et al.* High incidence of lung, bone and lymphoid tumors in transgenic mice over-expressing mutant alleles of the p53 oncogene. *Mol Cell Biol* 1989; **9**:3982–3991.

12 **Srivastava S, Zou Z, Pirollo K,** *et al.* Germ-line transmission of a mutated *p53* gene in a cancer-prone family with Li–Fraumeni syndrome. *Nature* 1990; **348**:747–749.

13 **Olivier M, Eeles R, Hollstein M,** *et al.* The IARC TP53 Database: new online mutation analysis and recommendations to users. *Human Mutation* 2002; **19**:607–614.

14 **Birch JM, Hartley AL, Tricker KJ,** *et al.* Prevalence and diversity of constitutional mutations in the *p53* gene among 21 Li–Fraumeni families. *Cancer Res* 1994; **54**:1298–1304.

15 **Frebourg T, Barbier N, Yan Y-X,** *et al.* Germ-line p53 mutations in 15 families with Li–Fraumeni syndrome. *Am J Hum Genet* 1995; **56**:608–615.

16 **Chompret A, Brugières L, Ronsin M, Gardes M,** *et al.* p53 germline mutations in childhood cancers and cancer risk for carrier individuals. *Br J Cancer* 2000; **82**:1932–1937.

17 **Birch JM, Blair V, Kelsey AM,** *et al.* Cancer phenotype correlates with constitutional TP53 genotype in families with the Li–Fraumeni syndrome. *Oncogene* 1998; **17**:1061–1068.

18 **Bougeard G, Limacher J-M, Martin C,** *et al.* Detection of 11 germline inactivating TP53 mutations and absence of TP63 and HCHK2 mutations in 17 French families with Li–Fraumeni or Li–Fraumeni-like syndrome. *J Med Genet* 2001; **38**:253–256.

19 **Ayan I, Luca JW, Jaffe N,** *et al. De novo* germline mutations of the p53 gene in young children with sarcomas. *Oncology Reports* 1997; **4**:679–683.

20 **Diller L, Sexsmith E, Gottlieb A, Li FP, Malkin D.** Germline p53 mutations are frequently detected in young children with rhabdomyosarcoma. *J Clin Invest* 1995; **95**:1606–1611.

21 **Iavarone A, Matthay KK, Steinkirchner TM, Israel MA.** Germ-line and somatic p53 gene mutations in multifocal osteogenic sarcoma. *PNAS* 1992; **89**:4207–4209.

22 McIntyre JF, Smith-Sorensen B, Friend SH, Kassell J, *et al*. Germline mutations of the p53 tumor suppressor gene in children with osteosarcoma. *J Clin Oncol* 1994; **12**:925–930.

23 Porter DE, Holden ST, Steel CM, *et al*. A significant proportion of patients with osteosarcoma may belong to Li–Fraumeni cancer families. *J Bone Joint Surg* 1992; **74-B**:883–886.

24 Toguchida J, Yamaguchi T, Dayton SH, Beauchampe RL, *et al*. Prevalence and spectrum of germline mutations of the p53 gene among patients with sarcoma. *N Eng J Med* 1992; **326**:1301–1308.

25 Chen P, Iavarone A, Fick J, *et al*. Constitutional p53 mutations associated with brain tumors in young adults. *Cancer Genet Cytogenet* 1995; **82**:106–115.

26 Chung R, Whaley J, Kley N, Anderson K, *et al*. TP53 Gene mutations and 17p deletions in human astrocytomas. *Genes Chrom Cancer* 1991; **3**:323–331.

27 Kyritsis AP, Bondy ML, Xiao M, Berman EL, *et al*. Germline p53 gene mutations in subsets of glioma patients. *J Natl Cancer Inst* 1994; **86**:344–349.

28 Li Y-J, Sanson M, Hoang-Xuan K, *et al*. Incidence of germ-line *p53* mutations in patients with gliomas. *Int J Cancer (Pred Oncol)* 1995; **64**:383–387.

29 Tachibana I, Smith JS, Sato K, Hosek SM, *et al*. Investigation of germline PTEN, p53, p16^{INK4A}/p14^{ARF} and CDK4 alterations in familial glioma. *Am J Med Genet* 2000; **92**:136–141.

30 Vital A, Bringuier P-P, Huang H, *et al*. Astrocytomas and choroid plexus tumors in two families with idenical *p53* germline mutations. *J Neuropathol Exp Neurol* 1998; **57**:1061–1069.

31 Zhou X-P, Sanson M, Hoang-Xuan K, *et al*. Germline mutations of *p53* but not *p16/CDKN2* or *PTEN/MMAC1* tumor suppressor genes predispose to gliomas. *Ann Neurol* 1999; **46**:913–916.

32 Børresen A-L, Andersen TI, Garber J. Screening for germ line *TP53* mutations in breast cancer patients. *Cancer Res* 1992; **52**:3234–3236.

33 Prosser J, Porter D, Coles C, *et al*. Constitutional p53 mutation in a nonLi–Fraumeni cancer family. *Br J Cancer* 1992; **65**:527–528.

34 Rapakko K, Allinen M, Syrjakoski K, *et al*. Germline *TP53* alterations in Finnish breast cancer families are rare and occur at conserved mutation-prone sites. *Br J Cancer* 2001; **84**:116–119.

35 Sidransky D, Tokino T, Helzlsouer K, *et al*. Inherited *p53* gene mutations in breast cancer. *Cancer Res* 1992; **52**:2984–2986.

36 Zelada-Hedman M, Børresen-Dale A-L, Claro A, *et al*. Screening for *TP53* mutations in patients and tumours from 109 Swedish breast cancer families. *Br J Cancer* 1997; **75**:1201–1204.

37 Lalloo F, Varley J, Ellis D, *et al*. Prediction of pathogenic mutations in patients with early-onset breast cancer by family history. *Lancet* 2003; **361**:1101–1102.

38 Wagner J, Portwine C, Rabin K, *et al*. High frequency of germline p53 mutations in childhood adrenocortical cancer. *J Nat Cancer Inst* 1994; **86**:1707–1710.

39 Varley JM, McGown G, Thorncroft M, *et al*. Are there low-penetrance *TP53* alleles? Evidence from childhood adrenocortical tumors. *Am J Hum Genet* 1999; **65**:995–1006.

40 Ribeiro RC, Sandrini F, Figueiredo B, *et al*. An inherited *p53* mutation that contributes in a tissue-specific manner to pediatric adrenal cortical carcinoma. *PNAS* 2001; **98**:9330–9335.

41 Latronico AC, Pinto EM, Domenice S, *et al*. An inherited mutation outside the highly conserved DNA-binding domain of the p53 tumor suppressor protein in children and adults with sporadic adrenocortical tumors. *J Clin Endocrinol Metab* 2001; **86**:4970–4973.

42 Malkin D, Jolly KW, Barbier N, Look AT, Friend SH, *et al*. Germline mutations of the p53 tumor-suppressor gene in children and young adults with second malignant neoplasms. *N Eng J Med* 1992; **326**:1309–1315.

43 Malkin D, Friend SH, Li FP, Strong LC. Germ-line mutations of the p53 tumor-suppressor gene in children and young adults with second malignant neoplasms. *N Engl J Med* 1997; **336**:734.

44 Shiseki M, Nishikawa R, Yamamoto H, Ochiai A, *et al.* Germ-line *p53* mutation is uncommon in patients with triple primary cancers. *Cancer Letters* 1993; **73**:51–57.

45 Cho Y, Gorina S, Jeffrey PD, Pavletich NP. Crystal strucure of a p53 tumor suppressor-DNA complex: understanding tumorigenic mutations. *Science* 1994; **265**:346–355.

46 Hainaut P, Hollstein M. p53 and human cancer: the first ten thousand mutations. *Adv Cancer Res* 2002; **77**:81–137.

47 Avigad S, Barel D, Blau O, *et al.* A novel germ line p53 mutation in intron 6 in diverse childhood malignancies. *Oncogene* 1997; **14**:1541–1545.

48 Barel D, Avigad S, Mor C, *et al.* A novel germ-line mutation in the noncoding region of the p53 gene in a Li–Fraumeni family. *Cancer Genet Cytogenet* 1998; **103**:1–6.

49 Lehman TA, Haffty BG, Carbone CJ, *et al.* Elevated frequency and functional activity of a specific germ-line *p53* intron mutation in familial breast cancer. *Cancer Res* 2000; **60**:1062–1069.

50 May P, May E. Twenty years of p53 research:structural and functional aspects of the p53 protein. *Oncogene* 1999; **18**:7621–7636

51 Cadwell C, Zambetti GP. The effects of wild-type p53 tumor suppressor activity and mutant p53 gain-of-function on cell growth. *Gene* 2001; **277**:15–30.

52 Hwang S-J, Lozano G, Amos CI, Strong LC. Germline p53 mutations in a cohort with childhood sarcoma: sex differences in cancer risk. *Am J Hum Genet* 2003; **72**:975–983.

53 Olivier M, Goldgar DE, Sodha N, *et al.* Li–Fraumeni and related syndromes: correlation between tumor type, family structure and *TP53* Genotype. *Cancer Res* 2003; **63**:6643–6650.

54 Kleihues P, Schäuble B, Hausen A, *et al.* Tumors associated with p53 germline mutations: a synopsis of 91 families. *Am J Pathol* 1997; **150**:1–13.

55 Nichols KE, Malkin D, Garber JE, *et al.* Germ-line *p53* mutations predispose to a wide spectrum of early-onset cancers. *Cancer Epidem Bio Prev* 2001; **10**:83–87.

56 Birch JM, Alston RD, McNally RTQ, *et al.* Relative frequency and morphology of cancers in carriers of germline TP53 mutations. *Oncogene* 2001; **20**:4621–4628.

57 Le Bihan C, Moutou C, Brugières L, *et al.* ARCAD: a method for estimating age-dependent disease risk associated with mutation carrier status from family data. *Genet Epidem* 1995; **12**:13–25.

58 Evans DGR, Birch JM, Thorncroft M, *et al.* Low rate of TP53 germline mutations in breast/sarcoma families not fulfilling classical criteria for Li–Fraumeni syndrome. *J Med Genet* 2002; **39**:941–944.

59 McNeil DE, Brown M, Ching A, DeBaun MR. Screening for Wilms tumor and hepatoblastoma in children with Beckwith-Wiedemann syndromes: a cost-effective model. *Med Pediatr Oncol* 2001; **37**:349–356.

60 Varley JM, Evans DGR, Birch JM. Li–Fraumeni syndrome-a molecular and clinical review. *Brit J Cancer* 1997; **76**:1–14.

61 IBIS Investigators. First results from the international breast cancer intervention study (IBIS-I): a randomised prevention trial. *Lancet* 2002; **360**:817–824.

Chapter 17

Other tumour predisposing syndromes

Fiona Lalloo and D. Gareth R. Evans

Melanoma

Introduction

Melanoma is an increasing problem in western Caucasian societies as the consequences of excessive sun exposure have their effects on melanoma incidence. Rates of melanoma for Europe are now 7 per 100 000 (1), with rates in the USA of 10 (2) and Australia of 35 (3) per 100 000 per year. This equates to a lifetime risk of 0.6 per cent in Europe and 2.8 per cent in Australia. Life expectancy is inversely proportional to the thickness of the lesion, with the result that early diagnosis and detection of precursor lesions will have a beneficial effect on long-term mortality.

Risk factors

- Sun exposure – increased sun exposure increases the risk of melanoma. There is a higher risk if this occurs at a young age and is accompanied by sunburn. Individuals with atypical naevi or with type 1 skin (fair skin, freckles and does not tan, often associated with blue eyes and ginger hair) are particularly susceptible to the effects of UV exposure.

- Melanocortin 1 receptor gene variants – fair skin is determined by the melanocortin 1 receptor gene and variants in this gene, irrespective of skin colour, are now considered as independent risk factors (4).

Familial melanoma

It is estimated that 10 per cent of melanoma is hereditary (5). Familial melanoma can be described if two first-degree relatives are affected or if there are at least three blood relatives in a kindred with the disease. The FAMMM condition (familial atypical mole malignant melanoma) is described where there are coexistent individuals with multiple, atypical moles and melanoma (6). However, it is becoming apparent that the presence of atypical moles in the context of a melanoma family does not necessarily indicate that an individual has inherited the main susceptibility gene. It is just that melanoma families are more likely to be identified when a melanoma susceptibility gene, such as *CDKN2A* (*TP16*), coincides with a probably separate gene predisposing to atypical moles.

Members of a family with malignant melanoma should be advised about sun avoidance and the use of sunscreens and referred for annual cutaneous surveillance.

Familial melanoma genes

The first evidence for linkage of melanoma families was to chromosome 1p (7). Whilst this has been substantiated in some studies (8), many others have been equivocal or excluded this locus. At the present time, a melanoma gene on 1p has yet to be identified.

The *CDKN2A-ARF* gene on chromosome 9p21 is implicated in the development of a variety of sporadic malignant tumours (9, 10) as well as familial melanoma (11). This gene encodes two structurally distinct tumour suppressor proteins by virtue of different 5′ exons spliced in different reading frames to common exons 2 and 3. Exons 1a, 2 and 3 encode CDKN2A (p16^{INK4a}), while exon 1b, spliced to exons 2 and 3 in a different reading frame and transcribed using a different promoter, encodes ARF (p19^{ARF}) protein (12). As a single gene codes for two distinct proteins and mutational events can cause loss of function of either or both proteins, the specific role of the individual proteins in the development of neoplasia can be difficult to assess. Inactivation of *CDKN2A-ARF* in sporadic tumours can occur by mutation (13), methylation of the promoter (14) or deletion of the gene (15). Germline *CDKN2A* inactivation is seen in approximately 50 per cent of kindreds with an autosomal dominant predisposition to melanoma (16). However, the complexity of the locus has meant that identifying the underlying mutation has proven troublesome. Recent evidence has shown that mutation of exon 1b, and thus specific loss of p19^{ARF}, can lead to melanoma susceptibility (17). *CDKN2A* is not a melanoma-specific gene and in addition to uveal melanoma does predispose to pancreatic cancer (18). The life time risk of pancreatic cancer may approach 17 per cent (5). Mutations in the *CDKN2A-ARF* gene may also predispose to breast cancer (19).

A small number of additional melanoma families have mutations in the *CDK4* gene, which alter the binding of CDK4 to CDKN2A (20).

Predictive testing

Although predictive testing is possible in families once a pathogenic mutation in the *CDKN2A-ARF* gene complex has been identified, there are a number of issues regarding the risks of cancer associated with each mutation. In the presence of atypical moles, a *CDKN2A* mutation will confer a high (approximately 80 per cent) lifetime risk of melanoma. However, the risk in the absence of such moles is unclear. Individuals with atypical moles who test negative may still have a risk of melanoma that is substantially higher than the population level, and probably high enough to continue cutaneous surveillance. The risk of pancreatic cancer, with the lack of proven efficacious screening, makes the decision to have a predictive test problematic. Uptake of predictive testing in melanoma families has, so far, been relatively low.

Hereditary paraganglioma

Introduction

Paragangliomas are rare tumours that arise from paraganglionic tissue derived from the neural crest in the head and neck. The parasympathetic paraganglia lie along the course of the parasympathetic nerves, in particular at their intersection with the large vessels. Their function is largely chemoreceptive. The majority are in the head and neck, with the most common sites being the carotid body, glomus jugulare, and glomus vagale (21). Approximately 4 per cent of tumours are thought to be metastatic. The proportion of tumours that are familial is poorly defined; figures vary between 5 and 50 per cent of tumours, presumably due to the reduced penetrance of the disease and founder effects. The incidence of familial cases within the UK is less than 10 per cent, compared to 50 per cent in the Netherlands (22). Familial cases are more frequently bilateral and/or multiple and are diagnosed at an earlier age (23). Whilst the majority of the tumours are benign, pressure effects cause major morbidity due to cranial nerve paralysis and may compress the brain stem. The treatment of choice is usually surgery.

Counselling and management

Familial carotid body tumours were first described in 1949, and subsequently a number of other families have been reported. Studies of pedigrees have suggested in some families that tumours only develop if inherited via the paternal line (24, 25), suggestive of genomic imprinting. However, families with both mother and child affected have been described. Counselling of patients therefore becomes complex as, if the affected parent is male, the likelihood of developing a tumour is much higher, although penetrance is not 100 per cent. However, given that cases of paragangliomas have occurred with maternal transmission, screening should be offered to all at-risk patients. Screening is by MRI spine of the head and neck at 3-yearly intervals and annual 24-hour urine analysis for VMA.

Molecular genetics of hereditary paraganglioma

Baysel *et al.* localized *PGL1* to chromosome 11 and subsequently demonstrated that this is *SDHD*, a gene involved in the mitochondrial complex II (26). *SDHD* encodes the small subunit of cytochrome b in succinate-ubiquinone oxidoreductase. Further studies looked at other genes encoding subunits of mitochondrial complex II and demonstrated that mutations in *SDHD* and *SDHB* account for 70 per cent of familial cases of paraganglioma (27). Interestingly, none of these genes appear to be imprinted. However, a recent paper has hypothesized that the mechanism of expression of *SDHD* with only paternal transmission (maternal imprinting) is due to loss of the wild type *SDHD* allele in tumours in association with the complete loss of the maternal chromosome 11. It is known that *SDHD* is biallelically expressed, and that normal paraganglia express the maternally derived gene. Therefore, the authors suggest that paternal transmission can be explained by a somatic genetic mechanism targeting both the *SDHD* gene on 11q23 and a paternally imprinted gene on 11p15.5, rather than imprinting of *SDHD*.

Mutations screening of *SDHD* and *SDHB* should be undertaken in families with hereditary paraganglioma.

Renal cell carcinoma

Renal cell carcinomas (RCC) account for about 85 per cent of all kidney malignancies, with the incidence in the general population increasing between 50 and 70 years of age (28). About 2 per cent of renal cell carcinoma is familial. As with other inherited cancers, these are more likely to occur at an earlier age and to be multifocal or bilateral (29). There are two different histological types of renal cell carcinoma, clear cell or non-papillary type and papillary type, both of which have different inherited forms.

Clear cell carcinoma

The majority of familial cases of clear cell carcinoma are due to von Hippel–Lindau (VHL) disease which is discussed in detail in Chapter 13. There are, however, familial forms of clear cell carcinoma that do not appear to be associated with VHL.

Families have been described with a constitutional translocation of chromosome 3 (30). Within this family the probability of a patient with the translocation developing RCC was over 80 per cent. A number of other families with translocations involving the short arm of chromosome 3 have also been described (31, 32). It has been suggested that loss of a gene at this translocation break point on chromosome 3 may be the cause of the RCC. There is also a suggestion that these translocations predispose to the loss of the terminal section of 3p in the tumours, which then involves loss of *VHL*. A recent study (33) cloned a translocation segregating with RCC in a family, t(3;8)(p14.2;q24.2), and demonstrated a 5 kb microdeletion, but without alteration of a specific gene. The authors therefore suggest that the mechanism for tumourogeneis in this family is unlikely to be deregulation of a specific gene.

Papillary renal cell carcinoma

Papillary renal cell carcinoma has been described in a familial form, both as isolated RCC (34) and part of Tuberose Sclerosis or Birt–Hogg–Dube syndrome (35).

Isolated familial papillary RCC has been described with mutations in the *MET* oncogene (36). *MET* is one of the tyrosine kinase family of oncogenes. Mutations in the *MET* proto-oncogene result in activation of the *MET* protein, which then results in altered cell growth. Most of the germline mutations within *MET* are missense mutations within the tyrosine kinase domain. Germline mutations have also been demonstrated within families without RCC, suggesting a low penetrance (37).

Birt–Hogg–Dube syndrome

Birt–Hogg–Dube (BHD) syndrome is an autosomal dominant condition characterized by fibrofolliculomas, trichodiscomas and acrochordons – small papules distributed over the face, neck and upper trunk (38). Lipomas, collagenomas and oral fibromas have also been described. Renal tumours include renal oncocytomas (benign tumours) and papillary renal cell carcinoma. BHD also predisposes to pulmonary cysts with resulting spontaneous pneumothoraces. There has been controversy over whether BHD predisposes to colonic neoplasms (39), but it may be associated in certain families (40).

BHD was mapped to 17p11.2 (41) and the *BHD* gene was found to encode a novel protein named folliculin (42). Mutations have been described in patients with BHD and exon 11 has been demonstrated to have a mutational hot spot (40).

Approach to renal cancer

- Take a three-generation pedigree and confirm the histology of tumours
- If clear cell histology, assess for other features of VHL, including a neurological examination
- If papillary, examine for skin lesions
- If clear cell, screen DNA for mutations in *VHL* gene and do a karyotype
- If papillary, screen DNA for mutations in *MET* or *BHD*
- Discuss implications for other members of the family and institute abdominal USS/CT scans or full screening programme for VHL (Chapter 13) if there are two or more proven cases of RCC.

Retinoblastoma

Retinoblastoma is the most common ocular malignancy in childhood, typically presenting before the age of 5 with leukocoria. Retinoblastoma is an autosomal dominant condition, although less than 10 per cent of cases have a family history. The high rate of new mutations means that even without a family history, 40 per cent of retinoblastoma cases have a germline mutation in the retinoblastoma gene. This is more likely if retinoblastoma is bilateral or multifocal and diagnosed before the age of 1 year.

The likelihood that an isolated, unilateral tumour is due to a germline mutation varies depending on the series. Draper *et al.* estimated the probability of a germline mutation as being 2.9 per cent (43). However, actual testing of cases demonstrated that 15 per cent had a germline mutation (44). As such, the risk to offspring of an isolated, unilateral case is 7.5 per cent.

Approach to bilateral retinoblastoma

+ Bilateral retinoblastoma is likely to be due to germline mutation
+ Examine parents for evidence of regressed tumours
+ Obtain blood samples for karyotyping and DNA for mutation screening of *RB1* gene; may need to obtain tumour tissue to clarify DNA results
+ Discuss risks to potential offspring and to sibs (depending on family history)
+ Discuss chance of non-ocular malignancy

Approach to unilateral retinoblastoma

+ In unilateral retinoblastoma, 15 per cent are due to germline mutation
+ Risk to offspring is 7.5 per cent
+ Examine parents if possible
+ Obtain tumour material for *RB1* studies along with DNA
+ Obtain blood sample for karyotyping
+ Discuss possibility of germline mutation with parents/ patient.

Early surveillance for retinoblastoma

Surveillance of those at-risk or mutation carriers should be:

+ Monthly examinations from birth until 3 months without anaesthetic
+ Three-monthly examinations under anaesthetic (EUA) until 2 years of age
+ Four-monthly EUA from 2 to 3 years and then 6-monthly EUA until 5 years
+ Yearly examinations without anaesthetic are then undertaken until 11 years
+ Early surveillance has been demonstrated to decrease mortality and to increase the chance of ocular survival and retention of vision (45).

Non-ocular tumours in retinoblastoma

Patients with a germline mutation of *RB1* have an increased risk of non-ocular tumour.

+ Pineoblastoma – this has been described as "trilateral retinoblastoma" as the tumour is morphologically similar to retinoblastoma. It is a rare but recognized association with retinoblastoma. The survival is poor, although early diagnosis by screening may improve this (46).
+ Osteogenic sarcoma – there is a marked increased risk of second tumours in children with germline mutations, with a relative risk of 30 (47). The highest risk is for the development of osteogenic sarcomas at all sites, although particularly in the radiation field. This risk is dose-dependant (48). The latency period between retinoblastoma and sarcoma varies in patients, with a shorter latency period within the radiation field (49),

• Other tumours – an increased risk of cancer at a number of other sites has been suggested, including soft tissue sarcomas, malignant melanoma and lung cancer. It has been suggested that patients with retinoblastoma have an increased risk of third and fourth primaries with a variety of sites. A recent study suggests a 5-year incidence rate of a third primary tumour of 11 per cent and a 10-year incidence rate of 22 per cent (50). The most common sites of malignancy were skin and soft tissues of the head.

Genetics of retinoblastoma

The *RB1* gene was cloned in 1986 (51) from chromosome 13, following reports of translocations and deletions involving 13q14. The gene consists of 27 exons encoding a 928 amino acid protein. The protein is a tumour suppressor gene, which acts as a cell cycle regulatory protein. Frameshift, nonsense, missense and splice site mutations as well as large deletions have been described throughout the gene. Splice site mutations appear to be associated with a lower penetrance phenotype (52). Mutation screening is now routine in diagnostic labs and predictive testing can be offered to direct management of newborns. Prenatal diagnosis is also possible.

Haematological cancer and lymphoproliferative disorders

As with most common cancers, a first-degree relative diagnosed with a haematological cancer or a lymphoproliferative disorder will increase the risk to the proband. However, clearly dominant predispositions to these disorders have not been fully elucidated.

There have been a number of studies suggesting a familial element to non-Hodgkin's lymphoma (NHL) with an increased relative risk to siblings. One large study suggested that the relative risk to siblings of either Hodgkin's lymphoma or NHL is 2.5, although some of the data in this series were incomplete (53). Other studies have also demonstrated an increased risk (54), and others have demonstrated a general increase in risk of both lymphomas and haematological malignancies, but with different histological types, suggesting a defect at stem cell level (55).

A number of recessively inherited conditions predispose to lymphoproliferative disease including: Griscelli syndrome (Online Mendelian Inheritance in Man database (56) (OMIM) 214450); Chediack–Higashi syndrome (OMIM 214500); Diamond–Blackfan anaemia (OMIM 205900); Blooms syndrome (OMIM 210900); and Nijmegen-breakage syndrome. However, all these conditions are rare.

References

1 Micheli A, Mugno E, Krogh V, Quinn MJ, Coleman M, Hakulinen T, *et al*. Cancer prevalence in European registry areas. *Ann Oncol* 2002; **13**:840–865.

2 Jemal A, Devesa SS, Hartge P, Tucker MA. Recent trends in cutaneous melanoma incidence among whites in the United States. *J Natl Cancer Inst* 2001; **93**:678–683.

3 Marrett LD, Nguyen HL, Armstrong BK. Trends in the incidence of cutaneous malignant melanoma in New South Wales, 1983–1996. *Int J Cancer* 2001; **92**:457–462.

4 Palmer JS, Duffy DL, Box NF, Aitken JF, O'Gorman LE, Green AC, *et al*. Melanocortin-1 receptor polymorphisms and risk of melanoma: is the association explained solely by pigmentation phenotype? *Am J Hum Genet* 2000; **66**:176–186.

5 de Snoo FA, Bergman W, Gruis NA. Familial melanoma: a complex disorder leading to controversy on DNA testing. *Fam Cancer* 2003; **2**:109–116.

6 Lynch HT, Frichot BC III, Lynch JF. Familial atypical multiple mole-melanoma syndrome. *J Med Genet* 1978; **15**:352–356.

7 Greene MH, Goldin LR, Clark WH Jr, Lovrien E, Kraemer KH, Tucker MA, *et al*. Familial cutaneous malignant melanoma: autosomal dominant trait possibly linked to the Rh locus. *Proc Natl Acad Sci U S A* 1983; **80**:6071–6075.

8 Bale SJ, Dracopoli NC, Tucker MA, Clark WH Jr, Fraser MC, Stanger BZ, *et al*. Mapping the gene for hereditary cutaneous malignant melanoma-dysplastic nevus to chromosome 1p. *N Engl J Med* 1989; **320**:1367–1372.

9 Pollock PM, Pearson JV, Hayward NK. Compilation of somatic mutations of the CDKN2 gene in human cancers: non-random distribution of base substitutions. *Genes Chromosomes Cancer* 1996; **15**:77–88.

10 Hussussian CJ, Struewing JP, Goldstein AM, Higgins PA, Ally DS, Sheahan MD, *et al*. Germline p16 mutations in familial melanoma. *Nat Genet* 1994; **8**:15–21.

11 Hussussian CJ, Struewing JP, Goldstein AM, Higgins PA, Ally DS, Sheahan MD, *et al*. Germline p16 mutations in familial melanoma. *Nat Genet* 1994; **8**:15–21.

12 Haber DA. Splicing into senescence: the curious case of p16 and p19ARF. *Cell* 1997; **91**:555–558.

13 Pollock PM, Pearson JV, Hayward NK. Compilation of somatic mutations of the CDKN2 gene in human cancers: non-random distribution of base substitutions. *Genes Chromosomes Cancer* 1996; **15**:77–88.

14 Gonzalez-Zulueta M, Bender CM, Yang AS, Nguyen T, Beart RW, Van Tornout JM, *et al*. Methylation of the 5' CpG island of the p16/CDKN2 tumor suppressor gene in normal and transformed human tissues correlates with gene silencing. *Cancer Res* 1995; **55**:4531–4535.

15 Cairns P, Polascik TJ, Eby Y, Tokino K, Califano J, Merlo A, *et al*. Frequency of homozygous deletion at p16/CDKN2 in primary human tumours. *Nat Genet* 1995; **11**:210–212.

16 Hussussian CJ, Struewing JP, Goldstein AM, Higgins PA, Ally DS, Sheahan MD, *et al*. Germline p16 mutations in familial melanoma. *Nat Genet* 1994; **8**:15–21.

17 Hewitt C, Lee WC, Evans G, Howell A, Elles RG, Jordan R, *et al*. Germline mutation of ARF in a melanoma kindred. *Hum Mol Genet* 2002; **11**:1273–1279.

18 Goldstein AM, Fraser MC, Struewing JP, Hussussian CJ, Ranade K, Zametkin DP, *et al*. Increased risk of pancreatic cancer in melanoma-prone kindreds with p16INK4 mutations. *N Engl J Med* 1995; **333**:970–974.

19 Hewitt C, Lee WC, Evans G, Howell A, Elles RG, Jordan R, *et al*. Germline mutation of ARF in a melanoma kindred. *Hum Mol Genet* 2002; **11**:1273–1279.

20 Goldstein AM, Chidambaram A, Halpern A, Holly EA, Guerry ID, Sagebiel R, *et al*. Rarity of CDK4 germline mutations in familial melanoma. *Melanoma Res* 2002; **12**:51–55.

21 Lack EE, Cubilla AL, Woodruff JM, Farr HW. Paragangliomas of the head and neck region. A clincal study in 69 patients. *Ca* 1977; **39**:397–409.

22 Astuti D, Hart-Holden N, Latif F, Lalloo F, Black GC, Lim C, *et al*. Genetic analysis of mitochondrial complex II subunits SDHD, SDHB and SDHC in paraganglioma and phaeochromocytoma susceptibility. *Clin Endocrinol (Oxf)* 2003; **59**:728–733.

23 Somasundar P, Krouse R, Hostetter R, Vaughan R, Covey T. Paragangliomas – a decade of clinical experience. *J Surg Oncol* 2000; **74**:286–290.

24 van der Mey AG, Maaswinkel-Mooy PD, Cornelisse CJ, Schmidt PH, van de Kamp JJ. Genomic imprinting in hereditary glomus tumours: evidence for new genetic theory. *Lancet* 1989; 2:1291–1294.

25 Heutink P, van der Mey AGL, Sandkuijl LA, van Gils APG, Bardoel A, Breedveld GJ, *et al*. A gene subject to genomic imprinting and responsible for hereditary paragangliomas maps to chromosome 11q23-qter. *Hum Mol Genet* 1992; 1:7–10.

26 Baysal BE, Ferrell RE, Willett-Brozick JE, Lawrence EC, Myssloreck D, Bosch A, *et al*. Mutations in SDHD, a mitochondrial complex II gene, in hereditary paraganglioma. *Science* 2000; 287:848–851.

27 Baysal BE, Willett-Brozick JE, Lawrence EC, Drovdlic CM, Savul SA, McLeod DR, *et al*. Prevalence of SDHB, SDHC, and SDHD germline mutations in clinic patients with head and neck paragangliomas. *J Med Genet* 2002; 39:178–183.

28 Motzer RJ, Bander NH, Nanus DM. Renal-cell carcinoma. *N Engl J Med* 1996; 335:865–875.

29 McLaughlin JK, Mandel JS, Blot WJ, Schuman LM, Mehl ES, Fraumeni JF Jr. A population–based case–control study of renal cell carcinoma. *J Natl Cancer Inst* 1984; 72:275–284.

30 Cohen AJ, Li FP, Berg S, Marchetto DJ, Tsai S, Jacobs SC, *et al*. Hereditary renal-cell carcinoma associated with a chromosomal translocation. *N Engl J Med* 1979; 301:592–595.

31 Bodmer D, Eleveld M, Ligtenberg M, Weterman M, van der MA, Koolen M, *et al*. Cytogenetic and molecular analysis of early stage renal cell carcinomas in a family with a translocation (2;3)(q35;q21). *Cancer Genet Cytogenet* 2002; 134:6–12.

32 Eleveld MJ, Bodmer D, Merkx G, Siepman A, Sprenger SH, Weterman MA, *et al*. Molecular analysis of a familial case of renal cell cancer and a t(3;6)(q12;q15). *Genes Chromosomes Cancer* 2001; 31:23–32.

33 Rodriguez-Perales S, Melendez B, Gribble SM, Valle L, Carter NP, Santamaria I, *et al*. Cloning of a new familial t(3;8) translocation associated with conventional renal cell carcinoma reveals a 5 kb microdeletion and no gene involved in the rearrangement. *Hum Mol Genet* 2004; 13:983–990.

34 Zbar B, Linehan WM. Re: Hereditary papillary renal cell carcinoma: clinical studies in 10 families. *J Urol* 1996; 156:1781.

35 Toro JR, Glenn G, Duray P, Darling T, Weirich G, Zbar B, *et al*. Birt–Hogg–Dube syndrome: a novel marker of kidney neoplasia. *Arch Dermatol* 1999; 135:1195–1202.

36 Schmidt L, Junker K, Nakaigawa N, Kinjerski T, Weirich G, Miller M, *et al*. Novel mutations of the MET proto-oncogene in papillary renal carcinomas. *Oncogene* 1999; 18:2343–2350.

37 Zbar B, Lerman M. Inherited carcinomas of the kidney. *Adv Cancer Res* 1998; 75:163–201.

38 Birt AR, Hogg GR, Dube WJ. Hereditary multiple fibrofolliculomas with trichodiscomas and acrochordons. *Arch Dermatol* 1977; 113:1674–1677.

39 Zbar B, Alvord WG, Glenn G, Turner M, Pavlovich CP, Schmidt L, *et al*. Risk of renal and colonic neoplasms and spontaneous pneumothorax in the Birt–Hogg–Dube syndrome. *Cancer Epidemiol Biomarkers Prev* 2002; 11:393–400.

40 Khoo SK, Giraud S, Kahnoski K, Chen J, Motorna O, Nickolov R, *et al*. Clinical and genetic studies of Birt–Hogg–Dube syndrome. *J Med Genet* 2002; 39:906–912.

41 Schmidt LS, Warren MB, Nickerson ML, Weirich G, Matrosova V, Toro JR, *et al*. Birt–Hogg–Dube syndrome, a genodermatosis associated with spontaneous pneumothorax and kidney neoplasia, maps to chromosome 17p11.2. *Am J Hum Genet* 2001; 69:876–882.

42 Nickerson ML, Warren MB, Toro JR, Matrosova V, Glenn G, Turner ML, *et al*. Mutations in a novel gene lead to kidney tumors, lung wall defects, and benign tumors of the hair follicle in patients with the Birt–Hogg–Dube syndrome. *Cancer Cell* 2002; 2:157–164.

43 Draper GJ, Sanders BM, Brownbill PA, Hawkins MM. Patterns of risk of hereditary retinoblastoma and applications to genetic counselling. *Br J Cancer* 1992; 66:211–219.

44 Lohmann DR, Gerick M, Brandt B, Oelschlager U, Lorenz B, Passarge E, *et al.* Constitutional RB1-gene mutations in patients with isolated unilateral retinoblastoma. *Am J Hum Genet* 1997; **61**:282–294.

45 Abramson DH, Beaverson K, Sangani P, Vora RA, Lee TC, Hochberg HM, *et al.* Screening for retinoblastoma: presenting signs as prognosticators of patient and ocular survival. *Pediatrics* 2003; **112**:1248–1255.

46 Kivela T. Trilateral retinoblastoma: a meta-analysis of hereditary retinoblastoma associated with primary ectopic intracranial retinoblastoma. *J Clin Oncol* 1999; **17**:1829–1837.

47 Eng C, Li FP, Abramson DH, Ellsworth RM, Wong FL, Goldman MB, *et al.* Mortality from second tumors among long-term survivors of retinoblastoma. *J Natl Cancer Inst* 1993; **85**:1121–1128.

48 Wong FL, Boice JD Jr, Abramson DH, Tarone RE, Kleinerman RA, Stovall M, *et al.* Cancer incidence after retinoblastoma. Radiation dose and sarcoma risk. *JAMA* 1997; **278**:1262–1267.

49 Chauveinc L, Mosseri V, Quintana E, Desjardins L, Schlienger P, Doz F, *et al.* Osteosarcoma following retinoblastoma: age at onset and latency period. *Ophthalmic Genet* 2001; **22**:77–88.

50 Abramson DH, Melson MR, Dunkel IJ, Frank CM. Third (fourth and fifth) nonocular tumors in survivors of retinoblastoma. *Ophthalmology* 2001; **108**:1868–1876.

51 Friend SH, Bernards R, Rogelj S, Weinberg RA, Rapaport JM, Albert DM, *et al.* A human DNA segment with properties of the gene that predisposes to retinoblastoma and osteosarcoma. *Nature* 1986; **323**:643–646.

52 Alonso J, Garcia-Miguel P, Abelairas J, Mendiola M, Sarret E, Vendrell MT, *et al.* Spectrum of germline RB1 gene mutations in Spanish retinoblastoma patients: Phenotypic and molecular epidemiological implications. *Hum Mutat* 2001; **17**:412–422.

53 Paltiel O, Schmit T, Adler B, Rachmilevitz EA, Polliack A, Cohen A, *et al.* The incidence of lymphoma in first-degree relatives of patients with Hodgkin disease and non-Hodgkin lymphoma: results and limitations of a registry-linked study. *Ca* 2000; **88**:2357–2366.

54 Pottern LM, Linet M, Blair A, Dick F, Burmeister LF, Gibson R, *et al.* Familial cancers associated with subtypes of leukemia and non-Hodgkin's lymphoma. *Leuk Res* 1991; **15**:305–314.

55 Shpilberg O, Modan M, Modan B, Chetrit A, Fuchs Z, Ramot B. Familial aggregation of haematological neoplasms: a controlled study. *Br J Haematol* 1994; **87**:75–80.

56 www.ncbi.nlm.nih.gov/omim/.

Chapter 18

The ethical and insurance issues of cancer genetics

Patrick J. Morrison

Ethical principles

A family history of cancer, particularly breast, ovarian and colon cancer or rare cancer syndromes such as multiple endocrine neoplasia type 2, is now recognized as the biggest risk factor for cancer after age. Testing is not always straightforward, as family dynamics differ within and between families. Experience of genetic testing for breast cancer over the last decade has allowed some ethical principles to be formulated so that a framework to guide procedures with can be utilized.

Four principles of medical ethics were advocated by Beauchamp and Childress (1) – beneficence, non-maleficence, autonomy and natural justice (Box 18.1). These provide a useful framework for medical ethics and can act as a checklist when confronting ethical problems. On their own, however, they may provide a full answer. Individually they may produce conflicting ways of approaching a situation – for example mutually exclusive answers may arise depending on which principle is considered paramount.

Gillon (2, 3) has recently argued that promoting respect for the four principles remains of great practical importance in ordinary medicine – however, the principle of respect for autonomy should be "first among equals" if one has to choose between the four. Genetics is much more complex than some branches of medicine when it comes to ethics. This is partly because new situations arise that have never been seen before (such as IVF, cloning, etc.) and partly because many situations don't just affect one

---

Box 18.1 **Founding principles of medical ethics**

- Beneficence
- Non-maleficence
- Natural justice
- Autonomy

Box 18.2 **Ethical concepts and principles**

- The *concept* of genetics solidarity and altruism
- The *primary principle* of respect for persons
- The *principle* of consent
- The *principle* of confidentiality
- The *principle* of non-discrimination
- The *principle* of privacy

---

person but a whole family or several generations. Often people will have to perform altruistic acts such as having a *BRCA1* or *BRCA2* test while suffering from breast cancer, perhaps not only so that their oncologist will be able to help tailor their chemotherapy or their surgeon discuss their risk of future cancers and preventative surgery, but also to allow genetic testing of other at-risk relatives.

Following this, and the realisation that personal genetic information is of a sensitive nature and requires special consideration, the Human Genetics Commission (HGC) in the United Kingdom introduced a new concept of genetic solidarity and altruism, plus five principles, to help provide a further framework the consideration of ethical problems in relation to hereditary disease (Box 18. 2).

The concept plus five principles approach is helpful but still may not provide all the answers needed in a typical cancer genetic consultation (3, 4). To try and cope with this complex area, most genetic testing centres will now have proper consenting procedures in place with careful counselling and full information and explanation.

The concept of genetic solidarity and altruism

We all share the same basic human genome, although there are individual variations which distinguish us from other people. Most of our genetic characteristics will be present in others. This sharing of our genetic constitution not only gives rise to opportunities to help others but it also highlights our common interest in the fruits of medically-based genetic research (4).

Genetic tests taken by a person may impact on others and testing may help others unrelated to a person or family.

The primary principle of respect for persons

Respect for persons affirms the equal value, dignity and moral rights of each individual. Each individual is entitled to lead a life in which genetic characteristics will not be the basis of unjust discrimination or unfair or inhuman treatment (4).

Every individual should be unhindered by unfair discrimination by insurers or employers.

Secondary principles of respect

The principle of privacy

> Every person is entitled to privacy. In the absence of justification based on overwhelming moral considerations, a person should generally not be obliged to disclose information about his or her genetic characteristics (4).

This applies not only to insurers or employers but also to the media and other persons in society. However, disclosure of genetic information to their relatives may be allowed against a person's wishes if a person declines to tell other relatives or refuses the release of information such as a history of cancer. Such disclosure in these circumstances should be following attempts to persuade the patient of the seriousness of the need for other relatives to benefit, and the reasons should be weighty enough to outweigh any distress which disclosure would cause to the patient. Discussion with professional colleagues is advised before proceeding down this route and it is recommended that the individual should be informed of this action before proceeding.

The principle of consent

> Private genetic information about a person should generally not be obtained, held or communicated without that persons free and informed consent (4).

Careful consent with explanation should be given in all cases. General Medical Council guidelines in the UK state that consent should be informed and be either oral or in writing. In the context of genetic cases, writing is preferable – however, a written note in the patient's chart stating the issues discussed and the patient's agreement may be sufficient. Specific consent forms are in use in most genetic centres and allow for use of information by other family members.

The principle of confidentiality

> Private personal genetic information should generally be treated as being of a confidential nature and should not be communicated to others without consent except for the weightiest of reasons (4).

The arguments for breaking confidentiality are few but are similar to privacy arguments above.

The principle of non-discrimination

> No person shall be unfairly discriminated against on the basis of his or her genetic characteristics (4).

An offence of DNA theft in the UK is being introduced to prevent unlawful use or procurement of genetic material or information.

Use of the principles – counselling and testing

One of the functions of a cancer genetics clinic is to provide clear information about the practical limitations of molecular diagnostics and about the issues to be considered before any individual family member proceeds down this road. The restricted availability of facilities for molecular analysis of *BRCA1* and *BRCA2* and other cancer tests imposes its own discipline on the practice of gene testing. As molecular technology advances, however, mutation detection may become rapid, efficient and widely available. There is a real danger that individuals may then embark on predictive testing without adequate counselling.

Over-the-counter testing is available in some countries, and recently in the UK recommendations were issued that over-the-counter tests should only be carried out by a recognized, trained professional such as a doctor, nurse or pharmacist, and in a location conducive to sharing genetic results (5). Internet access is, of course, unregulated but a system of "kite marking" suitable sites to show that they have government or professional approval would be useful, in the same way as we would select a plumber or other service based on some sort of quality assessment.

Several topics should be addressed in any genetic consultation and a checklist of possible areas to be covered is given in Box 18.3.

Familial cancer risk

Individual self-estimates of cancer risk among members of multicase families vary widely and are probably influenced by emotional responses to personal experience rather than assessment of mathematical realities. Widely quoted lifetime penetrance

---

Box 18.3 Elements to be considered in decisions about the use of genetic information

- What are the implications about use of information:
  - cost, therapy, danger to others.
- What principles need to be taken into account:
  - patient autonomy, the public health, costs.
- Who decided where and why the test will be done:
  - patient, employer, clinician, third party.
- Who decides what to do with the results:
  - patient, clinician, third party, government.
- What is discussed during the consenting process:
  - use and sharing of information with other family members and professionals
  - the nature of testing
  - length and complexity of testing process
  - storage and future use of samples
  - unexpected outcomes – parentage, support after testing.

figures of over 80 per cent, for *BRCA1* or *BRCA2* mutations (6), contrast with values of 40 to 60 per cent obtained more recently from population-based studies (7, 8). The same applies to colon cancer risks. Penetrance may be modified by other genetic and/or environmental factors (9, 10). Until these are defined the projection of risk, even for someone with a proven *BRCA1* or *BRCA2* or mismatch repair gene mutation, must remain very uncertain. Where this becomes important is in influencing decisions about management, for example when there is a choice between continued surveillance and prophylactic surgery.

Confidentiality of family medical history

A recurring theme in clinical genetics is the difficulty of balancing an individual's right to privacy against the duty to share relevant information with the wider family. The enormous increase in the potential for genetic analysis in recent years has raised public awareness of the risks of "genetic discrimination" in education, employment, insurance and access to health care. These are genuine concerns that society must address but the initial reaction, which is often to propose legislation that gives highest priority to confidentiality, may not secure the greatest good for the greatest number. Restricting access to medical records is well-intentioned but may achieve little in terms of protection of individual rights while negating efforts to gather epidemiological data of profound importance for improving the future health of all (11–16).

Family history

The very essence of clinical genetics is the taking of a verbal family history. At present, the prior consent of family members is not a statutory requirement and it is difficult to envisage a workable formula that would make it so. The family tree as described by the proband may well be both incomplete and inaccurate. Good medical practice dictates that the information given should be checked and amplified so that risk assessment, advice and management are as soundly based as possible (17–21). The great majority of families are co-operative and relatives readily give consent for confirmation of relevant diagnoses via hospital records or cancer registries. However, some family members may be difficult or impossible to trace, though the place and date of previous surgery may be known, or relatives may refuse permission to examine their hospital notes. Not infrequently, we must rely, at least partly, on unconfirmed data.

Existing and proposed laws often include a vague clause that permits release of information without formal consent "for sound medical reasons" but it seems that what is envisaged is protection of the public against infectious diseases or other identifiable medical dangers. There is no indication, as yet, that provision of genetic information to other family members would constitute a "sound medical reason" for obtaining limited access to the medical records of a third party (21, 22). It is interesting to note that organizations representing families affected by genetic disorders (i.e. those with the most profound stake in both the benefits and the disadvantages of medical secrecy) are among the strongest advocates of openness in recording genetic information (23).

Very occasionally, a family history of breast (or other) cancers may be concocted or grossly embellished by a patient seeking attention or as a variant of Munchausen's syndrome (24).

Confidentiality of molecular genetic data

Once a germline mutation (for example in *BRCA1* or *BRCA2*) has been identified in one family member then we enter more complex ethical and legal territory (25–27). A life assurance company is entitled to ask any questions it wishes about illnesses or causes of death among relatives (in much the same way as a clinical geneticist) and could repudiate cover if these were subsequently shown to have been answered untruthfully. The company's rights of access to predictive molecular genetics test results are, however, much less clear-cut and vary widely from country to country. Similarly, while there may be a moral obligation to share the test result with other family members, reluctance to do so can be justified on the grounds that, compared to family medical history, molecular information is much more likely to lead to unfair discrimination.

It is therefore crucial to obtain genuinely informed consent for disclosure of the result to relevant members of the family before setting in train the process of analysing DNA from one key individual. It has been argued that, once the result is known, that information becomes the property of the whole family (28) but this concept has yet to be validated in law. As predictive testing for a known mutation for a hereditary cancer gene proceeds through the family, it is quite possible that certain individuals will either decline to be tested or will refuse to allow anyone else access to their result (17). It is generally accepted that *BRCA1/2* and HNPCC testing should not be undertaken on minors since there is no proven advantage in knowing the result long before there is a measurable risk. Cases where this differs include multiple endocrine neoplasia types (MEN) 2A and 2B, where testing ideally takes place before the age of 5, and familial adenomatous polyposis (FAP) where testing may take place before teenage years. This is acceptable as the result of predictive testing will potentially alter management of the minor.

If a mutation is found in a "research" sample that has been handled many times, perhaps over several years, it is mandatory that the test be repeated in a hospital approved laboratory in a fresh specimen, ideally from the same individual or, if that is impossible, from another affected member of the same family. Once the mutation is known, virtually all centres insist on formal counselling before any at-risk family member is offered a predictive test. When agreement to test has been reached, it is important that there should be minimal delay before the result is obtained. Most clinics will make every effort to give the result in person rather than by post or telephone and follow-up counselling should be available to both mutation-carriers and non-carriers. As a result of the special position of molecular test results, in relation to life assurance and employment, there is some uncertainty as to how and where they should be recorded. Hospital notes are, by their nature, not particularly secure.

Duty of care

Failure to pass on now, to distant branches of a family, the fact that a *BRCA1* or *MSH2* or other germline mutation has been discovered could have regrettable consequences in 20 or 30 years time. Social trends suggest that family coherence is declining and worldwide mobility is certainly increasing so that opportunities for communication of relevant genetic information are unlikely to improve. Some legal cases exist (Box 18.4) (29, 30) but generally it is the duty of a physician to tell the patient of the hereditary nature of a disease and suggest that the patient informs relatives of the availability and need for genetic testing. A summary of the consultation with the patient in letter format copied to the patient as well as the referrer will allow discussion of the issues with various relatives who can then choose to attend a genetic or other clinic for further information.

The cases in Box 18.4 illustrate that legal decisions vary. Proper informed consenting practice and careful explanation of the results will usually avoid such situations. Proper education of all types of health care workers is needed. The genetic curriculum for several key professionals, including managers, pharmacists and nursing and other staff, has recently been looked at in the United Kingdom (31), and these groups are remedying the deficiencies and planning for the future.

Gene patenting

Despite existing law and directives on both sides of the Atlantic, the principle that gene sequences should be patentable is still being challenged (32–34). Many geneticists worry that clinically important research and development will be stultified by companies who hold patents on particular sequences and who wish to recoup their investment in this field by controlling access to diagnostic tests and to new therapies based on knowledge of these sequences.

Box 18.4 **Legal cases detailing 'duty of care'**

The case of Pate vs. Threkel 1995

A daughter of a woman was not informed of her mother's medullary cancer and sued the physician after she too developed medullary cancer, and the court held that the duty was to tell the mother of the potential risks but not warn the daughter.

The case of Safer vs. Pack 1996

A man died from colon cancer in the 1960s. His daughter, 25 years later, obtained the father's pathology slides, discovered he had FAP and sued the physician for not warning her that she had a 50 per cent risk. The court upheld the decision and decreed that the physician should have warned her directly even though she was a child at the time, perhaps even over the father's objections.

In relation to *BRCA1*, for which Myriad Genetics Inc. has held US patents since 1999 and European patents since 2001 (32), the company has been prepared to enter into relatively liberal agreements with publicly funded health providers so that current clinical practice is unaffected. In the longer term, however, the fact those genes may be "owned", even for a limited period, by any agency – commercial, governmental or charitable – is a cause of deep unease. It seems to contravene the principle that only a new invention should be patentable (35). A gene sequence is not an invention and its complete speci-fication is usually the end result of a long process that has involved contributions from a number of (knowingly or unwittingly) collaborating groups. There is ample scope for the invention of diagnostic or other applications of the sequence, and these processes may indeed be the subjects of patent applications. That would leave the field open for the development of newer, faster and less expensive alternative techniques. Something of that kind is going on at present in the field of *BRCA1* and *BRCA2* diag-nostics and there have been recent challenges to the Myriad patents in Europe (33–34). There could be major benefits for breast cancer families but, as matters stand, large-scale introduction of new *BRCA1*, *BRCA2* and other cancer tests could be impeded by the patent-holder. Patent holders also have recently (in the case of Myriad genetics) commenced direct marketing to consumers through the web and media (though a clinician is still needed to sign the sample form). This and other ways in which compa-nies will try to increase sales of their test or recoup costs may be in direct conflict with impartial information given by a qualified genetic counsellor or physician.

Paternity testing

The current perspective in clinical practice when non-paternity is suspected following mutation testing is not to tell the husband directly of a non-paternity result (36). The committee on assessing genetic risks of the Institute of Medicine in the US (37) recom-mended that the woman herself should be informed, as "genetic testing should not be used in ways that disrupt families". Raising the possibility at the outset, as this mini-mizes the ethical dilemmas encountered when the tests suggest non-paternity, solves most problems in practice. In Australia, this is often done with an information leaflet (38). Whatever way paternity is (or is not) broached following results, a sensitive approach to the discussion of the facts is needed. An offence of DNA theft is currently being introduced in the UK to prevent unauthorized testing for paternity or for other genetic disorders (such as testing by employers in susceptible persons or by the media in famous individuals to see ether they have fathered a child or have a gene for say Alzheimer disease). A government report on paternity testing practice is currently in preparation in the UK (39).

Large-scale DNA databases

Our understanding of genetics is often restricted to high penetrance genes such as *APC* or *BRCA1*. Large-scale genetic databases, such as the UK Biobank study (40), will allow the collection of data from large cohorts of patients over a long time span. Ethical implications differ depending on whether such data are anonymous or not, and safeguards need to be included, such as an independent monitoring committee and encryption of data to allow anonymization without having identifiers or links to individual patients. The consent at the outset is a crucial component of the research and patients should know exactly what use of their data is planned. This will need to be very specific with room for further consenting if data are not anonymous. Further reconsenting should not generally be necessary if full consent is obtained initially on anonymous data.

Insurance issues

The UK (where the health service is generally free, and not insurer based as it is in the US) has introduced a moratorium on genetic testing and insurance which allows up to £500 000 worth of insurance cover to be obtained for purpose of mortgage (house insurance cover) and £300 000 in cases of health insurance. This applies to approved tests. So far only testing for Huntington disease has been approved, although *BRCA1* and *BRCA2* testing is under consideration by the genetics and insurance committee (GAIC) (41, 42).

Huntington disease (HD), an autosomal dominant neurodegenerative disorder, has been a role model for this type of testing in adult genetic diseases. Several ethical and legal problems already have been recognized (43, 44). Clearly, there is a difference between more highly penetrant autosomal dominant diseases such as HD and diseases such as breast and colon cancer. Life tables and penetrance have been worked out for HD and it is possible to predict the age of death within a narrow range. A predominantly non-familial, common cancer, such as breast cancer, which may be due to single genes in only 5 to 10 per cent of cases, presents more difficulty as few accurate lifetime risk tables are available or are difficult to compile with limited accurate penetrance data (45, 46). If genetic tests, such as *BRCA1* and *BRCA2* or *APC*, are used in insurance they should only be used in conjunction with other information.

Family history data have been used for years and are generally accepted by insurance companies, although there may be considerable inaccuracy in these data. Using such history without good validated reasons is bad practice and should be challenged – further evidence is being collected to demonstrate whether such use is really fair or effective, as part of the moratorium in the UK.

In the UK, 95 to 97 per cent of life insurance policies are accepted at no increased premium. Only about 1 per cent is declined, and 2 to 4 per cent are rated up (47, 48). There is no analysis of these figures for specific diseases. The main reason for refusal or "loaded" premiums is the above average sum assured, and not the type of "high risk" individual assessed. Risks for insurers will be small if the policy value is low (49), for example under £100 000.

UK policy developments in insurance

Before 1995, the UK insurance industry paid little attention to progression of genetic testing. A House of Commons Science and Technology Select Committee reported on human genetics in 1995 and included insurance issues (50). The committee found a lack of published research on underwriting and adverse selection, with the insurance industry relying on the principle of the "right to underwrite".

Shortly after the publication of the report, the UK Government gave the ABI (the Association of British Insurers, a body representing around 95 per cent of insurers in the UK), one year to formulate proposals that would meet demands for access to insurance. At the same time, they announced the formation of a Human Genetics Advisory Commission (HGAC). The HGAC was established in December 1996 as a non-statutory advisory body to report to the government on various developments in genetics. It concentrated on insurance as its first task. The insurance industry, in 1997, announced the appointment of a genetics adviser and drafted a code of practice.

The first HGAC report was published in December 1997 (51). The report recommended a 2-year moratorium on genetic testing. The Government rejected their recommendations for a moratorium but asked the insurers to come up with a plan of action to remedy the situation. The ABI did this and a code of practice for genetic testing came into effect in January 1998. It had several important features and applied to all insurance, including life, permanent health, critical illness and long-term care and medical expenses (52). Most "relevant" UK insurance is life insurance linked to personal pensions and property insurance (mortgage cover). As the UK National Health Service provides free health care, health insurance is less frequently purchased than in the US, although there has been a recent increase in sales of personal health insurance cover policies. The situation differs greatly from the US insurance market, which is dominated by private health insurance.

The Government established a Genetics and Insurance Advisory Committee (GIAC) in April 1999 in an attempt to validate genetic tests proposed by the ABI. Initially a list of around 30 tests was drafted, but the list was later shortened to three autosomal dominant diseases. The list of conditions included MEN, breast cancer and FAP, and was never openly published. The role of GIAC was in validating the tests proposed by the ABI. Tests were defined (Box 18.5) and deemed suitable for use in assessing insurance proposals if they met three conditions (Box 18.6): technical relevance, clinical relevance and actuarial relevance. Only Huntington disease has been approved to date, however *BRCA1* and *BRCA2* and early-onset Alzheimer disease are under consideration.

The first condition to be validated, Huntington disease, was approved in October 2000 as reliable and relevant for the purposes of life insurance policies. The insurance companies accepted this ruling and disclosed that they would not use tests that were not received for approval by GIAC by the end of 2000. Two more conditions were submitted and are currently being processed – early-onset familial Alzheimer disease and

---

Box 18.5 **Definitions of a genetic test**

- A genetic test has been defined by the ABI as "an examination of the chromosome, DNA or RNA to find out if there is an otherwise undetectable disease related genotype, which may indicate an increased chance of that individual developing a specific disease in the future" (52).
- The UK Advisory Committee on Genetic Testing (ACGT) defines it as "a test to detect the presence or absence of, or change in, a particular gene or chromosome" (67).

Box 18.6 **GAIC criteria for relevance of a genetic test**

- Technical relevance – is the test technically reliable and does it accurately detect the specific changes sought for the named condition?
- Clinical relevance – does a positive result in the test have any implications for the health of the individual?
- Actuarial relevance – do the health implications make any difference to the likelihood of a claim under the proposed insurance product?

---

hereditary breast/ovarian cancer (*BRCA1* and *2*). Regrettably, the insurance companies took the view that although they had withdrawn other tests, including those for FAP and MEN, for which they felt genetic testing by middle age was not going to add much to family history and clinical examination, they refused to allow the results of negative (i.e. not carrying a family mutation) tests which would have been advantageous in securing normal rates in those penalized by family history of these disease.

Although there was a large amount of public opposition to the first approval of HD by the GIAC, the role of the GIAC has been useful in that it forced the ABI to consider the topic seriously, rather that its previous view that no problem existed. It also put the onus on insurers to produce facts and a case to submit evidence to the GIAC regarding reliability, and for just this reason most of the possible tests were dropped. The GIAC has all types of insurance as its remit and not just life insurance, which is most problematic in the UK, and has forced the consideration of health and critical illness and long-term care onto the agenda (issues which are particularly relevant in the US).

After another House of Commons Select Committee report on insurance and genetic testing progress, in early 2001 (53), the HGC published, in May 2001, interim recommendations on the use of genetic information in insurance (Box 18.7). These included an immediate moratorium on the use of genetic tests, which would allow

> ## Box 18.7 **HGC moratorium recommendations, May 2001**
>
> - No insurance company should require disclosure of adverse results of any genetic tests, or use such results in determining the availability or terms of all classes of insurance.
>
> - Recommendation is for introduction of a moratorium on genetic testing for not less than three years. This will allow time for a full review of regulatory options and afford the opportunity to collect data, which is not currently available. The moratorium should continue if the issues have not been resolved satisfactorily within this period.
>
> - The moratorium will not affect the current ability of insurance companies to take into account favourable results of any genetic test result, which the applicant has chosen to disclose.
>
> - HGC will address the issue as to how family history information is used by insurers.
>
> - An exception is made for policies greater than £500 000 as protection from significant financial loss.
>
> - Only genetic tests approved by the Genetics and Insurance Committee (GAIC) should be taken onto account for these high value policies. There remains a need for an expert body of this kind.
>
> - In view of the failings of self-regulation, independent enforcement of the moratorium will be needed. The HGC believes that legislation will be necessary to achieve this.

time for a full review of evidence and regulatory options (54). The use of family history information was allowed, but the HGC specified that they would discuss this and address how insurers use family history information. They also placed a ceiling on the recommended moratorium of £500 000, to protect the insurance industry from significant financial loss. They recommended that legislation might be needed to enforce the moratorium because of the failings of the current system. The ABI responded by issuing, on the same day, an extension to their existing moratorium to include all classes of insurance up to £300 000 (previously this only applied to mortgage-related policies up to £100 000).

The UK government response to both the House of Commons Select Committee report and the HGC interim recommendations was published in October 2001 (55, 58, 42). The key features are summarized in Box 18.8. The Government and the ABI announced a 5-year moratorium on the use of genetic test results by insurers. The moratorium applied to life insurance policies up to £500 000 and critical illness, long-term care

Box 18.8 Government and ABI agreed moratorium, October 2001

- There will be a 5-year moratorium on the use of genetic test results by insurers.
- The moratorium will apply to life insurance policies up to £500 000 and critical illness, long-term care insurance and income protection up to £300 000 for each type of policy.
- In policy applications above these limits, the insurance industry may use genetic test results where these tests have been approved by the GAIC.
- Legislation has not been introduced; however independent monitoring of the ABI code of conduct will take place through an enhanced role for the GAIC in monitoring both insurance compliance and customer complaints.
- The moratorium has not been extended to use of family history data.
- The whole moratorium will be reviewed after 3 years.
- The use of negative test results in obtaining normal premiums is encouraged by the insurer, subject to confirmation, in most cases, by a geneticist of the relevance of the result.

insurance and income protection up to £300 000 for each type of policy. In policy applications above these limits, the insurance industry may use genetic test results where these tests have been approved by the GIAC. Legislation has not been introduced; however, independent monitoring of the ABI code of conduct through the GIAC takes place for both insurance compliance and customer complaints. The moratorium has not been extended to the use of family history data, but the insurers and other groups are investigating evidence for use of this data, with the hope that by the end of the moratorium the position will be clearer.

The situation in other European countries

Several European countries have no legislation or guidelines on insurance and genetic testing. There is no legislation in Finland, Germany, Greece, Hungary, Iceland, Italy, Portugal or Spain. In Ireland, the situation is similar to the UK and, although there is no specific legislation, most Irish insurance companies have organizational links to the ABI and follow the ABI code where possible.

In countries that do have some guidelines, there is a moratorium on the use of genetic tests. Austria, Belgium, Denmark, France, the Netherlands, Norway, Poland, Sweden and Switzerland all have legislation, advice or recommendations that insurers should not use genetic data as a condition of insurance.

Regulation in other countries

In the US and other countries without national health services, the main concern is about health insurance, where a positive predictive test would have great relevance, although predictive genetic tests are rarely able to determine the time at which someone will become ill. In the US, most health insurance is purchased on a group basis by employers, and the unemployed or low income groups are often not insured. There is no obligation on an employer to insure a high-risk employee who would raise their costs. Thus 31 to 36 million people in the US have no health insurance (56). The most significant legislation is the health insurance portability and accountability act 1996 (HIPAA). This federal law provides some protection from genetic discrimination but only to employer-based and commercially issued group health insurance. President Clinton, in February 2000, signed an executive order forbidding the US federal government from using genetic information in general employment decisions (57). National legislation in the US to prevent discrimination was passed on October 14th 2003 with the introduction of the Genetic Information Non-discrimination Act (S 1053).

Australia has an Insurance Contracts Act 1984, which allows insurers to take into account existing genetic information as well as family history. Insurers generally are against forcing individuals to take genetic tests. The Life, Investment, and Superannuation Association of Australia (LISA) have revised further guidelines. The genetic privacy and non-discrimination bill 1998 explicitly prohibits genetic discrimination by insurers. Canada has no legislation and New Zealand issued guidelines in April 1997.

Benefits of cancer genetic testing

As in Huntington disease, if the genetic nature of the condition is well enough defined, individuals may be unable to obtain insurance because they are at 50 per cent risk, irrespective of DNA tests (44). This may prompt those at risk to request testing in the hope that their 50 per cent prior risk will be reduced to the point of being able to obtain insurance. This has not been found to be a particularly important reason for opting for a genetic test, nonetheless some women who test positive for *BRCA1* have had premiums reduced to normal after prophylactic mastectomy and oophorectomy.

The finding of negative predictive genetic test results (i.e. non-gene-carriers) has been used to lower already high premiums. In the UK, insurance companies cannot insist that applicants should have genetic tests. Many individuals at risk and on a higher premium will organize genetic tests at their own expense. Confirmation by genetic testing of a genetic cause for a cancer in an already affected person does not automatically increase the existing premium, as this may be based on existing family history or current health status, but a negative test result has led to a reduced premium for some applicants.

Some insurers consider that genetic information is not essential for underwriting life insurance and are not requesting information about genetic tests. Most applicants who were requested to provide further information were not rated at a higher premium or rejected. Some companies such as Standard Life, Virgin Direct or the Co-operative insurance, consider they can absorb this small extra load.

Insurance discrimination

A survey of European genetic centres involved in breast cancer testing showed that all the UK centres surveyed had had patients who refused testing because of fear of penalty or being unable to obtain insurance. Two (40 per cent) of the UK centres had experience of patients who refused genetic testing because of fear of employment discrimination (58, 59). None of the other centres had reported discrimination. A postal survey found that up to 33 per cent of UK respondents in patient support groups might have experienced problems when applying for life insurance (60). Such findings can easily be over-interpreted due to a high non-response rate by more satisfied customers.

In the rest of Europe, where most countries have restrictive legislation, there is little evidence of discrimination, although in Norway there is evidence of increased premiums for HNPCC, but not for *BRCA1/2* (61).

There is little evidence of discrimination in obtaining health insurance in the US for presymptomatic individuals (62), nonetheless health insurers are unwilling to pay for testing of, for instance *BRCA1*, with only 15 per cent covering the costs (63) and this is likely to increase if the tests are targeted in the high-risk situation, such as a family with a known mutation (64). Unless more is done to encourage insurers they may not to be prepared to pay for an FAP predictive test, for example, thus denying those on lower incomes the opportunity for testing in the first place. Further work in the US has also shown that insurance industry's fears about adverse selection may be groundless. Women testing positive for *BRCA1* mutations did not take out higher levels of life insurance (65).

In Australia, families with hereditary bowel cancer experienced genetic discrimination. In a survey of families on the hereditary bowel cancer register, Barlow-Stewart found 8 per cent had experienced discrimination – predominantly HNPCC related, and including a number of areas: refusal of life insurance, denial of an increase in life insurance for a pre-existing policy, refusal of income protection and trauma insurance, reduction of superannuation and loading on premiums for travel insurance (66). One interesting case was that of a civil servant who reported that her application for a senior position in the public service was subject to a negative FAP test result. She had to discontinue her application, as she would have been forced to have a test that would have revealed her mutation status. The issue had been picked up after she ticked a "regular colonoscopy" box on the health form. As a result of release of this evidence, the

Australian government has initiated several enquiries to determine the direction for future law or other policy development.

How can patients with a family history of cancer ensure the best possible management of their condition?

Patients, and their clinicians, should be aware of the regulations on insurance and genetic testing, the relevant contents of the ABI report and the recent moratorium on insurance and genetic testing within the UK. Most of these issues are complex and patients with a history of familial cancer need access to a clinical genetics service either by direct telephone or clinic contact, or through secondary contact via their medical practitioner or hospital clinician. This is particularly useful if the risk is being based on family history, as often the patient's knowledge of their own family history of cancer may be inaccurate. The introduction of the recent moratorium, and the safeguards contained both within it and by external monitoring of the genetic testing aspects by GAIC and the ethical and social aspects by HGC, are an encouraging step. Increased use of normal test results in setting normal premiums, and industry competition should improve access to reasonable insurance cover for hereditary illnesses and, as not all insurance companies belong to the ABI, good advice is to "shop around" using an independent advisor who may be able to negotiate very competitive rates.

Conclusion and the future

The rapidly evolving practice of clinical genetics is producing many questions to which we do not yet have clear answers. This is nowhere more apparent than in the genetics of common cancers, including beast and colon cancer, which is the fastest growing area of genetic medicine. Worry about misuse of genetic test information by insurers is a real concern and the recent discussions between the UK government and the insurance industry, leading to their moratorium, are to be welcomed. Little hard evidence exists to calculate risk assessment by insurers on either the predictive power of cancer genetic tests or on the use of family history as a rating factor. Further high quality, actuarial research evidence will provide a better understanding of insurance risk estimation and allow better actuarial practice in the calculation of insurance premiums in families with a history of cancer.

Future trends are impossible to predict – however there will be an increasing use of genetic results in determining the treatment of hereditary cancers, and tests for moderately penetrant genes will be introduced, leading to more widespread use of hereditary cancer testing in medium and lower risk cases. This, combined with dietary and other lifestyle advice, will allow a greater level of cancer prevention. Careful attention to the ethical principles outlined in this chapter, particularly autonomy and the proper consenting of patients undergoing testing, will need to be adhered to if this more widespread introduction of testing is to be introduced successfully.

Note

The United Kingdom 5 year moratorium on genetic testing was extended to 10 years in a concordat between the UK Government and the insurance industry in March 2005 (68, 69). It will be reviewed in 2008 before the 10 years ends on 1st November 2011.

References

1 **Beauchamp TL, Childress J**. *Principles of biomedical ethics*, 1st edn, 1979. Oxford, New York: Oxford University Press.

2 **Gillon R**. Ethics needs principles – four can encompass the rest – and respect for autonomy should be "first amongst equals". *J Med Ethics* 2003; **29**:307–312.

3 **Gillon R**. Four scenarios. *J Med Ethics* 2003; **29**:267–268.

4 Human Genetics Commission. *Inside information: Balancing interests in the use of personal genetic data*, May 2002. www.hgc.gov.uk/insideinfirmation/index.htm.

5 Human Genetics Commission. Genes direct: ensuring the effective oversight of genetic tests supplied directly to the public, March 2003. www.hgc.gov.uk/genesdirect/

6 **Ford D, Easton DF, Stratton M**, Breast Cancer Linkage Consortium. Genetic heterogeneity and linkage analysis of the *BRCA1* and *BRCA2* genes in breast cancer families. *Am J Hum Genet* 1998; **62**:676–689.

7 **Struewing JP, Hartge P, Wacholder S, *et al***. The risk of cancer associated with specific mutations of *BRCA1* and *BRCA2* among Ashkenazi Jews. *N Engl J Med* 1997; **336**:1401–1408.

8 **Thorlacius S, Struewing JP, Hartge P, *et al***. Population-based study of risk of breast cancer in carriers of *BRCA2* mutation. *Lancet* 1998; **352**:1337–1339.

9 **Narod SA, Goldgar D, Cannon-Albright L, *et al***. Risk modifiers in carriers of *BRCA1* mutations. *Int J Cancer* 1995; **64**:394–398.

10 **Burke W, Press N, Pinsky L**. *BRCA1* and *BRCA2*: a small part of the puzzle. *J Natl Cancer Inst* 1999; **91**:904–905.

11 **Peto J, Collins N, Barfoot R, *et al***. Prevalence of *BRCA1* and *BRCA2* mutations in patients with early onset breast cancer. *J Natl Cancer Inst* 1999; **91**:943–949.

12 **Vandenbroucke JP**. Maintaining privacy and the health of the public. *BMJ* 1998; **316**:1331–1332.

13 **Wadman M**. Privacy bill under fire from researchers. *Nature* 1998; **392**:6.

14 **Al-Shahi R, Warlow C**. Using patient-identifiable data for observational research and audit. *BMJ* 2000; **321**:1031–1032.

15 **Strobl J, Cave E, Walley T**. Data protection legislation: interpretation and barriers to research. *BMJ* 2000; **321**:890–892.

16 **White MT**. Underlying ambiguities in genetic privacy legislation. *Genetic Testing* 2000; **3**:341–345.

17 **De Vos M, Poppe B, Delvaux G, *et al***. Genetic counselling and testing for hereditary breast and ovarian cancer: the Gent(le) approach. *Dis Markers* 2000; **15**:191–195.

18 **Floderus B, Barlow L, Mack TM**. Recall bias in subjective reports of familial cancer. *Epidemiology* 2000; **1**:318–321.

19 **Theis B, Boyd N, Lockwood G, Tritchler D**. Accuracy of family cancer history in breast cancer patients. *Eur J Canc Prev* 1994; **3**:321–327.

20 **Kerber RA, Slattery ML**. Comparison of self-reported and database-linked family history of cancer data in a case-control study. *Am J Epidemiol* 1997; **146**:244–248.

21 **Steel CM, Smyth E**. Molecular pathology of breast cancer and its impact on clinical practice. *Schweiz Med Wochenschr* 1999; **129**:1749–1757.

22 **Reilly P**. Legal issues in genetic medicine. In: Rimoin DL, Connor M, Peyritz RE, eds. *Emery and Rimoin's principles and practice of medical genetics*, 3rd edn, 1996, pp.655–666. New York: Churchill Livingstone.

23 **Hunt A**. The patient's viewpoint. *Dis Markers* 1992; **10**:205–210.

24 **Evans DGR, Kerr B, Foulkes W, et al.** False breast cancer family history in the cancer family clinic – a report of 8 families. *Eur J Surg Oncol* 1998; **24**:275–279.

25 Human Genetics Advisory Commission (UK). *The implications of genetic testing for insurance*, 1997. London: Department of Health.

26 American Society of Human Genetics, Social Issues Subcommittee on Familial Disclosure. ASHG statement: professional disclosure of familial genetic information. *Am J Hum Genet* 1998; **62**:474–483.

27 **Muller H, Eeles RA, Wildsmith T, McGleenan T, Friedman S**. Genetic testing for cancer predisposition; an ongoing debate. *Lancet Oncol* 2000; **1**:118–123.

28 **Pembrey M, Anionwu E**. Ethical aspects of genetic screening and diagnosis. In: Rimoin DL, Connor M, Peyritz RE, eds. *Emery and Rimoin's principles and practice of medical genetics*, 3rd edn, 1996, pp.641–653. New York: Churchill Livingstone.

29 **Clayton EW**. Ethical, legal and social implications of genomic medicine. *N Eng J Med* 2003; **349**:562–569.

30 **Safer v. Pack**, 677A.2d 1188 (N.J.App.) appeal denied, 683 A.2d 1163 (N.J.1996).

31 **Burton H**. *Addressing genetics, delivering health. A strategy for advancing the dissemination and application of genetics knowledge throughout our health professions.* Public health genetics, Cambridge, UK, September 2003. www.phgu.org.uk

32 **Bennett RL, Hampel HL, Mandell JB, Marks JH**. Genetic counsellors: translating genomic science into clinical practice. *J Clin Invest* 2003; **112**:1274–1279.

33 **Benowitz S**. European patent groups oppose Myriad's latest patent on BRCA1. *J Natl Cancer Inst* 2003; **95**:8–9.

34 **Matthijs G, Halley D, Sperling K, et al.** Patents and monopolies on diagnostic tests: Europe's opposition against the BRCA1 patents. *Am J Hum Genet* 2002; **71**: (suppl1). 93.

35 **Knoppers BM**. Status, sale and patenting of human genetic material: an international survey. *Nature Genet* 1999; **22**:23–26.

36 **Lucassen A, Parker M**. Revealing false paternity: some ethical considerations. *Lancet* 2001; **357**:1033–1035.

37 Institute of Medicine, Committee on Assessing Genetic Risks. *Assessing genetic risks*, 1994, p.276. Washington DC: National Academy Press.

38 Medical Research Council. *Ethical aspects of human genetic testing: an information paper.* Sydney, Australia.

39 Human Genetics Commission. www.hgc.gov.uk/

40 Medical Research Council. www.mrc.ac.uk/

41 Department of Trade and Industry Office of Technology, and the Department of Health. *Government response to the Human Genetics Advisory Commission's report on the implications of genetic testing for insurance*, November 1998. London, UK: HMSO.

42 **Morrison PJ**. Insurance, genetic testing and familial cancer: recent policy changes in the United Kingdom. *Ulster Med J* 2001; **70**:79–88.

43 **Huggins M, Bloch M, Kanani S, et al.** Ethical and legal dilemmas arising during predictive testing for adult-onset disease: the experience of Huntington disease. *Am J Hum Genet* 1990; **47**:4–12.

44 **Harper PS**. Insurance and genetic testing. *Lancet* 1993; **341**:224–227.

45 MacDonald AS, Waters HR, Wekwete CT. The genetics of breast and ovarian cancer I: A model of family history. *Scandinavian Actuarial J* 2003; **103**:1–27.

46 MacDonald AS, Waters HR, Wekwete CT. The genetics of breast and ovarian cancer II: A model of critical illness insurance. *Scandinavian Actuarial J* 2003; **103**:28–50.

47 MacDonald AS. How will improved forecasts of individual lifetimes affect underwriting? *Phil Trans R Soc Lond* 1997; **B352**:1067–1075.

48 LeGrys J. Actuarial considerations on genetic testing. *Phil Trans R Soc Lond* 1997; **B352**:1057–1061.

49 Morrison PJ. Genetic testing and insurance in the UK. *Clin Genet* 1998; **54**:375–379.

50 Science and Technology Committee, House of Commons. *Human genetics: the science and its consequences*, 3rd report, HC41-I, 1995. London: HMSO.

51 Human Genetics Advisory Commission (UK). *The implications of genetic testing for insurance*, December 1997. London.

52 Association of British Insurers. *Genetic testing ABI code of practice*, December 1997. London.

53 Science and Technology Committee, House of Commons. *Genetics and insurance*, 5th report, March 2001, HC174. London: HMSO.

54 Human Genetics Commission, Department of Health. *Whose hands on your genes? A discussion document on the storage, protection and use of personal genetic information*, November 2000. London: Department of Health.

55 Department of Health. *Government response to the report from the House of Commons Science and Technology Committee: Genetics and insurance*, October 2001. London: Department of Health.

56 Brett P, Fischer EP. Effects on life insurance of genetic testing. *Actuary* 1993; **10**:11–12.

57 Josefson J. Clinton outlaws genetic discrimination in federal jobs. *BMJ* 2000; **320**:168.

58 Morrison PJ, Steel CM, Vasen HFA, *et al.* Insurance implications for individuals with a high risk of breast and ovarian cancer in Europe. *Dis Markers* 1999; **15**:159–165.

59 Morrison PJ, Steel CM, Nevin NC, *et al.* Insurance considerations for individuals with a high risk of breast cancer in Europe: some recommendations. *CME Hung J Gynaecol* 2000; **5**:272–277.

60 Low L, King S, Wilkie T. Genetic discrimination in life insurance: empirical evidence from a cross-sectional survey of genetic support groups in the United Kingdom. *BMJ* 1998; **317**:1632–1635.

61 Norum J, Tranebjaerg L. Health, life and disability insurance and hereditary risk for breast and colorectal cancer. *Acta Oncol* 2000; **39**:189–193.

62 Hall MA, Rich SS. Laws restricting health insurers' use of genetic information: impact on genetic discrimination. *Am J Hum Genet* 2000; **66**:293–307.

63 Anon. Private matters, public affairs. *Nature Genet* 2000; **26**:1–2.

64 Schoonmaker MM, Bernhardt BA, Holtzman NA. Factors influencing health insurers' decisions to cover new genetic technologies. *Int J Technol Assess Health Care* 2000; **16**:178–189.

65 Zick CD, Smith KR, Mayer RN, Botkin JR. Genetic testing, adverse selection and the demand for life insurance. *Am J Med Genet* 2000; **93**:29–39.

66 Barlow-Stewart K, Keays D. Genetic discrimination in Australia. *J Law Medicine* 2001; **8**:250–262.

67 Advisory Committee on Genetic Testing. *Code of practice and guidance on human genetic testing services supplied direct to the public*, December 1997. London.

68 Department of Health. *Concordat and moratorium on genetics and insurance.* Department of Health, London, March 2005 (www.dh.gov.uk).

69 Devlin LJ, Price JH, Morrison PJ. Hereditary non-polyposis colon cancer. *Ulster Med J*; **74**:(In press).

Index

Page references in *italics* indicate a table.